REVOLT AND CRISIS IN GREECE

BETWEEN A PRESENT YET TO PASS AND A FUTURE STILL TO COME

How does a revolt come about and what does it leave behind? What impact does it have on those who participate in it and those who simply watch it? Is the Greek revolt of December 2008 confined to the shores of the Mediterranean, or are there lessons we can bring to bear on social action around the globe?

Revolt and Crisis in Greece: Between a Present Yet to Pass and a Future Still to Come is a collective attempt to grapple with these questions. A collaboration between anarchist publishing collectives Occupied London and AK Press, this timely new volume traces Greece's long moment of transition from the revolt of 2008 to the economic crisis that followed. In its twenty chapters, authors from around the world—including those on the ground in Greece—analyse how December became possible, exploring its legacies and the position of the social antagonist movement in face of the economic crisis and the arrival of the International Monetary Fund.

In the essays collected here, over two dozen writers offer historical analysis of the factors that gave birth to December and the potentialities it has opened up in face of the capitalist crisis. Yet the book also highlights the dilemmas the antagonist movement has been faced with since: the book is an open question and a call to the global antagonist movement, and its allies around the world, to radically rethink and redefine our tactics in a rapidly changing landscape where crises and potentialities are engaged in a fierce battle with an uncertain outcome.

Contributors include Vaso Makrygianni, Haris Tsavdaroglou, Christos Filippidis, Christos Giovanopoulos, TPTG, Metropolitan Sirens, Yannis Kallianos, Hara Kouki, Kirilov, Some of Us, Soula M., Christos Lynteris, Yiannis Kaplanis, David Graeber, Christos Boukalas, Alex Trocchi, Antonis Vradis, Dimitris Dalakoglou and the Occupied London Collective. Cover art by Leandros. Layout and design by Klara Jaya Brekke and Tim Simons; edited by Antonis Vradis and Dimitris Dalakoglou, all of Occupied London.

REVOLT AND CRISIS IN GREECE

BETWEEN A PRESENT YET TO PASS AND A FUTURE STILL TO COME

Edited by
Antonis Vradis and *Dimitris Dalakoglou*

AK Press & Occupied London
Oakland, Baltimore, Edinburgh, London & Athens
— 2011 —

Revolt and Crisis in Greece:
Between a Present Yet to Pass and a Future Still to Come

An Occupied London Project
Edited by Antonis Vradis and Dimitris Dalakoglou
Co-Published by AK Press and Occupied London, 2011

ISBN: 978-0-98305-971-4
Library of Congress Control Number: 2011904668

For more information:
www.occupiedlondon.org | www.revoltcrisis.org

AK PRESS
674-A 23rd Street
Oakland, CA 94612
USA
www.akpress.org
akpress@akpress.org

AK PRESS
PO Box 12766
Edinburgh, EH8 9YE
Scotland
www.akuk.com
ak@akedin.demon.co.uk

The above addresses would be delighted to provide you with the latest AK Press distribution catalog, which features the several thousand books, pamphlets, zines, audio and video products, and stylish apparel published and/or distributed by AK Press. Alternatively, visit our web site for the complete catalog, latest news, and secure ordering.

Visit us at www.akpress.org and www.revolutionbythebook.akpress.org.

Cover illustration by Leandros.

Cover design by Tim Simons.

Layout by Klara Jaya Brekke.

Profits from the sale of this book will benefit anarchist printing and publishing projects around the globe, including Rotta in Greece and AK Press in the United States.

ACKNOWLEDGEMENTS

Thanks to everyone at AK Press and Kate, Lorna, Jessica, and Suzanne in particular for all their help; Bruce and Mikey (Oakland, US); Manny and Magpie (NYC, US); Shannon and Gabrielle (Montreal, Canada); Jaya, David, Daphne, and Yiannis (London, England); Catherine (Southampton, England); Harry (Edinburgh, Scotland); Christos and Yannis (St. Andrews, Scotland); Christos (Lancaster, England); Edward, Tom, Leila, Lia, Frances, and Emilia (Brighton, England); Evie (Madrid, Spain); Vasia (Patras, Greece); Haris (Thessaloniki, Greece); Leandros, Idris, Soula, Christos K, Christos G, Thanos, Stratos, Eleni, Hara, Vaso, Calamity, Achilleas, Yannis, Yiorgos, Dimitris, Evangelia, Katerina, Stefanos, Marilena, James, and Tim in Athens.

CONTENTS

ACRONYMS

ADEDY (ΑΔΕΔΥ) Supreme Administration of Greek Civil Servants' Trade-Unions.

ASOEE (ΑΣΟΕΕ) Athens School of Commercial Studies. This is the old name of Athens University of Economics and Business that remains, colloquially, up to the present day.

EFEE (ΕΦΕΕ) National Student Union of Greece.

ERT (ΕΡΤ) Hellenic Broadcasting Corporation. The state-run TV channel and radio station network.

GSEE (ΓΣΕΕ) General Confederation of Workers of Greece. The national federation of trade unions, founded in 1918.

KKE (in) (ΚΚΕ [εσ.]) Communist Party of Greece (Interior). The party that emerged from a major split of KKE in 1968.

KKE (ΚΚΕ) Communist Party of Greece.

KNE (ΚΝΕ) Communist Youth of Greece, the youth of the Communist Party of Greece.

LAOS (ΛΑΟΣ) Popular Orthodox Rally. An extreme right-wing, nationalist, and xenophobic parliamentary party.

MAT **(ΜΑΤ)** Public Order Reinstatement Units. The Greek riot police.

ND **(ΝΔ)** New Democracy. The major right-wing conservative party in the Greek parliament, in government between 1990–1993 and 2004–2009.

NTUA **(ΕΜΠ)** National Technical University of Athens. Commonly known as the Polytechneio or Athens Polytechnic.

PAME **(ΠΑΜΕ)** All-Workers Militant Front. The trade union federation under the control of the Communist Party of Greece **(KKE)**.

PASOK **(ΠΑΣΟΚ)** Panhellenic Socialist Movement. The social-democratic party in government between 1981–1989, 1993–2004 and 2009–present (winter 2010–2011).

SYRIZA **(ΣΥΡΙΖΑ)** Coalition of the Radical Left. A parliamentary coalition of Euro-communist, socialist, and radical left groups.

1

INTRODUCTION

Dimitris Dalakoglou & Antonis Vradis

You are a child growing up in Greece in the nineties. There is a high likelihood that one of your distant relatives, or even your aunt, your uncle, your grandfather, or your mother or father may be haunted by the memory of a few years in their life from whence no bedtime stories will ever arise. "Exile," "dictatorship," "civil war": these strange words ring about, yet remain lost behind the veil of the untold. Silent grandparents with lingering gazes, voters-for-life of a party that would repeatedly betray them over the course of a lifetime too far along to change its course. These were times past, hidden by the thick screen onto which the capitalist spectacle projected itself. By the mid-2000s, the spectacle had grown to Olympic proportions. The Games were here: development fever, a certain euphoria mixed with longing, the longing to become "Western," to finally "make it." For a brief moment in time it actually seemed to happen for some.

And suddenly the screen went blank. December 2008: the month when the country's divided past returned in full force. The time that followed was an animated reminder that class and political struggle had not been tucked away in museums or history books—and most certainly would not stand to be so any time soon. A sudden awakening. Or was it?

Contradictions, struggles, the ubiquitous feeling that history marches over everyday victories and defeats—the December revolt was the precise moment when an entire generation awoke to the realisation that the muted stories of the past had always been part of the present.

Revolt and Crisis in Greece: Between a Present Yet to Pass and a Future Still to Come is a collective attempt to map the time between the revolt of December 2008 and the crisis that followed. Most of us were children who grew up in Greece in the nineties. Some of us are still there, some are now elsewhere, and some have never even visited. For all of us, however, December is a key point of reference. It may have started out as a territorial reference, but it quickly moved beyond geographical boundaries; it became so much more. We feel that what is being played out in Greece poses some enormous questions that reach far beyond the place itself or the people who live there. We were told that it was "a bad apple," the first European country to see austerity measures kick in, to see the IMF arrive. But Ireland was quick to follow. Portugal was next in line, then perhaps Spain. The bad apples multiplied, like dominoes of unrest that did not seem to care much about border crossings or planned schedules. Revolts continued to spring up, seemingly out of "nowhere," at unexpected times. Think of Alexis Grigoropoulos's assassination in Athens and they days and months that followed. Or Muhamed Bouazizi, the street vendor in Tunisia who simply had enough. He lit himself on fire and set the entire region ablaze. Algeria, Egypt, Bahrain, Libya.... In a circle almost full, the flames of revolt have become visible from Greek shores once again.

Yet questions remain: What gave birth to the revolt on these shores, and what has followed since? Our collective exploration of these questions is divided into three parts. Part One, entitled "The Site: Athens," is the reader's landing strip, an introduction that sheds light on the context for these events. Part Two, "The Event: December," is a reading of the revolt of December 2008 traced through its remnants in the present, designed to illuminate not only what made those events possible, but also what those events made possible in return. The final part is called "Crisis." To be sure, this is about the global capitalist crisis as grounded and lived within the territory of Greece. But these concluding essays are also about the social antagonist movement's moment of crisis: even if the colloquial meaning of the word suggests a downfall, in its original (Greek) meaning, it refers to judgement and thinking—which means, in our case, some much-needed self-reflection.

The notion of crisis may also imply a moment of rapid change, a moment that marks and reveals an almost instantaneous transition towards something different. What remains an open question and a challenge, then, is to try to make sense of this transition—of how we position ourselves within it as anarchists, as part of the global antagonist movement, as people inspired by the December revolt who nevertheless want to be better prepared for the next Decembers that are sure to come.

THERE ARE NO PALM TREES IN ATHENS

When presenting or discussing events that took place in Greece to audiences in other countries, we have sometimes been confronted with what largely feel like awkward questions. "What is it like to live in an anarchist neighbourhood?" has come up often. So too has "Did people still go to work after the December revolt?" This is not radically different than the treatment our global antagonist movement has reserved for movements of armed struggle in distant times and/or places—and so, we felt that the first thing we needed to do was to break away from the mythical image of Greece as a politically exotic "Other." This is an exoticisation that is both distorting and dis-empowering for the struggles taking place here and now. So be assured, dear reader: there are no palm trees in Athens. That is to say, there is nothing politically exotic, mysterious, or alien about the city. True, if you were to cruise through its avenues there is good a chance you might see the dried-out remnants of a palm tree: one of the scandals of the Olympic Games was the planting of over-priced palm trees across a city where the climate was entirely unsuitable. But this proves our point precisely, that despite its particularities, Athens is yet another European metropolis. And, as all of the contributors to this book imply or explicitly demonstrate, there are no ideal political or cultural conditions for a revolt—it can happen anywhere at the right time.

So how did the revolt materialise in Athens in the first place? Vaso Makrygianni and Haris Tsavdaroglou's chapter offers some great insight into these questions. They show how the capitalist development frenzy after WWII shaped the appearance of Greek cities, in particular the capital, where near half of the country's population lives. They explain how a sizeable hybrid social class of workers and small-scale landlords formed within a few decades. They also explain how these six decades of capitalist urban development created the spatial and material site where the revolt of 2008 was realised. An extensive, day-by-day description of the geographical spread of the revolt in the city of Athens is followed by an exercise comparing December 2008 to the revolts in Buenos Aires, Paris, Los Angeles, and Milan.

In contrast, Christos Filippidis offers a fresh spatial analysis of Athens. He explores the experience of being in the urban jungle (the "polis-jungle," as he calls it), providing a reminder that cities are primarily produced politically—or, even better, that politics become spatialised and grounded via the practice of urban planning. Filippidis brings us straight up into the heart of the December revolt, revealing the endemic violence of the city. Though the discourse of sovereignty claimed that the violence of the revolt could not possibly belong to a "civilised" or "modern" city, Filippidis shows how Athens, and modern capitalist urbanity overall, is a machine of violence. The polis-jungle is not Athens alone; it speaks to every and any urban experience under the crisis of capitalism.

The first part of the book ends with a chapter on the everyday politics of the polis-jungle as formulated after the December revolt. Here, we wanted to read Athens through the political polarizations forming within it, by looking at the examples of two opposing political tendencies, each fighting to spatially define and materialise their own right to the city. On the one hand, there is a radical reclaiming of space and its transformation through guerilla gardening in a public park, all at the heart of the neighbourhood that gave birth to the 2008 revolt. On the other hand, in a square located just a few kilometres away, neo-Nazi groups have been trying to establish a "migrant-free zone" since late 2008. The moment of the revolt provided the opportunity, the perfect ignition for these two materialisations of everyday politics to erupt. What is at stake here far exceeds the mundane or the triviality often—but wrongly—associated with the everyday. Claiming a right to urban space becomes a challenge and a question of how to act politically in a city and society as a whole.

THE NOT-SO-SECRET LIVES OF DECEMBER

For many distant spectators, the events of December 2008 were a perfect storm in an otherwise clear sky. But the revolt was far from that. Our section on "The Event" opens with a chapter by Christos Giovanopoulos and Dimitris Dalakoglou, which traces the historical conditions that shaped the Greek state's "enemy within" over the course of the last three decades or so: the genealogy of the 2008 revolt. Beginning with the student movement of 1979–1980, they discuss key youth movements in post-dictatorial Greece and highlight how each contributed to the history of the Greek antagonist movement, noting the particular events that have shaped the collective memory of these youth movements since the end of the dictatorship in 1974. This collective memory is not something abstract: we can feel how tangible it is every time it accumulates, merges with momentary circumstances, and triggers the outpouring of fresh political activity back in the streets. Giovanopoulos and Dalakoglou point out some of the most significant ruptures on the surface of the post-dictatorial political regime, ruptures that were quick to become cracks and lead to the December eruption in return.

But ruptures are not caused by social movements alone. The past four decades have also seen structural tears in the political systems of governance—many of which are linked to the neoliberal reconfiguration of the conditions of labour, a process taking place simultaneously all over the planet. In Chapter Six, TPTG ("Children of the Galley" or, in Greek, "Ta Paidia Tis Gallarias"), an anti-authoritarian communist group from Athens, discuss the December rebellion and the developments in its immediate aftermath as aspects of the crisis of capitalist relations in Greece. TPTG put December in a different perspective, describing the recent neoliberal reconfigurations of the capitalist relation in the country and the extent to which these were linked to the revolt. Taking the global capitalist crisis as a point of departure, they turn their focus back to Greece, highlighting the particularities of the social and political crisis and the ways December made itself felt within them. They go on to describe the class composition of the 2008 revolt, illuminating the ways in which pre-existing class subjectivities were transcended to form an entirely new, spontaneous collective subjectivity in the streets and in occupied spaces. TPTG suggest that the revolt could not have been manipulated by reformist tendencies of the Left, neither could it have been represented in any way by armed struggle groups that emerged around that time, which were little more than a voluntaristic self-perceived vanguard who ignored the political dynamics of the collective actions of the revolting masses of December. Ultimately, TPTG address one of the central questions regarding December, namely: why didn't the rebellion extend to the places of waged labour? They try to formulate an answer by looking at the limited class composition of the rebellion in terms of the low participation of those workers who can be described either as "non-precarious" or as "workers with a stable job." Moreover, they try to explain why the minority of "non-precarious" workers who took part in the rebellion, as well as the "precarious" ones, could not extend it to their workplaces. Notwithstanding the limits of the rebellion, after December the state was quick to respond to the latent threat of the overcoming of separations within the proletariat through the enforcement of a whole new series of repressive measures, as well as through an ideological and physical attack against the marginalised/immigrant/delinquent proletarians who occupy the inner city area of Athens—all of which is an an attempt to demonise the reinvented "dangerous classes."

The landscape is changing beyond recognition: not only by the emergence of new movements in the face of neoliberalism's charge ahead, but also in terms of the tools these movements take on. Counter-information—that is, the diffusion of information on social struggles from below—has come to the fore as a key tool in the service of radical social movements in Greece. In Chapter Seven, the Metropolitan Sirens (a collective pseudonym for comrades involved in the practice of counter-information in Greece) talk us through the historical evolution of counter-information and its importance in the December events. It is not a coincidence that, shortly after December, MPs, ministers, and journalists attempted to shut down Athens Indymedia. A keystone of counter-information in Greece, the website received over ten million hits between the day of Alexis Grigoropoulos's assassination and the following one (6–7 December 2008), quickly becoming a central node for communication between those participating in the revolt and the diffusion of news about it. Beyond the internet tools used in December, occupied physical sites (mostly public buildings such as universities, town halls, etc.) also became nodes of counter-information, spreading the word of those who revolted throughout the country and beyond frontiers.

The genealogical approach employed in the first three chapters might suggest it that should have been possible to see the December eruption coming. Yet, still, the revolt was a surprise—not only because it was hard to predict such an enormous and widespread reaction to the assassination of Alexandros, but also because it would have been impossible to even imagine the political implications it would have. Yannis Kallianos begins Chapter Eight by establishing that what happened in December 2008 was unexpected for both those in power and for the social antagonist movement alike. Kallianos then provides an analysis of the actions that took place during the days of December in Athens, the ones that turned the revolt into a historical moment. In other words, Kallianos outlines December as a historical moment, one marking a transition and a certain social and political transformation.

Despite the enormous historical value of December's events, the lived experience of the revolt itself was multiple and even contradictory. These contradictions and reflections are discussed extensively in the next four chapters by comrades both inside and outside of Greece. Chapter Nine by Hara Kouki is addressed directly to each one of us. It is a reflexive text, critical of our collective self as people who were involved in the revolt, who were active in the antagonist movement before it and who continue to be. As many of our contributors explain, during the revolt people who were already politically active came suddenly into contact with the thousands who took to the streets for the first time. This experience was a unique moment marking life-crisis transitions— or as Hara Kouki describes it: "Your sole reaction was this sense of bewilderment at being together in the streets and an urge to do and write thousands of meaningful things that made no sense." Still, this sense of bewilderment and this connection between so many people who would not meet in any political project under normal circumstances did not last long. For this reason, a question that quickly emerged after the end of the revolt came into sight, in January 2009, was about the legacies December would leave behind. To a certain extent these legacies were appropriated by the mainstream while stripped of their radical political meaning—both because the systemic forces were already prepared to do so, and also because we as a movement did not manage to organise any follow-up. So, then, what remains of the revolt in the present, Hara Kouki wonders— and has quite a few answers to suggest.

Chapter Ten offers plentiful imagery from December: the barricades, the "carpet" of broken glass and stones in the streets, buzzing assemblies, hooded teenagers, older activists, burnt-out shops resembling archetypal caves by the morning after, collectively-cooked looted food, and insurgents sleeping in occupations, mass demos and clashes in the streets of Athens. Kirilov knows well the difficulties of talking about the revolt. Our own memories of the event betray us, and sometimes words are simply insufficient, even for those who can use language exceptionally well. What matters is not just what we articulate but also the stories of the revolt that remain untold. This in turn makes it even more difficult to put concrete thoughts on the revolt together without omitting parts of the picture that would be crucial for the author. Kirilov reminds us that "an explanation of insurrection demands a very different method of inquiry: a militant research that does not simply interpret and analyse reality, but modifies it."

How was the reality of the revolt experienced outside Greece? We asked two comrades from North America, to write about their experience. Their reply, that "Nothing happened," is a letter to friends in Greece that discusses their effort to interpret the events in the country while encountering the brutality of Canadian police apparatus at the same time. They talk about their faith in our common ideas and the joy derived from the events in Greece—but, at the same time, confess an apparently unavoidable depression and rage from the lack of such situations and activities in their own local setting. Soula M., a recipient of the Canadian letter, offers a reply: despite differences between those who experienced the revolt directly and those who witnessed it from afar, the mixture of feelings in the present is, if anything, quite similar. We all feel fear, faith and rage. Neither December nor the social antagonist movement in Greece are nearly as perfect as they may seem to some. The bottom line for her is that what matters for all of us (all those who experienced the revolt directly or indirectly, all who read these lines right now) is what we make of December and of our feelings about it. These two, the event and our feelings, are interwoven—and it is this interconnection that will bring about the Decembers we have yet to live.

CRISES

After the fury, the rage, and the joy of December, Greece entered the trajectory of crisis proper. The crisis had, of course, been looming before December and it was experienced by some of the most vulnerable parts of society—like the young proletariat—as TPTG makes clear, and yet it was not until 2010 that the state would officially admit that the wave of capitalist crisis had reached the shores of Greece, and acknowledge the massive accumulation of debt that marked capitalist consumption across Europe as a whole. Christos Lynteris discusses the economic crisis as an evental substitution, in a way engaging with Yannis Kallianos who opened the discussion several pages before by seeing an event in the December 2008 revolt. In Chapter Thirteen, Lynteris deconstructs the medico-juridical origin of the notion of "crisis," suggesting that it may be seen as a moment of truth, a moment when lengthier processes show their "real" substance. He expands this deconstruction to the political arena, explaining how crises are read as events that not only arise as a culmination, but which also define how entire processes will evolve, since they are—ostensibly— a moment of action and conflict. Regardless of whether the revolt was a genuinely course-changing event, the problem here is that in this moment of crisis that has followed, there is no single political tendency (Left, Right, or even anarchist) that is not going through a political crisis of its own—and none of them seem able to offer any viable alternatives as a result.

    In Chapter Fourteen Yiannis Kaplanis comes in to talk about the economic crisis on a tangible level. He writes about the economics of the sovereign debt crisis in Greece and describes how a country with an astonishing level of economic growth only saw this benefit very few. The economic data he presents shows how most people received a much worse deal even during the years of the "Greek miracle." This supposed economic "miracle" was based on credit expansion, the construction of public works, and the real estate boom, rather than well-planned developmental policies that would be for the benefit of the wider social strata. As a result, precarious forms of employment and job polarisation were on the rise, particularly for younger people and women. And so came the moment of December, after approximately a decade of long-drawn-out crisis experienced by the most vulnerable strata. Kaplanis contextualises this eruption within the framework of the ongoing crisis. What is more, this economy that excludes the many and benefits the few was not interrupted by the revolt; it lived on, leading to the eruption of the sovereign debt crisis, which, in turn, led to an even worse reconfiguration for the poorer strata—whose numbers were dramatically increasing all the while.

In Chapter Fifteen, David Graeber reminds us that no debt can exist without another party benefiting from it. One person's debt is another person's surplus—or, in other words, the surplus of other countries is intertwined with the Greek debt. Graeber shows that, historically, debt came before the invention of money, but suggests that monetary economy is directly linked to the existence of debt. Various political powers throughout history have managed to control the system of debt with a level of regulation that did not allow debt to spiral out of control. It is only in the current system of late capitalism that the control over debt has become so weak. In light of his historical analysis, Graeber proposes that this current politico-economic system has reached its limit: "the utter moral bankruptcy of this system… has been revealed to all," he suggests, and we are now inevitably in transition toward another form. As Graeber concludes, the trajectory of this transition will depend, among other things, upon the choices made by the antagonist movement and wider social fractions—and these will most definitely include the choice of approach toward debt itself.

Chapters Thirteen to Fifteen put the Greek crisis in context, whether historically (Graeber), economically (Kaplanis), or philosophically (Lynteris). Then, in Chapter Sixteen, TPTG attempt to place the Greek crisis in a global context. Here, they demystify the "debt crisis" by showing that it is the most recent expression of a protracted crisis of capitalist social relations, i.e. an exploitability crisis of labour power and a legitimacy crisis of the capitalist state and its institutions through a historical class analysis both on a global level and on Greece's national level. TPTG suggest that the so-called "'debt crisis' is intended to become a productive crisis: a driver of primitive accumulation, dispossession, and proletarianization, a linchpin for the terrorizing, the disciplining, and the more effective exploitation of the proletariat through the curbing of class conflicts, proletarian desires, and expectations." They go on to demonstrate all the measures of "shock therapy" applied to the proletariat in Greece until approximately September 2010 and the response of the working class up until then. The article concludes with remarks on the limitations of the current means of struggle in the fight against these attacks and the working class's relatively disproportionate reaction to the profound attacks against it.

Chapter Seventeen begins a subsection of critical discussion on the crisis of the social antagonist movement, exploring its practices and discourses in face of the wider economic and social crisis. For Christos Boukalas, the jumping off point is the murder of three bank workers on 5 May 2010 during the demonstration against the IMF/EU/ECB loan—one of the largest demonstrations Athens had seen in recent times. Identifying the event as a watershed moment for the anarchist movement, Boukalas looks back at its causes, and forward to its impact. He tries to find out what went wrong politically and ideologically, and how some fractions of the antagonist movement ended up causing what would lead to a tragic event in the midst of one of the most important demonstrations in recent Greek history. He traces its main source to the construction of a fetishised "revolutionary" socio-political identity, an identity that positions its bearer as separate from, and against, society. The political and ideological fallacies of these tendencies have profound impact on the entire anarchist movement. Boukalas tries to assess it by discussing the numerous anarchist reactions to the 5 May events. He sees the events as a rare occasion when the movement would be forced to undertake some critical evaluation of its attitudes and practices. His study of anarchist responses to the events seems to indicate that even this opportunity went begging.

In Chapter Eighteen, Alex Trocchi attempts a wider theoretical critique of our collective self as anarchists, insurrectionists, or other tendencies of the antagonist movement. In an age of crisis, and given the epochal apogee we lived during December's revolt, the question is not how to achieve insurrection but rather how to sustain it. Trocchi suggests that we need an outright change in our theory. Starting with the example of the revolt in Greece and the situations that followed, Trocchi's point is that for the insurrection to succeed we must perceive and do things far beyond the cliches of the anti-globalisation movement and other "protest" movements in the past few decades. One problem is the lack of a well-developed theory, which leads not only to identity-based politics and fetishising the insurrection itself, but to the trapping of anarchists within the regime of social war as enforced by late capitalism. As Trocchi puts it: "The insurrectionary question should change from 'How do we increase the intensity of the attack?' to 'How can the number of people involved in the attack increase?'" He ends by calling for the development of a new insurrectionist metaphysics, first of all amongst insurrectionists themselves. Revolts, as he concludes, have many more sympathisers than we may think. The question is how not to separate ourselves from them.

AN EXCEPTION NO LONGER

For many years we have grown accustomed to treating nearly everything coming out of Greece as somewhat mythical, or at least exceptional. Take its geography for example: the country is European, we are told, yet it is somewhat Oriental; it lies in the southern end of the Balkan peninsula yet it's in the West. Or politically: here is a European Union member-state whose laws resemble the bureaucracy of the Ottoman Empire, its finances edge closer to a "developing" country than the EU "core," and so on. And, let us not forget of course, the perceived strength of its anarchist and social antagonist movement in general: "They riot so often, and there are thousands of them in the streets"; "Well, that's just Greece." Here we have the peculiar Greek state, then, a state that has been perceived as—quite literally—a State of Exception, a territory in which all sorts of peculiarities, diversions, and anomalies can prevail. A haven on the edge of the Western world where social and class antagonism is still alive and kicking, a dissenting singularity standing as a reminder of the consensual veil falling over the political realm elsewhere. In his famous definition, Carl Schmitt reads sovereignty as the power to decide on the state of exception (1985: 5). The Greek territory had long ago joined the club of romanticised, far-away places in an imaginary realm decided upon and dictated by sovereignty itself: Chiapas, Buenos Aires, South Central, the French banlieues, Exarcheia…. Perceived as ultimate sites of anomaly, these were distant places (no matter how geographically close, in fact, you might happen to be to them), places supposedly playing host to struggles neoliberal sovereignty would never allow within its geographical core.

A strange thing happened after December 2008. From that moment on—that is, from that moment of absolute diversion from normality, of the ultimate exception—the Greek case was no longer exceptional. It would seem as if people across so many boundaries finally responded to Walter Benjamin's call for a real state of emergency (1942), a state of exception brought about by the oppressed, not their oppressors.

Sure enough, this was not just Greece anymore. So, then, was the Greek revolt a prelude to a European version of this global crisis? Or was it the last few words of the preceding chapter? By now, the question of what happened first matters little. More significant than the sequence of events is the occurrence of the events themselves. Blending in with global struggles, the moment of revolt was no longer a near-fantasy in a far-away place. And by being the first area in the Eurozone to ground the crisis so firmly, Greece was entering a global condition, therefore abandoning any exceptionality of its own for good.

A feeling of déjà vu, anyone? The U.S. government-backed military dictatorship of 1967–1974 was a crucial and failed experiment to determine whether Latin American-style military dictatorships could flourish on European soil. This time around, the same territory would once again host an experimental mode of governance in which powers are shifted away and above the level of national territory. Of course to us, as anarchists and anti-authoritarians, the distance from which orders come would not matter so much (more important is the fact that they are still coming!). But the landing of the IMF/EU/ECB "troika" in Athens as a key player in the everyday operations of the state is an experiment with repercussions reaching way beyond the ground on which we stand. What happens on Greek territory in the coming months and years may prove to be absolutely crucial. With the eyes of so many of our comrades in the social antagonist movement turned there during and after the December revolt, any perceived failure to halt the IMF's charge ahead could be incredibly demoralising. Yet in the face of this crisis, some of our comrades in the antagonist movement have been quick to dismiss our chances of victory in any possible way. One of the 20th century's major capitalist crises led to Fascism, then Nazism, as the argument goes, and thus there is supposedly a good chance that history will repeat itself. Of course history is never truly repeated and the outbreak of Nazism as a refuge of a previous capitalist crisis cannot act as any sort of indicator for its repetition.

Something new is about to be born. We live in a period that is not at all distant from its immediate past and is yet so alien, so monstrous. The gruesomeness of the monster lies precisely in its not-quite-human form of life: it resembles something human, but it is not quite the same. In this sense, our times are monstrous, but not for the first time. At the twilight of the rise of Fascism, Antonio Gramsci predicted from his prison cell: "The old world is dying away, and the new world struggles to come forth: now is the time of monsters" (Gramsci 1971). He was insightful enough to see that the world was changing and, even behind prison bars, he could feel the spectre of Fascism hanging in the air.

Yet take heart, for not all periods of transition create monsters. If they did, we might very well give up struggling and resign ourselves to the idea that history will continue to jump from one monstrosity to the next, even more appalling one. We remember Gramsci, but we also must remember what a "monster" is to begin with: it is a hybrid living being—usually part human, part animal. The fear it induces in humans is precisely due to its resemblance to them.

Instead of a conclusion, then, we want to close with the notion of hybridity as a metaphor for our time and place. The monster is the quintessential hybrid, a combination of life forms, human and bestial. Our own, collective position is also a hybrid one. As political subjects and as writers, all of us contributing to this collection stand simultaneously inside and outside the geographical boundaries of the Greek state and, of course, we stand between two points in time— between a present and a future, a fleeting moment, a moment that gives birth to monstrosities and the enormous potentialities contained in them. This is not a purely negative moment; living in these in-between times is not a threat, it is a potentiality. Breaking down the boundaries of present and future, we must read this relationship, following Georgio Agamben, as one between the outside and the inside: "the outside is not another space that resides beyond a determinate space," he says, "but rather, it is the passage, the exteriority that gives it access in a word, it is its face" (2007: 68). Let's take this as a metaphor for the present and the future: the future is not another time entirely outside our present; it is the exterior of the present, its façade—what gives it access, what allows us simultaneously to understand the limits of the present and to sense the move to the future. We are at that precise moment, dancing on that façade: A time when struggling for the way in which this transition will happen is more crucial than it has been for a long, long while. Wherever we are, we must quickly erect our antagonist social structures, as barricades ensuring this can happen on our own terms. For this transition, the place is here and the time is now.

PART ONE

_____

THE SITE: ATHENS

2

URBAN PLANNING AND REVOLT:

A SPATIAL ANALYSIS OF THE DECEMBER 2008 UPRISING IN ATHENS[1]

Vaso Makrygianni & Haris Tsavdaroglou

The revolt of December 2008 was not just a flare that lit suddenly or momentarily in the streets. It sprang from existing structures and relations among us and sowed seeds that are still very much alive. As soon as the news of Alexandros Grigoropoulos's murder broke, a surprisingly well-coordinated crowd of people managed to bridge existing territorial and social distances to create fields and forms of resistance no one had previously dared to imagine. The men and women rising up comprised a mixture of politically conscious individuals, university and high-school students, migrants, unemployed, and precarious workers who threw their identities into the melting pot of the rioting streets. December 2008 was unique mainly because the virus of contestation and resistance spread to every part of the city and deeply influenced the people who fought during the course of those days to claim back their lives. Greece, and Athens in particular, welcomed the revolt in their own way, different by far from the reaction to previous revolts as in LA, the French *banlieues*, or Argentina. In fact each *December* was and will be different as it emerges from varying places and invariably lays different roots.

This chapter does not constitute yet another more or less chronological narrative of December's events. This would have been impossible, despite the appreciable efforts that have been made to conceive the span and recurrence of the events in their entirety. Rather, it roams the Athenian metropolis before and during the revolt, attempting to illuminate those angles that ignited December's conflict. It sees space as a derivative of human relations, and cities as places of coexistence that can function as fields of resistance and as sites where everyday life can be reclaimed. Through a tour of Athens's particular urban characteristics, the chapter presents the territorial spread of conflict, examining the relationship between urban space and the events that took place in December and their consequent feedback into the city's vast web.

THE SPATIAL AND CLASS COMPOSITION OF ATHENS AFTER WWII

Greece's greatest urban transition took place after World War II and in particular after the end of the Civil War [the *emfylios*, see Glossary]. The post-war authorities, in their attempt to achieve social peace and to control the population, pushed for two parallel processes: first, a violent urbanisation[2] and proletarianisation of what was, by a vast majority, the left-wing rural population, and second, a certain amount of tolerance towards unlicensed building and construction. The latter was linked with the emergence of the system of *antiparochi* [a construction system that brought together landowners and building contractors—see Glossary]. In its promotion of private ownership and development, *antiparochi* would in fact comprise a spatial and social extension of the Marshall Plan[3], which aimed at the capitalist development of the country. The Plan's aim was the post-war elimination of communist visions—still popular at the time—by promoting a liberal ideology of economic development, strengthening small private property, and promoting specific new patterns of consumption.

Yet this strategy of unlicensed building in fact led—from the mid-1950s onwards—to extensive proletarian neighbourhoods and slums. Combined with already existing refugee[4] neighbourhoods and traditional working-class quarters, the new districts created sites with strong class consciousness. These districts had some very particular spatial characteristics: a high population density; low-rise, small buildings; narrow streets; limited communal public space; mixed land use; etc.

The state response to the emerging militant working class of the 1960s took the shape of the mandatory demolition of slums through the further promotion of *antiparochi* and the subsequent class transformation of some of the workers into petit bourgeois. Thus, from the mid-1960s and continuing through the 1970s, concrete apartment blocks began to dominate the cityscape of Athenian neighbourhoods. During the 1980s, however, Athens began to suffocate as a capitalist mega-machine. Its chaotic gigantism was not accompanied by the construction of the necessary infrastructure. The city was plainly not functioning effectively; it was short-circuiting (Michalis 2007). The Operation for the Reconfiguration of the Urban Plan (ORUP) and the 1985 Master Plan of Athens constituted the authorities' attempt to rationalize the city's development. Entire districts of buildings constructed without licences were legalised and vast pieces of land were allocated to the towns surrounding Athens, laying the foundations for future suburbanisation. In the case of inner Athens, the model of a polycentric city was applied.

The ORUP project involved an attempt to suppress the city's anarchist and far-left political spectrum by means of urban planning. The idea was to gentrify the very downtown district to where much of the city's radical political activity had been gravitating since the early 1980s: Exarcheia. The attempted modernisation project largely failed, partly for bureaucratic reasons and partly because the clientelist form of the state and widespread petty ownership prevented large-scale investments. These factors, plus the social struggles taking place in the area during the early 1990s, were not conducive to the gentrification of Exarcheia. Simultaneously, the bourgeois strata started to flee to the northern and southern suburbs. This movement would be accelerated during the 1990s and 2000s, when more than 500,000 migrants arrived in Athens.[5]

The 1990s and the early 2000s were the times of the so-called "powerful Greece"[6] with the country joining the European Union's Economic and Monetary Union (2001), its ruthless exploitation of the Balkans (1990s–2000s) and Athens's hosting of the 2004 Olympic Games. Gentrification and major infrastructure construction work became driving forces of the economy. Social movements' response came quickly, with the eruption of the 2006–2007 student movement. Alongside this, the schoolteachers' movement of 2006 would once again fill the capital's streets with people protesting against the neoliberal reconfiguration of education. The ultra-parliamentary left and particularly the anarchist and autonomous scene would simultaneously establish stable points of reference in the metropolitan domain, setting up gathering-places and squats. In addition, urban movements emerged in resistance to the environmental destruction caused by pre-Olympics building work. Finally, the first base unions—mainly workers in the most precarious labour sectors—were formed. These would play a key role in disseminating the December revolt into the wider social strata.

ATHENS TODAY

The metropolitan area of Athens-Attica

Contemporary metropolitan Athens covers an area of 3,375 km² with an official population of 3,740,051 inhabitants: one third of Greece's entire population.[7] The municipality of Athens covers 412 km² and has an average population density of 8,150 inhabitants/km². In some areas, however, this density exceeds 40,000 inhabitants/km². The city's gross domestic product (GDP) per capita was €17,823 in 2001, but more recent years have seen a significant increase: in 2006, the GDP per capita of the Attica region reached €26,212, surpassing the EU average at the time by 131.1%—ranking Attica amongst the 42 richest districts in the EU. In viewing the entire urban complex of Athens, one can clearly identify which neighbourhoods are working class, which are middle class and which contain bourgeois strata.

THE CITY CENTRE

The centre of Athens has a higher population density than all European capitals, including Istanbul. Only cities in Africa and Asia, such as Cairo and Mumbai, have higher population densities in their urban cores.[8] Besides this very high population density, Athens's distinctive features also include diffuse and mixed land use, increased urban density, lack of public open spaces, and high-rise blocks as the prime constituent units of the urban area.[9]

Although the historical centre of Athens during the 1990s was abandoned by many of its old inhabitants in favour of the suburbs

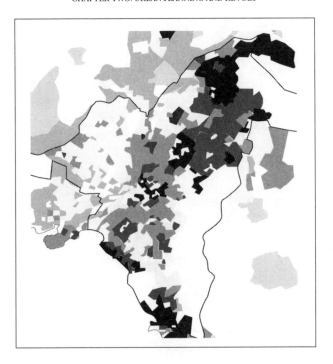

The class composition of municipalities in Attica, 2001. Concentrations of higher economic strata are shaded darker, lower economic strata lighter.
Source: Gortsos, K. Mark, A., P. Camoutsis 2008.

new "clandestine" residents would quickly settle there. Central neighbourhoods, therefore, are now largely migrant neighbourhoods. The centre of Athens is something between a site of vitality and a ghetto, where globalisation and racist attacks coexist. Just before the 2004 Olympic Games, a large redevelopment project was undertaken in the Attica basin, including central Athens. Areas of the centre such as Gazi, Psirri, and Metaxourgeio were gentrified, land values rose sharply, and the old residents were displaced in order to allow for gigantic entertainment facilities and accommodation for the nouveau riche. This process would involve the emerging "creative class,"[10] large contractors, real estate companies, the government, and "concerned citizens." Efforts to turn the centre into a controlled multiplex for tourism, entertainment, consumption, and innovative entrepreneurship are still ongoing, creating an even more mixed and complex situation.

The historical centre of Athens is the place where its administrative, police, and judiciary authorities are concentrated and where they coexist with commercial use, housing, education, culture, welfare,

33

Land use in the central area and urban complex of Athens: Areas of central functions are shown in dark grey, general residential areas in grey, and pure residential areas in white.

entertainment, and even industrial areas. Despite an ongoing attempt to remove all central administrative functions[11] from the centre of Athens, this does have a clear strategic importance when it comes to social-political struggles—hence the enhancement of policing and surveillance.[12]

PRIVATE SPACES: HIGH-RISE HOUSING BLOCK

The most common private residential space in Athens is the high-rise housing block (*polykatoikia* in Greek, literally multiple housing, see Glossary)—the primary cell of urban social reproduction. Although these housing blocks were a symbol of modernisation in interwar Greece, over the following decades they came to fulfil urgent housing needs.

The structure of the building contains the characteristics of vertical social class segregation: basements (low income), ground floor (shops), intermediate floors (middle-class homes and offices), penthouse (high income). Although originally specified as residential, the block of flats offers endless options through its flexible structural system: space inside the block may be used for accommodation, an office, a ministry,

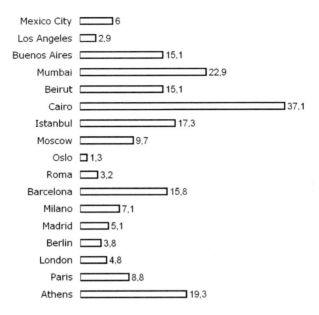

Population density and metropolitan areas, in 1,000 residents/km².

a shop, a warehouse, a restaurant, a workshop, a supermarket, a café, a bar, or even a garage. At the same time, because Athens only has a few public spaces and very narrow streets, these housing blocks absorb the city within them and in turn empty out their interior to the city (Woditsch 2009). Private and public life interact in its hallways, its balconies and façades. Flags hanging over balconies, scribbles on walls, stickers in elevators, slogans on walls—multiple signs of communication transforming the impersonal shell of the building into a dynamic living organism that constantly beats, yells, makes a multitude of noises, falls in love, and quarrels.

PUBLIC SPACES: STREETS

Green spaces in the city of Athens measure 2.5 m² per inhabitant, whereas in most European cities[13] the figure exceeds 15 m² per inhabitant. The largest part of public space in the city is its most authentic form—that is, the street. Streets as public spaces are alive for 24 hours a day, as the mixture of multiple uses permits and promotes such a situation. The street is a place of open-air trade, meeting, finding a job, and so on—while, of course, it is also the prime site of protest.

During the past fifteen years, nearly 500 demonstrations have taken place in the city annually.[14] Urban planning in Athens is

Metropolitan Areas	Average streets width	Average density cross roads
Berlin	15-120m	270m
New York	15-45m	245m
Los Angeles	15-190m	220m
Moscow	10-80m	180m
Beijing	5-160m	160m
Buenos Aires	10-135m	115m
Barcelona	5-60m	115m
Paris	6-70m	110m
Mexico City	10-60m	95m
London	10-90m	90m
Milano	5-55m	75m
Athens	5-50m	70m
Mumbai	5-45m	50m
Beirut	7-35m	45m
Istanbul	2-45m	40m
Algiers	10-25m	40m
Napoli	5-35m	35m
Cairo	3-70m	35m
Baghdad	3-70m	30m

The geometric characteristics of streets.

characterised by the small distances (an average of 70 m) between street intersections. This is owed to the small size of building blocks, which is in turn a result of the fragmented nature and small size of property-holding in the city. The frequency of road intersections has particular significance when it comes to the crucial moments of demonstrations and clashes with the police. Factors such as visibility, ambushes, or the ability to communicate are directly related to the physical and geometrical characteristics of urban space. So, for example, streets in "unruly" Exarcheia intersect every 45 m, while in the bourgeois neighbourhoods of the northern suburbs, junctions occur every 220 m.[15]

36   Compared to its western counterparts, Athens has much smaller blocks and many more streets. Its public space, which has to be under

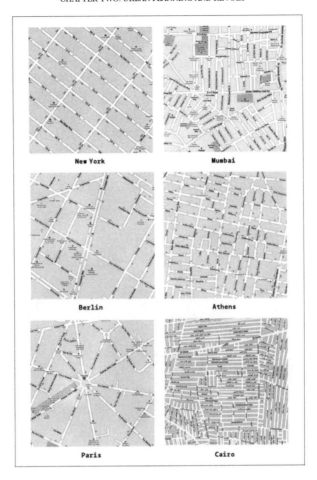

Sections of the city centres of New York, Mumbai, Berlin, Athens, Paris, and Cairo. The maps are at the same scale and cover areas of 600m x 600m.

surveillance and control, is therefore much larger and denser. In terms of urban planning and zoning, Athens is a pure failure. If anything, it may even come closer to the largely spontaneously-formed populous concentrations of the Middle East, India, and Africa.

MOVEMENT STRUCTURES, SQUATS, SOCIAL CENTRES, AUTONOMOUS SPACES

Squats and social centres emerged in Greece in the late 1980s and the early 1990s, the era of the high-school student movements of 1990–1991 and the emergence of the punk scene. Anarcho-punk squatters occupied abandoned buildings and turned them into spaces for subcultural activity, collective living, and dissident action (see c/krümel

2005). Yet it would take a decade for the practice of squatting to spread. Between 2000 and 2005, anti-authoritarian squatted places would spring up all across the metropolitan complex. At the same time, more than fifteen squats were created in cities outside Athens while many political, social, and student centres (*stekia*, see Glossary) appeared in every university city. These social and political centres and squats were preconditions for establishing an antagonistic everyday reality. December 2008 was the first time the dynamics of the social centres and squats found themselves organised in the streets, all across the country.

MOVEMENT STRUCTURES 2008

STARS INDICATE AREAS WITH SQUATS OR SOCIAL CENTERS

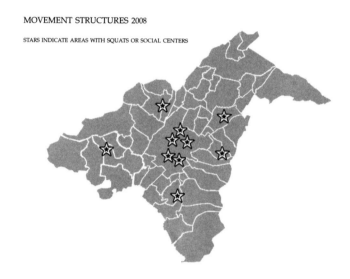

Squats and social centres in the urban area of Athens.

UNIVERSITIES

The first universities were established during the mid-19th and early 20th centuries in Athens, the then-newly-named capital of the young Greek state. They were located on what was then the *edge of the city* and comprised of small campuses of between one and three hectares (e.g. Kapodistrian, Panteion, Technical, Harokopion, and ASOEE). These first universities had a manageable size and a high density of students for the area and created an intense sense of community; by no means did they have the impersonal and chaotic characteristics of the large campuses of the later period. As Athens expanded and the universities were organically integrated into the urban fabric, they became inextricable entities in the city's everyday life. The liveliness of the universities and the political procedures that take place there are increased by the fact that the composition of the student community has spread across social classes. Yet due to a lack of space, and following the experience of the subversive student movements of the 1960s and the 1970s, university campuses built during the dictatorship or the post-dictatorial years would purposefully be built away from the urban core. Nevertheless, old university buildings in Athens and other cities are still prime places in which social movements organise. These buildings offer resources for meetings, events, concerts, and sites from which to organise the logistics of the movement.

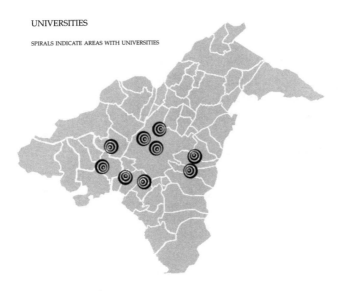

UNIVERSITIES

SPIRALS INDICATE AREAS WITH UNIVERSITIES

University faculties in the urban area of Athens.

TERRITORIAL EXPANSION OF A REVOLT

"A BURNING CITY IS A BLOSSOMING FLOWER"

Athens may have been the European metropolis with the most barricades in the first decade of the new millennium. December 2008 was not the first time that streets and public buildings were occupied, but it was one of the very small number of occasions when this took place in such a massive and coordinated way. Starting on the Saturday evening, the nuclei of revolt were mainly the streets, the schools, the university faculties, the public buildings, the social centres, and the occupations that spread across Athens and all over the country. These nuclei stayed in place for days; the remarkable nature of the revolt was the fact that the *revolted* [see Glossary] were simultaneously and constantly at countless points in the city.

GROUND ZERO—SYMBOLIC SPACE BECOMES REALITY

Saturday night in Exarcheia: Alexis's murder takes place in the "hottest" area of the city, at the "hottest" time of the week. The time and the place of the murder could not have been more symbolic and provocative. Only a few hours after the murder, as the news spread all over Greece instantly via mobile phones and the internet, people gather in the district of Exarcheia. It is clear, from the very outset, that the revolt is situated in the public space. People attack many targets, recognising that their enemy is not the one who squeezed the trigger but the system that created him. Therefore, they target not only the police departments but also everything that expresses the domination of the police. For years, Exarcheia has had a symbolic meaning for the antagonistic movement; there, any clashes or the very presence of police has been treated as an intrusion on to "a ground occupied by the antagonistic movement." Exarcheia can stay alive as long as its people can stay there. The murder of a place's people means the death of the place itself. Therefore, the murder of Alexis Grigoropoulos was interpreted as a murderous attack against the entire neighbourhood. People are gathering at the square, the reference point of the neighbourhood and the entire city, but also at the Technical University, the reference point for every emergency. What is known, "safe," and always expected is taking place in Athens during the following hours; clashes all night long, on Patision Street, starting from Athens Polytechnic. Those who had the fastest reaction times are running to the common confrontation areas in order to make themselves visible, to awaken the city, to defend their life. Exarcheia, the Technical University, Patision Street, have retained their character and their memories for years. The clashes are spreading easily, initially at a smaller scale compared to what the following days will bring. The streets are full of targets and the instantiation of nearby pillars is easy and sensible. Therefore, the Faculty of Law and the University of Economics (the former ASOEE) are being occupied, so that they can be turned into counter-information centres

and strongholds for clashes. The existence of a closed and clearly protected space helped but also captured the street revolted. The university
institutions have turned once more into nuclei of revolt. After the first
evening, another dimension of the events emerges, as the actions gradually move beyond the common routes. The news is travelling fast via
mobile phones and the internet. The points where the first "reactions"
gather are not randomly chosen. They were essentially central areas
of the metropolis where young people spend their Saturday evenings
(Monastiraki, Petralona, etc.) and they serve as a centre for people who
are looking for other areas besides Exarcheia. Clashes are now taking
place on Ermou Street, targeting commercial shops and the police station of the Acropolis district, near Omonia Square. So far, the targets
are known; police stations, banks, rubbish bins, the offices of the ruling
party, shops; easily-approached targets in the city centre. Nobody has
yet got closer to the crucial police station of Exarcheia, from where
the murderers started patrolling, or the police headquarters, where the
murderers took shelter afterwards.

NEW SUBJECTS = NEW PLACES OF CONFLICT VS. NEW PLACES OF CONFLICT =
NEW SUBJECTS

By the next morning, Sunday 7 December, had become clear
that the perpetrator of the murder, the police, would be targeted. The
make-up of the forming demonstration is a characteristic example of
demonstrations over the following days. Thousands of people are gathering, under the identity of a raging crowd. The target is the General Police
Department of Athens.[16] The location of the target in Athens is extremely convenient and this will always pose a problem for the city administration. Of course, the 2.5 km distance to it is greatly extended by the presence of hundreds of police officers, shop windows, and tear gas. This is
how space and time are doubled. On the way, Alexandra Avenue, a road
40–45 m wide, is literally devastated. Rage is actively expressed on every
corner of both sides of the street. Shops and petrol stations as well as
public buildings are under attack. Every space that represents trade, consumption, the city in its dominant form, must be destroyed as a means of
revenge, because in the end everything and everybody is responsible for
a death that symbolizes thousands of other deaths on the city concrete.
Of course the cops are not going to allow any approach to their fortress.
As the demonstration is disbanded, people are being chased towards the
upward narrow streets of Neapoli, while others will turn back, towards
the Polytechnic School. After a while, the police station in Exarcheia will
see its first attack. After all, it is only 700m away from Alexandra Avenue.

41

The police's tactic, to push demonstrations into the city alleys in order to decentralize the protesters' force, did not bear fruit this time. At the same moment, new, smaller fractions of resistance were created, and they spread with the same aggressiveness towards different parts of the city centre. Similar formations played a vital part in most Greek cities over the course of the following days. The people were determined, whether on an avenue or dissolved in the city alleys. For every different space, there was a different tactic. The situation was beginning to spread across the city, while the police strove to surround the perceived source of all evil, Exarcheia. Exarcheia, at that moment, was, however, more of a symbolic space, since the news had already spread across the streets and houses, through the television, to the balconies and rooftops from which the smoke of the burning Alexandra Avenue was visible. The situation spread, of course, across people's minds and consciences as well, something that is hard to restrict geographically. The real space of conflict was, at that moment, the city as a whole. The riots continued, eventually involving migrants who were living near Patision. For the migrants, Exarcheia itself and the Polytechnic School probably did not mean much; for them, it was about the neighbourhoods in which they lived and in which they were persecuted every day. At this exact spot, when the new subjects entered onto the field of battle, facts began to take a new form. Space, in its wider than material sense—urban space but also the social space of conflict and resistance—expanded even more, and it is at this point that the revolt began to look like a revolt.

The turmoil no longer belongs to Exarcheia. It now belongs to Athens and to the whole of the country, and therefore to the people who mostly experience its "ugly" side. As ever-expanding groups of people become involved, new spaces enter the topology of the revolt and new places of conflict emerge. Expropriation begins. In the city centre, expropriations take place near Piraeus Street, Koumoundourou and Victoria Square. These are places where migrants live, and they are familiar with violence and police operations.

The constituted presence of students marked the beginning of the third day of revolt, Monday 8 December. Many youth had already taken part in squats and riots, but on Monday, the first school day, they organise as pupils, recognising that the gun was turned against one of them and thus against them. The appearance of students and new residents changed the geography of revolt rapidly. Every neighbourhood has a school and a police station, and those places will bring the revolt to a peak, thus filling the map with spots of resistance.

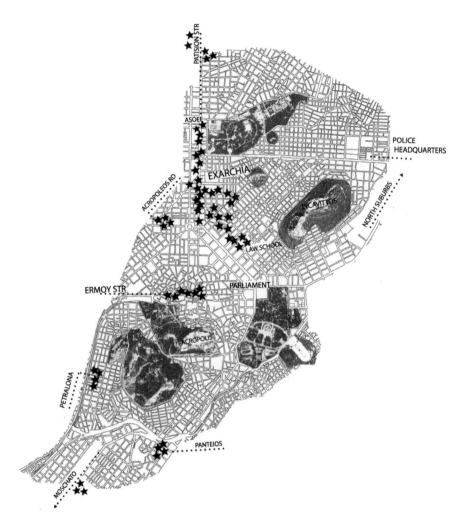

Districts of the demonstrations, clashes, and direct actions.

The student demos start from different parts of Athens, where the schools are located, and converge at a common place of reference, Propylea.[17] The metropolis is filled with targets, which are not hard to find. The telephone network and the internet, along with the school network, have proved to be of great use, as have with the three squats in the city centre. The Monday demonstration was a combination of all of the above and managed to fill the centre of the city for 3 km. On the same night, a unique situation, which will astonish millions of people, is created. During the next evening, on Tuesday 9 December, the down-town "aura" will reach Zephyri.[18] This night in Zephyri will be of great importance, since it is one of very few occasions when its residents will try to interact with events in the city centre.

The involvement of various subjects was a characteristic of the revolt. Although the people repeatedly gathered under pre-formed iden-tities, new identities arose through the December conflicts and everyday presence on the street: those of the struggling subjects, who meet and act together, creating a new collective We, ready to defend its everyday exis-tence on the streets of the metropolis. The revolt materialized because it concerned an ever-growing number of groups. In this way it spread all over the city, and for that reason it is of spatial interest.

THE STREET

On Tuesday the 9th, another spot is added to the map, a neigh-bourhood in the south, in Faliro, where Grigoropoulos is to be buried. On the streets, in the middle of conflicts after the funeral, policemen trying to defend the local police station will use their weapons. The vio-lence of the state has no limits and will reach almost all areas.

Until this point, the place of revolt has definitely been the street. It is one of the last intra-class places in town, where its residents coexist, although in a far from harmonious way. It is one of the primary places of control. The ruler of the street becomes the ruler of the city. Although the streets may constitute a continuous channel for the flow of commodities, they are easily transformed into a channel for conflict, since they are, most of all, places of communication and the meeting of people. The natural space in the city is still a protagonist in extreme cases. In states of emergency, that tend to become the rule in the mod-ern metropolis, an event must be made known through the presence of people in the most public part of town. Barricades are set up, the flow of everyday life is interrupted, and the streets and squares become the fields of an open public battle that now concerns everybody.

The occupation of university spaces, schools, and pre-existing structures functioned more to create bases than places that could absorb the crowd. The rebels had conquered the street during those days, and they would not leave it for any occupation. On the other hand, the road as a place of conflict is fluid and hard to demarcate. Therefore, even during the conflicts, the rebels will often seek the "safety" of a building, whether as shelter, as a starting point, or as a place for discussion and counter-information. The stability of a building against the fluidity of the street will always be an important issue for the antagonistic movement.

During the days of the revolt, and after them, the streets functioned in various ways. They served as channels of communication that daily transferred the message of revolt to the metropolis, as parts of a network that connected the distant neighbourhoods of Athens, but also as links among buildings that brought the revolt into the private spaces of the city. Their unlimited capacity always leaves all chances open. The streets of Athens hosted hundreds of demonstrations and events and thousands of people during the days of December. The continuous presence of the rebels on the streets caused enough problems to the circulation of commodities, and the market was literally paralysed.[19] The interruption of traffic and the conversion of road use takes place in many different, and sometimes inspired, ways. On Friday 19 December, a concert in Propylea is organized, and almost 5,000 people use the street as a huge music stage. A few days later, during the occupation of the Athens Opera House (Lyriki), the "rebel ballet" will shortly interrupt the traffic in Academia Street, in order to dance in front of the astonished drivers.

The assassination of Alexis Grigoropoulos happened in public, at the corner of Mesologiou and Tzavela Street. In the same public way, thousands filled the public space, claiming it as a space for meeting and "doing" life in the city, and not as a place of death for its residents.

COMPARING DECEMBER'S REVOLT IN ATHENS TO URBAN REVOLTS ACROSS THE WORLD

December's revolt in Athens started with clashes in the neighbourhood of Exarcheia, yet such clashes, demonstrations, and direct actions were quick to spread to the city's periphery. Distances within the Athens metropolitan area are small when compared to respective areas that have seen urban revolts in the past. Population density, on the other hand, is extremely high in Athens. The maximum distance of actions and clashes from the city centre were thus confined to a 5 to 13 km zone.

In order to better understand the importance of the spatial confinement of December's revolt in Athens we would like to use the examples of revolts in other urban areas: namely, Paris, Los Angeles, Milan, and Buenos Aires.

The revolt closest to Athens in terms of time is the Paris revolt of 2005. The sites where the clashes took place were the remote suburbs next to highways, the dormitory towns, the working-class migrant neighbourhoods: single-use *banlieues* ["suburbs" in French] with no commercial or other functions, cut off from the city centre, resembling the characteristics of a ghetto. The metropolitan area of Paris is three times as populous and five times as large as Athens. In Paris, the distance of the protesting suburbs from the city centre was between 13 and 25 km. Clichy-sous-Bois, the suburb from which the revolt began, lies 19 km east from the city centre; clashes spread northward to Goussainville (22 km from the city centre) and southward to Neuily sur Marne (20 km), while the closest nucleus of the revolt was Saint Denis, itself 13 km from the city centre. The revolt, for the most part, circulated between neighbourhoods on the perimeter of Paris and only threatened the city centre for the briefest moment. Similarly, even though the revolt inspired and ignited smaller-scale migrant revolts in other French cities, it almost completely failed to spread among other social groups (students, workers). The result being that the revolted, despite their enormous rage and fighting spirit (they engaged in clashes with the forces of repression for twenty days) found themselves isolated—and the revolt never became generalised.

Los Angeles, the city with the largest and most diffused metropolitan area in the USA, played host to the Watts Rebellion in 1965. Lasting for five days, the rebellion took place 22 km away from the city centre. The urban parts where it took place were migrant areas of residential use, where the narrowest streets are 20–25 m wide and avenues are up to 70–80 m. The revolt of 1992 took place in South Central Los Angeles, again in residential migrant neighbourhoods and with the distance from the city's financial and commercial centre exceeding 10 km. Despite its extremely violent characteristics, the revolt was quelled within six days.

In Milan in the seventies (from the heated autumn of 1969 to the generalised movement of 1977) a constant struggle was in process for the takeover of the city by workerist autonomy, the so-called "Indians of the metropolis," and the proletarian youth. This was the time that saw the transition from the vertical and centralised structure of leftist organisations and the "mass worker" to the threshold of the "social worker" and the diffused social factory. The spatial expression of this transition takes place with the decay of the headquarters of leftist organisations, situated exclusively within the administrative and financial centre of the metropolis (competing, as they were, with the institutional political status quo) and the parallel formation of street groups, occupations, and social centres in the perimeter of Milan. For the people in struggle, centralised place no longer comprises an identity, a becoming of the self, or a characteristic (Moroni 1996). The form of

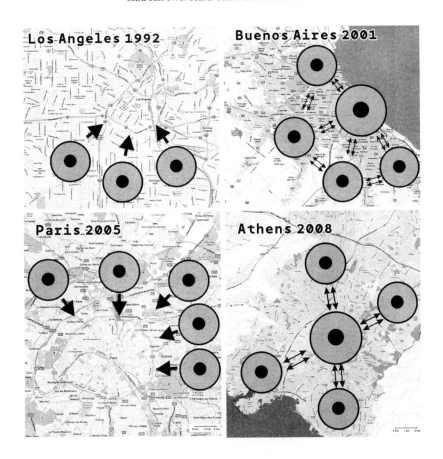

Nodes and flows of revolt.

the new subjects of struggle overlooks the city centre and treats it as merely a place where new tactics of auto-reduction are applied, along with appropriations and clashes. The places where the circles of the proletarian youth, punks, and "metropolitan Indians" grow roots coincide with the working-class suburbs and are situated on a perimeter of 7–15 km from the historical centre of the city. Subsequently, then, the direction is from the periphery toward the occupation of the centre. Additionally, apart from the vast working-class suburbs, hordes of people come from the hinterland of Milan to participate in the demonstrations. The movement in the metropolis of Milan never saw a moment of revolt; nevertheless, the entire decade of the 1970s was packed with periods of intense movement activity, struggle, clashes, and creativity.

The Argentinian revolt of 2001 and its course in Buenos Aires might be spatially closest to the Athenian example. However, what ig-

47

nited it was substantially different to the cases of Paris, Athens, and Los Angeles—since, after a prolonged period of financial crisis and supervision of the country by the IMF, what ignited the revolt was the freezing of bank accounts and the middle classes coming out on to the streets. The revolted, unlike most other cases of urban struggle, included a great range of politicised individuals, students, unemployed, and petit-bourgeois strata who came from nearly the entire city. On the very first day, they were able to take over the city centre and the Plaza de Mayo and to besiege the parliament. At the same time, more than 200 popular assemblies were taking place in nearly all the neighbourhoods and suburbs of the Argentine capital, over a radius larger than 10 km. The revolt in Argentina and Buenos Aires saw —besides clashes, appropriations, and direct actions—the occupation of workspaces (factories, hotels) and created structures of reproduction, a precious legacy for the generations to come.

INSTEAD OF A CONCLUSION

SPACE AS A FIELD OF POWER

Spatial dominance is of great importance for those in resistance—and not just for them. Urban space operates as a symbol of power and authority, as a signal of overall dominance in political and everyday life. What took place in Athens in December was a parallel struggle not only for territorial dominance but also for the control over meanings produced by the city space. A typical example was the struggle over the plastic Christmas tree in Syntagma Square. The revolted did not merely torch a plastic tree, but the symbol of Christmas for the entire city of Athens. This was considered a matter of major importance; in the days that followed, strong riot police forces would protect the new Christmas tree, following the Mayor's orders. A few days later, the Mayor himself would send bulldozers over to Kyprou and Patision Park [translator's note: the latter is one of the two parks taken over by locals in Athens after December's revolt], his aim being to create a parking space in one of the densest neighbourhoods of the city. The defence of the park and its trees by neighbours would be described as vandalism on the side of authority—yet the protection of the plastic tree was an act of the highest importance for the life of the city! Undoubtedly, in those days revolted were in large part dominating the city. And if the dominant is the person who has the capacity to change the rules (the capacity to install an exception) then the revolted were dominant over the production of their space; they were the dominant

48

producers of a rupture in the everyday life of the city. For many, this was a game of authority. The magic of control over the streets (the absolute public space) can lure even the most devoted anti-authoritarian. Yet for most, it was a change in everyday life beyond anything that had been imagined so far.

There is no central planning or strategy; tiny elements of this will make an appearance only in the aftermath of the events. The central stage belongs to the memory and experience of similar events but, above all, to the determination and acts of the thousands who met in the streets. In any case, what was typical of December's revolt was not a defensive stance against state violence (defence, after all, makes little sense in a revolt) but a constant offensive against all that resembles the presence of sovereign power. In the tiny space of one or two nights, the torching of the "old world" had to be complete, not to allow the slightest shadow of doubt over the fact that revolt had taken over every part of the urban whole.

FROM THE CENTRE TO THE CITY – THE LONG MARCH OF A REVOLT

"The wave" began from those places already bearing meaning, where everyone feels "familiar" with clashes, where tear gas and fire arouse the senses on an everyday level. Actions take place with a direction from the already-conquered centre toward the outside. This "exodus" from the centre was typical of the revolt movement. Despite the fact that perhaps the most "spectacular" actions would take place in the continuously-occupied centre, the "exodus" to the periphery and the rest of the country comprised an even larger spectacle—the assassination and the instinctive responses allowed not even a shadow of doubt that the situation concerned everyone. Alexis, after all, was "one of us"—whatever the repercussions of this might be. The involvement of new subjects was by then a given and crucial in putting the message across: "You will not shoot us in cold blood—and when you do so, expect anything in response." From the moment this was no longer a minority issue (e.g. belonging solely to the anarchists), it automatically escaped the symbolism of Exarcheia and ceased to be defined within a given "space," as authority would perhaps hope. In order for the intervention into everydayness to be "real," it had to be as close to everyday life as possible: to the family, the neighbourhood—not a "sterile cluster of freedom" in the centre. As the revolt was distancing itself from a mere clash between police and anarchists it would simultaneously try to inhibit other meanings. The revolted tried to touch as many aspects of the everyday life as they could, such as labour, public space, the arts, cir-

49

culation, and survival in the city—all by taking decentralised action in symbolic spaces. This is how the GSEE building was occupied, as well as the opera house, town halls, and schools; interventions took place at theatres, ticket validation machines on the public transport network were sabotaged, and so much more. In reality, the periphery of the metropolis was never immune to the "virus of freedom." For the first time, however, everything came under the same light—"co-ordinated," "simultaneous," and diffused. The actions taking place at the same time in countless places of the city created a labyrinthine network with a start but no finish. After December 2008, one can only suspect that, no matter how far centres of power relocate, future revolts will be possible, since the creativity of the revolted easily surpasses any imagination on the side of the planners of authority.

At the same time, the revolt traversed through networks of relationships and communication, but also via images and testimonies in places no one could have predicted. The place of the revolt expanded to reach France when, on 15 December 2008, the minister of education there temporarily revoked the educational reform plan, perhaps affected by the wave of disobedience in Greece. Zapatistas sent their very own message of support, while solidarity actions took place in more than 30 countries and 150 cities, from Japan to Argentina and from Cairo to Helsinki.

THE SPACE OF THE REVOLT

Most actions, occupations and marches of the revolt took place primarily in the central and southern part of the metropolitan area of Athens, in a zone with a 15 km radius—only a handful of actions took place outside this. The space of the revolt is situated primarily south of Attici Road, west of Immitus Mountain, north of the suburb of Glyfada, east of the Egaleo ring road. The countless occupations of schools and universities did not "trap" people inside these buildings. The space of the revolt was primarily that of the street, the public space, the park, and the square. It was also, however, the space of radio waves, of television (thanks to station occupations), of the internet, and the telephone. The countless blogs offered fertile ground for the circulation of ideas as much as the immediate spread of information. In this case, the internet and mobile phones greatly expanded the space of the revolt. If, then, space requires all senses in order to be produced and understood (Pallasmaa 2005), all senses were at the disposal of the events. And so the sound of a stun grenade would create space beyond the physical boundaries of an action, while the taken-over PA system of a shopping mall would transmit the message of the revolt even to those pretending nothing was going on. At the same time, newspapers with smashed shop fronts on their covers hanging outside corner shops,[20] the image of Alexis and of the torched Christmas tree would create the setting of a revolt even at the most "distant" point of the metropolis.

EVERYDAY LIFE AND RARE ACTS – THE RANDOM EVENT IN STATISTICS

Important acts are not always captured by statistics.[21] Indeed, during December possibilities opened up for everything to happen everywhere. The revolt was full of events against normality of which even the Situationists would be jealous. It was full of disruptions to the hourly schedule of the city, which no statistical analysis could predict. December sought (just like capitalism—and after all, December is part of it too) endless novelty, surprise. Space could not be policed by experts, whether these were on the side of the repression or the protesters. Everyone stood in a fluid space (Bauman 2007) and even experienced participants did not know what could happen. And this is where there are two sides to the coin. On one side, the side of authority, this was a "liquid fear" (Bauman 2006), a possible "lift" of the "security" condition. On the other side, however, possibilities opened up for each and everyone to turn desires into reality. At that point, exceptional things were born. The revolt was doubtlessly a rupture in the everyday, perhaps reaching its apogee at the moment when the everyday became revolt. This exact "reality" had so far been trapped within the island of Exarcheia but would now spread across the entire city—and so, a few days after 6 December, it seemed normal for someone to sit on a couch in the middle of a street while a bank was in flames nearby. Indeed, important acts such as those of December cannot be captured by statistics—we should never forget they are born from everyday life.

THE REVOLTED

> These people did not arrive here in an organised manner, that is, they did not come here with some social façade, bearing any social representation. They did not arrive and come in the building stating that they want to protest for anything at all.... [T]hese people then did not arrive in an organised manner at the ERT headquarters and I denounce them.... [A]t no point, to be precise, was there any occupation, no one occupied the broadcasting corporation. What happened was its storming by small unorganised groups which entered the TV studio by the use of force.... [T]hey also gave me a text with no signature, with no title, a non-paper with which they denounce the way in which various TV stations present the events... something which does not concern us at all.... [W]e cannot tolerate units and particular groups with no image, with

51

no face, which engage in a targeted operation to withhold the Greek people's right to information. It is a condemnable event with characteristics that exceed democracy.

—Panagopoulos 2008[22]

The outburst of the director of ERT reveals the unbelievable *thrasos* of authority to insist, even in the midst of a revolt, to define the form, the faces, and the rule of behaviour of the revolted. Yet it does something else too: it outlines in the most vivid of ways the ghost of the revolted as seen through the eyes of authority. It describes the complete confusion caused by the mix of the "faceless" protesting people. No koukoulonomos [the so-called hoodie-law, see Glossary] could ever hold when faced with such a crowd. Indeed, authority could not have done a better job in outlining the face of its enemy. And this surprise for the identity of the revolted was not felt only from the side of authority but also from the antagonist movement. Thousands met in the streets, not in organised groupings but in a crowd. The "old" correlatives were lost in face of a collective—and at the same time "peculiar"—"we." Whatever attempt to create an identity of the revolted failed. It is necessary for forces of repression to create a face for their enemy in order to target them more easily. And yet, the divisions that the voice of sovereignty would spit out through mass media, between the "good" and "bad," "justly" and "unreasonably" protesting, between migrants, looters, hooligans, anarchists, and "even young girls" that would be in the streets—these divisions were not entirely untrue. Indeed, inside this crowd there existed discreet "groupings" with their own practice. The "new urban residents" found themselves in their own neighbourhoods, destroying or looting what for them were not "carriers of alienation" but essentials of which capitalism had deprived them.[23]

Many were quick to distance themselves from such events. Others hid behind the identity of the concrete politicised subject, while some just kept on smashing things up. At the same time, public space would vindicate yet another aspect of its history. The conditional presence of gender, or even its exclusion, was a reality even in the "open and public" spaces of the revolt. We saw very few migrant women out in the streets. December was a part of everyday life as-we-knew-it and failed in breaking through the limits of gender sovereignty, despite the fact that the presence of anti-sexist discourse was particularly strong. Incidents of sexist violence occurred even in the demonstrators' blocks.[24] After all, the mere presence of subjects in the revolt would not automatically free them from whatever sexist or homophobic behaviour they had engaged in before. Nevertheless, December also comprised a field of apt questioning of machismo, the "Rambo" executor,[25] with many of the revolted, male and female, rethinking the roles socially assigned to them through all these years.

HANGOUTS, OCCUPATIONS, AND AUTONOMOUS SPACES

The hangouts and occupations that existed prior to the revolt played a crucial part in its first days. Because they were dispersed across nearly the entire country, they acted primarily as recipients and ignitions of the events. Most occupations and hangouts [steki, see Glossary] are in the central parts of cities, a fact that helped significantly in whatever organising there was on the side of the revolted, their coming together, and counter-information overall. Afterwards, they had more of an auxiliary role and something of an invisible character because the events had become everyone's business. In Athens, during recent years, there have also been attempts to put together such spaces outside the city centre. These "peripheral" steki played perhaps the most important role as sites of reference and getting together during decentralised actions, perhaps due to the easier connection with neighbourhoods. Even there, of course, it was primarily other meeting points that were chosen, public buildings that were less politically defined by the political identity of anarchism or the extreme left. This, in an attempt to approach local residents but also to spread the revolt to everything that is still considered "common." In those cases however, where relationships were developed between steki and local residents (such as in the neighbourhood of Agios Dimitrios, with its local town hall occupation), results were incredible.

DECEMBER IN ATHENS'S PRESENT

Contrary to commands for "gentrification" inundating the modern city, December's revolt reminded those feverishly trying to forget that coexistence in Athens cannot be a peaceful endeavour. It reminded one also that ghettos exist on both sides of the metropolis, that is, the ghetto formed by new city centre dwellers and the ghetto constituted by the old-money residents of Kolonaki [Athens's most bourgeois central neighbourhood—see Glossary]. December functioned substantially as a magnifying lens of the violence that thousands of the city's residents suffer daily. At the same, the ability of those who revolted to form new fields of resistance in the frozen metropolitan time and place came as a loud response to all those who acted concerned about the political characteristics of the conflict, pointing to what appeared to

53

be a glaring absence of any demands. In reality, December gave birth to a plethora of spaces and practices. The Skaramanga squat, Navarinou Park, graffiti, and stencils all around—these are only some of its spatial legacies. Mainly, however, it left behind human relationships that enable people to develop more acute reflexes in case their mass presence in the streets is called for once again. On the other hand, we cannot neglect the fact that December also bequeathed an individual-istic perception and attitude towards collective issues and structures, as it enhanced the perceived image of the protestor as a "soldier" and thus commanded the absolute destruction of collective objectives. The memories from those days are still alive in the turmoil of economic re-cession and will appear more useful than ever. Shadowed by economic crisis and IMF control, the period between December 2008 and the summer of 2010 displayed various pockets of resistance indicative of the wealth of the struggle: dock workers, lorry-drivers, railway workers, and air-traffic controllers went on strike, joined by committees against paying tolls. On the side of state authority, December left many new laws aiming to prevent the worst-case scenario—it has left the menace with which cops would uproot trees at Navarinou Park during one of their usual raids; the new Dias motorcycle police force, aspiring to win back the force's long-lost flexibility in urban terrain—and an even more bloodthirsty, murderous state, immune to the disdain for it that hordes of people seem to cherish.

Any presentation of the 2008 revolt is deemed to be incomplete and weak. This is simply because December was exceptionally multi-faceted; central and suburban at the same time; chaotic and structured; for some familiar, to others unique. In no way did December exhaust the forms and ways of offering resistance—on the contrary, it stirred the imagination and opened doors for new, even greater, gatherings. Its importance and contribution may only be fully understood in years to come—or then again, in the present crisis, this may come much sooner. In any case, as a genuinely "unfortified city," Athens will always vindi-cate its urban character thanks to its smaller and larger revolts.

NOTES

1 The present chapter is a shortened version of a booklet published by the same authors titled Athens, Unfortified City (2010, in Greek). Visit http://www.urbananarchy.gr for more information.

2 The period between 1952 and 1974 comprises the most notable urbanization in modern Greece. Within twenty years, the population of Athens doubled after 1.5 million domestic migrants relocated to the city.

3 This was the US aid plan offered to European countries after WWII (mainly during 1948–1951). On one hand, it aimed to strengthen national economies, yet on the other hand it would serve US foreign policy, in the sense that it also aimed to prevent aid-receiving countries from entering the Soviet Union's sphere of political impact. The initial recipients were those countries that—according to the US government—were in immediate danger from the expansion of communism, namely Greece and Turkey.

4 After Greece's unsuccessful expedition to Asia Minor, the Lausanne Treaty was signed in 1922. The Treaty dictated major population exchanges between Turkey and Greece. As a result, more than 200,000 refugees from Asia Minor (Turkey) settled in the periphery of Athens during the 1920s and 1930s.

5 According to the 2001 census, migrants comprise 19% of the population in Athens municipality. Today it is estimated that they make up 30%.

6 This term, frequently used by the government and corporate media during this period, became a widespread slogan.

7 According to ESPON.

8 Until the mid-1990s, Athens had the characteristics of a compact city with mixed land use, increased residential densities and clear urban boundaries. Trends of spread from urban to rural areas (urban sprawl) have only begun to appear during the last fifteen years, leading its metropolitan area to acquire the features of a diffused city. However, this suburbanisation is limited to Athens's metropolitan area, and in 2001 only 10% of the population lived outside its firm and relatively limited agglomeration. The percentage of suburbanisation in the metropolitan area stands at 10%, much lower than that of other metropolises (for comparison: Paris 81%, San Francisco 79%, Buenos Aires 77%, Los Angeles 75%, Milan 73%, Tokyo 68%, Barcelona 67%, Cairo 61%, Madrid 49% [Source: ESPON, Urban Audit]).

9 Even though the fourth CIAM took place in Athens in 1933—which praised the "functional city" and opened the way for "zoning" of cities globally through the "Charter of Athens"—the city of Athens itself was never zoned, which has given it the urban vitality it retains to the present day.

10 According to Richard Florida, cities that attract gay people, artists, and ethnic minorities are the new economic forces of our era, because they are the areas inhabited by creative people. Creative employees make up the creative class, have a high level of knowledge and skills, and are called in to solve problems by incorporating innovative solutions and ideas. The creative class seeks intense social interaction and the coexistence of many different lifestyles, emphasising "public life" over "community life"; it prefers quasi-anonymity, the presence of minimal strong social ties, and the potential to be surrounded by strangers and different types of people. "Cities without gays and rock bands are losing the race of economic growth," says Florida (see Florida R. *The Rise of the Creative Class*).

11 During the last decade, the Athens Stock Exchange and several ministries have been

relocated away from the centre, while there are plans for even the house of parliament to follow.

12 1,300 police CCTV cameras were installed in the streets of Athens on the occasion of the Olympic Games in 2004. Many have suffered extensive damage and destruction, during either marches or direct actions.

13 Proportion of green space per inhabitant: Sofia 169 m^2, Helsinki 146.6 m^2, Amsterdam 35 m^2, Berlin 27 m^2, Rotterdam 24 m^2, Rome 15 m^2 (Data available at http://www.urbanaudit.org/index.aspx).

14 Available at http://www.metopo.gr/article.php?id=1817 [in Greek].

15 In New York, the equivalent distance between road intersections stands at 245 m, making spatial control easy; in Barcelona it is 115 m, in Paris 105 m, in Berlin 270 m, but in Cairo it is 35 m. In the war zones of Baghdad and Kabul the equivalent distance is 30 m.

16 The General Police Department of Athens is located in a thirteen-storey edifice on Alexandra Avenue. The main building has stood since the 1970s like a beehive at the centre of the city, true to its Modernist principles.

17 Propylea, the square in front of the University of Athens, is a traditional place for gatherings. It is, at the same time, under the academic asylum regime and an open space in the heart of the city.

18 Zephyri is a greatly impoverished area in Attica, where many Roma live. In Zephyri, conflicts with the police are frequent, but there is an impenetrable barrier between the neighbourhood and the rest of the city. It is rare for events in the one to affect the other. On the night of 9 December, it could be said that Zephyri sent "smoke signals" towards the city centre, by driving a flaming vehicle straight into a police department in the area.

19 According to estimates of the Chamber for Commerce and Industry, 435 businesses in Athens suffered damage (37 were completely destroyed), at a total cost of €50 million.

20 Note: in Greece, newspapers usually are sold in kiosks. These kiosks are located on the sidewalks and squares.

21 Statistical laws only hold when we are dealing with large numbers and long periods. Unusual/important acts or events can statistically only appear as diversions from the rule (Arendt 1986).

22 Panagopoulos C. (2008) *Statements by the Director of ERT* [in Greek] available at http://www.youtube.com/watch?v=1niOJ4hlKYk&feature=related.

23 Of course there were also generalised looting incidents with the aim of profit/reselling of goods. We are in no position to know what exactly happened during those days. We can, however, imagine a few migrants watching TV without having to go to a public cafe in order to do so, or wearing new shoes and clothes they might have had otherwise needed to spend years saving to buy.

24 Language for example is never innocent; rather, it reproduces exclusions and phobic

behaviours. A typical example here would be the slogan "cop cunts, you kill kids" and the disputes between male and female demonstrators (See Riot Girls 2009 "This Revolt is Bollocks Comrades..." 9 January 2009 [in Greek] http://indy.gr/analysis/ar3c7idia-eksegersi-syntrofoi-3).

25 After all, the trigger of the revolt, the act of the assassination, was also part of the deeply patriarchal attitude of "machismo" and "male" survival, which overcame the cop and murderer Korkoneas and "pushed" him to shoot.

3

THE POLIS-JUNGLE, MAGICAL DENSITIES, AND THE SURVIVAL GUIDE OF THE ENEMY WITHIN[1]

Christos Filippidis

The law is not born of nature, and it was not born near the fountains that the first shepherds frequented: the law is born of real battles, victories, massacres, and conquests which can be dated and which have their horrific heroes; the law was born in burning towns and ravaged fields. It was born together with the famous innocents who died at break of day.

—Michel Foucault (2003: 50–1)

THE SPATIALITY OF THE JUNGLE

One phrase in the realm of common discourse undoubtedly exemplifies certain perceptual spatial and figurative images of popular understanding, whilst at the same time indicating certain particularly important political schemes. What the popular phrase "the city has become a jungle" principally articulates is, on the one hand, the practical difficulty of orientating oneself within dense urban environments and, on the other, the quotidian absence of encounter with any signs that might bear meaning. This unfocussed schema teeters between the practical impossibility of spatial cognition and symbolic impossibility and recalls in reverse fashion the unique possibility, as Walter Benjamin said, of losing oneself in the metropolis in the way that one gets lost in a forest.

"Not to find one's way around a city does not mean much," writes Benjamin (2003a: 352). "But to lose one's way in a city, as one loses one's way in a forest, requires some schooling." With this statement, the

German philosopher intended to evince the modern urban experience and the imposing position occupied by the (orienting) information held within it—perhaps announcing, in his own way, that the city requires of us an enormous effort if it is to be understood and lived as a jungle.

Beyond this territorial-urban reference, what seems to retain the greatest importance in the above formula is that the city is no longer to be understood as a field for the formation of a political construction, i.e. as a polis. Complicated and dense urban clusters evoke the impossibility of navigation through a dense jungle area but, beyond that, another covert operation is in progress. The political dimension of the metropolis seems to be violently brought into a state of doubt. The upshot here is the immediate reduction of urban social phenomena to counterpart events within the city's erstwhile communities of wildlife. Two objections are immediately raised from such a blatant reduction, concerning two separate misconceptions, which require some clarification in return.

A SOCIETY THAT IS WILD YET POLITICAL

The first objection is one that this article would not want to put under any scrutiny—this concerns the anthropological and colonial finding that the reference to "wild societies" does not set a ground for collective political subjects and that it instead invokes a treaty of war, at the heart of which individual interest triumphs. Conflict is organised upon this interest, always on an individual level. This claim on the one hand makes use of a Hobbesian[2] political interpretation: in the absence of any centralised authority, a mechanism of arbitration (read: rule) seems unable to understand other reasons for cohesion and/ or conflict. On the other hand it recalls a point from the Marxist anthropological tradition whereby the absence of coherent and distinct forces of production obliges us to talk only of pre-political and non-historical societies. Those who study the archaeologies of violence of Pierre Clastres (1989) or the nomadology of Deleuze and Guattari (1986) would clearly suggest that the main challenge in this Western anthropological anxiety has been and remains to confirm and validate the State's role as the only vehicle through which to establish a collective political entity. And therefore, what this anthropological and political tradition must display to the "savage societies" is the distance it keeps from such a centralised scheme.

The jungle, from which the modern metropolis derives its conceptual schemes, seems to therefore host a strange "primitive" condition. And as a sign of an anthropological centrifugal tendency it invites us to seek the very centre from which it has transgressive tendencies. For the Hobbesian tradition this centre is occupied by the imposing figure of the state, the only one worthy of carrying the commands of natural law or divine will. Therefore, by means of induction, we can only talk of the phenomena of the jungle in the absence of such a figure. Not about competing modes of political formation but wild pre-political phenomena. Not groups but individuals. Not about social heterotopias but social cannibalism. Thus, a jungle is born in those cities that fail to commit to the primary contractual oath, resulting in them giving host to centrifugal exceptions, abnormal behaviour and deviant properties: in other words, internal enemies, enemies within. This, then, is the city-jungle, where war reigns and the social contract is buried forever along with the thousands of corpses of an eternal and undefined war. Where competing political groupings are not recognised as such and where the state appears as the sole guarantor of the political constitution in question and as the exclusive arbitrator of political decisions.

WAR AS AN INSTRUMENT FOR THE CONTINUATION OF POLITICS BY OTHER MEANS

Our second objection concerns a hypothesis that has acquired the status of a certainty within the Western legal and philosophical discursive tradition: a certainty that establishes the State's fundamental truth and haunts anti-state discourse. A number of critical questions are born as a consequence and must be applied directly to the heart of this foundation. Suppose savage societies did therefore exist before "politics" and that their main feature was the war of all against all (in Hobbesian terms). In the first event, what does the exclusion of the phenomenon of war from the political sphere mean and what form does the argument "the city was a jungle" take? The problem therefore arises from the moment when this hypothetical case assumes the characteristics of an objective reality. And its profundity was never more visible than in those days of December. During those days we witnessed an unprecedented operation to exclude these phenomena of urban violence from the political sphere of the metropolis. In this effort, December united the orchestrators of bourgeois democracy who alleged that such violent phenomena were located somewhere in the state of nature.

Such an insidious attempt to apportion this mass outbreak to jungle phenomena of pre-political violence and instinctual delirium beyond any rationality made it clear that sovereignty, once again, was not prepared to understand these metropolitan riots as a potential field of

61

political formation—a formation that would most certainly be threatening to it. In this sense it forced these riots to situate themselves in the irrational maelstrom of the natural condition. The city-jungle, then, especially in those days hosted a double condemnation: first it strengthened and largely contributed to the desperate enterprise of consolidating the misleading shape of the "wild society" as a non-political society, attaching to it one more pre-political event. Second, it situated the metropolitan-political unrest in a vast area of wild (re-)representations and therefore in a forced, eternal, natural condition.

It makes sense to pause at this double conviction and reflect upon the value of those days. This was a pure reflex outburst of the youth which, after its first two or three days in the public eye, was attributed the typical characteristics of urban "thuggish behaviour" and indiscriminate violence; an apolitical outburst with angry shopkeepers as its victims. This outbreak did not escape a ton of always-at-the-ready bourgeois ink which wrapped these unprecedented events up in a veil of mystery, making sure to treat them as yet another violation of some supposed universal contract.

Such a move revealed a U-turn of the media which had initially come close to recognising political elements in a social phenomenon that has constituted to date an historical scourge of such dialectical thinking—that is, violence per se. Yet fortunately, once repented, they viewed things clearly and confessed: all against all, irrational violence against reputable merchants—i.e. a state of nature, or at least nothing that would resemble any political process. A brilliant social war was therefore within a matter of days transformed through a media delirium into some supposed "natural condition," that is, into a pre-modern drama containing absolutely no political content. No relation-commodity, no relation-state was able to magnetise the interpretations to guide the understanding, to declare war. It was therefore clear that the duty of the agents of communication was to highlight the absurdity of the extremely violent reaction next to the extreme reason of everyday legal violence. The only thing that could guarantee this was the bombardment of public opinion with images of damaged and looted "innocent" commercial functions. An image of "all against all"; the law of the jungle.

FROM THE INTERMEDIATE COMMENTARY ON THE CONCEPT OF THE POLITICAL...

62 Paradoxically, the concept of the "asymmetrical threat"—which conceptually refers to an uncontrolled war condition—was unexpectedly

"adopted" during the August 2007 forest arsons in Greece, yet it was not part of the communications arsenal of sovereignty in December, even though it would have suited it perfectly. This was because those responsible knew that what they were asked to address was not unbalanced. They knew exactly what gave birth to it and what it would host in the future. The ways in which it was manifested were perhaps asymmetric, but its sources certainly were not. The causes of the riots of December were therefore not at all unspecified and yet they had to disappear within the irrationality of the natural condition. Under this management regime, Giorgos Karatzaferis[3] seemed a worthy interpreter of the events and loyal to the theoretical tools of domination when on 21 December 2008—fifteen days after the outburst—he found himself vocalising angry calls for the "mature" political world to consider the establishment of special courts to prosecute acts that threatened democracy, "acts of war" as he called them. He therefore demanded a hybrid juridical scheme for "attitudes that have no place in the family of bourgeois democracy" and which cause a peculiar embarrassment to its political representatives. The embarrassment was detected in trying to deal with a political Enemy Within in ways and means that do not belong to the bourgeois political sphere, i.e. by wartime—military rather than by political means.

This is what Slavoj Žižek (2002: 93) seems to question when he refers to the paradox of al-Qaeda terrorists: "the enemy," he claims, "is criminalized if he simply defends himself and returns fire. A new entity is thus emerging which is neither the enemy soldier nor a common criminal: the al-Qaeda terrorists are not enemy soldiers, they are 'unlawful combatants'; but they are not simple criminals either—the USA was completely opposed to the notion that the WTC [World Trade Center] attacks should be treated as apolitical criminal acts. In short, what is emerging in the guise of the Terrorist on whom war is declared is precisely the figure of the political Enemy, foreclosed from the political space proper." This exclusion will be seen clearly later on through Schmitt's comments on the partisan.

By the same token, the "outlaw insurgents" in December were responding to this paradox. In this instance the paradox manifested itself in the fact that, at a moment when the riots in question constituted "attacks on the political stability of the country" and an "attack on the democracy itself" and were therefore closely politically related to the existing order, the leader of the extreme-right-wing LA.O.S. would dare to express the innermost fantasies of bourgeois democracy in articulating a radical concept: the idea that the entire political system should proceed united in the establishment of special military tribunals—in other words, it should activate the arsenal of martial proceedings to suppress political (and not mere criminal) acts that were nonetheless neither accepted nor perceived as such. He was therefore recalling once again the natural condition and arguing that we should mobilise military resources in order to maintain political stability. In so doing, he contradicted himself in many ways: whilst refusing to recognise any political attributes whatsoever to those in revolt, he would nevertheless demand the launch of a war against them with a clear political (sacred) purpose.

As a figure of the extreme right, Karatzaferis intimately knows the culture of the Decision, and this was confirmed in the request that he made. The moment of the establishment of a hybrid semi-bourgeois/semi-military court would be the culmination of the domination enjoyed by the bourgeois-democrats. And he would have repeated what has become absolutely clear in modern history—that is, that the one who dominates is not the person who establishes law but rather the person who decides on its suspension. Not the one who constantly negotiates the "criminality" of a diversion but the one who at a crucial moment will signal that the political game is over and that now is the time for war. An absolute moment, perhaps most eloquently described in Walter Benjamin's *Theses on the Philosophy of History*:

> The tradition of the oppressed teaches us that the "state of emergency" in which we live is not the exception but the rule. We must attain to a conception of history that is in keeping with this insight. Then we shall clearly realize that it is our task to bring about a real state of emergency....[4]

What does Benjamin mean when he talks about the true state of emergency? And how is Schmitt's famous definition of sovereignty reinstated in this context? Schmitt (1985: 5) declares in his political theology: "Sovereign is he who decides on the exception"—which confirms that in a time of crisis (whether caused by war, revolution or natural disaster) the dominant will seek to ensure the maintenance of law and order even if they must thereby declare, temporarily, its suspension (or not-so-temporarily as demonstrated in the Nazi example). This event therefore retains its own particular significance in history. This admittedly was the motivating force in the riot scenes of December. A just political event constituting nothing but a marginal conduit, a conduit that may nevertheless sometimes be placed in the service of the oppressed.

Seizing this tremendous opportunity, Panagiotis Kondylis[5] articulated his observations on the positions of Schmitt. If Schmitt reads the declaration of emergency as a tool solely serving the state, Kondylis invites us to rethink the importance of its limitations to the extent that such a tool might be activated to the benefit of the oppressed. And the moment of this paradoxical activation will escape the limits of domination since it will comprise a pure limit, a limit existing outside the state. Since this declaration leaves behind any imposition of law, it is no longer characterised by any anxieties regarding its perpetuation. This state of emergency, which according to Kondylis is a revolutionary moment, suspends the rule of law not in order to restore it later, nor to maintain it in the limbo of its own suspension, but, rather, in order to practise and claim something entirely new—something that is written "...in memory of the suffering of humanity and not in promise of a bright future; for revenge rather than eschatology." (Faraklas 1997: 32). It is precisely this vengeful route that comprised the ground for the negations of those days, giving the impression that if Kondylis was still alive he would speak of his famous "absolutist miracle." A miracle that for a fraction of a moment seemed real, a miracle that would not allow any return to the natural rule of law but would instead set a definite break with the historical continuum, the history of winners. This is the absolutist miracle for which Benjamin calls when he speaks of the true state of emergency in his eighth thesis. And it is to this call that those thousands of anonymous rebels seem to have responded—and sooner or later, it seems, will do so again.

In those days revenge circulated in the streets along with a reminder that history is not always written by the winners. That within the existing margins of the glorification of imperial achievements a war-fuelled discourse is born which is totally oblivious to natural law and enforced peace. And that right next to it, in an erratic and often frenzied manner, it prepares the ground for the totalitarian wonder. In those places and moments we were once again reminded that these outbursts are nothing but arrhythmias in the body of the ever-enforced/ obligatory social peace. Visible traces in the image of order, traces that loudly reveal that their peace is war, that it presupposes war and that this has been so since the 16th century. That peace needs to account for the war it produces and which is inherent to its survival. In this sense Foucault reversed Clausewitz's famous aphorism and declared that "politics is the continuation of war by other means"; that the political peace in which we live is war. For this reason he claimed that the challenge lies in identifying the "forgotten past of real struggles, actual victories, and defeats which may have been disguised but which remain profoundly inscribed... in rediscovering the blood that has dried in the codes and not, therefore, the absolute right that lies beneath the transience of history" (Foucault 2003: 15).

The riots of December showed that no blood was left to dry and they erupted as a worthy retaliation to peace's everyday war. Revenge while the blood was still fresh. The very vindictive preparation of the riots instantly lifted the burden of decision and declared that it would allow both mourning and celebration,[6] that it would allow space for both creation and destruction. And it hosted first and foremost in its illegal territory the purest—in a Benjaminian sense—form of violence.[7] The kind of violence that exists beyond the boundaries of law and that no compromise whatsoever can be reached with it. "The proper characteristic of this violence is that it neither makes nor preserves law, but deposes it and thus inaugurates a new historical epoch" writes Agamben (2005: 53). He then states that this violence resides outside the law, that is, precisely where the state of emergency does too. It occupies a void area of law that "seems, for some reason, to be so essential to the juridical order that it must seek in every way to assure itself a relation with it, as if in order to ground itself the juridical order necessarily had to maintain itself in relation with an anomie" (Agamben 2005: 51).

...TO THE INTERMEDIATE COMMENTARY ON THE CONCEPT OF THE SPATIAL

Beyond the temporal dimension of such development, however, it is important to observe its very spatiality since this marginal condition does not only suggest a historical break or a time interval from/within the linear-historical account of the winners but precipitates the unfolding of a huge range of elements entered directly into space. And this is precisely what arises from the positions of Agamben, too. For if one encounters pure violence in a non-juridical space, this violence simultaneously occurs in a natural-material place in whose territory dominant law remains—even temporarily—unable to show any force whatsoever. And this is what is shocking in true time: the fact, that is, that the sites of this violence are exempt from the legislative and administrative territory; in other words, that they produce an unlawful space—not to mention that this space may be unpredictable, sudden, and therefore uncodifiable, occurring in the heart of the safety of commerce and "Justice" like, say, in the heart of Kolonaki.[8] Moreover, the definition of Agambian deduction as an extra-juridical site does not only reveal a situation unable to find its place in the syntax of the philosophy of law but also a natural or artificial space at the limits of which this syntax cannot be implemented. The exception, therefore, is not only a place outside of the frame of law but also a material (three-dimensional) location outside the force of law.[9] This is what the Italian philosopher emphasises when he speaks of counter-laboratories of deduction/exemption, referring to the *favelas* of Latin America: highly specific, natural–artificial sites that inhibit the force of law, and more specifically sites that, on the one hand, do not allow the police to enter but, on the other hand, are also not subject to the dominant property relations.[10] These sites outline a peculiar and valuable space for present and future transgressions.

The very anomy then seems to generate its own site and appears to be placing it on the existing legal and spatial condition. It thus reclaims and expropriates temporary parts of applied law/justice. The more that these deductions multiply, the more frequently their temporary spaces occur. And, as these sites proliferate, the dominant site of law disintegrates. These sites are inhabited by external entities that obligate suspensions of the law and seem to be the same entities that make up the rugged scenery of the jungle. The same entities that seemingly manufacture and inhabit the natural condition they constantly fight. These martial exceptions eventually produce their own battlespace and this space takes us once again back to the jungle. The city as a jungle, then, is a city that hosts many of these exemptions but not the natural state. The war of all against all is not a war between individuals but a war between groups of people (and both Schmitt and the Boulaivilliers would agree on this). In particular it is a war of groups against the absolute group, that is, the state. This proves that there is no natural condition, only a diverse and unregulated field of political setting—conflict. The city-jungle therefore is at the heart of this field and appears dangerous for the dominant state of rule in the same way that Hobbes would hear the inarticulate cries of the "wild" to be dangerous too. If what Foucault argues truly stands, regarding the significance of war through the historic discourse from the 16th century onwards (which began to identify war in terms of the pattern in battle rather than the controversial two-tier mechanism of attacker/victim, winner/loser etc. [Foucault 2003: 199]) then one has to pay tribute to the city-jungle for the value of such an approach. The value of the open political process weighs above the natural condition. Where the Enemy Within flourishes and discipline loses its meaning. Where the city-jungle turns into a polis-jungle.

THE ASYLUM DENSITIES

If one characteristic is typical of the jungle, this must be density. This characteristic is therefore worthy of our attention in our attempt to interpret and analyse the functions of the jungle. Density was what was at stake in designing the city of the Enlightenment and the craving for density paved the way for the domination of commerce. The city that should allow both adequate blood circulation (read: the unimpeded flow of goods and people through its road arteries) and successful breathing (read: adequate ventilation of buildings and the likely presence of a green component)[11] was a city primarily obliged to manage densities (frighteningly similar to modern calls for bio-climatic design). And this demand for management was recorded, as history conclusively proves, in a broader demand for civilian control.

The doctrine of social control is based upon these biological functional necessities of breathing and blood flow. This is rather paradoxical, considering that the political Hobbesian demand for eternal escape from the natural condition presupposed natural functional frameworks. And that this denial of the natural pre-political condition could not ultimately be conceived outside natural, biological, or apolitical frameworks. The demand of dominant urban design from the Enlightenment onward therefore brought a "biological" type of warfare, attempting to rewrite the contract in space. And careful densities constituted the syntax for such a successful rewriting. This biological warfare had already been organised since the time of the Victorian city through a moralistic campaign concerning public health, and it subsequently annexed parts of the (micro)biological discourse to displace their "dark" neighbourhoods spatially and their "dirty" social life politically. Official medical town planning was therefore called to organise obedience in territorial terms and, in so doing, to eliminate the possibility of a territorial breach of the social contract. Yet nights and days like those of December serve to remind us how urban space was, is, and will remain a site of deviation too.

The Situationists were well aware of all of this when they wrote:

> if the city's history is the history of freedom, it is also the history of tyranny, of state administration controlling the countryside and the city itself. The city has so far only managed to comprise the territory of the historical struggle for freedom, not its acquisition. The city is the environment of history because it comprises simultaneously both a concentration of social power (which makes its historical undertaking possible) and a consciousness of the past. (Internationale Situationniste 1979: 120)

A consciousness that keeps alive the tradition of the oppressed found in Benjamin's eighth thesis, and which will explode within the uncontrollable density that hosts it. The Situationists, after all, seemed to be in need of these densities for their own games and wanderings for which they would probably not even bother to draw psycho-geographical maps should they be able to use Pikermi, Pilea,[12] or a French *banlieue* [suburb] as their sites of experiment. Which brings us back to the question of urbanity as such. "Our field is therefore the network of urban space, a natural manifestation of collective activity that is able to understand the creative forces unleashed by the decay of an embedded culture of individualism" (ibid.: 56).

The encounter of December's riots with the properties of urban densities restored for the oppressed the magical moment of committing an offence disputing urban formation itself. The problem for sovereignty therefore arises when some people decide to transform the city from a realm of commodity and spectacle into a public realm of war; from a site hosting the state relationship to a site that questions this very relationship. Amidst sovereignty's desperate attempts to evacuate areas, to split up neighbourhoods and normalise movements, outbursts of anger in memory of the suffering of mankind often render these spatial or territorial divisions useless. Consequently, in similar cases, any attempt to organise urban space according to security zones often retreats in the face of bold threats that may have even been anticipated. The emergence of the Enemy Within is spatially organised through the discourse about walls, about those walls that move into the heart of cities and which may be materialised either in the form of ring roads (see the example of the riots in the suburbs of Paris), red zones (see the temporary control and exclusion zones every time the heads of global domination meet) or, finally, actual physical walls (see the now-common blast walls of Fallujah, Baghdad, or the West Bank).

But what causes more outrage during such outbursts is the negation of principal spatial segregation and any structure in the midst of widespread lawlessness. Even more so if they do not enjoy the immunity of a large-scale event but instead develop within the bounds of their own singularity and produce a threatening and dangerous outstretched period of lawlessness for no obvious reasons in the eyes of the public— as the raid of Kolonaki[13] in broad daylight aptly showed. That is, without any "respect" for critical spatial or temporal pre-existing structures, nor for critical intangible spatial and temporal walls. Density, therefore, as a cover for such operations keeps alive the hope that conflict will inhabit cities *upon the ground of historical struggle for freedom*, as a problem that is rather difficult for sovereignty to solve.

MARTIAL SURFACES...

When Schmitt attempted to demonstrate the problems introduced by the appearance of the partisan on the backdrop of 20th-century war, he insisted on points that, along with their political specificity (how, for example, this strange figure would be included in the Geneva Conventions of '49), highlighted the spatial and chronological dimensions of this figure's actions. The importance of the partisans' arrival lies in a dual specificity. On the one hand, it violates the conventional limits of a warfare process with whatever repercussions for its inclusion in the dictionary of the war and the conditions that defend it and thus for the partisan's own visibility. On the other hand, it redefines the gravity of the subscription space, liquidating the relationship of the subject along with the necessary systems of spatial reference. The four criteria set in Carl Schmitt's theory on the rebel/partisan are particularly revealing for the new face of war-spatial approaches and are indicative of a starting point for the questioning of this "unorthodox" warrior.

The elements of non-regularity, increased mobility, growing political commitment and telluric character organise a discursive space that can only involve the spatial dimension from the very beginning (Schmitt 2007). Whether as a reference to strict coordinates, as static development for confrontation in a set territory to secure its defence or as a foundational process of motion and laceration/rupture, these criteria highlight the role of space; the importance that its strategy has always yielded. However, they soon shine upon it, and, in a manner that recalls a series of signs reminiscent of the fact that space had been crumbled through the lens of relativity, we can no longer speak in the same terms for the space of Sun Tzu and Clausewitz. Since, as Schmitt argues, a new dimension has been added through the rebel/partisan: the dimension of depth. A dimension articulated in space either, for example, through the underground burrows of the rebels in Kabul or through the vertical integration of (micro-)war taking place in the limited territory of a single building in Palestine. Something that points ultimately to the role of the vertical dimension in the outcome of modern military operations, something that caused Eyal Weizman (2002) to claim that geopolitics was traditionally a horizontal plane discourse (a flat discourse), a discourse that omits the vertical dimension. Inside the importance of this escape, its geopolitics no longer holds the perceptual flexibility that would offer the possibility of a complete mapping of the skyline of the future complex and flexible urban conflict, a mapping that will include the third dimension and therefore cannot be reduced to a two-dimensional reality. One that is reduced, that is, to figurative surfaces incapable of delivering the very decisive concept of depth.

Holding in mind the position that the concept of space tends to enjoy in such approaches then creates the impression that Schmitt's four "tools" ultimately illustrate not only the profile of a rebel, and therefore an idiom within strict space-time framework of a military process, but also a critical technical decryption of contemporary urban phenomena, if not the one and only "Survival Guide" in the city of flows and networks.

Such a theory recalls the notorious figure of the war machine as composed by Deleuze and Guattari in their essay on nomadology, which in turn also yields a prominent position in the dimension of space. Yet it is recalled paradoxically, since while the rebel in Schmitt resides in an embossed area, one that is particularly dense, organised in particular via tensions in terms of depth and verticality, Deleuze and Guattari imagine their own irregular war machine to slide in a smooth horizontal non-metric space (a smooth space) like the desert, the steppe or the sea (Deleuze and Guattari 1986: 32–34, 59–62).

In any case, this random individual or collective confrontational entity restores the Foucauldian position on the importance of the process of a battle/confrontation and, in a very heavy symbolism of the word *battle*, the concept of density is seen for the oppressed as a key regulator for its successful outcome. Schmitt's horror in the face of the organised emergence of a collective subject competing with the state forced him to illuminate perhaps the most competitive of them all, that of the partisan. And he led the drafting of his theory, giving him an honorary (for the partisan, not for Schmitt himself) attribute of the concept of interference in the political—that is, the intervention in the Friend/Enemy distinction (Schmitt 1996). This intervention has to do with the unorthodox partisan features that offer from the outset the option not to be visibly involved in the relationship between Friend/Enemy, within the political relationship *par excellence*: to remain, therefore, within a non-codifiable yet political sphere.[14] And, respectively, allowing it to construct a fluid space, using the density, installing temporary lawless zones like those in December, putting sites briefly outside law and ultimately making an equally critical interference in the concept of the Spatial. And this is of the utmost importance: the fact that the interference in the concept of the political can only be conditional and eventually lead to a corresponding sense of interfering with the concept of the spatial. For this reason both space and the physical presence within it will continue to assert their sense of conflict in the fluid

71

and impersonal conditions of virtual networks of information. "The relativity of space," writes Doreen Massey,

> ...with the opening means that the space always contains an unexpected degree, unpredictable. So, apart from the edges that do not meet, the place always involves an element of 'chaos' (not specified by the system). This is a 'mess' created by those accidental confrontations, those random separations, the often paradoxical nature of geographical formations in which some special orbits intertwine, and sometimes interact. The space, in other words, is inherently 'cleft.' Perhaps, above all, given the prevailing attitudes, the space is not surface. (2001: 34)

It therefore makes sense for someone to insist on a focus on this negativity. Space is not a surface (as illustrated by Weizman) because the city is not the seat of the contract alone. Space is discontinuities, gaps, but above all, it is the very relationships that it hosts and the "chaos" resulting from them. Urban densities indicate that they give space to relationships that do not fit the terms of the social contract and for this reason they have been fought historically and continue to be so. And they seem to create their own system of law; some system that has long ago cut its ties to the natural documentation but is in no case Singular. It is a multiple law of conflict and encounter and, in this sense, a concept of law that is constantly under question and mutation. And, within the infinity of this property, the densities in question are of unique value for the oppressed. Because these densities are where "exception" eventually finds refuge; where possibility is given to "minority" sexual preferences to manifest themselves, to criminals of all types to structure their own public sphere and to political spaces to establish their own sacrosanct arenas.

... AND THE EXTREME URBAN MAKEOVER

This is the city-jungle that frightens. And in the face of this fear the bulldozer often takes charge. Either through normalising non-beneficial and non-productive conceptually empty territories in Eleonas,[15] in the colonial logic of commercial gain, or through destroying buildings thanks to the unique ability of armoured D-9 vehicles (as in the refugee camp of Jenin) or simply by demolishing hubs of political resistance (see the recent example of the Ungdomshuset squat in Copenhagen). The remnants of these operations often show us that this destruction was in itself the aim, rather than a means to implement a plan (as the rubble of the demolished occupation Santa Barbara squat in Patisia, Athens, will remind us for some time to come). Urban destruction is after all a nodal point of urban redesigning within the framework of urban gentrifications and is always of crucial importance to geopolitical development. Conceiving this importance, the Modernist Movement in the iron grip of Le Corbusier testified—right between the two world wars—to its own proposals for the defensive deadlock that the war of nation-states carried with it. Again, density comprised the navigator of modern designs. Rare densities therefore came as a defence along with tall buildings that would enable cities between the two world wars to limit their losses in a potential bombing (Graham 2004: 38–41). Tight medieval urban densities, therefore looking vulnerable in face of the iron death that came from the sky, had to be levelled. A process that simply revoked the importance of geopolitical factors in the business of urban redesign and confirmed in its own way the leading role that densities hold in this undertaking.

Baron Haussmann, the famous demolition artist, seemed to understand this as early as the mid-19th century, and so the first thing he attempted was the management of densities. These were the densities that hosted the Enemy Within in the heart of Paris and had to mutate. The defensive deadlock they caused did not concern the potential development of an external war at this time but an internal one. Or more precisely, they concerned a strictly civil war, right in the body of the city. "The real aim of Haussmann's works was the securing of the city against civil war."[16] The unique protection sought first and foremost to inscribe itself upon space. The straight and extremely wide avenues that were opened up to cross over and through urban densities, to install permanent axes of control, eventually both settled the impossibility of the construction of a barricade and made direct military intervention all the more possible. Not accidentally, this urban renewal effort, with its political roots and extravagant spectacles, was dubbed "strategic gentrification."[17]

This is an oxymoron schema which in a way does justice to Foucault's position, namely that war is inherent to peace and the law that is born amidst the wrecks of demolished towns. A schema that shows how urban renewal is often an urban war at heart. The Communards of 1871, in defiance of this position, attempted to prevent the declaration (to cause, in Benjamin's terms, the real state of emergency and to build their own double-decker barricades) in the hope that this war would end with them rising as the victors in the diverse urban terrain. Ever since, every such outburst in any part of the world attaches to this war the historical significance to which it corresponds. Perhaps eventually these martial exceptions produce their own space: a novel contribution to the concept of participatory planning. As Mike Davis has pointed out,[18] perhaps vandalism is ultimately a true production of space. A bizarre production that claims its share in urban design and which understands the city as an unfinished work of art, as the site of relationships in continuous conflict, as a disputable historical object. In response to the events of the Commune, Walter Benjamin (2003b: 25) ultimately reached the conclusion that "the burning of Paris is an apt end to the devastating work of Baron Haussmann." It remains to be seen whether the burning of Greek cities in December was indeed an ending and to whose "devastating work" it would deserve to be so.

Christos Filippidis, May 2009

NOTES

1 A Greek version of this article first appeared in the Athens-based magazine *Hooliganizater.*

2 See the political tradition accommodated in Thomas Hobbes's book *Leviathan, or the Matter, Forme and Power of a Common Wealth Ecclesiastical and Civil.*

3 Karatzaferis is the leader of the ultra-nationalist far-right parliamentary party LA.OS.

4 See Löwy 2005: 57.

5 Kondylis is the translator of Schmitt's *Political Theology* into Greek. His translation includes an extended postscript commenting on Schmitt's analysis.

6 See the chapter "Feast, mourning, anomie" in Agamben (2005).

7 "[I]f beyond droit, violence sees its status insured as pure and immediate violence, then this will prove that revolutionary violence is possible…" (Benjamin 2004: 300).

8 Translator's note: Kolonaki is the most bourgeois neighbourhood in central Athens.

9 We are also reminded of this double meaning via the term "extraterritoriality," etymologically deriving from outside (beyond) jurisdiction. This could mean either non-conforming to the law of a given authority, or (and here the importance of the term shines through) the absence of limits within which this authority actually exists. Clearly however, the term under scrutiny here can mean, in both its component words (extra-territoriality), an exceptional territorial condition. Spatial metaphors during the symbolic-juridical formulation of the limit become strict territorial inscriptions. Similarly, the appeal to a notional-juridical site that will host the exception can only follow the literal application of the suspension of the rule in an entirely specific physical and material place.

10 See the conversation between Giorgio Agamben and Zygmunt Bauman at the conference *Archipelago of Exception Sovereignties of Extraterritorialities*, Centre for Contemporary Culture in Barcelona, 10–11 November 2005, available online at http://roundtable.kein.org/node/385.

11 For the biological-natural equivalents of urban functions, see primarily the chapter "The body set free" in Sennett 1994.

12 Remote suburbs of Greater Athens and Greater Thessaloniki respectively.

13 In March 2009, a group of anarchists went on a rampage in the area, destroying luxurious shopfronts and cars.

14 Schmitt's theory of the partisan and the notion of nomadology in Deleuze and Guattari could both be read, after all, as theories of an asymmetrical warfare—in the sense that they describe an entity that cannot be codified, that does not conform to common rules of combat and that is therefore not predictable. The elements that Schmitt focuses on in examining the partisan reveal the problem arising when he ignores the dictionary of war—and by extension, the terms of codification and recognition of the partisan's martial presence. Similarly Deleuze and Guattari describe a martial collective figure that has the exceptional ability of adjusting to any given conditions and of constantly redefining the terms under which it will negotiate and clash with them.

15 Translator's note: Eleonas is a vast area of approximately 9,000 m^2 in Athens, mostly unused at present and the subject of a great deal of speculation regarding its possible development as a sports ground or commercial site in the near future.

16 Walter Benjamin "Paris, Capital of the 19th Century" available online at http://www.newleftreview.org/?view=134.

17 Benjamin, as above.

18 "If you wanted to generate a theory of participatory architecture or urbanism, vandalism seemed to be the most common and popular form of participating in the built environment." See the interview "Resisting, subverting and destroying the apparatus of surveillance and control" with Mike Davis, on the Occupied London website. Available at http://www.occupiedlondon.org/davis/.

4

SPATIAL LEGACIES OF DECEMBER AND THE RIGHT TO THE CITY [1]

Antonis Vradis & Dimitris Dalakoglou

What grounds gave birth to December's revolt and most importantly, what new grounds has the revolt given birth to in return? The political background of the events of those days and their repercussions are discussed extensively in the next part of this book.[2] What we have tried to do here is to take a look at the *actual, physical* grounds of the uprising and its legacies—to read it, that is, through its inscription in the urban space of the city of Athens. To look at urban struggles in new sites of confrontation that have opened up there since; everyday reminders that *December lives.*

But why is the site of the uprising important and why should we concern ourselves with its spatial legacies? It is easy enough to answer this question—after all, the spontaneous gathering of thousands at the scene of the police killing in the neighbourhood and the reverberation of the protests across Greece and around the globe were driven by two main factors. First, the near-instant spread of the news of the police killing was made possible by grassroots media and particularly by independent media websites;[3] only hours after the assassination, impromptu demonstrations began taking place in dozens of cities inside and outside of Greece. Second, though, and perhaps most importantly, there was the political symbolism associated with the location of the murder of Alexis Grigoropoulos. Exarcheia is adjacent to the Athens Polytechnic, the epicentre of the anti-dictatorial student uprising of 1973 and the place where acts of political dissent and unrest in the country's post-dictatorial era (1974–present) have been centred since. The site of the ignition of the revolt was equally important to the breathtaking speed with which it spread.

The December uprising quickly became the focal point for an emerging radical movement. At the same time, it also became a reference point for both state authorities and reactionary non-state actors. Both have reconfigured their strategies in the process of confronting an empowered and confident radical social movement in the country. Beginning in the immediate post-revolt period (from early 2009 onward) the two sides in December's conflict have produced new relationships to public space as expressions of their own political identities and strategies. These new urban spatial practices are the main subject of our chapter. More precisely we consider the socio-spatial dynamics of two urban sites that emerged in Athens in the aftermath of the 2008 uprising: one, the self-organised Navarinou Park, born in March 2009 in Exarcheia; and two, the Ayios Panteleimonas Square, only a few kilometres away. Members of the neo-Nazi group Chrysi Avgi (Golden Dawn) have been attempting to establish since May 2009 a "migrant-free" zone in explicit cooperation with the police force permanently stationed in the area.

The conflicts at these small urban sites can only be seen as deriving from and at the same time reflecting wider social dynamics. We offer some thoughts on these two examples in the context of what has become an important current within social struggles in the metropolises of the West, including segments of the "social antagonist movement," within which we place ourselves. We are talking about struggles for "the right to the city" (RtC): by placing our two examples alongside both contemporary debates about the RtC and the original conception by Henri Lefebvre we suggest that these place-specific struggles can help us rethink the "right to the city" altogether.

A SANDBOX OF FREEDOM

On the morning of 7 March 2009, a mass of people armed with shovels and plants marched through the central Athens district of Exarcheia. They were heading for an abandoned parking lot just a few yards from where Alexandros Grigoropoulos was murdered. Breaking the asphalt surface of the lot, they quickly replaced it with plants. In the digging and planting that followed, the first self-organised park of central Athens was born thanks to the combined efforts of experienced activists, new activists politicized during the events of December, and "ordinary" local residents. But these are no ordinary times and this is most certainly not an ordinary neighbourhood: Exarcheia has a long radical tradition, partly due to the presence of the Athens Polytechnic and some premises of the University of Athens in its vicinity. Relatively cheap housing has historically allowed students, intellectuals, radical political groups, bookshops, and affordable eateries to thrive in the area. As the centre of the city's intellectual and political activity, the neighbourhood has long been a hotbed of radical action too. For the greater part of the country's post-dictatorial era both media and popular discourses have characterized Exarcheia as the heart of anarchist activity in Athens. In the coverage of the events of December 2008 alone, Exarcheia was portrayed as anything from a "volatile district"[4] and an area that "anarchists regard as their fortress,"[5] to "Athens's answer to Harlem"[6] and even a "ghetto."[7]

Yet for all the area's history and potential, it was not until after December 2008 that the Exarcheiots would dare attempt such a bold appropriation of public space, transforming it into a meeting point for the people of the neighbourhood—green and public space of a kind notoriously lacking in Greek cities. The park's organising assembly (a loose but regular gathering of people interested in running the space) explicitly traces its origin to December's uprising. People in the area often call the park "December's park," not only because it is close to the point where Grigoropoulos was assassinated, but also because the park would not have been born without the collective empowerment and confidence gained for radical activities in the aftermath of the revolt. Since March 2009, this experiment in freedom has seen a wide variety of local residents, individuals, and various radical political groups (many of whom played a key role in the December events) come together, overcome long-standing sectarian divisions, and use the new space for concerts, film screenings, meetings and info-nights, exhibitions and festivals. The open-air space has provided unprecedented visibility for many political groups: for example, the curious onlooker can stop and take a peek at the regular public screenings organised by the Haunt of Albanian Migrants, whose declaration of participation in the uprising was exemplary of December's spirit.[8] Besides such public events, people continue to gather almost weekly in order to carry out the work necessary for the maintenance of the park, which has also received positive coverage in some mainstream media.[9]

One year after the uprising, the "Self-Organised Navarinou Park" hosted a three-day event about the revolt. Similarly, several other

December-related protests, like the demonstrations in solidarity with the hunger-striker Iliopoulos (arrested in December 2008) started or ended there. This little park has become a new base of struggle for post-December grassroots political activities in Exarcheia and beyond. It is not surprising, then, that it has itself become an object of struggle: in the eyes of the authorities the park is an emblematic child of December, which continues to inspire various anti-authoritarian activities and must therefore be suppressed. In the first twelve months of its existence alone, the park had already claimed at least three major police raids (under both the conservative Nea Dimokratia government and, since their ascent to power in October 2009, the social democrats of PASOK). During these raids, police in full riot gear stormed the park and arrested and beat those who happened to be there at the time. Merely being present in the park has become a political act—and a punishable one at that.

WHEN THE NAZIS CAME TO THE SQUARE

This direct and violent suppression of the Navarinou Park coincided with the emergence of another space operating on completely antithetical principles. In May 2009, a mere two kilometres away in the neighbourhood of Ayios Panteleimonas, members of the neo-Nazi group Golden Dawn—along with right-wing populist partners—started visibly organising.[10] The area, which together with Exarcheia stands among the most centrally located residential zones of Athens, had seen a recent influx of migrants—many of Afghan origin. Most ended up there after having been pushed out of the more tourist-oriented central areas of the city by police "cleansing" operations in the lead-up to the 2004 Olympics. Anything deemed "dirty" by authorities, from stray dogs to undocumented or homeless migrants, street vendors, and drug users, was to be eliminated from public view.

Four years after the Olympic spectacle, neo-Nazis hijacked the area's so-called "local resident committee," an organisation that had been founded sometime earlier by residents of various political backgrounds. But this political diversity was soon pushed out as neo-Nazis—many living in other areas of the city—took control as of November 2008. It was at that time that they organised their first protests against what they claimed was the supposed occupation of their neighbourhood by clandestine migrants. Gathering at the Ayios Panteleimonas Square, the neo-Nazis argued that migrants without papers, the recent riots, self-organised parks, and all such things disorderly had to be confronted directly by so-called ordinary citizens. Members of Golden

Dawn envision a system of authoritarian rule that would make urban areas "ethnically and politically clean" through mass deportations of migrants and other means. Their aim was to rid the area of "undesirables," particularly the migrants who had found refuge there after the Olympic pogroms of 2004. What the Nazis lacked in numbers they quickly made up in support from authorities. Police-backed Nazi patrols ensured that the square's playground was locked up in order to prevent migrants' children from using it. A local church—located by the square itself—was forced to stop providing free meals to local migrants out of fear after direct neo-Nazi threats against the church's head priest.

On 26 May 2009, "persons unknown" set fire to the church's basement, where the priest had been offering shelter to homeless migrants. Weeks later, a parent who tried to break the siege of the playground along with his five-year-old son was physically attacked by neo-Nazis; police arrested the parent for "provocative behaviour" and detained him for hours in the local police department, which was besieged by a mob of a few dozen members of the "Ayios Panteleimonas Resident Committee" who threatened to lynch him. Throughout the summer of 2009 a number of anti-fascist demonstrations entered the square and temporarily opened up the playground only to be teargassed and pushed back by police units. In July 2009, the then-Vice-Minister of Public Order Christos Markoyannakis visited the square and met with the neo-Nazi-led resident committee—never hiding his sympathy for their extreme right-wing politics. Only minutes after the meeting ended, a small group of neo-Nazis left the square and headed for the nearby Villa Amalias squat only to be outnumbered and chased away by those defending one of Athens's oldest squatted buildings.

At the time of this writing (late 2010), the square is still effectively under neo-Nazi control. The playground is locked up, the "Ayios Panteleimonas Resident Committee" still organises its own anti-migrant patrols, and riot police units are still permanently stationed by the square to provide assistance in preserving their authoritarian rule. Throughout the past year, stories have surfaced in mainstream media about ruthless attacks on migrants in the neighbourhood. In late August 2009, a local Afghan shopkeeper was forced to close his café early in the evening "so that migrants would not mingle around it." The police have refused to take testimonies from migrants who have been assaulted.[11] The soothing words of the then-social-democratic Minister of Citizen Protection[12] (who called the situation around Ayios Panteleimonas Square "scary" in October 2009) have not been accom- panied by any concrete changes on the ground.

Contrary to the relatively unchanged situation in Ayios Panteleimonas, the Exarcheia neighbourhood quickly felt in its bone the rise of the social-democratic PASOK government in October 2009. From the government's second day in power, the area was besieged by police. The new government's intention became evident not only in the repeated raids on the Navarinou Park but also—and especially—in the daily siege of the entire neighbourhood in those days: restrictions on the free flow of people in and out, constant ID checks of passers-by, random detentions, forced detouring of people, etc. Yet the most important aspect of the Exarcheia operations after PASOK's rise to power has been played out at the level of representation. One only has to take a glimpse at mass media coverage of these operations to realise that the new government sought to simultaneously occupy the physical and representational space of the neighbourhood.

Bolstered by these media distortions, the new government took things as far as claiming that Exarcheia was *en route* to becoming a "Greek Montmartre"[13] (as then Deputy Minister of Citizen Protection Spyros Vougias had put it). Its interventions in Exarcheia were intended to demonstrate a capacity to enforce order and a containment of the riotous spirit of December 2008. This representational project has been aimed at two target audiences: one, a conservative segment that was to appreciate the state's show of force in the physical presence of police on the streets of this famously unruly neighbourhood; and two, the anarchist and leftist activists who, according to media representations, concentrate themselves exclusively in Exarcheia. The idea, it seems, has been to reassure the conservative parts of society by intimidating those who would dare to continue to resist after December.

THE RIGHT TO THE CITY

State repression aside, what is it that remains of an urban uprising after the dust settles? What can the cases of Navarinou Park and the square of Ayios Panteleimonas tell us about the articulation of an uprising's legacy through the new and more permanent sites of political confrontation it produces? And how do the emergent spatial practices in post-revolt Athens fit into the broader legacy of uprisings and riots in European and American cities more generally?

These questions must be approached in the context of a more generic one—namely: what is the potential of violent crowds to become agents of change and what might spatial practices linked with this potential social change look like today? This is a question that has been repeatedly posed by historians, from Eric Hobsbawm's (1965) descriptions of the "pre-political" urban mobs of medieval cities to E.P. Thompson's analysis of the "moral economy" of crowds in 18th century. A major turning point in the "revolutionary" potential of such crowd action occurred between the French Revolution of 1789 and the Paris Commune of 1871. And yet, at the dawn of the era of bourgeois democracy and industrial production, violent crowd action found itself out-manoeuvred by urban design (e.g. the so-called "Hausmannization" of Paris as the prototype for social control through urban planning),[14] outdated by changes in social stratification, with the crowd's spontaneity being "incompatible with the long-lasting solidarities" (Hobsbawm 1965: 124) of the then-emergent working class. It found itself outmoded by the supposed evolution of political representation since bourgeois democracy was widely considered to be "both an improved substitute for violence and altogether incompatible with any form of violence" (Moore 1968: 1). For all these reasons you could have expected city mobs, violent crowds, and urban riots to have all but vanished: it was for these reasons, in fact, that Hobsbawm had announced their "passing." (1965: 124).

But in the last decades of the 20th century this idyllic image of First World urban politics has been "shattered by spectacular outbursts of public unrest, rising ethnic tensions, and mounting destitution and distress at the heart of large cities" (Wacquant 2008: 18). The examples are many: acts of urban rioting have taken place in numerous metropolises including Paris (1968); Brixton, London (1981); Los Angeles (1992); Bradford, Leeds, and Oldham in the north of England (2001); and more recently Paris (2005) and, of course, Athens (2008). Academic efforts to grapple with this most recent upsurge of urban rioting have focused on the structural causes underlying each instance. These range, for example, from the perceived social policy failures that led to the French suburban uprisings of 2005, (see for example Dikeç 2007), to the interracial tensions that erupted into a string of urban riots in the north of England in 2001 (See Amin 2003 and Bagguley and Hussain 2008) and the long-standing animosity between police and members of the black community that served as backdrop to the outpouring of violence in Los Angeles in 1992 (see Baldassare 2004 and Jacobs 2000). The dominant approach has been to read acts of rioting primarily as responses to particular structural injustices and to focus on operations aimed at preventing their re-emergence. But there are reasons to think that another perspective, more attuned to spatial dynamics, might provide important insights about the legacies of urban riots and revolts.

Consider Manuel Castells's reading of the string of urban riots in the US of the 1960s as a form of urban social movement, with participants claiming the right to occupy and re-use certain urban spaces (the black ghettos) for their own purposes as a key "organizational basis of the revolt" (Castells 1983: 53). Individuals and collectivities participating in urban riots for this purpose might then be understood to be making a claim to a "right to the city" which, in Lefebvre's original conception, was a call for "a radical restructuring of social, political, and economic relations, both in the city and beyond" (Lefebvre 1996: 34). This original conception of the right involved the capacity to access urban services, but also considered a "right to appropriation"—that is, inhabitants' right "to physically access, occupy, and use urban space" (Purcell 2002: 103).

It is in this conception of the "right to the city" that a fundamental political and material-spatial difference between Navarinou Park and Ayios Panteleimonas Square can be seen. First of all, the Nazis who physically occupied the square lacked the explicit legacy of revolt that animated the occupation of Navarinou Park. The Nazis were simply reacting to the December event and its legacies, creating a field of artificial social tension in an effort to manifest their limited spatial and political presence in a city that was briefly overcome by anti-authoritarian revolt. However, and more importantly, the people of Navarinou Park had the power and the will to access, occupy, and radically alter the actual materiality of the former parking lot: they tore apart the asphalt, planted trees, painted the walls, transformed building walls into cinema screens, and threw away metal and plastic fences. In short, the people involved in Navarinou Park turned the site into a lived space, organically integrated into the life of Exarcheia while at the same time reflecting and affecting political developments in the country. On the other hand, by preventing migrants and anti-Nazi inhabitants from being in the square and using the playground, the Nazis in Ayios Panteleimonas altered none of the established materialities of the square's space. This was because they lacked the social legitimacy and power that the revolt offered to the Navarinou Park people and because, together with government forces, they concentrated exclusively on the politics of representation and symbolism rather than on the politics of lived urban space. The most that the authoritarian occupiers of Ayios Panteleimonas can stand for is the fragmented and local right of Greeks to use the square as opposed to foreigners, establishing a regime of fear and violent discrimination: a single-issue politics materialised with a very passive and limited spatial practice—that is, closure and fencing of the site where they want to root their explicit political project.

In contrast, the Navarinou Park project has reached beyond the representations of what can be achieved without the intervention of the state and when people self-organise. It is a spatial-material legacy of the revolt but it is now also a lived everyday space with a constant flow of people and events. Integrated within a broader framework of post-revolt political potential in Greece, it is open both socially and spatially to the transformations in Athens after the uprising. This becomes clear in light of the most recent police raid on the park that took place in April 2010, only days before the loan agreement between the Greek government and the International Monetary Fund, the European Central Bank, and the European Union.[15]

In December 2008, popular consent for the post-dictatorial political settlement broke down rapidly and spectacularly, bringing a simmering political crisis to boil; at its core was a rapidly fading faith in the political legitimacy of the Greek state and its apparatuses. Since the December revolt the Greek state has been confronted with some very tangible ruptures. Several segments of the population have emerged from December more confident about the potential of their own political identities and projects, which have a strong anti-state and anti-authoritarian character. Many of these post-December political subjects were brought together through the Navarinou Park occupation. While this site may be a relatively minor instance of urban reclamation, it nevertheless represents a significant resistance-scape[16] that poses a tangible danger for the Greek authorities and their political crisis (now presented as a fiscal one) because of its potential to evolve into a much broader escalation by some of the most progressive and militant elements of society.

Governance in the post-dictatorial period has alternated between the two main political parties, which have bred nepotism, large-scale corruption, and enabled the domination of the political landscape by a small number of families. The shifting of attention to narrow financial-administrative issues in the current moment can be read as an attempt by political elites to distract attention from this long-standing political crisis that was expressed so dramatically in the December revolt. Since October 2009, when PASOK came to power, an attempt has been made to create a war-like atmosphere of financial emergency. The state has exploited this sense of crisis to characterize protests, strikes, occupations, and similar actions as being not only opposed to the government and financial elites, but also to some imaginary common ("national") good.

On the night of April 12, 2010—one day after arranging the details of a major loan from the IMF, the ECB, and the EU (the so-called *Troika*, see Glossary)—Greek authorities sent hundreds of police special forces to raid the Navarinou Park where they beat up and detained more than seventy people. Because of its potential as a base from which the new policies and measures related to the Government-Troika deal could be opposed, the very first target the Greek state chose was the park. What defines the park is that it openly questions the consent that Greek authorities—along with the Troika—request from large segments of the society to work more, to be paid less and to come under increased surveillance. The park shows the possibilities of spatialising resistance and the potential of a radical conception of the "right to the city."

While many urban political groups from the left have invoked a version of this right to the city, the term has too often been mobilized in precisely the ways that Lefebvre would have warned against—that is, in the terms of single-issue politics. Even worse, the "right to the city" has at times signalled a narrowing of political forms from the global and national to the regional (specifically, the urban) arena—or even as an imagined exit from the milieu of politics altogether. In this sense Mark Purcell is quite right to point out that the right to the city has often been misinterpreted to describe groups applying "fragmented, tactical, or piecemeal resistance" (Purcell 2002: 101). Citizen groups looking to create more green spaces in their neighbourhood, for example, could do so in the name of a common good and as an act that is apparently not political, since it does not seem to produce any immediate political confrontation. Surely everyone is in favour of planting a tree!

Indeed, there are good examples today in which to see both the pitfalls and the potential of claims to the right to the city. For example, Critical Mass bike rides are seen by some of their participants as little more than a means to carve out space for bicycles to share the road with other vehicles: the right for yet another transport vehicle (the bicycle) to exist side-by-side with the emblematic vehicle of capitalist culture, the car. But this reading misses how these mass demonstrations can function as a challenge to the culture of capitalism. Within a broader political framework, the Critical Mass ride might serve as a key challenge to the legitimacy of an icon of capitalist culture: the socially isolating and environmentally destructive car and its capacity to provide the capitalist system with constant and speedy flows of people and commodities. Critical Mass rides—by the sheer volume of their participants, their slowed-down pace, and their attack on the individuality imposed by car transportation—challenge inherent and fundamental elements of capitalism and hierarchy more than many traditional demonstrations ever manage to do.

As we saw in the example of Navarinou Park the "right to the city" is not about rights, and it is not about cities; at least, it is not exclusively about either. If fragmented and narrowly understood "rights" were this concept's only criteria, then the Nazis' claim for the exclusive right of Greek citizens to access and use of the square and the playground might also qualify. The Navarinou Park version of the right to the city is much closer to more radical conceptions of a "collective human right" that have, according to David Harvey, emerged throughout history as responses to the fact that most notions of human rights "do not fundamentally challenge hegemonic liberal and neoliberal market logics, or the dominant modes of legality and state action" (Harvey 2008).

What has been happening in Athens since December 2008, then, is an attempt by some of the participants in the December uprising to make their own claim to the city, and through this process to subvert the authority of the state over everyday life and to experience an unmediated and unobstructed fulfilment of their needs and desires. This is no small order and, for this reason, the authorities' crackdown on these spaces should come as no surprise. After all, it is there, outside the margins set by authority, that the legacy of the 2008 revolt can be fought for and where it can be materialized on an everyday level.

NOTES

1 An earlier version of this chapter appeared in *Upping the Anti* 10.

2 See Part 2. The Event: December.

3 For an extensive discussion of the role of independent in media see the article by Metropolitan Sirens in this volume.

4 "Years of riots, clashes with police in Greece," http://www.reuters.com/article/idUKTRE4B61DW20081208.

5 "Greek police shooting sparks riot," http://news.bbc.co.uk/1/hi/world/europe/7769710.stm.

6 Helena Smith "In Athens, middle-class rioters are buying rocks. This chaos isn't over," http://www.guardian.co.uk/world/2008/dec/14/greece-riots-youth-poverty-comment.

7 "Children of the Revolution," http://www.guardian.co.uk/world/2009/feb/22/civil-unrest-athens.

8 Haunt of Albanian Migrants, "These Days Are Ours, Too," n.d. Available at http://www.occupiedlondon.org/blog/2008/12/15/these-days-are-ours-too/

9 Articles that report on the opening of the park appeared by and large in the mainstream press, e.g. http://www.lifo.gr/mag/features/1280 while some publications have also covered the state of repression the park quickly encountered, e.g. "Athens Voice," http://www.athensvoice.gr/the-paper/article/284/.

10 The term neo-Nazi is used relatively loosely here. Those involved in Ayios Panteleimonas include both neo-Nazi skinheads and more mainstream extreme right-wing nationalists. Golden Dawn is a small neo-Nazi organisation that openly participates in elections as a national-socialist party. Its agenda, aesthetics, and violent practices and discourses follow the international trend of Nazism. Along with the skinheads of Golden Dawn, there are various other extreme-right wing populist politicians in Greece with their own groups, press, and followers. These organisations trace their political origin to the Greek junta (1967–1974) and its para-state apparatuses. Several of these extreme right-wing populists hold positions in the full spectrum of right-wing parties. The most distinct extreme right-wing parliamentary party is the "Popular Orthodox Alert" (LA.O.S). However Nea Dimokratia (which governed the country between 2004 and 2009) includes several extreme right-wing populist politicians. These "patriotic forces" often ally with one another to promote common issues.

11 "Two new attacks on migrants," Ioanna Sotirchou in the *Eleftherotypia*, 26 August 2009b [in Greek] http://www.enet.gr/?i=news.el.article&id=76200.

12 The social-democratic PASOK government was quick to rename the "Ministry of Public Order" the "Ministry of Citizen Protection"—with the ministry's roles intact, including the command of the country's police and Coastguard forces.

13 The vice-minister was referring to the Montmartre district of Paris, which used to be a bohemian part of the French capital. Since the end of World War II it has been gentrified and is today one of the most popular tourist destinations in the city.

14 Baron Haussmann's radical renovation of Paris (1852–1870) involved, for example, the replacement of the city's medieval alleys with wide boulevards that cut through traditional working-class neighbourhoods while providing security forces swift access to the city—invaluable in the case of social unrest.

15 Only days before the final corrections and submission of this article, the first draft of which was initially written in spring 2009.

16 "Resistance-scape" refers to sites that overcome the ephemeral nature dominating several of the RtC-related activities. Resistance-scapes are being developed within the framework of the RtC activities, but they are becoming materially and spatially durable and form explicit resistance discourses and practices.

PART TWO

THE EVENT: DECEMBER

5

FROM RUPTURES TO ERUPTION:

A GENEALOGY OF THE DECEMBER 2008 REVOLT IN GREECE

Christos Giovanopoulos &
Dimitris Dalakoglou

In mid-December 2008, a teacher from Athens narrated the following incident: a few days before, her nine-year-old son had come home from school and asked her if she knew how to make a Molotov cocktail. The woman was surprised, but wanted to tease him so she asked him if *he* knew how. The boy replied that he did and started describing the process with confidence:

"You take a bottle of beer," the boy explained.

"Why not a bottle for orange juice?" his mother asked.

"No, no! It must be a bottle of beer; you drink the beer first and then fill the bottle with petrol, you put a piece of cloth on the top and you light up the cloth and throw it."

Although some readers may be surprised to hear of a nine-year-old kid accurately describing how to make a petrol bomb, the fact is that this story is indicative of the diffusion of political images and imagination across entire generations, including the very young, in recent Greek history. Many of the kids who familiarised themselves with these radical discourses and imaginations sooner or later helped to form or participated actively in the recent political movements in the country. Three high school and university students' movements in the last twenty years (1990–1991, 1998–2000, 2006–2007) confirm this radicalization of teenagers and people in their early twenties. Furthermore, the December 2008 events comprise a further confirmation, as students—who saw their peer being shot—made up the main body of the revolt.

There are various ways that one can conceptualize the social activism of young people in Greece today. For example, one could argue that it reflects the level of politicization of the rest of society. This is a politicization that is linked with recent history: the civil war (1946–1949) of two generations ago was followed by several decades of police-state oppression and pogroms against the defeated left, and of course there was the military junta (1967–1974), all of which have left a mark on the personal and family histories of most people in Greece. However, despite the historical continuities that we should take into account, we have to state clearly that the radicalization of the youth during the post-dictatorial period is very particular and takes on a different character in the post-1990s period. Although this period signifies the longest-lasting parliamentary regime in Greek history, there has also been a large concentration of social movements, coinciding with the introduction of neoliberalism in the country.

In this article we hope to demonstrate that this "restored" Greek parliamentary democracy could not afford to allow acts of disobedience or protest against its own ills and the ills which it inherited. The line of argument they have used against the young protesters is that those who have revolted and protested against the supposedly democratic state do not have the right to do so as they have no legitimate reason for protest. Especially the youth has been represented and criticized as the "lucky generation," living in a free society, in a "Europeanised" and fully modernised polity with social provisions, etc. Furthermore, according to some public commentators, the youth of the post-dictatorial period is the first generation to live in affluence in comparison to their parents' generation. This discourse was very popular amongst the reactionary journalists and academics in December 2008. They emphasised that Alexis was a private school kid, coming from relatively wealthy, middle-class parents.[1] This argument about wealthy kids revolting for fun has been used repeatedly against the youth who have chosen a radical and often violent way of resisting the authorities. Without fetishising the lower economic classes, one should notice that actually not a word was spoken about those kids who spread the rebellion to the poor, working-class suburbs of Athens and throughout Greece's rural, small, and otherwise quiet towns. Neither did we hear about the great number of young migrants or second-generation immigrants who also participated in December in large numbers. This meeting of youth from various paths of life in the streets in December 2008 did not come out of the blue. Since the end of the dictatorship and especially since the beginning of the 1990s in Greece a lot of young people identify with far-left and anarchist agendas regardless of their class or wider social origin, not least because the youth have been constantly the primary target by various neoliberal measures and oppressive state campaigns.

The reader has to bear in mind that our argument throughout this paper is that there exist several distinctions applied to the people involved in the post-dictatorial movements. The main distinction we will draw is between the more fixed political subjectivities of the pre-neoliberalism period (up to circa 1990–1993) and the people who were raised or even born after the establishment of neoliberal (called modernization) policies in Greece. Our purpose is to outline the momentous genealogies of the December 2008 revolt in Greece and show the gradual emergence of a new social agency, political subjectivities and political tactics that contributed to the unmaking from below of the political context of *metapolitefsi* (the post-dictatorial period, see Glossary). In that respect we focus on the "breaking continuities" (or, continuous breaks) that led to the December eruption, which we consider to have been a radical break with *metapolitefsi's* political structures. So our article aims to talk both about the political genealogy and the political formation of the actual *genea* (generation) of December's revolt.

The empirical historical part of this chapter cannot be exhaustive, as there have been many more movements in Greece than we could include in this text. Instead, we will focus on five moments of mass militant student and youth movements (1979–80, 1987–88, 1990–91, 1998–99, 2006–07) that moved beyond the established margins and challenged the dominant political configurations in each of these periods. Moreover, we will underline three critical moments (1985, 1990, 1995) as in-between instances where the intervention of youth outside of the mainstream politics was felt strongly.

THE 1979–1980 OCCUPATION MOVEMENT: THE FIRST BLOW

In 1979–1980 Greece saw the formation of a mass student movement that was led by the extra-parliamentarian left, mainly its Marxist-Leninist contingent. This movement forced the prime minister at the time, Karamanlis (senior), to announce in his national address on New Year's Eve the cancellation of the notorious 815 legal act, which pertained to educational reform. This movement formulated a militant political culture by actively challenging the political consensus of the "newly reborn" democracy of the early post-dictatorial period. The movement was also linked to the appearance of a new extra-university youth that referenced the autonomous and antiauthoritarian ideologies and met and mingled with the students in the occupied universities. This meeting occurred at a moment when the people's demand for real change and an end to the—still ongoing at the time—right-wing post-civil-war police state was gathering momentum. During this period, and largely thanks to the occupation movement, the structural weakness of the conservative government of New Democracy—albeit its clear parliamentary majority—became apparent.

Despite the apparent weaknesses of the regime, there were efforts by the institutionalised and newly-legalised mainstream left to control the youth movement and support the established order. For example, the socialist- and communist-youth-controlled National Students' Union of Greece (EFEE) decided to close all universities just before Christmas in 1979 in order to diffuse the movement's dynamic that had developed outside the union's control. Arguably, amongst the crucial political contributions of the 1979–1980 protests was that they exposed the role of the communist youth (KNE)—the strongest student organisation at the time—in applying the political pact of *metapolitefsi*. KNE not only condemned the occupations but its members tried to re-occupy the Chemistry School of Athens, which was already occupied by the students' assembly, in order to regain order. For this action they received the congratulations of the conservative minister of Internal Security. In fact, through the KNE the government could bypass the obstacle that the *academic asylum* (see Glossary) imposed on the intervention of the police. On the other hand, the occupation movement functioned as the next reference point in the line of students' upheavals since the anti-junta revolt of 17 November 1973. In wider terms, it expressed the surfacing social and political changes from below in the post-dictatorship era.

Nevertheless, despite the 1979–1980 movement's attempts to define and intervene in the processes of social transformations, it was not able to substantiate an alternative route. It seemed that it reached the peak of its potential on 17 November 1980 when the radical part of the movement attempted to break the ban on marching towards the US embassy that the conservative government had imposed on the commemorating demonstration for the anti-junta revolt.[2] The break of the ban led to head-to-head clashes with the police outside the Greek parliament and the death of two militants: Stamatina Kanelopoulou, a worker, and Iakovos Koumis, a student. While the 1979–1980 movement challenged the strict limits of the post-dictatorial democracy and exposed the demand for an end to the post-civil-war regime and for political change, what followed was characterised by a lack of strategy or the ability to take any further initiative. These changes culminated the next year in the victory for the first time in Greece of what was considered at the time to be a left party, PASOK: the populist social-democrats of Andreas Papandreou. Also faced with a dubious stance toward PASOK's left rhetoric (a year later), the movement suffered the dissolution of its most significant and large Marxist-Leninist organisations.

1981–1989: CHALLENGING THE "SOCIALIST" VERSION OF DEMOCRACY

After PASOK's domination for a number of years and despite the fact that a large number of activists remained active in higher education and at a local and social levels, the framework had changed. Although the political system of *metapolitefsi* was still intact, and more stable than ever, it was disguised in its most democratic gowns. Under this new condition a generation emerged, characterised by an anti-authoritarian sentiment, that challenged PASOK's hegemony and democratic credibility. It was a new breed that responded to the institutionalisation of the so-called *Polytechnic Generation* (see Glossary) and the November 1973 revolt. It was a youth critical of PASOK's modernisation and to the traditionalism and compliant integration of the left and the trade unions[3] whose ineffective forms of struggle were actively refused.

The disillusionment and the numbness that affected the majority of the radical left after PASOK's first season in government, was interrupted in 1985 by violent protests and the occupations of the Chemistry School and the Polytechnic after the murder of the fifteen-year-old school student Michalis Kaltezas by the police. Kaltezas was shot by a riot cop named Melistas during clashes with the police in the neighbourhood of Exarcheia on the anniversary of the revolt of 17 November. The events were a culmination of numerous moments of intervention by the far left and the anarchist movement in the previous period, which were characterised in practice by violent clashes with the police: university occupations (e.g. of the Chemistry School occupation prior the general elections of 1984), the attack on and cancellation of a neo-Nazi meeting with Le Pen[4] in Caravel Hotel in Athens (1984) or the conflicts for "territorial control" (i.e. resistance against the gentrification of the highly politicised Exarcheia square). Arguably, in this yet organisationally infant political culture, it was rather the subcultural urban identity politics that prevailed, interwoven with the phantom of a militant tradition and a prevailing antiauthoritarian sentiment. The

95

events of these years mark the first autonomous appearance of the anarchist/anti-authoritarian movement trying to establish a culture of direct action based largely on an anti-state and anti-police agenda. The intervention of this "angry youth" (as it was labelled at the time) signified an end to the golden years of PASOK. However it failed—or rather did not attempt at all—to create or connect with larger struggles, which to a large degree it despised. It was also during this time that the "annual rendezvous" with the police each 17 November was established. Thus, against the co-optation of the November revolt and the consumption of its ideals in the electoral terrain, one meets the mutation of the revolt to its simulacra, a formal repetition of the signs of revolt which created its own referential reality and political imagination that reached its limit in, or immediately after, December 2008. Nevertheless, the de-marginalisation of practices—such as school occupations—and their expansion outside the universities (or rather the gradual shift of the main subject of the youth movement from the politicised and organised university students to the more contingently mobilized school kids) marked another important difference of the period.

However, these events functioned as semiological and historical preludes to larger developments that the youth were at the frontlines of. The most significant phenomenon was the beginning of the de-alignment of notable parts of the Greek society from the political parties. Within the rigid polarisation of the post-WWII and the early *metapolitefsi* era, the struggles of those who were rejected by the state or prevented access to the goods of modernisation and democracy (e.g. the defeated of the civil war) coincided with the anti-right sentiment of political struggles, parties, and institutions. The memories were still very fresh and the political alignments were quite polarized on either side, that of the state and that of the popular resistance. Hence such polarity expressed an abstract and ideological subjectivity which was directly linked to the concrete conditions of people's everyday lives. Therefore the distinction between the social and the political was very difficult to make for several decades after the end of the civil war. This changed with the victory of PASOK in 1981; the coming of PASOK to power was portrayed as the reconciliation of the civil war and as a re-unification of the Greek society. Nevertheless, these politics of the so-called "national reconciliation" during the 1980s signified a process of consolidation that removed the basis on which previously socio-political subjectivities and affiliations were based on.

Thus the integration of the previous outcasts into the political establishment created considerable gaps, but not yet a vacuum. To be fair, the right/anti-right dichotomy was still active and long-lasting (manifesting itself indirectly even in the December 2008 revolt) and formulated the dominant bipartisan system (PASOK-ND) in the exchange of power. However, another mass youth movement of the 1980s, signified by a new round of university and school occupations in 1986–1988, marked the emergence of the so-called "party of the discontent," namely a youth with only loose reference to the previous politically-based identities. The mobilisation of this youth was motivated by its own experience, namely the eye-witnessing of the collapse of political difference between PASOK and ND in power, in their policies, discourses, and practices. A collapse those previous generations refused or could not apprehend, as the older generations still referred to those two poles in terms of imagined or actual differences. The collective and individual subjectivation of the 1980s movements was founded on this collapse and manifested itself with the spread of the action of occupation. Until that moment the occupation of public buildings, even universities and schools, was considered an act almost outside the limits of law (for the most conservatives it was an outwardly terrorist act), and certainly outside the "pact of *metapolitefsi*," which laid out the agreed-upon borders of social confrontation. The efficiency of the 1979–1980 occupations, which managed the cancellation of an already-passed law by occupying just four university departments, underlined the real and symbolic power of this form of struggle. The people involved in the 1986–88 movement, however, created different constituencies and an agency that was characterised by two new elements. The first was the prevalence of their everyday social needs (as basis for their subjectivity and actions) and not of their ideological position. This had as a consequence the second: a distancing from, and critique of, party-based youth politics. They had a critique expanded beyond the two poles (PASOK and ND) and encompassed the rest of the parties, including those of the left (KKE and KKE) who had dominated the "politicisation" of the Greek youth. The spread of the act of occupations in secondary and higher education, for first time in the majority of the main cities in the country, exemplified the retreat of the party-youth control of the movement.

This loosening of party affiliation and social background expressed within the universities was combined with the structural changes of both higher education and of Greek society broadly. The expansion of higher education in the post-1981 era brought changes to the demographics of university students that also affected the politics of the students' movement. Larger portions of students with working-class

97

origins did not translate automatically in stronger working-class-orien-tated student politics. On the contrary, at the level of student elections the results gradually converged with those of the general elections. This meant a retreat of the dominant communist youth representa-tion that won the student elections until 1986, and the ascent of the student group of the conservative-party-affiliated DAP, fuelled by the ideal of upward social mobility and the promotion of the neoliberal yuppie dream.

In this context, the non-party affiliated student formations of the radical left provided to the movement the organisational know-how and a political framework and analysis. The latter though was some-what distant for the majority of students. This was obvious due to the fact that, despite the rise of radical left activists and better results in the student elections after each occupation movement, the radical left groups failed to formulate a political subject or force, or to extend their hegemony at a social level. More importantly, this gap was obvious in the relationship between forms of activism and content. The more radical the former became, the less the latter, which was increasingly restricted to specific demands regarding education and provided less of an overall critique of the capitalist system. However, the spread of such radical practices of political contestation underlined deeper changes in Greek society, as the 1990s will show, with the main characteristic being the increased discrepancy between political institutions and social agency.

1990s: REFORMING *METAPOLITEFSI* AND CONTESTING NEOLIBERALISM

Structurally, the 1989–1990 period can be considered a transitional period in the reconfiguration of the dominant discourses and politi-cal establishment in Greece. This occurred as both the result of larger changes in world geopolitics (the collapse of the Soviet block) and of the antagonisms in struggles for internal domination between the emerg-ing neo-bourgeois sectors (expressed by PASOK) and the traditional ones (ND). This antagonism created a climate of violent interventions between competing economic groups and extrapolitical institutions (e.g. media corporations) through the eclectic disclosure of scandals in an effort to remake the social contract and political map of *meta-politefsi*. The "end of *metapolitefsi*" has become a permanent slogan since then. In reality, what was introduced by the three governments of the 1989–1993 period was an openly neoliberal restructuring of the Greek economy and society, which needed to disintegrate those social obstacles for the "modernization"—the second dominant slogan—of the country. These obstacles included the social and public services of a poorly-developed welfare state, employment rights, sovereign policy for economic development, and any organized, antagonistic social agency, such as trade unions.

This neoliberal offence was implemented by the conservative government of K. Mitsotakis (1990–1993). This wouldn't, however, have been able to occur without the consensus of the rest of the parliamentarian parties at the time. Indeed, the Mitsotakis's administration governed with a very thin parliamentary majority. He secured this through the tolerance of all the oppositional parties (from its arch-rival PASOK to the unified Coalition of the Left—SYNaspismos, namely the unified KKE and KKE) and their consensus for this "catharsis." The slogan, literary meaning a "clearing" of the scandals,[5] in reality regarded the direction of the reforms and each party's position in the frame of a reformed *metapolitefsi*. The collapse of PASOK's government (1989) under the weight of scandals and corruption led to two elections without any party gaining a majority. Thus after the first elections of 1989 a coalition government combining the right wing ND and the two unified communist parties (Synaspismos) was formed. While the latter was hoping that its participation would deepen the PASOK's crisis and eventually marginalise the social democratic party, it was considered to be a betrayal of the whole post-WWII struggles against the police state of the right.[6] Thus, instead, the result in the new elections two months later was that PASOK gained the lost ground and participated in a new "ecumenical" (national) government, which included all the parliamentary elected parties: PASOK, ND, and the unified Synaspismos.

1990–1991: MASS SCHOOL OCCUPATIONS

It was in this context that the 1990–1991 occupation movement emerged. It was preceded though, by the January 1990 monthly occupation of the Polytechnic. The Polytechnic was occupied by anarchists because Melistas—the cop who killed fifteen-year-old Michalis Kaltezas back in 1985—had just been cleared of all charges in his second trial. Although anarchists and anti-authoritarians initiated this occupation, it was supported by the decisions of the students' assemblies of the different departments of the Polytechnic and it was also reinforced by student occupations of other universities for a shorter period (1–2 weeks). This occupation, remembered as "the blossom of the Greek youth" (named after the proverbial slogan on the banner of the last demo), marks a qualitative difference within the anti-authoritarian movement and the anti-organisational anarchism of the 1980s, mainly due to the prominent role of the Athens squatters' movement. Despite being a relatively small group, the anarcho-punk squatters' organisational skills—gained from their DIY experience—were transferred into the running of the occupation. This meant not only a position against the destruction of buildings and university facilities, but also control at the gates, the setting up of a collective canteen, cleaning shifts, etc. This new spirit, along with the organised communication (mainly by way of leafleting and flyer-posting) to the schools outside the centre of Athens, allowed the occupation to last for a month and to gain a mass support. One could say that indeed the January occupation left some footprints that led to the school occupation movement that erupted in November of the same year and lasted almost three months.

The 1990–1991 movement was the biggest—almost universal—school occupation movement in the history of the country, involving hundreds of thousands of students and several thousand schools and higher education institutes. In fact, it was eclipsed only by the uprising of December 2008 as one of the most significant moments in the history of social antagonism and political contestation in the post-dictatorship era. In addition to its mass character, the 1990–1991 movement was distinguished by strong qualitative differences from previous ones and defines the entrance into a new era of antagonistic politics in Greece.

Demographically, this movement was made up of those who belonged to a generation of people who were born or grew up after the dictatorship and entered their teens under the PASOK government. This means that they had been severed from the first-hand memory of the radicalisation of the *metapolitefsi* years and its political culture, if not of the (institutionalised by now) 1973 Polytechnic revolt, too. While the political representation of the uprising consisted of university students—largely due to their ability to politically articulate the movement's positions, their experience, and their national networks— the real backbone of the movement consisted of secondary school students. The massive participation of schools and universities, reaching around 90%, meant that for the very first time every town in Greece had a secondary education school occupied. This invasion of school students in the forefront of social contestation meant that the political subject (not of one or the another party, but as such itself) was left to the social agency of those making the movement. Organised political groups were forced to follow the initiative of the youth, which in real-

100

ity set the agenda and exercised the real hegemony in the movement. Therefore the attempts to politicise the movement with larger aims and goals, or even analyses and perspective, failed. In the previously described atmosphere of disillusionment and de-alignment from political parties, the youth did not share much with the pre-1990s experience and posed its own kind of politics and culture of protest. Its political logic was unique; on the one hand it had the potential to revitalise those "old" and "stereotyped" methods, while on the other hand it asked for something different. In short, this first instance of the prevalence of social agency and rather unplanned responses (which were, however, not spontaneous despite being strongly intuitive), in comparison with the political subjects already active in the movement, provided a glimpse into the shifts that would emerge during the following years and expand beyond the educational sector. This movement also holds strong parallels with the December revolt regarding the relation between the "political" and the "social" subject, and regarding either what was called the "spontaneity" of the movement or its lack of concrete demands and political procedures of decision making.

Politically, the lack of any alternative within the system, either nationally due to the ecumenical government, or internationally due to the collapse of the Soviet Union and the bipolar world, was spotted clearly within this mass movement. Going beyond the wider acknowledgement that "everyone is the same"—a sameness materialized very tangibly by the coalition and the ecumenical governments—this movement tried to constitute its antithesis to the political system by the slogan: "when you [the mainstream parties] agree in the parliament, the only opposition is us." In that way, it reworked and subverted the promoted and dominant, at the time, anti-populist and anti-political discourse that propagated the need of technocrats and specialists to be at the helm rather than politicians. A discourse (of ignoring the political cost) that aimed at the marginalisation of the energetic politically Greek populace.

In this context, the 1990–1991 occupation movement managed to reconfigure the promoted system of political indifference amongst all the parliamentary parties and turn it into a condemnation of the political system as a whole. They did this by drawing and emphasizing an explicit line between the strategically-unified political personnel and the people who had taken over the streets and the education institutions. The workers' and teachers' struggles in the following years (1991–1993) against the de-industrialisation of the country and the privatisation of the public services in one sense resisted and derailed the neoliberal reformation of *metapolitefsi*. As result it deepened the internal contradictions of the political establishment, contradictions that were based on a developed clientèle system that absorbed social discontent and maintained electoral power. However, the contraction of the state apparatus and the deregulation of the working market shrunk this system's abilities to provide favours. This contradiction was given a radical form by the current IMF intervention that has exposed and shaken the political system in Greece to its foundations.

The contribution of the 1990–1991 movement to the legitimisation of a series of political practices was immense. Most notably, the perception of building occupations and road blockades as marginal behaviour used mainly by extreme revolutionary political groups was radically altered as a result of the movement. At the same time, the dissolution of the Youth of the Communist Party (KNE)[7] allowed space for more immediate, or rather unmediated, expressions of social anger and more radical and inventive forms of resistance to emerge. One could suggest that the characteristics of the 1990–1991 movement, as they appeared in its slogans, actions, and organization, were more in sync with the movements of the French youth in 1986 and of the Italian students of the "panther" movement in 1990 than with the hitherto political culture of the radical students of Greece.

In that sense, the entry of a new generation, without the political links of the previous one, refreshed the logic and the vocabulary of political protest in Greece but at the same time was lacking the ability to articulate concrete demands or perspective. Namely, its demands were mainly defensive. This was not a new feature, only now it had become the dominant one. Due to the lack of any alternative proposal, the demands were very specific and were articulated against the most obviously reactionary elements of the proposed "white paper" for education. So the movement's most popular demands were a refusal: to pay for their textbooks, to return to the regime of school uniforms, to cut the days of school holidays, and to decrease the ceiling of the allowed absences from school. Their limited aims were directed against the economic consequences and the disciplinary functioning of the educational system. Nevertheless, larger demands or platforms connecting such consequences with the deeper restructuring of education failed to be embraced or prevail. But the unity and strength, both in numbers and morale, that these specific aims gathered showed the ability of the movement to expand, endure, and eventually succeed.

A second distinct element was the lack of the confrontational character that past youth movements had applied, a logic of force that was exercised not only against the system but also for acquiring power within the movement. This does not mean that the 1990–1991 movement renounced or did not use force or violence, but rather that it did so as a last resort. Confrontation was not prioritized in its political practice. Instead, argumentation, inventiveness, ridicule, humour, and collective participation were the main attitudes of the movement and these things encompassed even its violent moments. And yet, the disruption that this movement caused was much greater than any other until then—both in terms of time and space. However, blocking the roads with their school desks in order to inform the public of their demands and creating "functional occupations"—namely staying in their schools and creating their own spaces that they cared for, cleaned up, and maintained—were tactics clearly distinct from the destroying of systemic symbols. Such tactics of spatial reclaiming proved so effective that the usual rhetoric of vandalism was unable to break the public support for the movement, to allow the success of legal or more radical anti-occupation actions organised by authorities and vigilante groups, or to unease and mobilise parents against their kids.

The political practice that this movement produced manifested a different set of ethics, subjectivity, and agency that, retrospectively, one could argue had more in common with the ethics of the first days of the anti-globalisation movement—ten years later—than with the previous experiences of youth mobilisation in Greece. Its non-violent, or rather, non-destructive attitude was manifested even in its slogans, which gave it an integrity that was instrumental for its endurance and final success. One must also underline the determination of this movement to resist all attacks by the government and the state. Integrity and determination were fundamental elements for the maintenance of its mass character and support, as well as its unprecedented endurance— expressed with the slogan "I endure"—that kept the schools open and occupied during the Christmas break. It was also effective in resisting the government's attacks on the refusal of the movement to negotiate with it, and in mobilising masses broader than the youth.

Then at the beginning of January 1991, three days and nights of clashes with the police in the major cities of Greece erupted, marking, to a certain degree, the end of this movement. The event that had triggered this revolt was the murder of Nikos Temboneras, a teacher who had, together with his students, defended his school's occupation from the right-wing vigilantes who were trying to break it.

In addition to the aforementioned particularities of the 1990– 1991 movement, it is important to underline a number of other novel, 103 albeit minor, traits that it bore, as they have since become constant features of the emerging political culture. Something striking about this movement was the difference of its slogans and banners from the previous ones. The highly-politicised slogans and demands had been replaced with slogans that expressed feelings, attitudes, and sometimes visionary truisms: "When injustice becomes law/resistance is [our] duty" or "Our dreams will be your nightmares," etc. Also, instead of declaring political organisations or mere educational institutions, the banners declared the location of the schools and thereby linked the groups with their neighbourhoods, suburbs, towns, or villages.

Moreover, in terms of the spatial allocation of the marches one could also notice differences: Until then the white banners of the student unions—usually controlled by the youth of the Communist Party—were at the head, followed by the red banners of the ultra left students, with the anarchists tailing off the march. The 1990–1991 marches, however, had no particular order.

Moreover, the use of political slogans and their distinctive rhythm, while still present, had been sexed up by rhythms and slogans brought in from the football pitch. Famously, the slogan "Never, never, never" (shouted to the opposite team to suggest that they will never score a goal) became a dominant one in the political movements that followed, suggesting that the proposed reforms which the movement resisted, would never be enacted. This refreshing of the slogan culture, joined by more upbeat demonstration "performances," underlined a paradoxical return of the social to a waned political rhetoric and vocabulary. The newly involved masses of school kids brought their musical preferences in as well. A typical example of this was the slogan suggesting that "It's better to be the generation of chaos[8]/than in Afto-kinisi [a hip club at the time] and dance to house [music]."

One can argue that the movement of 1990–1991 had a rather "positive" or "constructive" character in comparison to the December revolt. However, the movement of 1990–1991 had the doubtful "privilege" of being the first one to act against the newly formed neoliberal regime, and was not yet defined by the violent conditions that neoliberalism would soon produce. The movement was composed of youth who, while experiencing the impasse of social policy and its incompetence to fill its promises, stood against the neoliberal destruction of their future. They defended, albeit intuitively and politically incoherently, their right to the future, before its vision collapsed entirely, as it had for the December youth eighteen years later. If the 1990–1991 generation had something to defend (or loose), the December generation had nothing. December's generation was born and grew up during and after the introduction of neoliberalism and was formed within its context—in terms of both its individual and collective subjectification—a context that produced subjects with a generalized marginality as antagonistic subjectivity and of a "deregulated" political action.

RECOMPOSITIONS CONCLUDING THE 1990s

The 1990–1991 student unrest functioned as the model for following school occupation movements opposing the further attempts at neoliberal educational restructuring made by both conservatives and by social democrats. The next important moment was the 1998–1999 school occupation movement. However, before we get to 1998 we should outline a number of developments that followed the 1990–1991 movement. Firstly, there were the workers' struggles against the deregulation of the labour market through deindustrialisation and privatisation. Most notably, the strike of the public bus drivers (the EAS strike), including its "All or none" (workers would stay at work) slogan and its dynamic and confrontational character against the state and police. However, the other trade unions did not actively support the strike despite the mass solidarity demonstrations that saw tens of thousands taking to the streets even in the vacation season of August. Parallel to the general disappearance of the official trade unions came the radicalization of the struggles of various sectors of workers—at least as far as forms of struggle are concerned. Thus, in the 1990s, there were two big farmers' movements with road blockades that split the country in two for weeks; multiple month-long strikes by school teachers; and a lengthy blockade of the port of Piraeus by dock and sea workers—to mention but a few struggles. However, these mobilisations remained isolated and unsynchronised with each other, despite having developed simultaneously at times.

A second development is that within the atmosphere of emerging struggles in 1990–1993, the Communist Party split between those who wanted to stay within the SYNaspismos coalition and those wished to see the Party regain its autonomy. The official pretext for this divide was the agreement by SYNaspismos to the Maastricht Treaty. In reality, part of the top cadre of the party saw opportunity in the vacuum that developed between the rising social discontent and the political formations of the 1989–1991 transitional experiment to a post-*metapolitefsi* era. Thus, they aimed to fill this gap and control these new constituencies, seeing a renovated role as a way to cushion social tensions before they got out of hand. So on one hand the Communist Party organisations were mobilized especially amongst farmers, construction and port workers struggles that at times tested the tolerance of the system's limits; on the other hand, in the decisive moments they always retreated or replaced the real conflicts with symbolic ones. These symbolic conflicts included mock and controlled occupations of ministries (executed by assigned squads of party members) or other "dynamic" imitations of direct action. This new configuration of reformism that used means of struggle that had been previously condemned as acts of provocation reveals once more the extent to which the "pact" of *metapolitefsi* had by that point been broken down under the pressure of the people's movement.

A third moment that ought to be recounted is the 1995 Polytechnic occupation by the anarchist movement that followed the 17 November annual march. The fierce clashes with the police around the barricaded Polytechnic, the burning of Greek flags (demonstrating an anti-nationalist agenda), the solidarity expressed with the continuing revolt of the inmates of Korydalos Prison, and the besieging and eventual arrest of 530 young people—a large majority of whom were school students—were all aired on live television channels. The newly-funded private TV channels, alongside the state-owned ERT, undertook a new role that they have kept up with since: to create a social consensus for the police offensive that aimed to silence a radical part of the youth that had been gaining ground since 1991. The state aimed to make an example of the protestors—arresting everyone who was present in the occupation—and to renegotiate the "academic asylum," which prevented the police from entering university grounds. Nevertheless the hostage-like situation that the arrested and their milieu were thrown into was indeed a blow to the anarchist movement, though it also marked an internal transformation. It forced, in one respect, a part of that movement to develop different strategies from those of the singular scheme of police-state-banks vs. society, leading to a renegotiation of the tactics of violent confrontation. Thus a number of social centres (*steki*) were established at universities and in neighbourhoods. This relatively new anarchist activity led to the introduction of new people who had been politicized within the post-1995 atmosphere, while the pre-1995 radicals gradually returned or found themselves in a scene that was rapidly developing. Eventually, anarchism in Greece made an impressive comeback during the anti-globalization movement's struggles of the 2000s, and today it is considered one of the largest anarchist movements in Europe.

106   What we have labelled the youth movement did not calm down during the 1990s. New waves of students entering high school con-

tinued to resist new educational reforms. Thus, in 1998, the Arsenis's generation (named after the PASOK minister of education) managed to build the next big school occupation movement. By now, the communist youth had managed to reconstitute itself and supported the occupations. Its presence, however, only divided the schools between those that followed a national coordination assembly controlled by the KNE and those that ascribed to the independent school coordination initiative in which leftists and anarchist students, among others, were represented. Despite the dominating presence of the KNE's coordination, the group was for the first time forced to adopt occupation as a means of struggle, though they avoided such tactics whenever they could. Still, they were unable to marginalise the non-KNE schools and students. The threat that the latter posed to the KNE, and the real attitude of the KNE towards them, became obvious at the beginning of the so-called Arsenis movement. In 1998, once more on 17 November, the riot police—with the active assistance of the KNE—arrested, without reason, around 160 people who were marching with the anarchist bloc, the majority of them secondary school kids.

The KNE managed over the course of the following years to become the first organised left force within universities—electorally speaking, as it is still weak in the general assemblies. It quickly returned to its orthodox position of condemning the occupations, but yet it fails to convince even its own members of this position when the issue comes up. During the latest student movement (2006–2007), in support of the constitutional Article 16 (which prevents the foundation of private universities, an article that the conservative government of ND wanted to change through constitutional reform), the Communist Party was adamant that they did not support occupations. Similarly, and even more vociferously in December 2008, the KKE (Communist Party of Greece) received official congratulations—by the right-wing government and the extreme-right party LAOS—for its denunciation of violence and its respect for the government's right to impose "law and order." "In the revolution, not even a shopping window will be broken," the KKE's general secretary Aleka Papariga declared in December 2008 in the Greek parliament.[9]

As previously mentioned, more radical forms of action have been established as the norm throughout the last two decades. A typical example of this was the so-called ASEP strike of 1997–1998. ASEP was the name of a new state organization that used written exams to determine a teacher's right to work. ASEP was pushing hiring practices towards a market-oriented evaluation process that would replace the previous system of placement based on teaching experience and academic merit. After numerous strikes, the movement decided to physically prevent the new exams from being administered. This meant three days of occupations of the exam centres and it meant clashes with the police. The fight was lost, but the movement, despite its organisational shortcomings, raised the stakes to an unprecedented level. It was one of the few cases in which a formal trade union decided to make use of direct action, which shows how particular dynamic practices had become legitimised forms of action.

2000s: TOWARDS THE UNEXPECTED

The Greek far left and anarchist movements participated actively in the various anti-globalization gatherings that followed Seattle during the late 1990s and early 2000s, most notably in Prague (2000) and Genoa (2001), which several thousand activists from Greece travelled to and participated in. The same model was repeated in December 2001 in Brussels and it was followed by an anti-EU demonstration in the Greek city of Thessaloniki in the summer of 2003. This international experience gave the chance for the Greek movement to put some of their tactics into a new perspective, to compare and to solidify them in order to project them within an international framework. New international points of reference were added to the logic of the Greek movement and new codes emerged. At the same time, this globalization of the movement has to be seen in parallel with the changes that globalization brought to Greek society itself. A typical example is that of an increasing number of youth migrating for studies and thus increasing the international links between the youth of Greece and the rest of Europe. Moreover, this was happening as a drastic inflow of immigration was taking place in Greece at the same time, particularly since the early 1990s. Migrants' rights and solidarity were added to the agenda of the movement while a lot of migrants—particularly second-generation—started participating in secondary school and university movements.

It was during the 2000s when, for the first time, a sizeable group of people emerged into the terrain of social and political struggles on such numerous fronts as local issues regarding environment and free urban spaces, official or grassroots union struggles, anti-racism, anti-war, anti-imperialism, and international solidarity campaigns, etc. This so-called "social left" identified with some of the objectives and strategies of political groupings (from radical left to anarchist ones) but did not wish to become explicitly part of them, although many hold anti-hierarchical or/and anti-authoritarian views. This part of society became visible quite suddenly in May 2005 when, at the closing demonstration of the European Social Forum of Athens, more than 70,000 people participated. The sudden appearance of this part of society and in such great numbers not only surprised everyone, but it catalysed the kick-off of the "Defend Article 16" movement.

This university-centred movement took place in 2006 and 2007. It was a year-and-a-half-long campaign against the aforementioned change of the constitution's Article 16, which secures a free and public higher education. The movement represented an important moment because it showed an attempt of political subjects, especially on the side of the radical left within the education movement, to correspond to and mould themselves to social shifts and aspirations in a militant movement. The broadness of this movement was a successful—though a weak and contingent—meeting of the political subject and social discontent. Of course, it is not coincidence that this occurred in the realm of the education sector in which a long tradition of mobilisations had established patterns of cooperation between different parts of the movement. It was this wide inclusion and unity of focus that made this movement successful in the end and even enabled it to revitalise hope for the potential of the intervention of the radical left in the central political scene. This was also supported by the unification of different tendencies within the left that could not have been previously imagined. These two last statements refer particularly to the project of SYRIZA (Coalition of Radical Left).[10]

However, when these ruptures became an eruption in December 2008, the social movements and the people more actively involved met with their limitations and had to deal with events that, while they may have contributed to, were beyond their reach. The role of this radical social left in building new sites for the antagonistic movement, and in acting as a national network of activists distributing a different political culture, must not be neglected in the effort to discern new shifts in the formation of social antagonism in Greece. Not in the least because it manifests the changing relations between social agency and political organization, even within the left.

A second development, closely paralleling the first, was the expansion of and further integration of the anarchist/anti-authoritarian movement over the past few years. In other words, anarchist groups, organizations, media, publications, and activities started appearing in more cities and towns than they ever had been before. Simultaneously, anarchist groups started getting more involved with wider social issues such as labour relationships or neighbourhood demands, and for first time during this period we have a much wider dissemination and popularization of anarchist ideas within society. One must recognise the role of new media and technology (particularly Athens Indymedia) in both acting as a "centre" (not exclusively, but primarily) for the anarchist/antiauthoritarian movement while at the same time multiplying its decentralisation and creation of its experience and practices (e.g. social centres). It is obvious that this spread of the movement and the increasing fluidity of the terrain of various local or national-scale struggles diversified the anarchist movement even more and created a whole group of activists that refuse any fixed ideological position. This shift manifested in the participation of "anarchists/anti-authoritarians/autonomists" in the movement for Article 16, in contrast with their previously hostile attitude towards the student movements. As such, the 2006–07 movement provided more than just the confidence inspired by its victory, but also a fresh memory and organising experience for the generation that revolted a year later.

POST-DECEMBER '08: "MOVING BY ASKING"

This text began with the story of a teacher and her son. Although the two of them had different demographic cohorts, they both seem to have experienced moments of political ruptures during their school years. Then we described some moments in the political genealogy of revolts in post-dictatorial Greece and the emergence and development of the practices and discourses that could be seen during December 2008. December, although it surprised everyone, did not come out of the blue. Although social injustice and social rage had been accumulating at the time, the event bore with it a legacy; a legacy not in terms of direct physical links—although these too were part of December 2008, as older activists who had not been on the streets for years ended up in the demonstrations, at the barricades, and in the occupations—but in terms of semiology, practices, discourses, and imagination. In other words, December 2008 was an intensive materialization of previously constructed images and experiences.

Moreover, in this chapter we have tried to demonstrate that, although the post–dictatorial political ruptures have often been portrayed and perceived in continuity with previous movements, they actually also carry some distinct qualities. First of all, they took place in what was formally the longest-lasting democratic period in modern Greek history and at the same time reflect the neoliberal restructuring that has affected every sector of Greek society since 1989–90. The frequency of these mass movements and the rebellion of students and young adults that occurred in the last twenty-five or so years also released a social dynamic that at the same time reflected and propelled such shifts on many levels. Most importantly, the emerging political subjectivities of the neoliberal era of Greece challenged the political structures that corresponded to the pre-neoliberal conditions as they had been formed after the collapse of the dictatorship.

The December 2008 events constituted the full disintegration of such political superstructures, following the complete removal (thanks to neoliberal restructuring) of the social grounds over which they stood, resulting in their violent collapse. However, in the eruption of December 2008 and during the previous ruptures, this depositioning of the social in relation to its political abstraction (representation and state) was not articulated into a coherent social alternative. It was articulated as a violent, non-directional (or rather multi-directional) "re-alignment" of the political with the social terrains of the dismantled previous structures, forced into being by "the street." It is in this sense that those who revolted in December completed the work of previous moments of social antagonism that had challenged the "limits of protest" that the democratically-elected regimes had imposed. Those previous moments had caused several cracks in the political establishment of the post-dictatorship state that led to the eruption. December also signifies one of the first revolts within the latest global economic crisis, marking in one sense the end of the neoliberal hegemony by exposing its remnants.

Throughout the post-dictatorial period, and especially over the course of the last twenty years, movements in Greece had been building towards an end that December 2008 materialised and fulfilled. But as we know, there is no end that is not also a beginning—the only question is of what sort. What kind of political logic, agency, field, and discourse has December 2008 produced? To confine this only to the participants of December 2008 would be an act of evasion. It would be evasive to not try to understand, face, and deal with the results of that great unmaking, of what the December 2008 revolt produced by penetrating all levels of the Greek society, not only those who participated in it. Failing to frame the action within the larger shifts in the post-December 2008 picture would be an attempt to avoid the questions that December 2008 has raised, questions that we need to face if we really want to turn the momentary grasp of the impossible, that we all felt, into a real potential. That, however, is another article. What we address herein are

111

the discernible changes that December 2008 has produced as (part of) its legacy, both in the still-active social subject that was formulated by experiencing (or, rather, making) it and in the larger political culture within the antagonist movement.

Occupations and violent confrontation as dominant forms of political activism drew a formal line between revolutionary practices and reformist ones. However, we argue here that the gradual demarginalisation of these tactics, as part of consecutive political and social struggles, met its own end in December 2008. In one sense the "absolute" domination or exercise of these tactics meant also their end as political indexes of radicalism (if they ever were as such by themselves). December 2008 challenged their limits and, by trespassing the borders of the most radical or maximal forms of political action, laid bare the nakedness of the political discourses and identities that had been build around their formality. This was something that was unfortunately realised with tragic consequences a year and a half later on 5 May 2010. On that day, three bank workers died in a fire set, allegedly, by "black bloc" activists, during an anti-IMF general strike.

At the same time, the December 2008 revolt reproduced such forms at their highest fidelity, realising them as simulacra. Thus the "non-result" of December 2008—which far from being non-productive, produced something that was and is of a different order—revealed not the inadequacy of such forms of action necessarily, but the political vacuum beneath or behind them, in that they were not supported by, nor did they support, an alternative way of doing or imagining things. That suggests that the December 2008 revolt was rather the expression of a social implosion rather than of a social explosion. It is within this context of implosion that one can detect the December 2008 revolt both as disruption and as a missed opportunity. Or as a slogan on a wall in Athens during those days put it: "December was not an answer. It was a question."

One could argue that any attempt to return to the pre-December 2008 political normalities is impossible at any level and for any actor in Greek political life. What followed the December revolt was a culmination in the intensification of the Greek crisis,[11] the neo-colonial regime of the IMF-EU imposed rule, and the unmaking of *metapolitefsi* from the top down through the forced collapse of any social and public regulations, the development of a securitised state, and the popular resistance to it. Even if the resistance is inefficient and lacking when compared to the size of both the attack and the social anger, the threat of a new eruption is still a visible phantom over Greece. It is not only the social anger that boils. Since the post-December struggles a new militant subject is emerging, one whose political culture cross-cuts the existing radical and revolutionary political actors and changes their qualities. There are developments that, in any case, have accelerated and condensed socio-historical time so much that they have made incomplete any critical discourse on December 2008 that doesn't project it in the context of more recent events. Having said that, one should be equally cautious not to underestimate the similarly incomplete, but real, social potential that the revolt opened up, a potential that still burns and re-shapes both the political culture at large and the antagonistic movement in Greece.

NOTES

1 For a typical example of such a position one can see in *The New York Times* a text by a Greek professor at Yale named Stathis Kalyvas, under the title "Why Athens is Burning," published during the December revolt. See: http://www.nytimes.com/2008/12/11/opinion/11iht-edkalyvas.1.18595110.html

2 The ban had been in place since 1976 and respected by the institutional left (PASOK, KKE, and KKE), until November 1981 when, under PASOK, the ban was lifted. It is still a contested of the US embassy each year. The US embassy is the destination of the annual 17 November demonstration because the US government backed the Greek junta.

3 It is important not to forget that this is also the era of the "farewell to the working class" among the disillusioned social democrats, leftists, and anarchists, the era of alternative social movements, and the era of the ascendancy of the neoliberal agenda and culture as expressed by the yuppies. This is not a minor point: the processes of pre-neoliberal politics and the emergence of neoliberalism as political structures/field have defined, to a certain extent, the production of its negation and its opposing social subject.

4 Jean-Marie Le Pen, leader of the extreme-right National Front party in France.

5 The Greek equivalent of the Italian "operation clean hands" that changed drastically the map of Italian politics to date. However, in Greece, it was merely a caricature as the two-party system of corruption and carried on.

7 A few months earlier, the majority of KNE had been kicked out of the Party because they disagreed with the collaboration between the Party with the right-wing ND.

8 Generation of Chaos (*Genia tou chaous*) was the name of an anarchist punk rock band of the 1980s.

9 This congratulation of the KKE was repeated by the current minister of education

in October 2010. When a new school occupation movement began, with the potential to put the IMF-subdued social democratic government in a difficult position prior to the start of elections, the KKE was quick to separate itself and to condemn those kinds of actions.

10 This was particularly obvious in the case of SYRIZA, a left coalition party with parliamentary presence. SYRIZA was the only parliamentary party that explicitly expressed its solidarity with December's revolt. Moreover, parts of SYRIZA had a visible and active participation in December. SYRIZA increased its electoral strength during the 2006–2007 students' movement. However, the full project is now falling apart, as some parts of the coalition have broken away from it.

11 We consider "the Greek crisis" to be something that is not merely an economic, but is instead an organic systemic crisis, and we see and the December 2008 revolt as its first grand moment. December 2008 was the first instance of an implosion of the system, rather than a social explosion due to its internal socio-economic contradictions (on the international level) and the specific socio-political discrepancies (on the national level) that together formed the current crisis in Greece.

6

THE REBELLIOUS PASSAGE OF A PROLETARIAN MINORITY THROUGH A BRIEF PERIOD OF TIME

THE DECEMBER REBELLION AND THE POST-REBELLION DEVELOPMENTS AS ASPECTS OF THE CRISIS OF CAPITALIST RELATIONS IN GREECE

TPTG

AN EPOCHAL CRISIS?

Since the mid-1970s there has been a worldwide permanent crisis of re-production of capitalist relations in all their forms (political, economic, and ideological). As we understand it, this crisis has two aspects: it is a crisis of over-accumulation of capital, which means an inability, on the part of the capitalists, to increase the rate of exploitation and reduce the cost of constant capital and so increase the rate of profit demanded by an advancing capital accumulation. At the same time this is a legiti-mization crisis—that is, a crisis of the political and ideological forms that guaranteed the discipline of the labour power. We could therefore talk of the inability of capital and its state to put forward a new global productive/social model that would replace the post war Keynesian deal, hard hit both by the struggles of the planetary proletariat and the capitalist policies against them.

During this long, drawn-out crisis of reproduction there have been periods of cyclical depressions. Capital in general has tried to deal with them in various ways: by changing the global institutional and legal framework of the movement of capital and "liberalizing" the markets, by promoting a mixture of neoliberalism and Keynesianism through war, by decreasing wages and institutionalising the precarisa-tion of labour, by accomplishing new enclosures, by putting the "dangerous classes" under penal surveillance and/or integrating them into the credit system through a policy of "privatised Keynesianism."

Despite temporal recoveries, the ultimate failure of all the above strategies and tactics—aimed at deferring the aggravation of the crisis—has in the long run turned this crisis of reproduction into an epochal one, as many would argue.

During the last two decades the crisis of reproduction in Greece has been dealt with by capital and the state by successive reforms of the education and welfare system, by promoting the precarisation of work relations, by continuous legal attempts to discipline immigrants and control immigration flows, by cutting down allowances, wages, and benefits and replacing them with bank loans. All these measures aiming at devaluing, disciplining, and dividing the working class and making workers pay the cost of the reproduction of their labour power have not succeeded in decisively reversing the crisis to the advantage of capital— this, despite the fact that during the period between the mid-1990s and the mid-2000s capital had managed to increase the rate of exploitation and expand its profitability.

In Greece the crisis of reproduction has manifested itself most explicitly as a crisis of legitimization of capitalist relations, either through the permanent crisis in education in the last thirty years (see our text on the primary teachers' strike in 2006 and the student movement in 2006–07)[1] or a lot more through the December rebellion. The rebellion was a clear expression of proletarian anger against a life that is getting more and more devalued, surveilled, and alienated. However, the December crisis cannot be directly connected with the recent depression that started manifesting itself in Greece in September 2008.

THE REBELLION: ITS CLASS COMPOSITION

We won't describe here thoroughly the various things that happened during the rebellion as we have done this elsewhere.[2] As far as the class composition of the rebellion is concerned, this ranged from high school students and university students to young, mostly precarious, workers from various sectors like education, construction, tourism and entertainment services, transportation, even media. (Of course, it is not easy to distinguish students from precarious workers.) As far as factory workers are concerned, there can be no accurate estimation about their individual participation in the riots since no reports from such workplaces became known. Some of the students and the workers were second-generation immigrants (mostly Albanians, although there were also some immigrants of other nationalities). There were also many older workers with more or less stable jobs, but they were a minority. Some of the students and the workers that participated in the riots were also football hooligans. Last but not least, we should mention the participation of "lumpen" proletarians, junkies, for example, mostly during the first days of the rebellion. In general, it was precisely those segments of the class that have directly been experiencing the violence of the state surveillance and the deterioration of work conditions that were more active in the rebellion. On the other hand, many older workers that had just started experiencing the so-called "financial crisis" (layoffs, wage reduction, etc.) were very sympathetic towards the burning down of banks and state buildings, but were mostly passive.

It might be interesting to add that because of the motley composition of the multitude and its violence a lot of politicos (even some organised anarchists) found it too "uncontrollable" and distanced themselves from what happened—especially on the third day of the rebellion, when violence reached its peak.

The high percentage of immigrants in the rebellion requires some explanation. The influx of many Balkan immigrants, especially Albanians, in the last twenty years has changed significantly the composition of the working class in Greece. At the same time, due to the immigration policy of the Greek capitalist state, a whole generation of young immigrants, mostly Albanians, that were born or grew up in Greece are not considered Greek citizens. The legalisation of all immigrants is undesirable for capital and the state, because in their world immigrants are only needed when they constitute an insecure, cheap, and obedient workforce. The so-called process of "legalisation," in Greece and other countries has long been considered as necessary for capital and its state only in order to control and keep track of immigration flows. That is why even second-generation immigrants cannot easily get a green card; on the contrary, they have to prove their "ability" to stay and work in the country every five years at most and of course they do not have the right to vote. Not to mention that their work conditions are the worst as far as wages and social security are concerned. But despite racism of both social and state origin most second-generation immigrants are quite well integrated—especially Albanians, who comprise the majority of the immigrant population in general.

Second-generation young Albanians fitted in very well with the rest of the native rioters. They felt more "comfortable" taking part in confrontations with cops, in attacks against state buildings and banks, and in lootings alongside Greek young proletarians than other immi-

117

grants—mostly Asians and Africans who still live on the fringe, isolated in their ethnic communities. For the latter it was easier and less risky to participate in the riots through looting or frequenting the open National Technical University occupation in the centre of Athens where big communities of them live in areas resembling ghettos: when the riots erupted near "their" neighbourhoods that was the way they "contributed" to them. They received the most violent onslaught from both the police and media propaganda. They were presented as "plunderers" and "thieves" and in some cases there were pogrom style attacks against them by fascists and undercover cops.

THE REBELLION: ITS CHARACTER AND CONTENT

The rebels who met in the streets and occupations temporarily superseded their separated identities and roles imposed on them by capitalist society since they met not as workers, university or school students, or immigrants but as rebels. They may not all have used a proletarian language, they may not have been able to go on strike, except for the high school and university students, but what they really did was to create *proletarian communities of struggle* against the state and capital. The spontaneous and uncontrolled character of the rebellion was proved precisely by the lack of any political or economic demands whatsoever, by a complete negation of politics and trade unionism. This proved to be the strength of the rebellion: the fact that it was impossible to be represented, co-opted, or manipulated by political mechanisms that would make bargains with the state. The extra-parliamentary left organisations that participated in the occupation of the Faculty of Law tried to impose some political demands (ranging from disarmament of the cops and resignation of the government to granting interest-free mortgage loans), but found no reception.

Here we will quote from the first account of the rebellion we wrote in late January:

> Judging from the slogans and the attacks against the police, an overwhelmingly anti-cop sentiment was dominant during the days of the rebellion. The cop stood for power and particularly the brutality and arrogance of power. However, it was as symbols of a certain power—the power of money, the power to impose the exploitation of labour and deepen the class lines separating Greek society— that big stores, banks as well as state buildings (town halls, prefecture buildings, ministries) were attacked, burnt down, or occupied. So, we could speak of a dominant and widespread anti-cop, anti-state, anti-capitalist feeling. Even the intellectuals of the left acknowledged the class element of the rebellion and some mainstream newspapers admitted that "young people's rage" was

not expressed only because of police violence. The cops were rather the most visible and crudest tip of an iceberg made of government corruption scandals, a security-surveillance state—armoured after the 2004 Olympics—that does not even hesitate to shoot in cold blood, a continuous attack on wages, an increase of working-class reproduction costs through the gradual demolition of the previous pension and health system, a deterioration of work conditions and an increase of precarious jobs and unemployment, a load of overwork imposed on high school and university students, a tremendous destruction of nature, a glamorous façade consisting of abstract objects of desire in malls and on TV ads, obtainable only if you endure a huge amount of exploitation and anxiety. In the first days of the revolt you could almost smell all these reasons in the air and then a lot of texts, articles, leaflets followed, written both by insurgents or sympathizers and "commentators" to acknowledge that there was "something deeper." This "deeper thing" that everybody was talking about was the need to overcome the individual isolation from real, communal life [*gemeinwesen*], an isolation that all the above historical reasons have created.[3]

Six months later it is still important for us to lay emphasis on this last point because many comrades abroad think that the movement only attacked the cops and the institutions of control—the "tip of the iceberg." The rebellious experience was more than that. It was the *common* activity of an emerging subversive undercurrent that *knows* that—alongside the sphere of immediate production—school, family, consumption, politics, prison, and the police *do* produce and reproduce classes. The rebellious experience, the material community of struggle against normalisation—when one deviant individual became the mediator of another deviant individual, a real social being—mediated emotions and thought and created a proletarian public sphere. This open sphere is the necessary presupposition of the decisive moment of social subversion: the communisation of the means of production and intercourse. But this decisive moment, the point of no return, was never reached. After all, this was just the rebellious passage of a proletarian minority through a brief period of time and not a revolution. However the feeling that there lay "something deeper" in all that, the idea that the issues raised by the rebels concerned everybody was so dominant that it alone explains the helplessness of the parties of the opposition, leftist organisations—even some anarchists as mentioned before.

Here, just because high school and university students were such a significant subject of the rebellion, we should be more analytical about the load of overwork imposed on them that we mentioned before. Education, as the main capitalist institution that shapes, qualifies, and allocates the labour-power commodity in a continuously developing capitalist division of labour, has been expanding in terms of student population since the 1960s in Greece. This development has given rise to new "popular" demands, expectations, opportunities of social mobility, and individual "successes." It has also led to the accumulation of tensions and contradictions, frustrations, and individual "failures" (also called "failures of the schooling system"). The mass production of expectations (and the corresponding rise in white-collar proletarians and new petit-bourgeois strata in the 1970s and 80s) caused by the democratisation and expansion of education created an inevitable structural crisis in the hierarchical division of labour and a crisis of discipline and meaning in school; in other words, a legitimisation crisis that hit state education hard. No matter what you call this crisis—a "crisis of legitimacy," a "crisis in the selective-allocating role of education," a "crisis of expectations," or a "crisis in the correspondence of qualifications to career opportunities"—the truth is that education has been seriously crisis-ridden. As the recent massive student movement of 2006–2007 showed, this situation has exploded. It is possible to understand both that movement and the rebellion if we see them as expressions of the accumulated dissatisfaction a whole generation of working-class youth has been experiencing since the previous reforms in the 1990s. These reforms were instrumental in imposing intensified work rates in the school and in the realm of proper wage labour. This generation could not be stopped from expressing its discontent for a life that is increasingly characterised by insecurity and fear. At the same time, they revolted against an everyday activity that looks similar to any other kind of work. This *revolt against student labour* was given a boost by a significant number of students who already directly experience exploitation and alienation as proper wage labourers.

SOME FORMS OF ORGANISATION THAT CAME OUT OF THE REBELLION

From the first day of the rebellion three universities in the centre of Athens were occupied and were used effectively as "red bases" of the movement from which subversive actions were organised[4] and where rebels could seek refuge if necessary. These occupations ended just before Christmas. In direct communication with them, several local assemblies appeared gradually, linked to occupations of public buildings in some neighbourhoods. As we said in the same text mentioned above:

> In all these activities, the common new characteristic was an attempt to "open up" the rebellion towards the neighbourhoods. These assemblies were understood as "neighbourhood assemblies of struggle" or "people's assemblies,"

as they were called. In most cases, there appeared distinct tendencies inside this social "opening," particularly as the rebellion was simmering down. One tendency wanted to organize a community of struggle broadening the issues of the rebellion, another one preferred a kind of activity more orientated towards dealing with local matters on a steady basis. In the beginning, the assemblies looked pretty innovative and lively. There was not a formal procedure of decision-making or majority rule and initiatives were encouraged. However, by the end of January, the occupations of buildings—whether public, union or municipal ones—did not flourish any more.... There was a lot of sympathy and interest for the insurgents but very little active involvement on the part of the "population."[5]

Some of these assemblies are still going on but with fewer and fewer people involved, mainly activists. Their main interests nowadays are the expression of solidarity with those prosecuted by the state and with immigrants, the defence of the occupied spaces in the city, as well as the organisation of several activities connected to current struggles (e.g. the new anti-motorway movement).

THE SPECTACULAR SEPARATION OF ARMED "STRUGGLE"

The need to mediate proletarian anger politically, even if it is to mediate it with an armed mediation, was not something that stemmed from the struggle itself but it was something that was being imposed on the struggle from the outside and afterwards. In the beginning there were two attacks by the so-called "armed vanguard," one on 23 December after the peak of the rebellion and one on 5 January, when the resurgence of the rebellion was at stake. From a proletarian point of view even if these attacks were not organised by the state itself, the fact that after a month all of us became spectators of those "exemplary acts," that had not at all been part of our collective practice, was a defeat in itself. The "armed vanguard" avoids admitting not only that they were not the first ones to target the police but also that no "armed vanguard," anywhere, has forced the police from the streets, or frightened individual cops from carrying their official identities with them for a few days. They can't admit that they were surpassed by the movement. Claiming that there is "a need to upgrade" violence, the so-called "armed vanguard" essentially tries to downgrade the socially and geographically diffused proletarian violence and violation of the law; the latter are the true opponents of the "armed vanguard" within the movement and, as long as such practices go on, no interventionism of "upgrading" things can find a fertile soil. It is on that basis that the armed struggle allies with the state: both are challenged by the

121

proletarian subversive activity, the continuation of which constitutes a threat to the existence of both.

The proletarian subversive activity in the rebellion gained a temporary but not so superficial victory: an insubordination that weakened the security-surveillance state for a month and proved that we *can* change power relations. This became possible since the rebels targeted the social relations in which they are forced to live, something that no "armed vanguard" has ever managed to do.

Considering the range and intensity of all the December events, the state repressive apparatus proved practically weak. Since they had to deal with a de-legitimisation of the institutions of control and not just bullets and grenades, the infamous zero tolerance became a simple tolerance towards the rebels' activities. The state counterattack could actually become successful in January only by making use of the "armed vanguard" operations: first, on an ideological level, by equating the state murder with the wounding of a riot cop, thus re-legitimising the police and the security-surveillance state in general. Secondly, on an operational level, intensifying its repression. They even exploited the place of the attack (Exarcheia), presenting the rebellion as a spectacular vendetta between cops and "anarchists," as a grotesque and banal performance staged in a political ghetto.

As the rebellion was dying away there was a notable proliferation of attacks against banks and state buildings by several groups that cannot be placed in the same category with the "armed vanguard's" "deeds," since most of them do not claim to be part of the actual movement (although they do not necessarily lack a voluntaristic or arrogant posture).

However, the return of the "armed vanguard" proper with the execution of an anti-terrorist-squad cop in early June 2009, when even the memory of the rebellion had weakened, has given militarism and the escalation of pure violence a pretext to present themselves as an attractive alternative to a portion of those who participated in the rebellion—if we are to judge by the political tolerance of the anti-authoritarian milieu towards this action. The limited class composition of the rebellion, its restricted extension beyond the level of the de-legitimisation of the security-surveillance state and the gradual weakening of several communal projects in the centre and the neighbourhoods—mostly in Athens—led to the flourishing of a separated kind of blind violence as a dangerous caricature of "struggle," or rather a substitute. As certain important subjects of the rebellion were gradually leaving the stage (the high school students, the university students, the immigrants), its social content got weaker and weaker and political identities were again strengthened as was previously the norm. The violence of the "armed vanguard" is just one of these political identities, even in its naive and nihilistic form, appearing in an era of a generalised crisis of reproduction when the state and capital are unable to offer any social democratic type of "remedy" to heal the wounds of the rebellion. It's not important for us now to doubt the real identity of these hit men with the ridiculous but revealing name "Revolutionary Sect"; what causes us some concern is the political tolerance of some quarters towards them, given the fact that it's the first time that in a Greek "armed vanguard" text there's not one grain of even the good old Leninist "for the people" ideology but instead an antisocial, nihilistic bloodlust. The crisis of neoliberalism, as a certain phase of capitalist accumulation and legitimisation crisis, seems to lead to a deeper crisis (even to serious signs of social decomposition) and not to any signs of revival of reformism. Even the recent electoral failure of the governing party combined with the high percentage of election abstention (the highest ever in an excessively politicised country like Greece), which was an indirect result of the legitimisation crisis that the rebellion expressed and deepened, have not led to any concessions on the part of the state. With all its own limits, the rebellion made the limits of capitalist integration even more visible than before. The slogan "communism or capitalist civilisation" seems timely more than ever.

THE REBELLION, THE WORKPLACES, AND THE RANK AND FILE UNIONS

To discuss the reasons why the rebellion did not extend to the places of waged labour—a question often asked by comrades abroad—we need first to be more analytical about certain segments of the proletariat. From our empirical knowledge, those workers who can be described either as "workers with a stable job" or non-precarious, had very limited participation in the rebellion—if any. For those stable workers who actually took part in the rebellion to try to extend it to their workplaces would mean engaging in wildcat strikes outside and against trade unions since most strikes are called and controlled by them, although their prestige has been undermined for a long time now. In the last twenty years many strikes have been called in the public sector (education, public utility services, some ministries). These past struggles have shown that the workers were not able to create autonomous forms of organization and let new contents emerge beyond the trade unionist demands. Occupations of workplaces have only taken place as defensive struggles against closures or relocations, mostly of textile factories. But even those, as well as most strikes, in the previous years have by and large ended in defeat.

Capitalism in Greece is characterised by a low concentration of capital resulting in many small firms where even fewer than ten people are employed and there is almost no unionism. The precarious waged workers, one of the main parties involved in the rebellion, who mainly work in such places, do not consider them to be a terrain of proletarian power and mobilisation. In most cases these workers are not attached to their job. Possibly it was precisely their inability or even unwillingness to mobilise on the job that made young precarious workers take to the streets. Moreover, like we said before, this first *urban rebellion* in Greece was, like all modern urban rebellions, a violent eruption of de-legitimisation of capitalist institutions of control and, what is more, a short-lived experience of a *communal life against separations and outside the workplaces*—with the notable exception of the universities and the municipality of Aghios Dimitrios. In the case of precarious workers, extending the rebellion to their workplaces would mean wildcats and occupations and nothing less. Given the practical possibilities there and their subjective disposition, such activity was both unfeasible and undesirable.

However, many rebels realized these limits and tried to make such a leap. The occupation of the central offices of the General Confederation of Labour of Greece (GSEE) stemmed from the need for workplace action and to undermine the media coverage of the rebellion as a "youth protest at the expense of the workers' interests." Besides, it offered an opportunity to expose the undermining role of GSEE itself in the rebellion. The initiative was taken by some members of the rank and file union of couriers, who are mostly anti-authoritarians. However, during the occupation it became obvious that even the rank and file version of unionism could not relate to the rebellion. There were two, although not clear-cut, tendencies even at the preparation assembly: a unionist-workerist one and a proletarian one. For the unionist-workerist tendency the occupation should have had a distinct "worker" character as opposed to the so-called youth or "metropolitan" character of the rebellion, while those in the second tendency saw the occupation as only one moment of the rebellion, as an opportunity to attack one more institution of capitalist control and as a meeting point of high-school students, university students, unemployed, waged workers, and immigrants, that is as one more community of struggle in the context of the general unrest. In fact, the unionist-workerist tendency tried to

124

use the occupation rather as an instrument of the union, and the idea of a base unionism, independent of political influences, in general. This didn't work. That's why some of them remained there just for two days.

As far as the rest of the "independent" left unions are concerned, things were even worse. There was only one assembly of trade unionists in the Faculty of Law on December 10th where several left bureaucrats stressed the need for a "political prospect" in the rebellion, meaning a political and unionist mediation expressed in a list of mostly populist demands. They rejected any proposals for violent action and pompously called for extraordinary general assemblies and agitation at the workplaces for a general strike after one week—needless to say that nothing of the sort was ever tried.

In January the media workers that had participated actively in the rebellion occupied the offices of the corporatist journalists' trade union. The Union of Editors of the Daily Newspapers of Athens (ES-IEA) is the main journalists' trade union in Greece. It includes journalists from the major Athenian newspapers—many of whom are, at the same time, employers because they are TV producers or they own newspapers—but it excludes those journalists who work with precarious contracts or are hired as "freelancers." The occupation of ESIEA focused broadly on two issues: the first was work relations, in particular the widespread precariousness in the media industry and the fragmented form of union organisation of the media workers; the second was the control of information by the official media, the way the revolt was reported by them, and how counter-information could be produced by the movement.

After the end of the occupation the same people created an assembly of media workers, students, and unemployed that organised a series of actions against layoffs or attempted layoffs at various workplaces, and reported on demos and other activities of the movement in a way that was against the dominant propaganda. Many members of this assembly are former students of the Faculty of Mass Media and Communication and took part in the students' movement against the university reform in 2006–07. Some of them had for years attempted to create a new union that would include all media workers. Right now workers of the media industry are organised in fifteen different unions (photographers, journalists, camera operators, clerical staff, etc.) The idea is to create a union that will include all workers, regardless of their position, from cleaners to journalists, and their labour contract, from full-time employees to "freelancers." Recently they tried to coordinate their activity with that of the laid off workers of the newspaper *Eleftheros Typos*.

On 22 December in Petralona, an old working-class neighbourhood in Athens, a Bulgarian immigrant cleaner, Konstantina Kuneva, the General Secretary of the Janitors Union (PEKOP-All Attica Union for Janitors and Home Service Personnel), was the victim of an attack with sulphuric acid by goons of the bosses while returning home from her workplace, a railroad station of the ISAP public utility (Athens-Pireaus Electric Trains). She was seriously wounded, losing the use of one eye and of her vocal chords and, at the time of writing, she is still in hospital. It is worth mentioning that she had also visited the occupation of GSEE since her previous activities had led her to a confrontation with the leadership of the confederation bureaucracy. The attack on Konstantina took place a couple of days after the end of the occupation of GSEE and that was one of the reasons why there was such an unprecedented mobilisation of people. After the attack a "solidarity assembly" was formed. Using direct action tactics, they organised a series of actions (occupation of the headquarters of ISAP, demos, sabotage of the ticket machines so that the commuters could travel for free). The assembly, despite its internal divisions, played a vital role in inspiring a remarkable solidarity movement that expanded throughout Greece, demanding not only the prosecution of the perpetrators and the instigators but also the abolition of subcontracting altogether. We should add here that outsourcing cleaning services has become the norm for public sector companies and that these companies do not hire cleaners any more: contractors are now the employers of thousands of janitors, mainly female immigrants, who clean hundreds of public utilities, hospitals, rail road stations, schools, universities, and other public buildings. Regarding the character of cleaning sector jobs however, these were always precarious and until recently it was regarded normal and natural for a woman to be a janitor or home service worker. Moreover by equating subcontracting or precariousness in general with "slavery," the majority of this solidarity movement (mainly comprised of leftist union activists) tried to equate certain struggles against precariousness—one of the main forms of the capitalist restructuring in this historical moment—*with general political demands*. These were of a social-democratic content, understanding the state to be a "reliable" and preferable employer to private subcontractors and thus putting the question of the abolition of wage labour *per se* aside.

THE DEPRESSION IN NUMBERS, THE STATE STRATEGIES, AND THE CLASS

As we said in the beginning, the signs of the depression in Greece were evident from last year already. In order to have a clearer idea of the signs and the consequences of the most recent phase of the crisis, some data concerning the situation of the working class are necessary.

According to Eurostat, Greece had the highest percentage of the population living in households that had mortgages in arrears. According to a study by the Bank of Greece in 2007, 6 out of 10 Greek households had been in arrears with mortgages, 7 out of 10 had been in arrears with consumer loans, and 1 out of 2 had been in arrears with credit cards. Apart from credit, 7 out of 10 households had been in arrears with rent and 6 out of 10 had been in arrears with utility bills. The number of households on credit exceeded 51%, meaning that 2.15 million use some kind of credit. So it is evident that taking recourse to credit has started reaching its limits. As far as wages and unemployment are concerned, indices are also revealing. 50% of waged workers received less than €1,030 gross. The basic wage in Greece is the lowest one in Western Europe (50% of the EE-15 wages). Youth unemployment reached 25.7% in 2008 and, as far as women are concerned, they are the most hard hit by unemployment in Europe. About 800,000 workers fall within the so-called 500 euro generation: 300,000 of them are "freelancers;" 295,000 work part-time; 180,000 were officially unemployed in 2008; and 80,000 people were expected to join the state Stage programmes (extremely low paid jobs at the public or private sector without social security and which supposedly offer training) for the years 2008–09.

In the first quarter of 2009, Greece's rate of growth was just above zero because of a decrease of investment of private capital, but stabilised there only through state investments. Due to the depression 160,000 people have become redundant and that number is about to increase to 300,000, mainly in small and very small firms.

In certain sectors now the situation is as follows: In the shipping trade a lot of sailors have not been paid while their wages will be frozen. The public sector workers will have their wages frozen too. In industry and in textile factories, in particular, redundancies of permanent and contract workers, a shorter working week with less pay, and delay of payment have both become more and more common. In the construction sector there is a high rate of unemployment and a 17% decrease in production. Tourism, the sector with the biggest share in GNP, has

127

already been hit with high rates of unemployment and a 9% drop in tourist arrivals.

Although the situation is certainly bleak, workers' reactions have been less than moderate and certainly too weak to counterattack the capitalist restructuring. There have been quite a few mobilisations in response to the mass layoffs, to delay payments or closures of companies, mostly in the form of short strikes or work-stoppages in some factories. Quite a few occupations of factories or companies (in a paper mill, a telecommunication company, and a furniture factory) were isolated and did not create contacts with other laid-off workers; the path of bilateral agreements between the workers and the company or the Ministry of Labour is preferred instead. It seems that in most cases the management of the depression/restructuring is of a standard pattern. While precarious workers just get fired, those older workers agree to resign and wait for early retirement. Thus no mass layoffs are visible while the state "guarantees" these social expenses now only to announce again the "collapse of the social security system" later—a recurring state motto of the last twenty years—which would entail "new sacrifices" and so on and so forth. Such a trick can prove valuable for the state at the moment, since it can save time and postpone a generalised explosion. But for how long? And how many can be satisfied with such manoeuvres?

In fact, while the depression/restructuring is deepening and capital and the state reduce the direct and indirect wage while increasing precariousness and layoffs, they are trapped in a vicious circle whereby they are compelled to let the legitimisation crisis deepen even more. At the same time as the "war on terrorism" is still ongoing, trying to deal violently with the accumulated problems of the previous phase of neoliberal war deregulation,[6] the Greek state (that has troops in central Asia) is currently "raided" with floods of refugees that it, itself, contributed in creating. Faced with the nightmare of a new December, fiercer this time as the crisis prolongs, and with the undesired masses of thousands of "surplus proletarians" from Asia and Africa, it only has one card to put on the table: the strengthening of its repressive mechanisms that triggered the December rebellion and created the dangerous mixture of both native and immigrant riots in the first place! Yet its recourse to discipline and the intensification of its zero tolerance dogma is inescapable since no social democratic strategies for the extended reproduction of the proletariat can be proposed any more. Selling "security" to natives against "invading" foreigners used as scapegoats has been the only "social offer" on the part of the state. Indeed, new divisions are on the agenda through the creation of new "folk devils" and "moral panics."

128

In the beginning of March, after a cop got killed during an armed robbery, many high-ranking police officers warned about the rapid increase of armed robberies since January (almost forty each month) attributing this both to the release of many convicts (as a measure to relieve congestion in prisons) and the "disruption" caused in December.

It was then that the launching of new repressive laws, passed just recently, started being discussed. First, in order to "protect police prestige," an old legislation, introduced during the dictatorship in the '30s, was put in practice again against the crime of "defamation of authority." The famous slogan of the rebellion, "cops, killers, pigs," can now lead ex-officio up to a two-year imprisonment. A second legislation targeting the December rebels refers to the "faking of one's facial features," meaning practically the use of hooded outfits. Along with the formation of new police forces and more regular patrols, these acts aim at more than a counter-attack on the favourite symbols of the rebellion. The demonisation of the "hooded rioters," starting with anti-authoritarians and anarchists, increases separations among the rebels and between the rebels and the rest of the proletarians who remained passive during the rebellion. If the penalties imposed were not that serious one could be tempted to laugh at the furious effort of the state to deal with a social rebellion on the level of its slogans and dress code!

Exploiting the generalised sense of social insecurity that the capitalist crisis itself has created, the second "enemy" fabricated by the state are the refugees and illegal immigrants that suffocate in the "hybrid ghetto" of Athens. The repression mechanisms do know that a large part of the revolting multitude that took over Athens streets those December days and nights and again in May during a Muslim small-scale riot consisted of immigrants hailing from nearby neighbourhoods. This "ghetto," mainly situated within the historical inner city, resembles the American ghettos in aspects such as the "vertical segregation" among inhabitants—in other words the non-uniform social character, or the policies of "planned shrinkage." It also resembles the West-European working-class suburbs in aspects such as the multiracial/ethnic mixture. The above-mentioned similarities, or better said analogies, should of course be treated with caution especially due to the rather large differences in scale. A media barrage full of passionate articles and heart-breaking TV reportages, focusing on the environmental and financial degradation of the inner city neighbourhoods, which was mostly related to the uncontrolled/unorganised housing of thousands of illegal immigrants, the presence of junkies, prostitutes, and other "lumpen" proletariat, signalled the first phase of this new warfare. It should be noted though that this media barrage had started a bit before December's uprising.

The second phase was a far more direct and violent one. Physical attacks on immigrants and people supporting them by members of a neo-Nazi group were coupled with massive arrests by the police, which led to imprisonments and deportations. Local assemblies of right-wing "indignant citizens" and petit-bourgeois merchants, organised by the only parliamentary ultra-right-wing party have protested against the presence of immigrants in their neighbourhoods and have even taken direct action against them, as in the blockage of one local playground where lots of immigrant children used to play while their parents hung around. Moreover, under the pretext of "public health protection," lots of old and/or abandoned buildings in the inner city area where thousands of immigrants are lodged had been registered and then evacuation orders were issued. Here, the constant "clean sweep operations" against immigrants and "lumpen" in the centre of Athens must also be seen as an effort to gentrify those areas in the "historical centre" that still remain "undeveloped" and resist turning into expensive, sterile, museum-like non places like in most West-European cities.

Apart from all this, the Greek government has also announced that it plans to construct eleven "concentration camps" all over the country, similar to those already established in Italy, where arrested immigrants will be detained while waiting for their deportation. It recently passed a new legislation whereby the time of detaining illegal immigrants until deportation rises to six or twelve months and any foreigner who is charged with committing a crime that carries a prison sentence of three months or more can be deported immediately, classified as "dangerous for public order and safety."

The recent speech of the Greek prime minister who linked "criminality" to "illegal" immigrants and "hooded rioters" points to a continuation of the—already failed—neoliberal management of the crisis; the reinvention and demonisation of the "dangerous classes" is to be used as a weapon for the further division and discipline of the proletariat in order to accept the deterioration of its living conditions because of the restructuring. However, the list of "criminals" may broaden dangerously and include in the near future those who were just "sympathetic" towards the rebels in December. Since the "social contract" has been breached but no return to the previous social democratic strategies appears on the horizon, the capitalist social relation cannot be adequately reproduced and maybe those "sympathisers" will have a million reasons to prove right the fears of the planetary bosses about the December rebellion as a prelude to a generalised proletarian explosion in the course of the global crisis of reproduction.

TPTG, June 2009

NOTES

1 *The Permanent Crisis in Education* at http://www.tapaidiatisgalarias.org/?page_id=105.

2 See our chronology of the December events at http://www.tapaidiatisgalarias.org/?page_id=105.

3 *Like a Winter with a Thousand Decembers* at http://www.tapaidiatisgalarias.org/?page_id=105.

4 Some of them—expropriations, acts of sabotage, etc.—are mentioned in our chronology of the December events, see above.

5 *Like a Winter with a Thousand Decembers.*

6 See our text *War, Peace and the Crisis of Reproduction of Human Capital, Part B: The "War on Terror"* (2003) at http://www.tapaidiatisgalarias.org/?page_id=105.

7

THE (REVOLT) MEDIUM IS THE MESSAGE:

COUNTER-INFORMATION AND THE 2008 REVOLT IN GREECE

Metropolitan Sirens

INTRODUCTION

It is not that we want to remember December in this way; it's just that it really was something phenomenal. All of a sudden, an entire country was only discussing and thinking about the assassination of Alexandros Grigoropoulos and the reactions that followed. The wave of mobilisations was so strong that it paralysed—quite literally—the heart of Athens for days: in the commercial centre of the city, shops were shut and no one at all would wander around aimlessly. Of course, the images were the same in most other Greek cities.

What made this event so special? How can anyone explain why Korkoneas's finger triggered the largest and most explosive mobilisation (a true *revolt*) in recent Greek history? Many interpretations have been offered already, largely based on the notion that the two bullets that killed Alexandros were simply the final straw on the camel's back. A mob that was out of control took to the streets, first full of compressed anger and then, a few days later, full of angry creativity. People revolted for all the reasons in the world: for the political scandals revealed in a domino fashion, for their gross exploitation and muck-around by power...

In this article, however, we want to put these causes aside and look at another aspect, one that, we feel, has been examined to a much lesser degree: that is, the mediums of the revolt. We want to talk about the contribution of *counter-information* to the revolt—what we feel is the most valuable tool in the hands of the antagonist movement. We also want to discuss the facts introduced by new technologies, facts that are new to the antagonist movement as a whole. In other words we want to interpret how and to what extent new mediums of communication can contribute to our social movements and whether they can alter the forms of struggle, of coordination, and of organising and we want to do so, of course, by focusing on the recent Greek example.

We decided to approach the matter collectively and based on our personal experiences with the hope that we would put some vivid images to paper. Starting with a historical overview of counter-information in Greece, that mostly covers the period from the mid-1970s to the end of the 1990s, we reach year 2002, which is when the first IMCs (Independent Media Centres) were launched in Athens and Thessaloniki. Everyone would admit that the landscape of the movement's communications was radically reshaped that year—regardless of whether they would support the new reality in question. Having painted a picture of counter-information in Greece during the past few years we then use this as a starting point from which to make some estimates about the role of counter-information during December's days of revolt. Did the new mediums of communication contribute to the spread of the revolt? Would mobilisations of such scale be possible without these new technologies? The aim of making these questions is not of course to remain at the level of pure theoretical analyses, but rather to use a lively example as this in order to gain tools and understandings that will strengthen our struggle for individual and social emancipation.

COUNTER-INFORMATION IN TIME

It is necessary to sketch a historical overview of mediums of counter-information in order to fully understand how they functioned in December as well as the needs that gave birth to them. First of all, the term "counter-information" is not an officially recognized one. When we say "counter-information," we mean information "from below." In other words, we mean that on the one hand there exists dominant information that offers the view of authority on events—and often even shapes them. On the other hand, there are parts of the society that are competitive and hostile toward authority and that organise their own channels of information in order to promote their own, essentially class-based interests. There are then two main elements in what we name counter-information: first, it is organised from below and, sec-

134

ond, it serves the needs of the movement that is competitive and hostile toward authority and by extension, it stands in competition with mainstream media since the latter serves the interests of authority.

The anarchist milieu in Greece started to formulate in an organised manner after the fall of the dictatorship (1967–1974), in the last years of the 1970s. During that time there was a liberal sentiment in the Greek society inspired by the French May '68 but also by the great revolt of the Athens Polytechnic in 1973. At this time the first collective attempts for the publication of magazines and newspapers started springing up carrying updates on current affairs from the viewpoint of the anarchists, along with translated texts from the anarchist movement mostly in Western Europe and North America. These first attempts were truly noteworthy and important since for the first time since WWII, the anarchist perspective on history and reality made its appearance within the Greek antagonist movement. It must be noted that these first publication attempts were always short-lived with no regular presence and small print-runs. They were aimed primarily at a small readership, mostly of a young age, and in the country's largest cities.

A core element of the anarchist milieu was that aside from theoretical work, it would try to put its ideas into practice. In the 1980s there were the first attempts to occupy abandoned buildings. These sites, apart from other intended usages (public events, concerts, etc.) acted as permanent nodes of counter-information. Those attending the occupations would be informed about events, discuss and exchange opinions, and collectively form positions. At the same time, by putting together many open social events, the occupiers would try to reach out to their neighbourhoods, to publicise their opinions, and therefore invert the image created by the dominant mass media about anarchists.

Understanding the importance and the necessity for counter-information the anarchists went one step further. Groups and collectives would publish posters, distribute brochures, use public address systems to inform people of current affairs in crowded public locations, and spray paint messages in the streets. In central Athens and other Greek cities, many walls are covered with graffiti and stencils portraying anarchist and anti-authoritarian messages.

In other words, up until the early years of the new millennium the counter-information of the anarchist milieu would seep out into public discourse through the cracks that its own actions opened up in the slick veneer of dominant propaganda. Despite the repression it was subjected to, it repeatedly aimed at social communication while at the same time sending strong messages to the political and financial

REVOLT AND CRISIS IN GREECE

elite. Whenever the level of violence was increased from the side of the state, the anarchist milieu would upgrade the characteristics of its own actions to make its voice heard louder: from symbolic occupations of public buildings and radio stations to mass "hit and run" actions of even 200 people, or simultaneous attacks against multiple targets, at day or night, against ministries, financial institutions—the message itself would become the target.

In the Greek territory there exists a strong tradition of armed struggle, one which continues today. This form of action has not always come solely from the anarchists or the far-left; during the dictatorship, even social democrats would commit bombing actions. For example, the socialist ex-prime minister (1996–2003) Costas Simitis participated in armed struggle groups during those years, which aimed at the fall of the regime and the installation of a bourgeois democracy in its place. Armed struggle was therefore used as a medium of propaganda and counter-information by many groups despite the sharp critique they received at times by parts of the anarchist milieu, concerning their negative impact.

After each action such armed struggle groups would issue a communiqué that was, in most cases, published in the bourgeois press. Yet some groups preferred to distribute their texts through a network of people, for example the guerrilla group Revolutionary Popular Struggle (Epanastatikos Laikos Agonas, ELA), which acted in the country for approximately twenty years (1975–1995), and infrequently issued the journal *Counter-Information* (*Antipliroforisi*).

ANARCHIST MILIEU AND MASS MEDIA

After the restoration of bourgeois democracy in 1974, bourgeois media were divided in two camps, broadly the "conservative" and the "progressive" ones. The first represented the right, ex-king sympathisers, junta sympathisers, and right-wing nationalists. We would undoubtedly file *Rizospastis* (meaning "the uprooter"), the newspaper published by the Stalinist KKE under this category. These media treat anarchists as "enemies of the nation," "traitors," or even "deviant provocateurs" (a favourite expression of *Rizospastis*). They ask for the repression and imprisonment of anarchists and, if possible, their disappearance from the face of the Earth.

For the progressive media that belong mostly to social-democrats and the non-Stalinist left, the situation is altogether different. Anarchists are often treated with sympathy, sometimes as quaint and other times as deviant children. The anarchist milieu has contact with some of these newspapers. Some journalists personally know anarchists and these connections are often utilised—for example in order for an anarchist communiqué to be printed, or for a more favourable stance to be taken on a particular issue.

Until the end of the 1980s there were only state-run TV stations in Greece, for which the anarchist milieu was non-existent. There only were minor references to anarchism in periods of mass turbulence. The means for any kind of non-studio TV coverage were extremely limited at the time. Things would start to radically change following the emergence of private TV stations in the late 1980s.

Certain types of anarchist action, such as the "spectacle" offered by Molotov cocktails and flaming barricades, would quickly become a favourite topic for private television stations. Coverage of such events was extensive and would often reach beyond of the country's borders; for example, the riots during the visit of US president Bill Clinton in 1999 were covered internationally. Of course, this coverage was always accompanied by misinformation, slander, and the omitting of the true reasons behind the actions. The image of the anarchists to the wider social strata was prey to the mass media. Supposedly "friendly" media would turn their back on the anarchist milieu at crucial moments in order to serve, as expected, their class interests.

The role and the power of mass media did not go unnoticed by anarchist and anti-authoritarian collectives. Discussions were held, analyses of the phenomenon were written, and for many years the handling of information, journalism, and mass media was a main topic of discussion. Nearly all anarchist collectives were quick to form a common stance massively against mass media, refusing any transaction with them and criticising the supposed dichotomy of "good" and "bad" mass media. This critique was to take a material form in the early '90s. At that time, professional photo-journalists, reporters, and TV camera crews switched positions at demonstrations: while before they would stand on the side of those demonstrating when photographing and documenting the events, they moved behind the lines of the police, as their cameras had, by that point, become a target of the demonstrators.

Meanwhile, the end of the decade saw a spectacular rise of internet use in the country as much as abroad. By this fact alone, the antagonist social movement acquired a weapon that was to break through many information barriers. At the demonstrations in Seattle the internet was used to the benefit of the movement, giving birth to the Indymedia platform. From that point on new paths and capacities opened up, rapidly changing the counter-information landscape.

For a long period, of course, the use of the internet as a propaganda medium was ignored or even demonised in Greece, since anarchists would focus on the directness of their message and therefore choose the streets and neighbourhoods as the sites of their action. Yet slowly, as had happened about a century earlier with printing presses, the anarchist milieu would attempt to form its own internet structures, which it would operate under its own rules.

THE FLAGSHIP OF COUNTER-INFORMATION: THE EXAMPLE OF IMC ATHENS

In order to explain the role Athens Indymedia held as one of the main informational gateways of the December revolt, we think it is vital to mention some facts about its earlier steps.

The first discussion about forming an Indymedia platform in Greece took place in July 2001 on board a ship carrying demonstrators who were returning to the country from the anti-capitalist demonstrations in the streets of Genova, against the G8 summit of that year. A need existed, it was felt, for non-commercial information that would be based on a bottom-up, anti-hierarchical, and horizontal mode of operation and be free from the manipulation and control of information by established politicians and financial authorities as well as the police. And so, in November 2001, the first two independent media centres were launched in the two largest Greek cities. In practice, it was shown that athens.indymedia.org and thessaloniki.indymedia.org did not aim to replace action in the streets but rather, to act in an aiding manner in the revealing of reality through the eyes of demonstrators and activists—in particular, through personal accounts verified by visual material. Gradually the community of users that was created acted as a trans-communicative node of information, not only for demonstrations, but also for other events that would have otherwise been unlikely to come to light.

TURNING INDIVIDUAL SILENCES INTO A COLLECTIVE SCREAM

As the medium was becoming more well known to the anarchists and to leftists, mobile phones, cameras, and computers turned into informal weapons transmitting real time information, against all attempts for a cover-up. Think tanks, mostly state and police-run, were now denied the precious time to manage the crisis that follows the revealing of a truth. At the same time this would alert mainstream media to rush to the point of the event in order to record images and testimonies.

The need for counter-information beyond local boundaries was so enormous that soon enough the medium started being used by individuals and groups from other cities—and so, information coming straight from the movement would challenge the myth that there were only localised reactions to important events. Often Indymedia comprised a pool of ideas and managed the coordination of events with common themes and toward the same target, resulting in local struggles or events causing chain solidarity reactions in different parts of Greece or even abroad by diaspora Greeks in coordination with local activists.

As more and more users and collectives from across Greece were compiling their information and political wording on the Athens Indymedia platform and therefore creating an assortment/combination of political information, the medium was transformed into a main node of interaction and communication with hundreds of independent connecting chains. In this way, the limitations of physical material were largely overcome (e.g. printing costs) and the readership of communiqués, analyses, posters, etc. was dramatically increased.

Over time, various revealing events and original visual materials were posted on IMC, including, for example, those that made public the often-occurring torturing of migrants in police stations. Breaking the mainstream media oath of silence, which would until recently refer to Indymedia as "the well-known website of the anti-authoritarians." Indymedia became known to an even broader audience that had little or no connection to anarchism, the left, or activism. With tens of thousands of visitors per day, Athens Indymedia is today placed in the ten most popular websites in the country.

COUNTER-INFORMATION DURING DECEMBER: WIDENING THE CONTRIBUTION OF NEW MEDIUMS

When we talk about counter-information during December's events we do not by any means speak of a solid or homogeneous flow of information—quite the opposite. What gave shivers of hope to some and fear to others was the fact that the communicative explosion—mirroring the explosive reality in the streets—was uncontrollable, with many nodes and means of transmission, different codes, diverse transmitters and receivers. After all, the people in revolt were not a single, coherent social group but rather, a mosaic of social subjects. The wealth and the width of counter-information was schematically marked by this fact also: on the same central Athens street (Patision Ave), three occupations that acted as bases of struggle set different priorities and acquired different characteristics while nevertheless producing a wording that was mutually complimentary.[1]

Overall, in December the entire spectrum of communication mediums was utilised (banners, slogans, stencils, texts, communiqués) in initiatives and actions that were "transplanted" with much creativity from the streets to many aspects of public life—schools, radio stations, theatres, the Acropolis, and so on. Here we need to add a comment concerning the many communication capacities that have developed on the internet: corporate social media platforms such as Facebook, Twitter, YouTube, and Flickr are radically different to collectives of independent media information such as Indymedia or indy.gr and to websites created to cover specific events from a political viewpoint (such as occupation-specific blogs), forums, personal blogs, and so on. The aim of this article is not to record or to examine the communicative ditigal explosion that was triggered by the assassination of Alexis. Rather, we want to focus specifically on counter-information, which is first and foremost a political act. There exists, of course, a common denominator in all the examples above: unmediated communication. Here, the capacity exists for independent organising, especially because mechanisms of authority are difficult to form within such network structures, since they are constantly evolving and largely based upon anonymity.

PANDORA'S BOX OPENS

Let us take things from the beginning, from the night of Alexis's murder. The statistics for Athens IMC are indicative of the strength counter-information gained, perhaps for the first time to this extent: the day before the murder the website had 601,313 hits; on 6 December the number rose to 1,380,551 and on the 7th, it sky-rocketed to 9,089,939, transferring 253.24 GB of data in a single day. The explosion of posts on Athens IMC, and on the Greek internet in general, can lead us to two initial conclusions. First, that the mainstream media was questioned—perhaps even distrusted—by a considerable part of the Greek-speaking audience. Second, that despite the occasional criticism against online counter-information networks, these had gained the trust of a significant number of internet users. Consequently, at 9:10PM on 6 December 2008, the moment young Alexis was shot by cops in the heart of Exarcheia, an undefined network of hundreds of people who had acquainted themselves with the function, directness, and aim of this medium was already in place. Moments after the first shock and numbness when everyone found difficult to believe what had happened and as rage started building up inside us all, the first news on the actual facts were reported on Athens IMC via a phone call—eight minutes after the shooting (9:18PM). This was an immediate signal for people to storm the streets. In order to conceptualise the counter-information network that had been set up, we should mention that first piece of information, a mere eight minutes after the murder, came from the other side of Greece—from the island of Crete.[2]

The news was quickly posted on several other websites (Twitter, indy.gr, etc.) minutes after the incident, and a vast flow of information and cross-checking by witnesses and neighbours followed. In sharp contrast, it took no less than forty minutes for the first "breaking news" bulletin to appear on a private TV channel—and even this was to transmit the state propaganda. News bulletins would, at that point, still report that a group of youngsters had harassed passing policemen by attacking them with sticks, stones, and Molotov cocktails and that the policemen fired in the air with the aim to intimidate the youths in response. To the contrary, eye-witnesses talked about two unprovoked shots aimed directly at the boy. By the time the first news bulletin was on, anarchists had arrived at the hospital where the boy had been taken, before strong police forces cordoned it off, and reported on Athens IMC his name, age, and that he was already dead.

People's need for real information was such that, from that point onwards and throughout the revolt, the Athens IMC server would crash every few minutes under the burden of so many simultaneous readers, besides the malevolent cyber-attacks.

The internet however provides many alternatives, and so new technological platforms and cyber communication tools helped keep the information flowing. New technologies brought to the surface a new chaotic non-linear public discourse that intersected in thousands of internet nodes: the youngest sibling of Athens IMC, indy.gr, which has a more leftist approach; hundreds—if not thousands—of blogs by political groups and individuals; accounts on Twitter, Facebook, Youtube, and Flickr all interacted non-stop in sharing calls for actions, first-hand information, photos, and videos. In this way, a multi-dimensional and compact network was formed that enabled information to flow incessantly, even when some would temporarily crash.

THE EMPEROR IS NAKED

From the very first moments it became obvious that the mainstream media was unable to cope with the situation. The political and media elite were quick to read the violent outburst in terms of some sup-posedly meaningless reflex reaction by "hooded anti-authoritarians," hooligans, and other deviant groups. The extent to which the state and mainstream media cooperated in distorting information however, was only revealed in full on the next day, when a video filmed at the time of the murder was posted on-line. The video captured the two gunshots and the two policemen leaving the site on foot—which practically proved that there was no police car around, let alone that it had been attacked with Molotov cocktails, as the mainstream story would go.

A series of texts and pictures continued to unveil the distortion of the truth by the mainstream media in the next couple of days: school students pelting local police stations, the police headquarters (GADA), and the Parliament with sour oranges and stones; migrants erecting barricades and expropriating stores; people of all ages taking part in demonstrations and clashes; occupations in many cities and in various neighbourhoods of Athens. All around one could see department stores and waste containers on fire, streets paved with stones and the remains of Molotov cocktails, rage...

The Greek media, confined to their conventional perspective and dependent on systemic information sources (police, state authori-ties, etc.) largely failed to present and interpret what was going on in a comprehensive way. Yet, practically speaking, it would not have been possible for them to have so many available cameras to film the numer-ous simultaneous actions and clashes anyway. Some media went as far as to question if a revolt was even taking place—this, at a time when police stations and other government buildings were coming under attack in many Greek cities. Their failure was of historical significance since a lot of people, and especially the newer generation, rejected them and saw right through them for what they really are: commercial corporations that distort or conceal truth for their own benefit.

As the dominant discourse seemed all the more incoherent, vertical information structures started losing ground to horizontal ones, in other words to information "from below." The swiftness with which that first-hand, unmediated information and comments were published and disseminated affected the pace in which actions were coordinated, as well as the breadth of their impact.

School students would mainly text each other or use Twitter and Facebook, sending messages from friend to friend as if it were from mouth to ear. Social network platforms, which are mainly associated with the abuse of privacy, served as political communication nodes. Mobile phones also proved to be a powerful tool since they connect separate networks of people (i.e. contact lists) quickly and with no outsider intervention.

Nobody could have foreseen the organisation and subsequent massive participation in the student demonstrations of the morning of Monday, 8 December, during which local police stations were attacked. A second example: the demonstration on Sunday, 7 December was held in the early afternoon only hours after the murder and had thousands of participants—although it had been organised exclusively through the internet, phone calls, text messages, and face-to-face contact.

Leaving the various social media groups aside, it is interesting to examine how counter-information made use of the internet. The ventures that sprang up back in those days—regardless of how long they lasted—would set up a blog and an e-communication channel (email, forum) and quickly network with "sibling" e-ventures. Counter-information in December was decentralised and helped decentralise action in return. Each occupation became a counter-information hub and all these initiatives came together both on the streets and on the internet, in the form of links. This enabled networking and the possibility for a massive exchange of information.

In other words, the internet developed into the informal headquarters of an information war between the "in-line-with-the-state" mass media and a new antagonistic subject, internet users.

Throughout the revolt, users regularly posted first-hand information, news, and comments and coordinated interventions in the public space. Yet when the strength and the speed in which counter-information spreads turns from a thorn into a pointed arrow, the regime acts promptly to crash it. And so, on 16 January 2009, under the fear of a potential resurgence of December's events, the Greek vice-minister of education, Spiridon Taliadouros, ordered on behalf of the government for the Indymedia server be tracked down and deactivated. Athens IMC became a favourite subject of discussion in parliament and mass media during the following months. The first complaints were lodged: the basic accusation was that the website constituted the operation centre of the December revolt, easily proving those in power had not quite understood the reasons that gave birth to the revolt.

COUNTER-INFORMATION HUBS: THE EXAMPLE OF OCCUPIED PUBLIC BUILDINGS

In the face of the complicity seen between the state, journalists, and consumers of the official propaganda, and against their common effort to conceal and slander the struggle, those revolting occupied public buildings from the early days of the revolt. Their aim was to create hubs for the exchange of counter-information and the coordination of actions. On the actual night of 6 December, there were calls to gather at the central university buildings in various cities around the country. When the first police forces attempted to repress them, the occupations became permanent. As the first clashes with the forces of repression began, more and more people gathered at these occupations.

News of clashes outside these buildings started to circulate around the media and the internet. As access to the buildings themselves became increasingly difficult, due to the presence of forces of repression around them, people started occupying new buildings in different parts of the city, thus creating new nuclei of social antagonism.

The first occupations comprised the connecting threads in the consecutive explosions of social mutiny. They tried to act as points of reference, of equal gathering and discussion, self-organising, and mutual shaping of ideas and action. After the universities, the wave of occupations spread to schools, town halls, labour union and confederation buildings, trade councils, theatres, cultural centres, municipal organisations, etc.—with the eventual aim being the mutual shaping of words and action. The occupations would usually last between a few days and several weeks and would spring up one after the other, passing on the counter-information relay up until February 2009. They multiplied, with the state seemingly unable to quell them.

Along with the days-long occupations of various public buildings, there were numerous hours-long occupations and interventions (in public transport buildings and vehicles, radio and TV stations). The apogee was the intervention and interruption of the main news show of NET, a state-run TV station, at the time of the prime minister's speech.[3] The actors and cinematographers who undertook this action were holding banners calling for the people to take to the streets and demonstrate. There were also moments when, after the attacks by police against neighbourhood demonstrations, residents would respond by occupying the local town hall, with the aim of highlighting the repression against them and mutually shaping their response.

It is important to highlight that counter-information was not limited to the act of the assassination (which was quite obviously a common thread across the occupations) but rather, it highlighted a series of other subjects, either more theoretical or regarding current affairs at the time (the bombarding of Gaza by Israeli troops, the murderous attack against syndicalist migrant cleaner Konstantina Kuneva with sulphuric

144

acid, regional environmental matters, etc.) For many, the revolt was not an everyday image on their TV screen, cut off from the reality each individual lived; it had social, financial, and political causes that touched people's own lives and neighbourhoods. In a conjuncture where the stature of mass media had been widely challenged, as we previously mentioned, people were thirsty for other sources of information—texts would appear in an instant: at the Athens Economics School occupation alone, approximately 350,000 pages were photocopied in eighteen days of occupation.

The occupations utilised the capacities offered by new media as an additional tool. The blogs of the occupations would aid posters, texts, publications, stencils, and slogans on the walls. The events would unfold and take shape in their natural location, the street. The internet, on the other hand, offered the capacity for instant communication and aided the coordination of the mobilisations. It offered the medium for the word of the revolted to spread instantly, beyond the country's borders. Of particular importance here were translation collectives, blogs covering the events in Greece abroad and of course, maintaining contact with comrades abroad. Reversely, solidarity actions abroad would inspire Greek mobilisations and would become known instantly. The "Greek Solidarity Map"[4] marks with black/red stars the numerous actions of solidarity in Greece and abroad: it is worth noting how synchronised these were in such a broad geographical breadth.

Cyberspace knows no borders and the power of counter-information can hardly be limited geographically. Even when the word of the revolted was limited to the Greek-speaking audience (and despite the importance placed on the translation of texts), videos and photographs would largely cover gaps in information. The images circulated in those days were so powerful (for example, the Christmas tree on fire on Syntagma Square, by Parliament) that the mediation of words was rendered unnecessary for meanings to be transmitted. Hundreds of expropriated images from corporate news agencies would be circulated around, while solidarity videos posted around were uncountable—it is worth mentioning the revolutionary greetings of Subcomandante Marcos to the "insurgent youth of Greece."[5]

This uncontrollable circulation of information created fears for a possible spill-over of the revolt into other parts of the planet. We would like to be reminded of the retreat of French president Sarkozy during those days (who repealed the law for educational reform in high schools) under the fear of generalised mobilisations—this, at the same time when Greek authorities would not even admit they were dealing with a revolt.

In parallel with the occupations, an important number of neighbourhood assemblies were born. These assemblies, in the spirit of self-organising, dealt with current affairs as well as local matters. From the occupations and local assemblies of the time, some were later transformed into permanent local or labour collectives with a permanent meeting space, and some permanently occupied abandoned buildings. Many of these incentives continue their action today.

ADVANTAGES, WEAKNESSES, AND SOME CONCLUSIONS DRAWN FROM DECEMBER

One of the greatest advantages of new media, in terms of the practices of the antagonist movement, is interaction—since the roles of the transmitter and the receiver are hereby dismantled. Communication with fewer mediators is enabled and anonymity largely frees individuals from the forming blocks of imposed social roles. There is also the advantage of a useful "internet archive"—even if some websites are no longer active, they are still available online. It is also very important to mention the formation of collectives that handle servers belonging to the movement, such as espiv.net and squat.gr—therefore allowing for the necessary security for the movement use of the internet to be deployed.

On the other hand, internet-based communication obviously entails some weaknesses. It is impersonal and partial. Under no circumstances can it replace human contact and the wholeness of communication (verbal and otherwise), face-to-face. It can give one the illusion of participating in a group, when in reality the connection with others is temporal. On a political level, web communication has been criticised for making idle, rather than increasing, reflexes whilst websites such as Indymedia are critiqued for becoming centres that manage anti-authoritarian action. Above all, however, the technologies of information are not immune to control—on the contrary. The networks of electronic communication are openly available for intense electronic monitoring, causing a series of security issues. Overall, we should not confuse the *capacities* offered by new technologies to the social antagonist movement with a *de facto* positive development. Political and social processes are those that define the use of mediums.

INSTEAD OF A CONCLUSION

146 Looking back at the days of December, we see that the centres of co-ordination were occupations and open assemblies. They are where all

mediums came together and where actions, for the most part, were organised. Counter-information via the internet came to strengthen the spread of the word and the action that was born from direct democratic procedures. The new mediums may have reshaped the landscape, but did not affect the forms of action in their essence. Today, as always, the streets are where we meet and make history.

It is difficult to make any safe estimates, yet the legacy of December is rich here, too: the revolt scored a huge blow against dominant structures and carriers of information, while at the same time widened the use of the internet for the movement and brought dynamically to the fore relevant matters and discussions. At the time, when these lines were written, espiv.net is also organising an event in Athens on freedom of speech, security, and self-organising and self-management online. The use of the internet as a tool of social struggle is a reality; what remains is for all of us to utilise it toward the direction we wish.

There is no use in idealising the mediums nor their capacities, nor of course December itself. A fertile self-criticism concerning the limits of material mediums—in the end, our own selves—is a valuable and even necessary prerequisite for the Decembers to come.

THE FIRST POSTS ON ATHENS IMC AFTER THE ASSASSINATION OF ALEXANDROS GRIGOROPOULOS

URGENT! SERIOUS INJURY AT MESOLOGIOU STREET (EXARCHEIA)
by ORA MIDEN 9.18 pm, Saturday December 6th 2008
I just received a phone call by a comrade who told me there have been some clashes at Mesologiou Street and one kid has been injured by a rubber bullet of a cop and that he is in critical condition. An ambulance has arrived and is transferring him to Euagelismos hospital… Those of you in Athens please confirm the information.

SOME EYE-WITNESSES DO NOT TALK OF A RUBBER BULLET BUT A PROPER ONE
by Tar 9.32 pm, Saturday December 6th 2008
(meaning the type of bullet is not as of yet confirmed)
A police car drove by, it was given abuse, the cop felt like he had much authority, tension increased, and then he shot. The kid shot was not breathing.

CLASHES IN EXARCHEIA
by nikos 9.38 pm, Saturday December 6th 2008
clashes at the square with the critical condition of the young comrade

now confirmed. We should not let the atrocity go unanswered… anyone who can should make it to Euagelismos Hospital whether doctor or lawyer.

PHONE CALL WITH
by comrade 9.42 pm, Saturday December 6th 2008
From a phone call with a comrade, who just arrived without having any suspicions at Mesologiou. The street is accessible, fires all around, riot police in the periphery.

NEW PHONE CALL WITH
by comrade, 9.52 pm Saturday December 6th 2008
up until a few seconds ago sporadic clashes with the cops in a large part of Exarcheia. First they would take the stones "without a complaint" (as the comrade put it…)—a little while ago they began with the tear gas. Now for the kid: the image that eye-witnesses had was not that "optimistic" about its condition. There were a lot of negative things heard (about its condition always) but no-one saying so was a doctor, so…

FROM THE SQUARE
by Phone 9.59 pm, Saturday December 6th 2008
It is said that a police car was crossing a main street of the area with many well-known bars and there was a minor confrontation between the injured person who seems to be under-age and policemen in the car, one of whom pulled a gun and shot in cold blood.

HE IS DEAD
by Tar 10 pm, Saturday December 6th 2008
It has just been announced by the hospital and the homicide department, he is being transferred for post-mortem, he seems to be a 15–16 year old, his name is Alexandros Grigoropoulos.

THE 15-YEAR-OLD IS DEAD
by Anarchist Hammer and Sickle 10:02 pm, Saturday December 6th 2008
People are heading to the centre. Everyone to Exarcheia, to stop them from blocking off the area…

DEAD SOS
by nm 10:17 pm, Saturday December 6th 2008
people at the polytechnic, clashes in Exarcheia, patision ave is accessible,

the kid is 16 years old, take to the streets everyone, it is confirmed

LATEST INFORMATION
by ORA MIDEN 10.35 pm, Saturday December 6th 2008
the young boy was called Grigoropoulos Alexandros Andreas. When the ambulance arrived at Euagelismos Hospital he was already dead. The cop shot him in his chest, since before someone had thrown empty beer bottles at the police car. The cop is one of those with the blue uniforms. The deceased will have to be transferred to the popular hospital for the post-mortem. Riot police units have encircled Exarcheia.

THERE IS ALSO A RIOT POLICE UNIT AT THE EUAGELISMOS HOSPITAL
by ORA MIDEN 10.38 pm, Saturday December 6th 2008
All the above from the phone-call of a comrade who went to Euagelismos.

GATHERING AT THE LIONS SQUARE NOW (CRETE)
by mercy... 10.42 pm, Saturday December 6th 2008
Gathering at the lions now for the assassination of the 15-year-old in Exarcheia

INFORMATION FROM THE CENTRE
by Tar 10.45 pm, Saturday December 6th 2008
Up until a little while ago there was a riot police van exactly outside the metro and the bus stops at Euagelismos. They were checking everyone going in or out of a bus.
3 riot police units, blue and green, at the war museum, 1 riot van at Rigilis Street, 1 at Mesologiou Street, 1 at Benaki Str, 2 at Exarcheia square 1 at Themistokleous Street, in the small streets surrounding the polytechnic.
A while ago people were trapped in the polytechnic by the Riot Police. There has been an attack by Riot Police on Tsamadou Street. At Exarcheia square stones were hurdled along with chairs against the Riot Police and tear gas was thrown [in response]. There are slogans heard everywhere, "the blood runs, it seeks revenge."

CREDIBLE INFORMATION BY AN EYE-WITNESS AND EVANGELISMOS
by until when 10.45 pm, Saturday December 6th 2008
Unfortunately I have the luck to have two friends who are doctors, one who was in Exarcheia and one on duty at Euagelismos Hospital.
From the friend at Euagelismos: He is dead shot straight at the heart. He is 15 years old. Euagelismos is encircled by riot police units.
From the friend who was in Exarcheia and offered first aid to the

injured: The confrontation was verbal. The kids were few in number (2–3, maybe a few more, but definitely not 25 [as some media claimed—trans.]). The policeman got out and shot straight at the heart.

12.00 IN ALL CITIES
by forward 10.52 pm, Saturday December 6th 2008
I propose that gatherings take place between 12 and 1AM in all cities in Greece. There are people everywhere. I propose this publicly.
At 12, in cities with anarchist presence, there should be gatherings of rage.

FROM PATISION
by euri 10:51 pm, Saturday December 6th 2008
you can enter the polytechnic from patision street, there are approximately 200 people there already.

NOTES

1 The occupations of the university of ASOEE (Economics School), the Athens Polytechnic, and the building of the General Confederation of Workers (GSEE).

2 The first posts that were published on Athens IMC are included here in detail.

3 Footage of the intervention is available at http://athens.indymedia.org/local/webcast/uploads/katalipsideltiounet.avi.

4 http://greekgreeksolidaritymap.blogspot.com/.

5 http://www.youtube.com/watch?v=GIYBUCrV534.

8

DECEMBER AS AN EVENT IN GREEK RADICAL POLITICS

Yannis Kallianos

IMPLOSIONS AND EXPLOSIONS

The chessboard is set. All the pawns are in position. The moves are predetermined and the strategy will rely upon these moves. The lines are the world. Black and white are never confused, never interchangeable capacities. White cannot be black, the opposite, the deviant, the unpurified. A game based on strategies, a civilised game.

The white pawn moves first, it separates itself from the white row of pawns by moving from a black square to another of the same colour, two squares ahead. The pawn's move resembles a disciplined effort. Diverging from the natural endeavour of a body that moves forward in the thrall of instinct, this pawn embodies the value of obedience to specific rules. The answer from the black side is instantaneous. The knight follows his routine move and lands on a square of the opposite colour. The game is taking some shape. The bishop, encouraged by the opponent's move, traverses the chessboard from one side to the other, sliding in white, as only a bishop is allowed to do. For quite a while, both kings remain in the same position, they discern the moves of those pieces of lesser importance and envisage a glorious victory. Coevality. This is a key concept. The pawns never congregate; they are always coeval with each other but never coexist in the same square. They meet, though, imaginatively, in a point of intersection between two opposing needs, two confrontational desires to exist. There, in these points of interstices, they meet, but only for a while. Their encounter means the end of existence for one. The other will take its place in the square, establishing another narrative but with the same discourse, that of the open battlefield.

A move by the black rook, though, disrupts our concentration. The rook has moved diagonally, neither in a vertical nor a horizontal line. This is obscene, a rook moving diagonally! Normally the game is not played like that. At first we laugh, a laughter revealing an inner understanding of the game of chess; nevertheless, it cannot conceal a slight concern, an agony and a doubt. There, between the eyes, lies fear.

Only after the pawn has learned its moves, only after it has been disciplined, can we continue the game. But our laughter is short. It drowns in a million hollow sounds. The rook's obscure move now follows a white pawn's unwillingness to hold to the rules, and thus it moves diagonally, crossing the board from one side to the other. The rules of the game are contested. Something has changed. The battlefield is no longer delineated. One abnormal move follows another, making the next move indiscernible to the opponent. When the embodied condition of game rules no longer applies for the chess pieces, the game's very existence becomes uncertain.

The objective of this short allegorical preface is to engage the reader with the notion of rupture in a game. Unable to foresee this rupture, the player is forced to engage in the game under new situations where the previous rules do not apply. In terms of the anti-authoritarian community in Greece, December was a situation of this kind. To make sense of it, the political subject had to resort to a familiar setting, the political imaginary.

THE QUESTION

The essential idea of this paper is that what happened during the days of December 2008 belongs to the site of the unexpected not only for those in power but also for the Greek radical political milieu. By arguing this, I do not claim a lack of awareness of the historico-political conditions that created the insurrectional events of December on that milieu's part. Rather, my argument focuses on the new schemes of action that were developed during those days as part of the insurrectional practice which established December 2008 as an event. More specifically, I examine the modalities of the relation between subject, time, and the social field from the side of the radical political community.

Since I take this relation to be constitutive, I aim to examine how people were able to act/react in the emergence of an unexpected event.

Before I continue, I would like to make clear what I mean by "unexpected." My knowledge of the unexpected is based on two different versions of this spatio-temporal frame. The first takes into consideration situations that are moulded by past experiences, in our case, by practices that belong to a long political tradition. This conceptualization makes a situation more expected than unexpected or, in Hannah Arendt's words, part of the process of action that makes a situation the "unexpected that can be expected" (Arendt 1998: 178). The other notion of the unexpected, which I employ here, deals with the unexpected as a situation that instantaneously disengages the subject, and thus the subject's relation with action, from the patterned process of past experiences. Therefore, this constitutional format focuses on the events of December as a point of excess/surplus in time; a moment in time that can actually only exist out of time, beyond the bounds of time. This is interpreted as a formation which functions out of the domain of the past, the present, and the "forthcoming." This analytical framework is concerned with December '08 as an unexpected event and its purpose is to unfold the modalities of opposing the rules of the social game within a non-authoritative political frame.

BARRICADING AUTHORITIES, CASTING IMAGINATIONS

On 6 December 2008, Saturday, at 9:18, a post in Greek on the Athens Indymedia website informed readers of a young boy, no more than sixteen years old, shot by police with a rubber bullet in Athens, Exarcheia. I translate:

> Emergency! Serious injury in Mesologiou (Exarcheia)
> from ZERO TIME 9:18 p.m. Saturday 6 December 2008
> serious injury to a young person
> I just received a call from a comrade, stating that clashes took place in Mesologiou and one boy was shot by a cop's plastic bullet, and he is in a very serious state, an ambulance arrived and he is being taken to Evangelismos. Those in Athens confirm the information.[1]

What seemed to be another brief confrontation between two police officers and a small group of youths in Exarcheia ended up becoming the origin of the most formidable radical force that has appeared on the Greek streets in the last thirty-five years.[2] The incident was caused by the cops transgressing an imaginary borderline that designates the line between opposed categories and at the same time an existent spatial limit imposed on the Greek police. Even though the state immediately classified the incident as isolated and accidental, several eye-witnesses and even video footage from a mobile phone very soon proved them wrong. The 37-year-old policeman calmly extended his hand, aimed, with real ammunition, and shot the 15-year-old boy in the chest.[3] The boy's death was confirmed a half-hour later.

This information is not revealed in such detail to provoke emotions or sympathy, far from it. In fact, this detailed description encompasses the experiences of a political field almost thirty years old; the place Exarcheia,[4] the subject of deviance—young people, the definite "Other"—the police forces/the state/the authorities. Within these three very distinctive positions, and in the incident itself, we can identify a whole series of forces, discourses, and actions that have come into play and been exercised throughout the years.

When Alexandros Grigoropoulos's murder was confirmed, an uncontrollable chain reaction was set in motion. The activities that formulated the chain of events were of the same essence. Demonstrations, marches, protests, clashes with the police, skirmishes, looting and squatting all together formed a kaleidoscope of action that nonetheless led up to a concrete framework of political activity. In more than thirteen cities in Greece, demonstrations, marches and several other actions took place immediately after the murder. These demonstrations had primarily an offensive disposition, targeting police stations in their region. In Ioannina, a city in the northwest of Greece, a group of people attacked the local police station with stones and flag bats. In Volos, central Greece, the demonstration attacked the police station, more than twenty banks, a municipal police car, the town hall and other buildings. In Chania, Crete, banks and other offices of prestigious private corporations and companies were targeted and attacked. In Thessaloniki, Greece's second-largest city, in the north of the country, several people marched towards the main police station in the city centre and attacked it ferociously.

During the first night of the events, three University buildings had already been occupied in Athens: the Polytechnic,[5] the Athens University of Economics and Business (ASOEE), and Athens Law School (Nomiki). These events took place only a few hours after the young student's death. Could this have been a well-organised response? Looking at the pattern of action dispersed all around Greece, the answer might be yes. However, my argument is that these practices follow a pattern of radical political action. This pattern is understood and deciphered if examined through a habitual political disposition that provides the subject with a feeling of participation in a game (here, the political game). This sense in the game is what allows the subject to acknowledge the pattern that is drawn from her position in the present to a certain "forthcoming." For Bourdieu the notion of the forthcoming is inseparable from the notion of the game itself. "The sense of the game is that sense of the forthcoming of the game, of what is to be done ('it was the only thing to do' or 'he did what was needed') in order to bring about the forthcoming state of the game that is visible there for a habitus predisposed to anticipate it, the sense of the history of the game, which is only acquired through experience of the game which means that the imminence and pre-eminence of the forthcoming presuppose a disposition which is the product of the past." (Bourdieu, 2000: 211–212) Elaborating on this idea, Bourdieu acknowledges that the forthcoming "is already present in the immediate present and not constituted as future." (Bourdieu 2000: 210) The forthcoming then is part of the process of making the present. Taking that into consideration the outline of action during the first hours belongs to a long tradition of anarchist/ anti-authoritarian action in Greece. The agent did what "needs to be done" as a necessary response to an incident where the state's oppressive power has been nakedly exposed. Nevertheless, the expansion and dynamic of the socio-political force expressed in such a short period as counter-violence against state oppression is of a unique kind in the history of Modern Greece.

During that time, the rapidity of action and the diversity of both method and practice made any attempt at interpretation almost impossible. Within these first hours the normality of the city was disrupted. What is important in this respect is the ultimate attack on authoritative discourses, power relations, systems of discipline and punishment, and imposed schemes of perceptions. The state, authorities, the prevalent system of law and order were immediately identified with the normality in the city. Therefore, the disruption of normality had the qualities of challenging all the above altogether. In addition, the targeted attack against police is strongly connected with ideas of emancipation and liberation in the course of action. A twenty-five-year old, second-generation immigrant told me a few weeks after the insurrection:

> This was my first time ever to cast a stone, first time I covered my face. After learning about the event it came naturally. I had been before in demonstrations and protests but never before I had participated in riots. It was something like an initiation for me and I have to admit I felt liberated you know. It made me feel like I regained control over myself. I was the one who decided for me.

155

One question arises immediately: how does a subject, especially a political subject, construct reality when "something new is started," here the insurrectional events? Considering the new as always appearing in the guise of a miracle, Arendt appreciates it as emerging from human action in terms of the "unexpected that can be expected." In this sense, the improbable becomes probable in the realm of action. For her, action always implies a new beginning. Considering that, I ask how someone who is nurtured towards a political rebellious attitude deals with the immense force (both in terms of numbers and dynamic) of December. This question, that has dogged me ever since those days, will act as a guide here for the analytical interpretation of those events. By no means will I treat this new beginning as an autonomous point in time. Instead, I aim to study it as a fabric in process, as a material that is woven and interwoven to challenge the *laws* of action, and thus the rules of a wider game, the social game.

MAKING THE EVENT

To view the unexpected from the side of the anarchist/anti-authoritarian milieu, I turn to the incidents of Monday morning (8 December 2008) as the new beginning that disengaged the subject from any previous experience.

On Monday morning, workplaces closed earlier than usual and schools were occupied by students. In many cases, 15-, 16-, and 17-year-old students occupied their schools. They made up slogans, prepared banners, and took to the streets. In several districts of Athens, students formed small demonstrations and attacked police stations with stones and bricks, smashed police cars, or stood outside shouting slogans. The geographical and geopolitical wave of attack obeyed its own laws. The unrest in secondary schools occurred in various places that do not share similar class characteristics. Outside the police headquarters what the political movement failed to do a day before, the students achieved easily; the massive building in Alexandras Avenue was besieged. The Greek parliament became another distinctive place of protest gathering for students. In their arrival most of the students would wear their hoods and cover their faces and approach riot police chanting slogans. In Piraeus, Greece's largest port, students attacked the general police headquarters and the city's town hall, overturning several police cars. Attacks on police stations and general disruption and unrest spread from the city centre to the periphery. Students attacked police stations in Ilioupoli, Kifisia, Egaleo, Patision, and Galatsi. Several of these districts, such as Kifisia, are considered very high upper-class districts, whereas others have middle- and working-class profiles.

The distribution of information was a major contribution to the unwillingness of this section of society to return to normality. This opened the path for the illegalisation of the official political scene and the destabilisation of the social stage. SMS and the internet (especially social networks such as Twitter and Blogspot) proved to be excellent tools for organising action on a large scale. "He was only fifteen years old," "it could have been one of us," "1,2,3, Fuck the police," "cops, pigs, murderers," and even "revenge" were slogans that students shouted repeatedly on that Monday morning. These slogans are the evidence of their anger and state of mind, as well as, of the conscious attempt to degrade the official mechanism. Some of these slogans belong to the discourse of the milieu and what is interesting here is their immediate assimilation by students. Monday became the passage from one period to another, from a specific use of political action to a generalized critic and decomposition of social values.

That afternoon, several leftist groups and the assembly of Nomiki had called for a central demonstration in Athens at one of the most customary points for demonstrations to begin, Propylaia Square. The gathering time was set at 6 pm. However, even before then, a number of people had started to concentrate in the area and clashes with police had already taken place in the nearby streets. At around 7 pm, more than 50,000 people were marching towards Omonoia (Amity) Square. Even though the march was supposed to cover the usual route from Propylaia Square to Parliament, it quickly broke into smaller pieces. It soon became obvious that the crowd that made up the body of the demonstration was very diverse. Several small groups broke away and attacked either commercial or state targets. When smoke appeared on the horizon and the first flames had been set, the crowd started to back up. By then, information spread like a gunshot. Information about everything and everyone: "*The fascist weapon store in Omonoia has been invaded and looted.*" "*The Ministry of Foreign Affairs is on fire.*" "*Police have attacked the demonstration in Omonoia.*" "*The fascists are outside their offices, protecting them.*" "*Nomiki* [Athens Law School] *is a safe place to be, people are going there.*" Information seemed to have no source and was simultaneously everywhere and nowhere. It traversed the crowd and, in its very course, changed emotions, attitudes and perspectives. Resembling an autonomous system of knowledge, it seemed to feed on nothing but simultaneously fed the surroundings.

Almost an hour after the demonstration had begun, the city centre was in flames. Several department stores were burning and a number of other buildings were destroyed. When the demonstration broke up, some sections of the crowd continued until they reached the Parliament, others found shelter in Nomiki and yet more tried to leave the city centre. The atmosphere was suffocating, the familiar noises were everywhere; fire alarms, ambulances, police cars, explosions from the stores that had been set on fire, shouting, slogans, and the distinctive noise of the police radio surrounded the city. The last image of the night has been symbolically displayed ever since as the main icon of the milieu's disruption of normality in the city; in Syntagma Square, just across from the Greek parliament, the grand Christmas tree was set on fire.

What then goes on to occur in the next few days will be classified as an insurrection. The dynamics developed in the social field, the multiple and diverse political practices performed during those days and the destabilisation that these schemes created in the socio-political institutions meant hope for change became tangible. Those in radical politics, subjects who supposedly had the capacity to recognise the political value of a situation, took action at once, but their practice was still part of a habitus of political reaction. Even though it was very dynamic and dispersed, it was not before Monday that the political subjects started to talk about "something else," something that had not been there before, the unexpected. At that moment, socio-political practices began to be evaluated and reconsidered. Why most students took to the streets during those days and what were the elements that developed this dynamic counter-force against authorities are questions that need further study. Yet, the radical political milieu's inability to foresee the forthcoming political change must be examined through these groups' historical consciousness and the social relations that constitute it. Only a few days ago, the milieu's critique had talked about an uninterested society for the collective issues/*koina*, about young people in the realm of the apolitical. In the accounts of "where did they come from?" we found, besides astonishment and enthusiasm, an attempt to cope with an unexpected reality. Nevertheless, the disjuncture created in the event was a burden that the milieu had to carry with it all along the insurrectionary path.

POSITION AND EVENT

158   In my endeavour to explain how an unexpected situation disengages the subject from past experiences, I turn to Badiou's notion of the

event. Examining the insurrection of December 2008 as an event establishes it as a moment of rupture for the milieu. Therefore, I use Bourdieu's *habitus* in order to look at the event as seen in the relation between subject time and field. In addition, I examine how the event which does not belong in the domain of intelligibility is reconstituted through its fidelities.

Badiou argues that the event "is ontologically formalized by an extraordinary set.... But the axiom of foundation forecloses extraordinary sets from any existence, and ruins any possibility of naming a multiple-being of the event. Here we have an essential gesture: that by means of which ontology declares the event is not" (Badiou 2005a: 190). In *Being and Event*, Badiou sets forth an intensive examination of that which does not exist, namely the event for which there is "no acceptable ontological matrix" (Badiou 2005a: 190). For Badiou, "the event is attached in its very definition, to the place, to the point, in which the historicity of the situation is concentrated. Every event has a site which can be singularized in a historical situation" (Badiou 2005a: 179). This conceptual formula implies that the multiplicity of historical points and signs of the local determination of a site in the event are simultaneously represented with a singular format. The notional formation that arises from this theoretical framework and concerns us here recognises the event as a point in the relation between time, space and being that is not expected. In other words it is a moment in time that is only recognised as such because it is simultaneously out of time. This means that, in the process of making sense in the political milieu, the event is not recognised as part of the process that creates the forthcoming, the domain of expectations.

At this point, Bourdieu's habitus is helpful in exposing this transition from the frame of the expected to that of the unexpected. If we look at action from the point of the strategically-informed body, the event acquires transparent qualities. The relation between action, time and the social field provides us with a solid ground to look at how embodied political practice functions within the unexpected. *Habitus* as an apparatus interprets the event as unexpected because it is not part of the illusion that creates the forthcoming; it is, in its totality, a rupture in the relation between illusion (the interest in the game) and making sense of the game, since it is not predicted, because it is not constituted through the formula *illusio*–illusion. Here the event cannot be discerned with this formula. At its core, December '08 is an event because it exists outside this rational formula of habitual representation. When the students took to the streets on Monday morning and besieged several police stations and when thousands of youths took shelter in the Technological Institute of Athens (Polytechnic) to clash with riot police, the site of political action thus expanded, changing the milieu's position in the events. What has been said many times since is that "events surpassed us." Bearing this statement in mind, I argue that the event is exactly what it is not in this formula. In what follows, I shall focus on the relation between the subject and action in the field of the unexpected.

FIDELITIES OF DECEMBER

By applying the theory of the event as Badiou conceptualises it to examine the insurrectional situation of December 2008, my purpose is not only to establish it in the realm of the unexpected but also to look at how the milieu makes sense of the event. Therefore, working with Badiou's theoretical construction, the event is placed further into the domain of intelligibility and into a discernible awareness, making it transparent in its non-transparency. Looking at December '08 through Badiou's theoretical formula, the event has no objective existence. It is through what Badiou calls "interpretive intervention" (Badiou 2005a: 181) that the event occurs as such. It is only in the eyes of the actors that December '08 acquires an objective nature and can be re-processed as the event. The event emerges along with the subject who recognises it and classifies it as an event. Thus, the state of the situation that is recognized as an event by the agents is not merely a "reflection of the situation. It is separated from the situation" (Badiou 2005a: 275). What concerns us here, then, is the state of the representation of the event.

Having said that, I argue that the state of the situation exists in the metanarratives of the event where it is formulated. These metanarratives dissociate the state from the situation and re-configure it in the excess of the situation: in the void of the incident and its context. It is in the metanarratives that we can see what Badiou calls fidelity to the event. It is exactly in this set of relations between the actors and the unexpected where the event is first recognised. "I call fidelity the sets of procedures which discern, within a situation, those multiples whose existence depends upon the introduction into circulation (under the supernumerary name conferred by an intervention) of an eventual multiple. In sum fidelity is the apparatus which separates out, within the sets of presented multiples, those which depend upon an event. To be faithful is to gather together and distinguish the becoming legal of a change" (Badiou 2005a: 232). At the same time, fidelity is not constituted in a domain of abstraction; on the contrary, it is configured where a definite logic is formulated. For example, when on the morning of 8 December several secondary schools were occupied by students who then took to the streets, this worked as the definite sign of irreversibility for the political milieu: "*nothing is the same anymore.*" Simultaneously, in the assemblies of the occupied universities, the question "*should we continue?*" shifted to "*how should we continue?*" This change was the first sign of recognition of an event. It worked as the indication of adapting to the situation, thus making sense (rationalising) any praxis taking place in the situation. For Badiou, the event is not in itself unintelligible; it is unintelligible in regards to the means of prediction, of forecast or of continuity of the situation. What creates the intelligibility of December is the fidelity to the event. From this perspective, fidelity is essential in the formulation of the event. In a sense, it is even more important than the event itself. It is fidelity that provides the human being with consistency in a set of changes. Through fidelity in a situation/practice/knowledge, the human being becomes an actor in the social field Fidelity reaffirms and reconfirms a certain continuity of thought and action. Thus it makes discernible the forthcoming as a future affected by our position in the present and our past experiences.

These fidelities were also constituted in the realm of possibilities, at which the connection between December and its fidelities now become even more obvious. To go a step further, the event is a rupture in time. It belongs to the void created in the excess of the situation in a social field. This rupture has the capacity to violently separate the past from the present situation. This does not mean repositioning the event in ahistorical and apolitical space. It is understood as the transformation of the relation between subject and action as identified during previous events. That said, December '08 does not only exist as an unexpected situation but simultaneously functions as the apparatus making the subject's position in the present irrelevant, thus trivialising any expectations of the forthcoming. Everything was possible in those days. The framework of possibilities was vast. In the participants' eyes, the limit was the "impossible" (a documentary released after December by collectives that had participated in the insurrectional events bore the title "the potentiality of storming heaven"[6]). This can be seen in all the practices displayed and performed during those days. In particular, several of the actions could not even have been conceptualised if it was not for the existence of excess in the December situation.

However, even though the excess is not measurable, it can be recognised in its effects. From this point of view, the excess emerged from the situation where the state revealed its oppressive power: "whenever there is a genuinely political event, the State shows itself. It reveals its excess of power, its repressive dimension. But it also reveals a measure for this usually invisible excess. For it is essential to the normal functioning of the State that its power remains measureless, errant, unassignable. The political event puts an end to all that by assigning a visible measure to the excessive power of the State" (Badiou 2005b: 145). It is in the relation between state, subject, and action that the excess first becomes intelligible when looking back in the insurrection of December 2008. From this point of view acting in the excess of the situation is like surpassing the laws of the situation. The event is simultaneously in place and out of place/in excess of the situation. That is because it is disconnected from all the rules of the situation. In the course of acting outside the rules, the fidelity of the new situation re-positions it within the field of the legality, making the change of the situation official and "grounded in law." Therefore, when I say that *December*, as an event, exists out of the situation, it means that the transition from another reality/situation has been legalised. Thus *December* can function as a concept able to formulate political consciousness.

This being said, the event, being an excess in time, tore away the normative logic of practice from the habitus of action, re-positioning it on the level of the radical political milieu's social imaginary. Therefore, all actions that appeared in the event or through the event are constitutive of the event itself. Otherwise these actions could not have existed if the past experiences had still applied in the present situation. These potentialities of December are clearly recognised in its fidelities. The fidelity of December contributed to this subversion of power symbols, thus contributing to the construction of the Event as the ultimate change; from the values of the norm to the values of an insurrection. It is in this function that we recognise the event as the topos of challenging the *laws* of the social game as much as it challenges the process of action in the radical political field.

CONSTRUCTING DECEMBER '08 AS A POLITICAL CONCEPT

It is noteworthy that, as time went by, the discourse produced by the milieu about the events of December '08 was less conflicting and contradictory than in other cases. If one were to try to formulate a unified discursive line that could be the following: full of rage in the very beginning, then excited and passionate with the new reality (counterworlds), explorative of the new field in latter stages, only to finally transform into the rhetoric of *"December leads the way."* This last rhetorical formation is anything but accidental. Two layers in this discursive form must concern us. First, the sentence *"December leads the way"* is actually based on *"November leads the way"* in the context of Greek radical politics. This former discourse refers to the rebellious events that took place in November 1973 during the military coup d'état (1967–1974) at the Technological Institute of Athens (Polytechnic). My argument is that this discourse reveals a continuation in the radical political milieu's consciousness rather than a substitution. However, this continuation can only happen if the fidelities of the past event have been saturated only to re-emerge exactly as fidelities to the new event. These fidelities interleave with a past situation to which the political subjects are no longer faithful, yet it has not been rejected. This can be seen in other discursive formations during that period: *"Fuck May '68, fight now"*[7] and *"We are an image from the future."*[8] Both slogans, written during December, connote a rupture with the past.

If examined from Austin's point of view, these utterances, and many others produced during December, imply, encourage and denote action in the context of December. Since, according to Austin, every one of these utterances is constructed within a specific context that for-mulates the kind of action (Austin 1975: 100), these slogans acquire a certain meaning only within the context in which they are being ut-tered. Yet, if studied from a semiotic perspective, the signified concept that completes the political sign is identified in the relation with the past; first, as a connotation that recognises a certain significance in an-other past event (May '68), even in referential analogies, and second, in the notion of the image from the future. This, it could be argued, refers not so abstractly to a revolutionary forthcoming. Having said that, what is interesting here is political subjects' attempt during that time to create an image which is neither motionless (we-the-subjects-of-an-uprising) nor is its message concrete (the future). How, then, is the message con-veyed if the image is not detected? The only way to see the image, then, is to understand it as a representation not of an image from the future but of an image from the past. The *"image from the future"* is created upon a long tradition of radical political events. In other words, this *"image"* encompasses and corresponds to what Lowy frames as the "oppressed of the past" (Lowy 2005: 90). This is because when Benja-min makes the distinction between historical time and clock time (*On the Concept of History*) he reveals a structural link between past and present that is obvious when revolutionary events take place. There-fore, the future is not the faraway but rather the process of invoking the "oppressed of the past." In Lowy's words the oppressed of the past are those who have come back to haunt the future. Only then does the word "we" make sense, because it encompasses all those who recognise in *the image from the future* the *"oppressed of the past."*

What emerges through these discursive formations is the absolute fidelity to the event. In the process of the milieu to discursively establish December 2008 as *The December*, or in other words establish the insurrectional events of December '08 as an event, the insurrection is assimilated into the long tradition of radical political events. *December*, then, takes its place in a long list of events referred to by the name of the month in which they occurred: Dekemvriana (December 1946), Iouliana (July 1965), and of course November (November 1973). In this process, December loses its autonomous essence and through fidelity is assimilated into the historical structural process of political matter. Altogether, December becomes a concept. Stating that *"December leads the way"* or *December* did this, that, or the other is to give it as a concept "the power to act in history as the words that designate them act in the sentences of historical narrative, it personifies collectives and makes them subjects responsible for historical actions" (Bourdieu 1990: 37).

Through that analytical framework, I consider all later formative political multiples after December 2008 to have been influenced by the event. From this perspective, the event was a rupture in Greek radical politics both because it affected radically all later socio-political relations constituting the milieu and because for a moment it disengaged the subject by his/her past experiences. Identifying the rupture, both for the milieu and the general social sphere, is to contextualise what one person said at a main assembly in mid-January 2009: "*[During December] it had become so difficult to find targets to attack or actions to perform, since when we were discussing doing something, this something was already happening or had already happened at the hands of students and young people.*" By being a rupture, the event established in the social the essence of the political. Altogether, December 2008 became the space where every aspect of daily life was inseparable from political attitude.

NOTES

1 The first post created on the site http://www.athens.indymedia.org informing readers of the death of the 15-year-old boy in Exarcheia, Athens. The translation is mine. Source: http://athens.indymedia.org/front.php3?lang=el&article_id=933042.

2 After the Athens Polytechnic uprising in November 1973 Greece has been the terrain for multiple incidents of social unrest. However, these incidents were only of interest to particular sections of society (for example, education workers in 1998, the student movement of 2006–07) that never found points to intersect with other agents in the social field. What is distinctive in the case of December is the diversity of subjects, agents and individuals that participated in the events.

3 Source: http://tvxs.gr/news. This is the description that the witness Lito Valliatza has testified on the court in the course of the ongoing trial.

4 Exarcheia has been the space of Greek radical politics for more than 25 years. At the beginning of the 1980s, the formulation of radical practices was still in an experimental stage and various political actions and protest techniques were being re-evaluated, re-adjusting to changes on both a political and social level. Exarcheia, being the most primordial space of these configurations, which ranged from the squatting of buildings to violent clashes with the police, was straightforwardly classified and distinguished as *imperium in imperio*. "The main square of Exarcheia is an Anarchist kernel.... They have occupied the district. As if the problems of the residents are not enough, they now have to deal with corruption, with the 'anarchists,' drug dealing, prostitution...." (*Rizospastis*, 16 December 1980. A description of the district by the official journal of the Greek Communist Party). In another newspaper in 1984 we read "Exarcheia: After the drugs and the anarchists came the punks with shaved heads" (*Ethnos*, 14 September 1984). In this discursive formation of the imaginary of the district, the state had an active role, not only in trying to control the neighbourhood but also by introducing abstract narratives to the public. In 1986, the former General Drosogiannis, the new Minister of Public Order, stated in the media: "*I will not tolerate a state of anarchists or any others in Exarcheia. The main square will become like any other and everybody will be able to walk freely*" (*To Vima*, 18 May 1986).

5 Built in stages from 1862 to 1957, the National Technical University of Athens (Polytechnic), one of the most significant Modern Greek architectural constructions, bears the elusive signs of Modern Greek history, since it is connected with the uprising (14–17 November 1973) that stood up to the military Junta (1967–1974). Since then, the building has symbolically connoted more than a revolutionary past, since its space is still used as the primary place for major assemblies by different political groups. In addition, the building's use during the latest uprising of December 2008 indicates the revolutionary imagery that is imposed on such spaces.

6 A video presentation of the December insurrection through the deeds and discourse of the participants. The video was made in Thessaloniki on January 2009 and was shown for the first time in an assembly at the occupied public library of Ano Poli.

7 Slogan on wall, December 2008, Athens.

8 Slogan that first appeared at ASOEE (Athens School of Economics and Business).

9

SHORT VOYAGE TO THE LAND OF OURSELVES[1]

Hara Kouki

The days of December 2008 seemed like a long—extremely long—moment of rupture that deeply and entirely shattered our normality. We saw before us the possibility of things happening: thousands of people taking to the streets every day, writing hundreds of calls to protest, occupying public buildings and interrupting theatre and music spectacles, participating in severe acts of civil unrest and violent rioting that shattered spaces and symbols that had been taken as firm and eternal realities. We shared space and anger and became engaged in a common fate. For a few days we saw our life as it is and we even saw ourselves taking part in it.

For instance, we saw the Athens Christmas tree, the "tallest and most beautifully lit tree in the whole of Europe," standing in Syntagma Square like every year. But this time it was guarded by heavily armed police in order to hold angry citizens back from burning it down or throwing rubbish at it. We realized, then, that the police were not guarding the tree. They were protecting us from facing the image of our reality denaturalised. We could now see what this represented and who those besieging it were; we could see the order of things naked, the terms of the game unmasked and instantly reverted.

A massive student protest was handled as a problem of "order" by police; the rage of thousands of citizens was labelled as violence and extremism, social conflict was trivialised as irrational, and we, protest-

167

ing, became the outcasts to be thrown out of the urban frame. On the other hand, police repression and the brutal treatment of immigrants, a failing educational system and rising unemployment, degenerated institutions, injustice and corruption, nonexistent social security, and rising economic crisis—all those were perfectly legitimated, presented as "common sense," the pillars of our living democratic experience. The blissfully-illuminated tree became a battlefield of stones and meanings. Collective action versus lawful peacefulness, nihilism versus democracy, citizens versus police and institutions, evil versus good.

> And he is good who does not outrage, who harms nobody, who does not attack, who does not requite, who leaves revenge to God, who keeps himself hidden as we do, who avoids evil and desires little from life, like us, the patient, humble, and just....[2]

If that is the frame of understanding, then, what is to be done? What is to be said?

Well, nothing, really.

THOSE DAYS (DECEMBER IN OUR LIVES)

1) LANDING WHILE CREATING OUR LAND...

We interrupt a live state TV news broadcast and silently raise a banner to silence this representation of reality.[3] We call on people to stop being viewers, to step out of their homes, to take to the streets, to resist. The black and white banner that some of us held for eighty seconds articulated no claim, no plan and no certainty. No indication of where to go, what to do, at what time, with whom, and for what. Against the anxiousness to explain, against the guilt of failing to predict and foretell, to plan and rationalise and fit in, to summarise and nicely narrate violence, we opposed our living thrill of collective and direct action against an absurd but confident reality and said nothing, really.

All Different, All Together

Because, at the moment, we did not ask ourselves who all those people next to us were. We just knew that they were our comrades—the thousands of frustrated secondary education and university students, unemployed graduates and employed boys and girls of the €600 generation, and then the leftists and the anarchists, of course it was them, but they seemed so many, didn't they? But we could also see some pensioners, and for the first time we could see immigrants out in the streets next to us, and also some middle-aged couples (they must have been parents worried about their kids, or simply people fed up with every-thing)—there was also the lady who cleans our offices and the guy who works in the bank opposite our school, and this old woman on the bal-cony crying out against the cops, it was everybody, wasn't it? During the demonstrations, the sit-ins, the looting, while shouting slogans and writ-ing texts, attacking policemen, throwing stones, burning and disrupt-ing movement, during every single moment we felt that we were part of a collective that did not have to ask of its members anything more than being there, because they and everyone together actually were the event. And this was massive, extraordinary, beyond imagination, and, at the same time, the only thing that made sense.

Before December, each one of us belonged to a certain group, had a role, a function, a place, and all of those well-defined parts formed an ensemble that also arranged things into the common and the pri-vate, the visible and the invisible, the permissible and the unthinkable, where properties, responsibilities, opinions, and disputes were ascribed to specific socio-economic identities or age groups. This way of count-ing at the same time implied the available ways of being, doing, and speaking and their appropriate limits. But once we took to the streets, we had no need to include ourselves within any group, to move closer to the ones who resembled us in terms of skin colour, income, dress code, or ideology, no need to explain, or even imply, who we are. No one was representative of any group, but everyone was represented; nothing of what we asked for could be articulated in the language of political de-mands, but everything was said. Our need for belonging somewhere that had made us part of a whole dissolved in a few seconds and we immediately stopped feeling dispersed and alone. We formed neigh-bourhood assemblies, primary unions, groups of solidarity with people we would have never imagined standing next to us. Being different was not a reason to stay separate, but to mount a multiple collective not re-ducible to the strands that brought us together. By living an egalitarian moment, we changed in one night the terms of inclusion and exclusion. We were transformed from invisible solitary figures rambling around in our urban misery into political subjects who managed to challenge, not the solutions that had to be applied to a situation, but the situation itself.

New Spaces

And then, there was nothing to say, because in that moment we did not ask ourselves where to go, with whom, and for what. We just had to take to the streets with other people, even if there was no fixed meeting, no prearranged destination, no gathering point. We simply felt impelled to start marching with our classmates towards the nearest police station, destroy the ATM outside our offices, smash the CCTV camera placed above our cars, shout against the policeman standing every night at the corner of our homes, remain immobile in the middle of the avenue when police forces were ordering us to move away, paint the ugly wall next to our friends' house in colours that did not match, and not feel repelled by the sight of those cars in flames. We just had to talk to people from our neighbourhoods we had never spoken to, to those young parents who live opposite us, to the math student who rents the house at the corner, and the lady who used to be a famous actress, to speak with urgency about what is to be done, about the park that is about to be demolished and that abandoned public building outside of which homeless people are sleeping, and break the door down and intrude and feel responsible and start writing a text and create a web page and send messages and receive others from other places and communicate with everyone in the city in order to be a part of them and for all of them to be a part of us. All of a sudden, we were there, next to other people, and it was the only thing that could have ever happened.

Before December, each one of us lived in one place and worked in another and we were all divided into groups that formed clear networks of representation that would address themselves to other groups higher in the hierarchy that would decide when to vote, where to demonstrate, and how schools, workplaces, malls and bars, airports and supermarkets will be distributed around the country. This urban arrangement ascribed places to regular possibilities and prohibited others, structured our movement in a legal way, and put surveillance mechanisms in place to protect our cities that were ever more besieged by individuals in need of drugs, money to survive, a place to stay, or a country to live in. But once taking to the streets and feeling part of a living community of people, we couldn't but occupy our cities in a different way. This experience of socialisation could not fit inside our offices and TV screens, coffee shops, shopping avenues, and secured square metres designed for us to live in. Our coming together violently spoiled the façades of all those urban places that actually cancel out our possibility of interaction and chain us to the role of a non-citizen; it gave birth instantly, instead, to self-organised groups, non-hierarchical gatherings, community events, fluid networks of people and horizontal counter-information, a multiplicity of small new personal relations of trust, commitment, and direct action that had to invent new localities so as to materialize and develop. During the days of December, we did not transform the spaces given to us, but we created new ones where we could also let ourselves be created.

Stateless Words and Actions

And there was nothing to say, after all, because in that moment we did not ask ourselves what to do, what to ask and from whom, who was leading us and why exactly we were doing what we were doing. There was no way to predict or classify this fluid and violent wave of people, no political organisation to lead the mobilisation, no uniform ideology to set its tone, or a political demand to put forward so as to be negotiated or rejected by the government. Our sole reaction was this sense of bewilderment of being together in the streets and an urge to do and write thousands of meaningful things that made no sense. We saw ourselves acting in ways we could not imagine, we became illegal, inaudible, unacceptable, ineligible, ferocious, and wonderful. It was not despair or disillusionment—we were never allowed to believe in something after all. It was acting beyond ourselves and what has made us so far understand the world around us. During those days we experienced the feeling of our coming together, of fighting for and not against, and for the first time we could make a difference. Everything was possible, as it should have always been.

Before December, we knew it already—no one was to be trusted, politics was corrupt, things were getting irreversibly worse all the time and there was nothing to do about it. But then we took to the streets, we found each other, and there was actually no need to read what other people wrote and do what other people had arranged to do and wait for others to think about what we want, no need to articulate demands and ask for marginal benefits so that they could understand, no need to adopt argumentative strategies and representative ethics so as to reach a rational consensus, no need to have a meaning within this frame, because we had no need of this frame, we created our own meanings. Our relating to each other in an equal way and the spaces, words and actions we formed rejected common sense, because they were not just directed against the state; this was a politics of resistance and solidarity that was bluntly stateless.

For a few days we set out on a voyage to a land where we were all different, but all together. The moments of this brief encounter form the story of December—a story that could not have been predicted and which cannot be unravelled. The before and after became indistinguishable, the effects caused causes and put together words, images, places and people so as to produce this true utopia, this utopian reality, 171 a living madness, *the wordless evidence of the thing given in itself, the exact coincidence of word and thing.*

2) FOREIGNERS TO OUR LAND

Journalists, politicians, intellectuals, academics, and citizens attempted to identify the groups that participated in those moments of revolt, and relate the events to both local and international contexts and trace the reasons for them (see Sotiris 2010; Gavriilides 2010).[4]

a) So there were some, certainly not the majority, who tried to understand and come to terms with the events, or even express solidarity with the protesters. Attempting something close to social analysis, they insisted on the conditions of globalisation and neoliberalism that produce rising inequalities, a crisis of values and youth insecurity, while others attributed the causes to the fallacies of Greek state corruption and political clientelism, an underdeveloped civil society, problems in the educational establishment, an institutional crisis, and the loss of state legitimacy.[5] There were those who, aided by social movement theory, looked for the organisational basis and membership of the protest events, and for any predetermined strategies that would possibly aim at the expansion of the political context or the institutionalization of the movement itself.[6] After December, some foresaw the "end of politics" brought about by mass individualism and nihilism and gave up their analysis; some others, led by revolutionary emotionalism, did exactly the same, but this time in the name of this sublime Event that will itself automatically lead to change and to the "return of politics."

All these explanations insisted on the centrality of politics and saw December as a movement meant to mobilise part of the population that felt more or less socially excluded. By confirming already existing inequalities, however, they proved unable to go any further than constantly rediscovering them.[7] This world is unequal, but this is an intangible given. It is as if those interpretations called on people to provide capitalism and existing state structures with a radical and more humanistic content.

b) But then there were those who stated in a much more vociferous way that what took place in the streets of the country during December was certainly not a "revolt," but something that paved the way to more violence and illegality. The protesters, each one led by a different motivation, had nothing in particular to say or to ask for. Their anger was short-lived and did not reflect or give birth to anything new.

In any case, things went back to normal immediately afterwards. As for the youngsters performing "a chain of irrational and openly anomic" acts of violence, they felt legitimated by a public discourse of resistance against authority that has become justified, if not glorified, in Greece since 1975. This was not a social movement, not an insurrection of the youth, not even a reflection of any deeper social, political, or ideological causes; it was only a culture of violence with which the state had proved incapable of dealing. It comes as no surprise, then, that Greece remains a pre-modern, primordial, and underdeveloped country.[8]

What was repeatedly asked for was zero tolerance to all forms of violence, nihilism, and abuse so as to maintain regime normality. As a result, consensus, law and order, as well as the Athenian Christmas tree, must be safeguarded and the cities cleansed of trash, vandalism, and extremism.

c) At the same time, the demonstrations and riots obviously became headline news for every single newspaper, TV, or radio station in the country. Media coverage stated that this was one of the most massive events taking place in the country, which was not the responsibility of the "usual suspects," but of much broader groups of people. The pattern of treatment for those "unique" events, however, was the same as ever: everything was framed around the issue of "violence," as conducted by both police and protesters; no attempt was made whatsoever to understand why such protests were taking place at this specific moment and on the streets, why they were embracing so many and such different people and taking this form and with such intensity. Media attention was directed to the teenagers protesting; those young people bearing no conflictual or politically-charged memory could easily appear as the only innocent and thus true political subjects of a world in disarray.[9] Vivid images of the city in flames and of citizens being beaten by security forces generated an urgent need to protect the country both from an abusive state power and from anarchist violent practices. Social tensions were obscured, neutralised, and depoliticised so as to let the national community emerge as a suffering body, united in its need to resist "violence" of all sorts.

The analyses offered by state representatives, public intellectuals, and the media attempted to link the events in a linear way so as to reach a point where the relation of cause and effect would be clear enough to explain them. In this way, they failed to offer an understanding of what happened. They managed, however, step-by-step to strip this voyage of ours of its content; we were told we were not there, because we were too many and we were too dispersed to be seen; we were denied a vital space, because we had burnt down what could possibly make sense; we were given no political role in the game, because we did not play according to the rules. In pronouncing December to be non-existent, or a failed appointment, this exhaustive series of possible explanations managed to come to terms not with the dynamics and the contradictions of the events per se but with preconceived realities already at hand. Most analyses were rational, confident and often aggressive, others paternalistic but also nervous to explain, while some were benevolent or even comprehensive. But, at the very end, this "prose of counter insurgency" (Guha 1983) was fearful of December as something that could not be grasped, that was not supposed to have happened, as something that was an exception to the rule.

What about life after December, then?

THESE DAYS (OUR LIFE AFTER DECEMBER)

3) DEPARTING FROM THEIR LAND OF CRISIS

The King is Naked

It was soon revealed, however, that it was not the exception to the rule that was to be feared, but the rule itself. A violent crisis, first financial and then all-encompassing, surfaced in the months following December, effectively shattering all the arrogant confidence of the system. During the last twenty years, the two major political parties in the country—right-wing and socialist—had been attempting to construct a central space beyond ideologies, where politics would be performed by sceptical liberals and responsible technocrats. This consensual universe was supposed to appease grievances and avoid conflicts. However, it had been gradually pushing to the margins a growing majority of people who could no longer expect to be incorporated or represented within its limits. Hitherto latent social antagonisms were revealed and became polarised, while their negotiation through established institutions was unmasked as a dead-end endeavour. The political establishment started to tremble and collapse, as did any alternative or dissenting options within its context, in either their reformist or leftist political form. And while the social fabric is being torn apart throughout the country, massive numbers of immigrants and refugees are waiting beyond or within its borders to be either naturalised or repatriated, while neither can happen. Cities around the country had been besieged throughout the last ten years by an ever-growing number of individuals in need; their disquieting presence had unsettled transport and education habits, workplace environments, housing, and urban normality. This has become an everyday reality that now directly relates to the overall deformation of the given frame of life, as it grows ever harder for people to be represented within it.

It was revealed, thus, that there was no life after December, because it was our own life that brought about December. People all over the country started realising that, however different their anxieties might be, their problem is common—the unequal way in which structures have been erected around them—and thus can no longer be tackled through the usual form of politics. Citizens emerge, not divided into different parts, but as one group subject to an institutional structure and power distribution that threatens their existence in different ways. Due to this crisis of representation, every opinion, criticism, or protest directly challenges the core issue of power and becomes instantly politicised. There is no longer space left for a commonplace student or anti-racist mobilisation to develop, or for a syndicalist demand to be put forward; truck drivers blocking avenues and workers fired from publishing houses, contractual employees of the Ministry of Culture occupying the Acropolis, and basketball players on strike—all those groups have single-issue claims that unavoidably acquire broad political connotations and challenge the overall framework in an explicit way. Meanwhile, the cities are inundated by growing numbers of asylum seekers, homeless people, drug addicts, and many more individuals that simply do not fit in, revealing the unequal way the state has until now defined the spaces assigned to its citizens. Interrupting the normal flow and spatial arrangement of things, people start becoming self-organised alongside those around them by occupying public spaces, mounting community events and forming neighbourhood assemblies. Local communities, which have been erased of any political content since the very foundation of the Greek state, appear now as an alternative political agent.

In the months following December, we, along with many people next to us, have started to acknowledge the surplus refugees that we ourselves are within our country (Agamben 1995: 119), within our towns and districts, and while the structures sustaining the world around us still remain intact we gradually become radically predisposed to understanding ourselves beyond their cognitive frame.

Dismantling Opposition

In stripping the system of its normality and legibility, this crisis made what we experienced throughout December all the more visible 175 and real. And, for this reason, our words and actions became dangerous for the maintenance of a system feeling insecure.

In the late modern conduct of affairs, conflict is declared to be finished, or impossible, and departs from politics in the name of rationally-achieved consensus. Any dissenting voice or communitarian attempt that shatters this contract seems like a relic from the past, or a temporary regression, so as to remain fragmented. But antagonisms and inequalities do not vanish and when conflict returns, as it recently did in a vulgar way in Greece, it can only be understood as radical evil and can only take the form of irrational violence or intolerance of the culturally different. Thus, the only remaining alternative way to represent and understand non-capitalist resistance is to push it to the margins and equate it with the label "extremism"; devoid of political content, which can equally be filled in with racist attacks, religious fundamentalism, or ultra-right-wing violence. Such pre-political violence can only be fought with repression, by introducing laws against "extremism,"[10] allowing for more police impunity, enhancing security forces and surveillance mechanisms around the country, and criminalising critical thinking and hitherto permissible protest activities, such as syndicalist protests and demonstrations. At the level of public opinion, state and media discourse violently attack protest mobilisations on a daily basis in an attempt to discredit and negate radical action and collective ethics as a political option. Power mechanisms must become more authoritarian so as to purge extremist forces and prevent the financial, institutional, and moral collapse of the country.

For the present order of things to be maintained, however, power also must respond somehow to the actual problems of the people suffocating within its contextual constraints. In any case, that is how capitalism managed to face the radical critique at the end of the 1960s and 1970s. Demands for autonomy and liberation of creativity, critique of hierarchy and bureaucracy—these were oppositional themes articulated during the "May events" that the system managed to recuperate. By mobilising pre-existing protests whose legitimacy was guaranteed, opposition was disarmed, initiative regained and a new dynamism discovered (Boltanski and Chiapello 2005). In today's crisis, the critique of the state as an apparatus of domination and oppression is gradually becoming a legitimate discourse written, heard, and communicated by many. Moreover, the demands for decentralisation and self-organisation emerge as a sound alternative to institutions that are corrupted and politicians who fail in making our lives any better. From right- and ultra-right-wing parties, socialist spokesmen, and NGOs to mainstream newspapers, free press, arty fanzines, and TV talk shows, public discourse gives birth to a new citizenship culture; while the boat is sinking, you must take things into your hands and do not expect anything from the state; defy governments and politics, mobilise beyond public institutions, challenge them by believing in yourself and friends, stop criticising others, "do it yourself," make your neighbourhoods look cleaner and safer, organise your own workplace, disgrace old-style ideologies, scientific analyses and revolutionary promises, act now, look alternative, be disobedient, be marginal.[11]

So, while direct action and political protests are persecuted and stigmatised at the level of political and social demands, anti-authoritarianism becomes at the same time a lifestyle in everyday culture endorsed and promoted by authorities themselves.

If that is the brave new world of wild possibilities and mortal challenges, then what is to be said? What is to be done?

3) OURSELVES BECOMING FOREIGNERS TO OUR LAND

During December, *After was turned into the Now and we were faced, as they were, with the Real.* For years we, the anarchist, anti-authoritarian, or libertarian movement, had been talking and shouting, acting irrationally, and believing passionately in self-organised communities of people and imaginative creativity in human relationships, in unmediated participation and committed action in everyday life, in decentralisation and re-occupation of vital urban spaces, in emancipation and solidarity, in violent resistance and never-ending revolt. It was due to our radical critique of everyday life that we had been cruelly criticised, marginalised, and persecuted for a long time and at every moment, it was due to our radical actions that we had been left alone. And then, December erupted. There it was—*reality denouncing the vanity of words and just what the words led us to expect. Beyond the analysis of the oppression or the feelings of duty towards the oppressed, there it was. The signs by which a gaze comes to recognize reality as exemplary of the idea and the idea comes to incarnate itself in a living landscape,* the lines and shadows of which created a new imagination for a world hitherto without images.

After December, we were faced, as they were, with what we had been aspiring towards for so long. And what we did at this liminal point is return to normal. This is not because the post-December realities disillusioned us; it is because we started gradually *to link the landscape we had experienced with our habits of belief, because we persisted in our gaze and reworked the way we knew all along to put together words and images*. After all, all those people around us were not critical enough, they did not have the experience and radicalism required to persist and the courage and commitment to go on, some of them had made compromises we detest and opted for ways of life we had been fighting, the majority of them are participants, after all, in the system we mean to demolish. Things did not happen as they should have and will not develop as they must, because, at the very end, they, and the others, cannot understand what we have been doing for so long. And we already knew they would not.

And so, we gradually lost what had bound us together with the rest of the people and we returned to the place we had always been. We kept on mounting individualised struggles that did not manage to touch upon overall political and economic conditions, when we had to relate to new realities and reinvent our tactics. We even kept on believing in manifestos for the reorganisation of society that failed to relate to society itself, when we had to communicate our principles and relate with people around us, we never ended up forming relations. We kept on rediscovering inequalities and never stopped speaking about an omnipotent present that contains no positivity other than an imagined negation, and failed to convince ourselves and others that we can do something more than be defeated. We started again to direct all our energy in fighting against the cops and the state, reoccupying the role of the marginalised and socially excluded that the system itself has prepared for us, a space reserved also for extremists and fascists working alongside the state. We destroyed and acted in symmetry with our repressors, when we had to move beyond the frame set by them. We kept on proclaiming self-organisation and decentralisation as our goals, when we had to make them our presupposition. We thought they did not see us, when they were already absorbing our critique and effacing our political agency. We vociferously shouted that we were against the system, when we had to create and reinforce non-capitalist, non-hierarchical, free and equal relationships, and multiply our stateless spaces and practices. We distrusted everybody, when we had to be in solidarity with everyone.

But we did not really care; we were used to being on the margins, after all. We believed that December and ourselves were both an exception to the rule.

But December emerged not because of us. It revealed, instead, that in an unjust universe the repressed learn to communicate without speaking, to step forward without moving, to resist without resisting. Throughout those days, all of us discovered ways to imply, to bewilder, and to be part of a whole, not to put into words, not to fit into words, ways to choose the margin and act in the centre, not to catechize or offer a paradigm, but to (re)open the eternally open and living area of possibilities, to be equal and to feel free. December, far from being an exception, contained the only normality that makes our living possible. This eternal present showed us the path towards a land not of fear and problems to be resolved but of collective illusions to be realised. *Under our gaze, to the rhythm of our steps, the images of the new world came into being and passed into the distance.* Now, it would be better to re-member how it was to be ready to win everything and lose nothing, to be no longer invisible, to relate endlessly with each other, how it was to set out on this voyage of moments never to return, *hanging until the final leap on the improbability and unpredictability of an encounter, 'the union of a long sentence with a bit of reality that is not.'* Local and contingent, mad and real, this land of ours *is on the point of disappear-ing and, thus, perhaps also on the point of reappearing.*

NOTES

1 I owe the title and parts of this text (in italics) to Jacques Rancière's introduction to *Short Voyage to the Land of the People* (Rancière 2003). Thanks to Regina and Giorgos for their comments and ideas.

2 Nietzsche, *Genealogy of Morals*. Or, in the words of Philip Roth (2004: 180–81), "My father chooses resistance, Rabbi Bengelsdorf chooses collaboration, and Uncle Monty chooses himself."

3 http://uk.youtube.com/watch?v=PK9lpMk7fiY&eurl, 16 December 2008, 15.12.

4 See also Radical Desire (2009) "Dossier: December: On the prose of Counter-Insurgency," [in Greek] http://radicaldesire.blogspot.com.

5 For example see Mouzelis, N. "Social Explosion and Civil Society," *To Vima*, 21 December 2008, [in Greek] http://www.tovima.gr/default.asp?pid=46&ct=72&artId=241057&dt=21/12/2008; Papatheodorou, Y. "The Symptom and the Crisis," *Nea Estia*, 1819, pp. 285–293, 2009 [in Greek]; Voulgaris, Y "The Rage of Impotence," *Ta Nea*, 11 December 2008 [in Greek] http://www.tanea.gr/default.asp?pid=10&ct=13&artID=4491662; or Alivizatos, N. "The Challenge of Violence: a Defeat of the Reformers," *Nea Estia*, 1819, pp 196–201, 2009 [in Greek].

6 For instance, the Contentious Politics Circle organising a related conference in December 2009; see http://contentiouspoliticscircle.blogspot.com.

7 Whether the Greek educational establishment, for instance, leads to the reproduction of inequality or to a possible reduction of inequality, the effect is still the same. See

Rancière 1991: vii–xxiii.

8 Main exponents of this perspective still are Kalyvas, S. "The culture of the *metapolitefsi*," *Kathimerini* 14 December 2008 [in Greek] http://news.kathimerini. gr/4dcgi/_w_articles_politics_2_14/12/2008_296059; Kalyvas, S. "…and what it was not," *To Vima* 6 December 2009, http://www.tovima.gr/default.asp?pid=2& ct=114&artid=303459&dt=06/12/2009; and Maratzidis, N. "Farce grecque: bilan d'une fausse révolte," *Le Monde* 28 April 2009 [in French] http://lexandcity.blogspot. com/2009/04/2008-monde.html and "The December events as farce," *To Vima* 21 December 2008 [in Greek] http://www.tovima.gr/default.asp?pid=46&ct=72&artId= 241058&dt=21/12/2008. See also Kanellis, I "The December culture," *Athens Review of Books* 3, 2009 [in Greek] http://www.booksreview.gr/index.php?option=com_ content&view=article&id=66:2009-12-23-12-57-03&catid=39:-3-2009-&Itemid=55.

9 The same seems to apply to the public narratives referring to the fall of the Junta, which is attributed consensually to the young generation of the time, while the participation of other groups of people is usually silenced.

10 See for instance the declaration "Fight against Extremism: Achievements, Deficiencies and Failures" passed by the Parliamentary Assembly of the Council of Europe on 5 October 2010, in which racist violence, religious fundamentalism, the anti-globalisation movement, and protests against repression (mentioning the case of demonstrations in Greece in 2009) are all labelled as "extremism." For a full text, see: http://assembly.coe. int/Mainf.asp?link=/Documents/WorkingDocs/Doc10/EDOC12265.htm.

11 In Greece, for instance, the ultra-right-wing parliamentary party incites citizens to take the law into their own hands and organise local assemblies so as to "clean" districts of homeless refugees, the Prime Minister congratulates youth NGOs that decide to mobilise on their own initiative in order, for instance, to make their neighbourhoods greener, TV shows wonder whether living in communitarian-style occupations is the solution to these individualistic times of ours, and well-known fashion companies persuade consumers that buying their products is so cool that "governments will hate you."

10

PAPER RIFLES

Kirilov

Four burnt cars, browned by flames, grayed by soot, are each stacked parallel; side by side by side by side, passenger doors laying face down on the pavement, driver's windows supinely watching the sky. The night before I arrived in Athens, the cars were overturned from their normal resting places and set ablaze to barricade the riot police from the gated entrance of the National Technical University. In a group of three we stood alone in front of the Polytechnic, granted with a rare and uncharacteristically quiet moment for that December, where only the sun, in a pitched battle with the clouds, gave any hints of a conflict. To finally settle on a mood, the day slowly deliberated upon a victor, and I took the same time to stare at the sedans, standing in a row perfectly equidistant from one another, resting like dominoes ready to fall with a child's nudge, and decided that the symmetrically aligned wreckage seemed more like an outdoor art sculpture commissioned for a city park than the aftermath of a revolt. Instead of black clad insurgents, I imagined druids—maybe the real-hooded ones, the *koukouloforoi*, reported by the Greek media—forgoing massive boulders for scorched cars and working unnoticed throughout the night to construct some sort of Brutalist Stonehenge. In my daydream these "known unknowns" labour carefully but efficiently, leaving the night undisturbed, to ensure the city will wake surprised in the quiet morning to an automobile monument devoted to the rebellion.

Savouring the fleeting calm, we're betrayed by our path, as the walk up Stournari street on a carpet of stones and shattered glass makes silent steps impossible. Drifting into Exarcheia, carried by something outside of myself, the spray-painted slogans and the colourful posters decorating what's left intact of the remaining architecture lose the competition for my attention to the charred skeleton of what was once a five-story building. Like a cancer spreading so fast its growth is visible, dark embers invade the remnants of the multiplex's walls. Last night's inferno robbed this former computer megastore of its façade, swallowing its silicone merchandise, replacing the edifice with a gaping, hollow cave. As caves will be caves, whether natural or man-made, playing out their role since antiquity, transmitting allegories, delivering messages, with blinding lights I came to recognize the foolishness in imagining this scene as a product of meticulous craftsmanship. Clearly, this was, and could only be, the unmistakable result of fury.

An excessive fury, an unremitting fury, a fury that cuts through space, crumbling windows, plucking throwing-stones from the concrete and finally burrows into people; shaking their inner-core like hands after a fist-fight. Once inside, the fury alters as it's altered, becoming wholly different while reciprocally evolving its inanimate host, molting its off dead, rotten layers, revealing new life. Abiding by a rationality unto itself, it travelled on a seemingly sporadic course, entering and escaping bodies, seeping into everything it encountered as the scent of sex soaks into whatever is present in a lover's hot summer bedroom. The swallowed razors, force-fed from birth, which regardless of our wish, we all painfully harbour inside us, from work, to school, to prison, and back to a home that's almost indistinguishable from the latter, were at last placed firmly in our hands. And that which was exempt from our slashes, those fragments of this filthy, miserable world we didn't hack to bits, were left to be enveloped, as the evil passions burrowed their way into the very substratum of reality, violently making changes at the level of pure substance, effacing each and every thing from the inside out.

> In this context of absurd and insupportable communication in which each is fatally held as in the trap of a paradoxical injunction—to 'speak' one must renounce 'communicating' and to 'communicate' one must renounce 'speaking'!

—Curcio and Franceschini (The Historical Founders of the Red Brigades)

Insurrection enters as much into people as into the depths of society. In their urgent task of demolition, the insurgency succeeds in taking the static, immutable nature of man as one of its many victims. Humanity is then approached as a real creation, a potential to be fulfilled in the constructed present. With the unfolding of new forms of life blossoms new ways of experiencing; of perceiving the environment and time, and new relations between people; interactions and communication. Displacing objects from their names, the signified from their signifier, rebellion empties out the things, which reality, in its perpetual surge, throws at our feet like the useless remains of shipwreck. Rather than re-establishing deeper meanings and alternative reference, new and unprecedented modes of human expression develop to coincide with the manifold changes, by instead, opening onto a field of possibilities.

Corralled back into the debilitating normality of everyday life, undermined by the armed peace that continually degrades legitimate experience and levels communication into flat information, I'm now nearly unable to recount what I witnessed during that warm December in Athens. Each attempt unfailingly descends into flowery hermeticism and jargon, coupled with unwanted verbal chiaroscuro effects: superlative and anecdotal exaggerations. To put this glossolalic condition in a far more blunt manner, one could say that the taste of freedom can never be articulated in a tongue accustomed to boot-licking.

Nevertheless, after countless unsuccessful efforts, what follows are a few more pale renderings of the images, emotions, and memories, which may have only been adequately depicted, during that all too brief period in my life, when I, amongst others, believed that anything could actually happen. Like stained emulsions held to dim light, each story intends to describe negatively the ineffable transformations in people, by detailing the inessential to somewhat delineate the essential. Unavoidably, this method produces inverted representations, where the light must appear dark and darkness appears as light. Thus due to the damage of time, the inevitable outcome of my offering is now the blurriest of portraits, pictures that could have only been seen clearly, while undergoing similar changes, from within those same lost moments.

> The time has come to reinstitute
> the morally just as the ultimate praxis.
> To make life into a poem.
> And life into praxis.

—Katerina Gogou

Unable to keep pace with the speed at which the events unfurled, my memories tend to blend and sometimes even collide with one another; as an effect, erasing from my mind instances I wish I could recall. And so, I can't remember exactly when I met him, yet thinking back to the demonstrations, the assemblies, and the gatherings I can often place him there. He was handsome, with a height that crouched slightly when he spoke to you, and like Orwell's Italian anarchist in *Homage to Catalonia*, his striking features told stories, detailing his personality; so swelled with candour there was no room left for ferocity. Without any of the fabled Italian's justified viciousness, his face was likely more moving and it also made you immediately like him. More importantly, I wanted him to like me; because he had a distinct way of greeting you with a smile that made you go inside yourself to recognize your very own uniqueness. Far too humble to command it, respect was instead willingly bestowed, not only due to the way he carried himself but likely because everyone else wanted a smile from him also.

During the last large demonstration in December, after the procession had ended, a clash had predictably erupted, only to be momentarily ceased by the riot police's Israeli tear gas searing open a sizeable space between them and us. From within the crowd, at a safe distance from the cops' batons, I could faintly make out something, that seemed like it was a universe away, moving in every direction except in line-formation with the MAT. You can suspect me all you want of over-embellishment, even condemn me of the charge, but I swear, this almost indiscernible object appeared to my two tear gas burned eyes as a star, enmeshed in all the instability and chaos of a ternary system. Given the complex dynamic between the MAT, the boulevard, and this nebulous mass, the way in which they repelled and attracted each other, emitting and exchanging waves of force, I cannot be convinced otherwise that what I observed was none other than the disorderly interaction of celestial bodies.

It wasn't until the triplet moved closer that I recognised him, alone. Rather than flashing his sought after smile, he instead, through a gas mask, bared his teeth at the line of riot cops like a careering ram set upon by bees. With more bestial qualities than human, he head-down crashed into their shields with the impact of a wild herd, and instantly after the collision, with a slight pivot, veered to the side and thrust himself into a bank with the same power, only to continue repeating the entire motion again and again.

With his back turned to the group of onlookers, he inched toward us after each smash, and from where I stood, I came to understand the Greek expression "gallons on his shoulders," as it became obvious he could carry us all in his backpack, unburdened by the weight, and continue fighting with the same intensity. Along with a few other internationals, I made a futile attempt at rushing in behind him only to be immediately pushed back, not by batons or concussion grenades, but by the energy the police let off as they moved in forward. Now only a few steps away from him, I could see that he was somehow granted with an extraordinary ability to relinquish any worn, rigid designation and transform into whatever suited him and his purpose at the moment. And after what proved to be a very careful selection, with the strength and agility of an athlete he charged into a bus-stop advertisement, and once it cracked to bits, with the beauty and grace of a dancer, he drifted past the riot polices' lunges and swings, to other side of the street. He then proceeded to hammer open the driver-side window of a sedan fortuitously parked at his destination, and while others came up to join him, his hand confidently reached into the car to yank it into neutral.

Now, look. I can go from city to city, or traverse the whole earth, by foot if necessary, surveying original works of art and seeing first-hand the monuments and wonders that entice us to reconsider the heights of mankind's aptitude. I can let my imagination place me in the audience of Théatre de Champs-Elysées to experience the original shock of a scandalous Nijinsky performance, or simply, lie down and dream the most fantastic dream. Yet measured against what occurred in that demonstration, the effective blurring of possibility and actuality, the powerful unification of what we are with what we can do, each of these, in comparison, would appear languid, uninspired, and even a bit hideous; merely subordinate images of beauty coloured by the subordinate existence assigned to us. Henceforth, from that day on, I can hereby state, with an unrivalled certainty, that all else is rendered an utter disappointment when judged next to the true experiment of living, where for him "the streets became brushes, and the squares became palettes"; the maximal dimension of human creativity which can only be conjured by invoking the Shiva-ite dance of destruction.

And to everyone's amazement, and with perfectly choreographed execution, the car was shifted into the middle of street, and with one sure heave, toppled at the line of equally astonished riot police, who finally stopped dead their advance only a few feet away.

> We'll be new, love,
> we'll wash away what is old and depraved,
> the putrid petty-bourgeoisie tendencies and vices
> with blood.

— Giaconda Belli

After almost two years of reflection and several return visits, I'm only now becoming capable of sifting through everything I witnessed to separate it into either cross-cultural phenomena, the specifically Greek, or relegating it to the bizarre happenstances wholly peculiar to insurrection. Since my introduction to Greece happened to also coincide with my very first uprising, some reflections still manage to be intractable combinations of the three, like for example, hearing for the first time the epic howls of Antartika, Greek Civil War music, blaring from the speakers of the occupied GSEE. Ceasing the passive reception of the senses which were instead felt intensely and antagonistically, the pulse of insurrection has the effect of amplifying commonplace circumstances that would normally fall into the former categories: I to this day still long, with an almost burdensome nostalgia, for the taste of the collectively looted food, and for the warmth, the odour, and the sound of dozens of exhausted insurgents, huddled together, sleeping in the first quiet place they could rest.

As for the rally that took place in front of the central Athens police station, it refuses to be classified amongst the others I've attended both past and present, standing as an example unto itself; not only because of what happened at the gathering but more importantly due to who showed up to it. That is to say, I'm completely sure that I'll never again see a rally with that many children, and I mean, literally, children, some as young as 10 or 11. And of all kinds, different attitudes and subcultural allegiances, including styles that scream apathetic and apolitical no matter the country: emo-kids, high-school football stars, prom kings and queens. From a distance, you could barely notice the leftist blemishes in the sea of kids, as the old paper-peddlers were almost indiscernible from the taller seniors of equal height. The rebellion had joyously lifted all the seriousness from the usually solemn ritual, and while some, in tiny groups laughed, chatted, and gossiped in that way that only school children can do, others took to playfully humiliating the cops, pelting them with eggs, tomatoes, and oranges.

After looking backwards to ensure that their friends approvingly watched, the braver ones lobbed stones at the police guarding the station. Once the trend caught on, the MAT, unable to bear the smallest reprisal for their daily behaviour, fired a tear gas canister into the crowd. After the shot, a riot ensued and people dispersed and scattered without any preset plan or direction, in and out of the side streets and back and forth from the main boulevard. The shuddering explosions of concussion grenades, the heat from the flames, the shrieking, screeching snaps of the riot police shields split by stones, each vying for pronunciation within the chaos.

Given the randomness of the situation, we made a totally random turn onto a seemingly deserted street, which would have been completely isolated had it not been for the presence of an adolescent boy, around the hard-to-pin-down age of thirteen. We almost failed to recognize him, as the only part of his little frame that appeared to us were his feet dangled inches above the ground. The remainder of his body was swallowed whole in the mouth of a large garbage dumpster. Likely due to inexperience, it was taking him an unexpectedly long time to light the contents of the bin on fire. The consequent frustration totally absorbed him in his task, which at the same time, made him unaware of anything happening in his periphery. Thus, he failed to notice a woman, dressed in a business-casual suit typical for her age, slowly approaching him from behind. The woman, who could have easily been his mother, had taken shelter in a shop once the riot began, yet assuming the worst of the storm had passed, she ventured into the desolate road. Very gently, she reached her hand into the dumpster to place it on the boy's shoulder. We were too far away to hear exactly what she said to the startled boy, who abruptly turned toward her quite surprised by the touch, so we rushed in towards them, only to gradually slow our pace once we realised the woman was only interested in chastising the child with the same maternal affection a young mother scolds her own adorable, yet troublesome, toddler.

If the jolted boy had been a seasoned militant, grasped from behind by someone he didn't immediately recognize, especially while in the process of committing a crime, he would have responded to her reprimands with a firm crack to the jaw, in order to clear a path for escape. Instead, he stared confidently into her eyes, unresponsively; the words aimed at him each time missing their impassable target. His newfound self-assurance did not arise from the affectations of a hardened militant, yet neither did he react with the disposition of a normal child, who commonly shrinks under the castigation of a superior. Declining his fixed role in the usual exchange between authoritative adult and minor, the boy remained in a subtle limbo, rejecting the attribution of another character. Furthermore, it became obvious he was unwilling to accept any other imposed mode of conduct or behaviour. Swelling with disobedience, you could practically see his person fraying at its edges. The power released by his rejections began to mount a tension. So confusing and uneasy was the tension that I couldn't decide whether I wanted to it continue or end. Never cowering or releasing the now baffled and disturbed woman from his stare, he finally broke the suspense, and told her, very matter-of-factly, "Fuck you and your capitalist dreams."

Briskly turning his back to the woman, who so rudely interrupted him, he instantly set back to work trying to ignite that all too stubborn trash on fire.

> Class struggle… is a fight for the crude and material things without which no refined and spiritual things could exist. But these latter things, which are present in the class struggle, are not present as a vision of spoils that fall to the victor. They are alive in this struggle as confidence, courage, humour, cunning and fortitude, and have effects that reach far back into the past. They constantly call into question every victory, past and present, of the rulers. As flowers turn toward the sun, by dint of a secret heliotropism, the past strives to turn toward that sun which is rising in the sky of history. The historical materialist must be aware of this most inconspicuous of all transformations.

—Walter Benjamin

As often as I'm asked to share my experiences from December, I'm just as frequently asked to give some sort of explanation as to how and why it happened. Yet to provide an adequate response, similar problems once again arise. For insurrection, by its very nature, refuses to be situated or interpreted: it is the unforeseen inception of the new that can never be translated back into the terms which preceded it. The event itself is a splitting off from, a fracture, a total break with causality. The shocks of its rupture multiply into a crescendo of lawless swerves counteracting any preconceived forms of determinism, circumventing placement in mechanistic models. Its effects are wholly irreducible to the previous conditions—and so, all the mindless €700 generation talk is an exercise in nonsense. Attempting to restore linearity after the fact amounts to nothing more than a plot to rob the uprising of its novelty—a plundering of what made it singular and unique. Any worthwhile explanation undoubtedly must rely on a notion as conceptually untameable, uncategorizable, and idiosyncratic as the rebellion itself; that being, the struggle.

"What strikes me in the Marxist analyses," Michel Foucault once noted, "is that they always contain the question of 'class struggle' but that they pay little attention to one word in the phrase, namely, 'struggle'." And the same can be said for all pacified answers to the social question; that is, when communism rusts into people's republics and anarchism retreats into bland anti-authoritarianism, each tendency, in their ossified form, will focus mainly on defining class, its boundaries, membership, and composition, leaving aside the far more important complexities brought forth by the antagonistic confrontation between the opposing classes. Following the icy road laid by abstraction, the ideologists, regardless of their intention, cross over into the enemy's ranks, joining the other courtly scribes of democracy's kingdom. The host of specialists, the psychologists, the sociologists, the journalists, etc. (all more aptly described as morticians), each in their own servile way, quench Power's need, on both a macro and micro level, to continually produce, convey, and disseminate its truths. This process of systematisation, on the one hand, works to represent order and its institutions as a functional requirement, a natural necessity: "What appears is good; what is good appears." On the other hand, it disqualifies incompatible modes of understanding; sanitising rebellion, reconciling the irreconcilable, rendering the ever present possibility for resistance unthinkable.

An explanation of insurrection demands a very different method of inquiry: a militant research that does not simply interpret and analyse reality, but modifies it; the excavation of truths that not only dismiss those ordained and sanctioned, but also undermine their procedures of legitimisation; knowledges that are not simply attained, but instead strategically and tactically deployed. The struggle itself therefore becomes a matrix of intelligibility deriving its explanatory capacity incisively from the life and death combat between the oppressed and the oppressors, the dominated and dominators, the exploited and the exploiters. Through the lens of aggression, tension, and hostility, the evolutionary vision of history dissipates, replacing the illusions of progress with a new frame of reference, which instead views the past as an uninterrupted and permanent war that rages even in seemingly tranquil periods. From the standpoint of the engaged conflict, the previous eras are then correctly conceived as a succession of victories and defeats in an ongoing war where, 'til this day, the winner still remains undecided.

This actively-elabourated coalescence of theory and practice enables one to understand the past, present, and future, as well as the secret bond between them. Thereby, the relation between today and yesterday ceases to be unilateral: in an eminently reciprocal process, the present illuminates the past and the illuminated past becomes a force in the present. The past is lit by the light of today's battles, by the sun rising in the firmament of history. In the above quote, Benjamin employs a double metaphor about the sun, to elude to it also as the traditional image of the German worker's movement, as in the anthem of the Social Democratic party: "Brothers, to sun, to freedom!" But instead of a flower, in regards to the Greek experience, we would find a more ligneous plant with "a dint of a secret heliotropism." Mimicking insurrection's bifurcation of society, the binary division which follows the open declaration of civil war, the striving flower should thus be replaced by the tree described in a poem by Yiannis Ritsos, which "never produced flower or fruit, only a far-stretching shadow that split the garden in two..."

An ancient olive tree, with a trunk with many rings and much history: here the German invasion, and here the Civil War and after that the regime of the Colonels. Here the partisans led by Velouchio-tis, and here the first Dekemvriana [See Glossary] and the Polytechnic Uprising, and here the Resistance, and more Resistance, and more and more Resistance: terror, civil strife, the mountain of Gramos, the islands of detention, and the death camps. Victories and defeats. Year by year a glorious history, a whole history, and throughout the years, the starving and the dispossessed, the disabled and thoroughly dead. And here, among the finer rings, are the riots of '85 and '86, the student unrest and murder of Nikos Temponeras, the dismal mass arrest at the Polytechnic, and the past decade's revitalised movement. Amidst the finest rings, the lean years are the children, all the young *antartes* [partisans], taken away to Tashkent, the Queen's "Children Cities," and the detention camps, and others left to die; here we find Michalis Kaltezas and Alexis Grigoropoulos, never to grow up to go grey, and to wrinkle, and to shrink, but to be fifteen forever—never to outgrow their heroic age.

To stretch this metaphor somewhat more, I might add that the bulk of the trunk is mostly comprised of a lighter wood, a negative space separate yet adjacent and bordering on the annual rings. And if we liken the rings to the efforts of historians, scribes, archivists, and even the memories affably shared by friends, then that lighter, less pronounced area in the bole that surrounds the concentric circles ought to coincide with everything that has escaped our memories, the records, all the books and news reports, and with that which has even exceeded our collective consciousness. This is exigency; it is that which must remain unforgettable, even if no one remembers it. It consists of the heroics of the far too modest comrade who now, after the fact, refuses to trade boastful December stories; the wild and rebellious, yet month-long, life lived by the shy school child who, pressured by society, has now returned to her desk and back within herself; and the presence of the unknown immigrants who were arrested, and subsequently, deported back to their native countries without legal process or court identification. We'll, of course, never "know" them, but without them, we would have never known a December 2008.

Furthermore, if every instant of that month were to be catalogued down to the very last second, there would be that which would nonetheless evade capture, fleeing into the shapeless chaos of the forgotten which is neither inert or ineffective, but rather, persistently follows reality; surrounding it, tracking it, haunting it. This exigency encroaches on the normal state of affairs, demanding its proper possibility, awaiting the revelatory moment when civilisation is once again exposed as one long, extended and barbaric catastrophe, to then reappear with all the destructive vengeance of a biblical storm. No way does this entail patiently waiting for the day of reckoning when the repressed return, in fact, it dictates the opposite; an active and inextinguishable fidelity to the mass of the forgotten. That is, a responsibility to respond to exigency by allowing it to shape each of our pursuits, whether individual or collective.

In the case of human communication, the faithful response does not simply mean commemorating the forgotten by bringing that which was lost back to life in words, or rather, constructing alternative histories and traditions to restore the memory of the oppressed and defeated. These attempts at reviving the forgotten are as futile as the earlier mentioned attempts to recount their welcomed re-emergence during revolts, uprisings, and insurrections. Conversely, history and tradition as such are only possible and transmissible due to exigency itself as it founds, determines, and underlies the status of all knowledge and understanding. It persists in the infinitely greater value found in what is left unsaid by what is said, by what is ineffably shown as opposed to what has been clearly articulated in any essay, poem, or page of sheet music worth the tree from which it came. To position the unspoken remainder, surrounding the enunciated letters and sounds, inside the text is both impossible and improper. The only importance of that which is spoken relates to the mass of the forgotten indirectly, as a contribution to the preparation for their return: a push towards the full completion of the revolutionary project through the destruction of the realm they refuse to inhabit. If I have here fallen short of this responsibility, because my powers are insufficient to cope with the task, then, to paraphrase Titos Patrikios: let each of these pages be converted into paper rifles used to overthrow regimes. With lips sealed and pens serving only as lances, let silence dominate. Until then, on the eve of every general reshuffling of society, the last and only words will be: "Combat or death: bloody struggle or extinction. It is thus that the question is inexorably put."

—Kirilov

11

NOTHING HAPPENED:

A LETTER FROM ACROSS THE ATLANTIC

Some of Us

To our friends in Greece,

We've been meaning to write to you for some time, to answer your call. We've never managed to. In fact, we'd never really tried—until now. The truth is, we haven't been doing too well. We realized we don't have a lot to say about what happened in Greece. Nothing happened here.

It is not that people weren't watching, thinking, and talking about those days of fire, yet it seems to us now that the uprisings and occupations brought into focus our own impotency. We questioned our faith, we stared at our own banality. It is embarrassing, the degree to which nothing happened here, and in fact, the degree to which nothing happening has become the norm. A norm we reproduce with each tired demonstration, each rush towards the cops, each poster promising something else which has no footholds, no traction on the real terrain in which we live.

What were we doing in 2008 when Greece was on fire? In an airport lobby, one of us wanted to switch flights, hop on the plane to Athens. A few others kept a blog, translated, and spread updates. Still others made posters and graffiti. There was talk. Greece echoed against the spontaneous riots that happened in Montreal two months earlier after cops killed a young man, Fredy Villanueva. We thought that something might be about to ignite here too.

A support demonstration for Greece was organized, people "attended." We were there too; we walked, we shouted slogans. People were throwing shoes at an image of Bush outside the American consulate just down the street from the Greek consulate on the day of the solidarity action. Truth be told, it was depressing. We became part of a charade in which all meaning was void before action had even begun. While Greece was burning and being re-occupied, we passed text messages of what was happening during an event organized for Fredy Villanueva. At the Villanueva demonstration, we took part in a simulated game of dice, what the kids were playing when the cops killed the fifteen-year-old boy. It was surreal. A stage-play in which no one knew anymore who were the actors and who were the stage-managers. We became lost in the labyrinth of our lack of faith.

The crisis deepened. We felt the rupture and we felt the continuity. We were still surrounded by the banality.

WE WERE SURROUNDED BY OUR OWN BANALITY

We wondered what it felt like there. Did it feel less banal? Were the fires in the streets warming the relations between people, were there real cracks opening in the possibilities of democracy, of anarchism, of communization?

When we think of you now, we remember that the news from your side of the world did resound with meaning, gave us shivers and gusts of hope, made sense to us, resembled us, spoke a language we knew and wished to speak.

Watching the insurrection and the occupations unfold that December was pure joy. A genuine anti-capitalist rebellion was underway with a serious critique of social relations, of the commodity, and the state. We watched attentively as sites of state domination and capital accumulation were attacked, as normality was ruptured, as objects and spaces were subverted, reappropriated. Banks on fire. Cops, police departments, ministries, department stores, state buildings. The enemy was everywhere and everywhere under attack. Universities, workplaces, and public buildings occupied. New networks forged, alliances made and acted upon. Lines of communication opened, popular assemblies flourished. Things had meaning, actions connected to concrete realities. At least temporarily, the state seemed uprooted from absolute power. It seemed to us, even if only in small ways, that the world was being re-inhabited by people who shared our love and our rage. We know it was not simple or easy, those days, but these tangible solutions and articulations ignited our imaginations and inspired us. It was a force that we had never experienced here, and before that time, we must admit, a myth we hardly believed in anymore. Yet that December we felt a part of it. It felt like us, our time.

Since then, we have also watched the recapture. "Austerity," imposition, debt, fiscal terrorism, recession, strike, class struggle, oppression, division. These are our times too.

Back here, we try to hold onto those concrete inspirations. But every space is colonized by absence, every image a numbing device, every word a prison. The response to our sad gestures is a terse, "too bad," or a swift dousing by large amounts of cops, infiltrators, surveillance systems, and violence. Quebec Prime Minister Jean Charest reacted to the outcry against drastic cuts in social spending with a "they'll have to live with it." At the G8/G20 in Toronto, the predictable smashing of a few shop windows justified the largest mass arrest in Canadian history.

This was only the culmination of a long process, leaving us stranded, exhausted, and clearly under tight surveillance, amplifying the sense that we, too, are living under a fast-growing fascism. Twenty thousand riot cops for three thousand demonstrators. A billion dollars spent on summit "security." Over a thousand arbitrary arrests and detentions, sexual and physical threats and abuses towards those that were arrested. Prominent social justice activists from across the country charged with conspiracy against the state. All this won the movement little outside a few open letters and editorials in the press, now duly processed in recycling facilities. Left movements to wage costly, arduous, and only modestly useful legal battles.

THERE IS NOTHING NEW HERE

We recognize that you are no less constrained than we are by these powerful global forces. We know you live in this desert too. We are not making excuses for ourselves, just trying to speak honestly to make sense of where we find ourselves, now.

We would love to provoke eruptions of life, material or symbolic perturbations of the ambient normality. Yet it seems suicidal to throw ourselves into the mega-violence of the state, or vain, likely to be re-territorialized by the yuppie art scene, the municipal government, or the like. Often, actions that do happen end up feeding the spectacle that salivates for the next anarchist threat, or worse, providing a ready-made, creative "solution" to urban "problems" for institutional planners. Either hardly constitutes a force. While writing this we were interrupted with phone calls about more ongoing secret security visits to the homes of our friends. Even the traditional anti-summit demonstrations in which we still sometimes feel a duty to participate are met with a large-scale military apparatus and energy-consuming criminalization.

More and more what we understood as social death looks like social killing. It is an active machine. Living in the desert of social death is hard enough; now any actions in contestation to the state are met, anticipated even, with killing devices.

THESE KILLING DEVICES, THEY MAY BE NEW

Even the liberals are starting to understand as they too are parcelled out, denied, abused, and discarded. But we still avoid facing our impotence. We feel lost. Is the terrain shifting or static?

We must start from where we are. A landscape riddled with foreclosed homes, environmental genocide, and corporate violence, where every aspect of bare life must be paid for. The problems are so transparent that the targets should be obvious. Yet how to engage?

We know the impotence we see is not strictly our fault, or the fault of the movements we often participate in. It is not only because they should have been better, quicker, faster, or more militant. This impotence is merely the shadow we throw as we stand in this desert, and it grows as the desert extends, and the desert sun saturates us.

We are the crisis, but we are also in crisis. We reproduce the time and space of an increasingly crazy capitalism, organizing flash actions around the flavour of the day. We run after emergencies, act out spectacles. The crisis has many faces.

Some of us rush towards the ascetic, becoming the priests and nuns in the high church of a purified ethical living: wearing the black costume of the righteous, fleeing from affective connection, afraid to touch one another, to infringe upon one another, guarding a liberal individualist space. Where your freedom ends, mine begins. We know that activism is its own virulent liberalism, that it recreates the isolation we fled from in the first place, why do we keep forgetting? We recoil at its tyranny. We become indignant or indifferent.

Some of us chase ambulances—follow the violent eruptions of capital and the state, accumulating and appropriating oppressions, unable out of the sheer fatigue from our running to create a real centre, a focal point, beyond the march, the meeting, the controlled protest. We chase some of these ambulances just in the hopes of meeting each other again before returning to our lives. We even sometimes feel excited to say, "Let's meet at the barricades." We report again with outrage the latest injustice from the sidelines. Tire ourselves demanding small concessions that the state gobbles up, sometimes spits back at us.

THIS IS THE ONLY SITUATION; THEREFORE THERE IS NO SITUATION

From this absence, we watched you irrupting into dreamtime—the insurrectionary moment. We felt so disempowered, if inspired. These days, we don't dare hoping for an epic insurrection. It is not coming here. We have entertained this myth, this understanding of insurrection as *the* moment of possibilities with no before, and a hazy after. It will not emerge from our Hail Marys. Neither from our theatrics. Our insurrection must be de-sanctified.

What did you do after the fires had gone out? In asking this, we ask ourselves, too, what do we find in our quiet days, in the shadows of resistance, which still inspires and renews us?

We need a code, a genealogy, connecting insurrection to our everyday. Revolutions cannot be reduced to the moment of culmination and release. Rather a continual breaking from the absence and a rupture from normality. It is the moment when something happens and subverts, but also, that persists. A mode of being that grows, a commons that disposes us towards action.

And so, amidst the desert and the killing, the flattening out and strangling of life, we must wonder how to resurrect, create, protect, and enrich our dispositions and possibilities.

We can no longer participate in propping up this absence, maintaining the minimal "necessary" adaptations and changes that restore our faith, but only help manage the abstractions that govern our lives. We want to find our faith in the present. We want to inhabit it. To push these multiple and intersecting crises towards their limits.

Within the desert, there is no dialogue to entertain, no roads to be paved, no future to expect, no choice to make, not even a refusal to hide behind. And beyond it all, we still want to share our dangerous, beautiful gifts. To elaborate a way of being together.

Communization, a whisper of revolution. Even here we feel shyness, an embarrassment. But no, we will not "collectivize the means of production" or recreate the totalizing community. If we hear words as signs, potential sites where we can meet, commons and communization point towards a way out. Dis-objectification, de-subjectivisation, sensualisation, singularisation. The sensuous world cannot be possessed, be it by one or many, but only bears histories, memories, affects. 197

There are no singular beings that are definable, categorisable, predictable, or commandable. There are only sites where memories, histories, feeling, affects, and potentials converge as a force that manifests. This is the language, the gestures, we have recognized in your actions. Perhaps this is what we share—what we want to share.

WE ARE LEFT WITH MANY MORE QUESTIONS THAN RESPONSES

Maybe we shouldn't have taken up the pen at all, tonight. We have failed, we are failing. But we hope we are not too far-gone into the heat and toxicity of the desert to be of use. We need to intensify the communication. We want to seize something we will not surrender. Can we cross borders, or does this un-ground us from the places and ways we must re-inhabit our lives and our territories? Are territories themselves imaginable anymore? We will push our translations across these frontiers. This will un-ground us. We will re-ground. We will de-inhabit and re-inhabit. For now, perhaps we can only be honest about our positions, failings, dreams, and desires. Try to build strength among us that might create the conditions for firmer, more fertile ground.

Ignite, friends,
Some of Us

12

THE COMMONALITIES OF EMOTION:
FEAR, FAITH, RAGE, AND REVOLT

Soula M.

During December's revolt a single phrase was being repeated in smaller or larger groups of people, in assemblies, forums, and amphitheatres. *What is happening here exceeds us.* What did this phrase describe? Who would expect to process the revolution, who could ever expect to have complete control over a concurrence such as December?

What traversed this question was the dominant masculine and bourgeois ideology of having control even of a revolt. What traverses this stance in return is the belief that the revolt expresses you to the fullest extent. No rupture or crack, no doubt or hesitation can question the justness, the truth of the revolt—neither, in return, your belief in it. Even the way in which one might view the dynamics of social relationships cannot help but be affected by these taken-for-granted beliefs. In an article referring to an occurrence parallel to that of December (without going into much detail, since this does not concern our present subject) the comrade, writing straightforwardly, concluded he did not see any fear in the faces of those who stood next to him in struggle.[1] Of course, feelings are expressed to the extent they are allowed to be. And for them to be allowed means they are de-fetishised —that is, that the social relationships producing them are unveiled. The importance of their subjectivisation rests with the fact that they are not limited to the private sphere but rather, they are produced, accrued, reproduced, and fulfilled in the public sphere, where we live ourselves and our relationships as they are and as we would not know them to be until we got in touch with others. After all, what we are describing here is not a phobia (even though we would not mind such reactions too). 5 May was a sad proof that fear is objective, that there are indeed risks and dangers for which no one wants to claim responsibility. Quite the opposite: at that moment, after the shock of the deaths in the Marfin bank, we rushed from different viewpoints to distance the means from our goals, to question the unity of the movement, to wonder about the monsters the rage of the revolted can ferment, to target the spectacular misanthropy, nihilism, and antisocial stance—all of which become ideological and, without being analysed, are uncritically headed in inexplicable directions. That moment comprised a sad occasion to put forth critiques and analyses that prioritise the socialising of our premises, the formation of structures of self-organisation, and the importance of social liberation.[2]

After 5 May we can say that even if there was no fear during December there probably should have been. Yet masculinity, which describes the dominant imaginary of the revolt of the metropolis and the violence with which this is expressed, knows how to take risks without claiming responsibility.[3] And this is probably the reason why there was no fear in the faces of the revolted.

On 15 December 2008, the Haunt of Albanian Migrants published a text on assassinations preceding the one of Grigoropoulos which did not see this kind of mourning in response.[4] Its title was "These Days Are Ours, Too" and it said the following:

> These days are for the hundreds of migrants and refugees who were murdered at the borders, in police stations, workplaces. They are for those murdered by cops or 'concerned citizens.' They are for those murdered for daring to cross the border, working to death, for not bowing their head, or for nothing. They are for Gramos Palusi, Luan Bertelina, Edison Yahai, Tony Onuoha, Abdurahim Edriz, Modaser Mohamed Ashtraf and so many others that we haven't forgotten.
>
> These days are for the everyday police violence that remains unpunished and unanswered. They are for the humiliations at the border and at the migrant detention centres, which continue to date. They are for the crying injustice of the Greek courts, the migrants and refugees unjustly in prison, the justice we are denied. Even now, in the days and nights of the uprising, the migrants pay a heavy toll — what with the attacks of far-righters and cops, with deportations and imprisonment sentences that the courts hand out with Christian love to us infidels.

Another group that appeared during the days of December were the "Purple hoodies." In a text read out during a public concert in Athens they wrote that they also add to the list of victims of state terrorism and police violence (brought to the fore by the assassination of Alexandros Grigoropoulos) the twenty women assassinated, after 1980, by their policemen husbands and lovers—in most cases in honour kill-ings and without the assassins facing any consequences whatsoever.[5] December's gender is analysed in detail in an article by the group Ter-minal119, "Did December Have a Gender?"[6] and for this reason we will not elaborate further here. Yet as this analysis shows, December was masculine and therefore it was neither the same by all nor for all.

Our rage then, the rage of the revolted, was from the start a product of what the revolted would "impromptu" destroy. "Women" and the "foreigners" are both often and in a stereotypical way distanced and categorised as partial and thematic issues for some of the tenden-cies of our movement. And it was they, in other words, who came to identify the partiality, the limits, the contradictions and commonality of December's events. Without meaning to write off the importance of this revolt, its beginning might have signalled its end, since its meanings were entrapped in a given normality—and therefore faced their own limitations in return. On the other hand, December was the ground upon which such a critique and self-critique could stand; some ground that does not polemically isolate two parts but instead stretches the lim-its of the existing and conceived space of our movement.

The importance of December, after all, is confirmed by this endurance of its meanings, which were so strong as to exceed even the conjuncture itself and its subjects, without shaking either to the ground. Without these politics being competitive, they are forced to compete with a politics that has priority and, since it claims for itself the univer-sal, excludes all those for whom we were not enraged enough, neither we smashed everything up. December exceeded us as many things do—just like its evolution, its result and even its beginning also did. Because this beginning did not entirely depend on "us." Its result and its analysis however stand in correlation—if not some direct connection—to our action and contents.

Many creative initiatives followed the days of December. Thankfully so, since the slogan-chanting and the clashes in the streets seem inadequate to open up new horizons in the movement, unless they are complemented or preceded by structures of reproduction, the imagination and socialisation of which can potentially widen the move-ment's fields of action and creativity in directions that street action and current affairs alone can't—apart from a social mark and the neces-sary commitment to existing and urgent conditions of power. A beloved writer would say that she writes by letting her subconscious run free while keeping control at the same time.[7] This seems to be a recipe true for every temper, for creativity that is not limited to a single moment but commits itself and takes the responsibility not to control things but to offer them meaning—that is, to radically change their condition. Or else: "If Marxism is a direction, anarchism is life. Even if we know (being the adults that we are) that we must give direction to our lives, we should also remember, since we want to become children whilst maturing, never to stop giving life to the direction."[8]

Bourgeois propaganda attempted to claim December as its own and will continue doing so for as long as the politics of human rights keeps aestheticising "revolution," having the means, the words, the armies, and the weapons, and above all, the consciousnesses on its side. We saw December become Greek and masculine. We saw the plexus of the bourgeois continuum claim the revolt, talking of the innocence of the assassinated child, depoliticising the explosions of the social war.[9] We saw the people in revolt imaginarily inscribe the culture of spectacle with and upon its body, we saw it limit itself within given ways of life, action, practice, politics and relationships which set limitations to, (anti-)normalising our lives.

If there is one qualm we have with the lucrative response of the comrades from Canada, it would be the fetishising of December. That nevertheless beautiful December, which by now signals not some distance in space and time (for which we second the sadness or nostalgia) but a loss, some void highlighting the decontextualised present. December became that which we had not thought possible to live. And we were there in order to change ourselves and December at the same time. With our privileges, our inequalities, our contradictions, our looted subconsciousnesses, our authoritarian behaviours. Since the relic not recognised by the authoritarianism of dialectics is the space of subjectivity—that is, the only opportunity offered to us, to an extent, to exercise our freedom. And for as long as it happened, December would keep becoming something more twisted, more scared—and it keeps constantly becoming something else, something less known, the more it becomes distant and we continue reading it. It becomes the "other" December we have yet to live.

NOTES

1 http://lapositiondutireurcouche.blogspot.com/2010/11/rocky-road-to-dublin.html

[in Greek].

2 Without accepting the style nor the self-referentiality of the text "The morbid explosion of Ideology," the analysis of the treatment and functions of violence from parts of the antagonist movement seem to us to be extremely accurate: http://www. occupiedlondon.org/blog/2010/05/11/289-the-morbid-explosion-of-ideology/.

3 See "Masculinities: Stories of the Gender and Other Relationships of Authority," issue 4, page 12, http://www.qvzine.net [in Greek].

4 http://www.occupiedlondon.org/blog/2008/12/15/these-days-are-ours-too/.

5 http://katalipsiasoee.blogspot.com/2008/12/blog-post_1744.html [in Greek].

6 http://www.terminal119.gr/show.php?id=524.

7 We refer to Margarita Karapanou and what she said in a TV interview.

8 http://radicaldesire.blogspot.com/2011/01/blog-post_12.html [in Greek].

9 Regarding the political character of the assassination of Alexis and the attempt to de-politicise it see the article "I Seek You in the Shiny Abattoirs of the Streets," http://katalipsiasoee.blogspot.com/2008/12/blog-post_1343.html [in Greek].

PART THREE

THE CRISIS

13

THE GREEK ECONOMIC CRISIS AS EVENTAL SUBSTITUTION

Christos Lynteris

A year after everyone in Athens was talking in terms of an uprising, today everyone is talking in terms of a crisis. A concept that seems only natural by now, crisis has in fact been an exceptionally complex medico-juridical invention of Western civilisation. As Michel Foucault (2006: 237) taught in his 23 January 1974 lecture at the Collège de France, in Greco-Roman medicine and in much of medieval alchemy and its related medical practices "there is always a moment for the truth of the illness to appear. This is precisely the moment of the crisis, and there is no other moment at which the truth can be grasped in this way." The contribution of Foucault here is crucial: if we are used to seeing the term crisis within economic or political discursive contexts, the fact that its position there seems natural or even intrinsic and inescapable is due to a much older cultural familiarisation with the term as a phenomenon of human physiology and pathology. Crisis, as it appeared for the first time during the classical age, comprises the opportunity [*kairos*] *par excellence* of truth, the time when all phenomena and illusions give way before a momentary and fully recognizable explosion of the true substance of the human condition. In other words, *krisis*, both crisis and judgement, is a concept that brings to the surface a new kind of truth, a new series of techniques of capturing the truth, and, of course, a new subject of securing the truth. As Foucault (2006: 237) noted, according to the classical medical model this "truth is not lying there waiting to be grasped by us; it passes, and it passes rapidly, like lightning; it is in any case linked to the opportunity, to the *kairos*, and must be seized." This truth is *rare* precisely because it appears exclusively as an evental truth (or a truth-event *chez* Foucault); because it "belongs not to the order of what it is, but to the order of what happens, a truth, therefore, which is not given in the form of a discovery, but in the form of an event" (ibid: 237). As a consequence this truth "does not call for method, but for strategy," which Foucault (2006: 237) elaborates on as a belligerent-predatory and at the same time ritual relation to the ailment under examination. Crisis is that event which at the same time forces us and allows us to structure a strategic fidelity with regard to a general-historic truth that it underlines and which is nothing less than the void of the previous situation responsible for the crisis: the structural weakness, the anomaly or pathology that is the symptomal kernel around which all the truth of the patient is structured and sustained.

As Alain Badiou has demonstrated, an event is never an autonomous incident independent from the struggle of decisions that unfolds on the basis of the imaginary field of its causes and effects. Slavoj Žižek (1999: 140) writes in *The Ticklish Subject*, in explication: "A true Event emerges out of the 'void' of the Situation; it is attached to its *element surnumeraire*: to the symptomatic element that has no proper place in the situation, although it belongs to it." Badiou's formula posits the connection of the event with that "for which" it comprises an event, as *the void of the previous situation*: "What do we mean by that? We mean that in the centre of every situation, there lays, as its foundation, an in-place void, an element around which is organised the fullness (or the stable multiples) of this situation" (Badiou 2007: 76). Thus, according to Badiou, the formative characteristic of an event is that it is "simultaneously *in-place*, it is the event of this or that situation—and *in-excess*, thus totally separate or disconnected from all the rules of the situation" (ibid: 76). This in-place void is no less than the habitus of the decision that constitutes the event as such. For as Žižek (1999: 136) argues, "the undecideability of the event means that an event does not posses any ontological guarantee: it cannot be reduced to (or deduced, generated from) a (previous) situation: it emerges 'out of nothing,' the nothing which was the ontological truth of this previous Situation."

The event is thus "always recognised as such retroactively, through an act of Decision that dissolves it—that is by means of which we already pass over it" (ibid: 137–138). In other words, it is constituted via the struggle regarding the void, the imagined fundamental truth of the preceding situation leading to its constitution. Likewise, in classical medicine crisis as a physiological event was not some objective moment in one's medical history, but the result of a decision, or more correctly of the struggle of decisions that constituted the preceding situation as a field where no substantial decision could be made as the revelatory evental truth remained latent or dormant: "Prior to Decision, we inhabit a Situation which is enclosed in this horizon; from within this horizon, the Void constitutive of the Situation is by definition invisible; that is to say, undecideablility is reduced to—and appears as—a marginal disturbance of the global System. After the Decision, undecideability is over, since we inhabit the new domain of Truth" (ibid: 138). Thus the crisis must be seen, with Lukács (2000: 55), as "a situation whose duration may be longer or shorter, but which is distinguished from the process that leads up to it in that it forces together the essential tendencies of that process, and demands that a *decision* be taken over *the future direction of the process.*" Hence, classical medicine was organised around the truth of the crisis, as the liminal state of the illness where all that is potential becomes concrete: "The crisis is the reality of the disease becoming truth, as it were. And it is precisely then that the doctor must intervene" (Foucault 2006: 243).

In this perspective, the crisis is not merely some acute moment in a linear development of deterioration of a pathogenic condition, but a real moment of battle, a moment where the outcome of battle is decided: the battle of the body with its own pathogenic elements, the battle of solids with humours, or in today's post-Fordist terms the battle of the immune system with the disease (Foucault 2003: 242). And like every battle, the crisis can be necessary or simply possible, but it always comprises an intrinsic characteristic of illness or of war. This is then the true discourse around crisis that at the end of the 18th century found itself more and more marginalised in medicine and yet in an ever more central position within political economic thinking, so as to acquire a power of exegetical hegemony in the writings of Karl Marx, as exemplified in the third volume of *Das Kapital*, which in the last few years has become the prayer-pillow of every good capitalist. Reflecting the power-knowledge of classical medicine, Marx held crisis to be a structural trait of the economy with its own particular rhythm which one should study and listen to in order to intervene effectively on the very truth of any given economic pathogeny, including capitalism *qua* capitalism. Based on the belief that "when the crisis occurs, the disease breaks out in its truth… appears in its own truth, its intrinsic truth" (ibid: 242), the only way to seize the opportunity [*kairos*] presented by a crisis was in Marx as in Hippocrates through the study of the rhythm of pathogeny which can allow one to predict the crisis so as to reinforce the power of nature (the organism, the economy, the political system) against the disease. This however must not happen before the crisis, for then the disease will not express itself and will endure (in a most Lacanian sense), possibly leading to even worse results in the future or even to a chronic state. The classical doctor as much as the modern economist must thus predict the crisis and arrange things in such a way that it will appear at the right moment, at the right opportunity. Bearing in its heart the predicting technologies of power-knowledge, this truth discourse, so piously reproduced in the political economic thinking of the 19th century onwards, said that the crisis can arrive on a favourable day, but can also arrive at on ominous day, and this difference is crucial for the battle with the disease: "the role of the crisis, is both intrinsic feature and, at the same time, the obligatory opportunity, the ritual rhythm, to which event should conform" (ibid: 243). We can thus provisionally conclude that the transformation of any event into a crisis presupposes a decision of a most sovereign nature, which renders it thinkable and intelligible, and at the same time a field or object of action, in terms of a *rhythm* in the most classical sense of the term: as a stasis, a formation of manageable stable schemata out of an ungovernable flow of movements (Kuriyama 1999).

Having reviewed in brief the truth-effect disseminated by classical medical and modern political economic discourses on crisis, glimpsing how it functions so as to render the event actionable and thinkable by objectifying its trace and thus freezing it in time, we can return to the heart of the problem today. If December 2008 was experienced as a totally-unexpected-event, an event that in all its force (beautiful or horrible, but certainly a force) shook all the conceptual, imaginary, political, economic, and desiring chains of social formation in Greece, in the spring of 2010 we stand before an officially sanctioned and governmentally organised Economic Crisis, a structural-counter-event that we always-already anticipated. A counter-event that, if it fails to explain December 2008, certainly manages to substitute it as the true field of decision, as the real crisis, imposing its rhythm on the social. In other words, the organisation of today's Economic Crisis objectively comprises a governmental fidelity to the December Uprising, a fidelity which, rather than problematising December itself, rises against it as an apparatus of problems that demand immediate solutions, emergency measures, and sacrifices under the star of national unity as the necessary rhythm of the social, as the general and always enduring debt/ guilt towards society.

The rising Economic Crisis, with an already ominous body count on its bills, in the form of the three bank workers killed by anti-capitalist militarism on 5 May 2010, has caused a ground-breaking deterritorialisation away from the social imaginary of *political agency* (the root of December, its hopes and miscarriages) and towards the realm of a social imaginary of *survival*. If, in other words, December was a real undiscernable event in the sense that it introduced in a radical way a non-decideable relation at the heart of the social, the Economic Crisis renders every decision always-already pre-emptively decided and unambiguously discernible. This return to the *pre-decided* is the role of neoliberalism as a strategic field and process that secures the "uniformity of effect" (Badiou 2007: 105). Through a prohibition of the contradiction which is the social, its effect is to render the latter unthinkable as what it really is, as the gap between the actual parts counted by the governmental enclosure and the "integrality of the one-effect" (ibid: 109) represented by it. It is precisely this debt/guilt towards uniformity which is the work of the counter-event called Economic Crisis. All the more, as the above mentioned prohibition becomes a condition for the reproduction of the state-relation as a security state under the light of December which temporarily short-circuited the relative autonomy of the state as a mode of class domination, forcing it to create the ground for new class alliances, for new strategic-hegemonic relations, for new governmentalities.

According to the currently ruling social-democratic discourse, both the event of December and the Economic Crisis stem from the same void of the previous situation: the anomic condition of the post-junta transition to democracy, the so-called *metapolitefsi*. It is this generalised anomie institutionalised in the founding of the Third Greek Republic in 1974 that has supposedly led on the one hand to a "culture of violence" amongst the masses and, on the other, to a "culture of corruption" amongst the ranks of the state. Here the social-democratic enclosure of really existing problems facing Greece is typically crafty. By simultaneously pointing at two real symptomal wounds of Greek social-formation, and paradoxically constructing its legitimacy on the promise of a "liberation from the *metapolitefsi*" (i.e. from what is largely its very own socio-political child), the Greek social-democracy mounts an operation of governmental reformation based on notions of unmasking, purification, and purging, a constant theme in what Nikolai Ssorin Chaikov (2003) has described as the technology of the deferred state characteristic of Soviet-type totalitarian regimes; a narrative of persistent state-failure, which constantly reproduces state-formation as the

211

key to solving all social problems. Within this context, the real innovation of the current social-democratic administration is that, rather than simply reproducing this fundamental mechanism of governmental autopoesis, it attempts for the first time to negate all traditional promises of an ideal relation between civil society and the state as always-already doomed, as the very source of today's sorry predicament. The work of the social-democratic administration is, in other words, the rupture and disrepute of the very social contract of the *metapolitefsi* era which had until now functioned as the measure of state present failure and future success, as the means of the very reproduction of the Republic.

If Greece were France, surely this would have been achieved through the pompous announcement of a Fourth Republic. Yet in the case of Greece, the numeric upgrading of republican polities is achieved by means of long dictatorial intervals, and this is not a likely outcome in the present liberal democratic European environment. Thus the proclaimed end of the *metapolitefsi* and of the sum of rules of negotiating civil autonomy vis-a-vis the state is largely conceived and talked about in terms of *culture* rather than in terms of a juridical or constitutional transformation. According to the social-democratic discourse disseminated through the media, what both December and the Economic Crisis have demonstrated is that Greece is permeated by an "anti-democratic culture," which posits individual and group interests against the General Good, thus endangering the good function of the state and the very cohesion of society and its economy. Drawing on the very origin of the myth of the Greek state and its supposed "struggle" with local/clannish interests—when in reality the Greek state has always been a board of strategic balance between those and never an autonomous agent—social-democracy thus attempts to portray a totally chimeric reciprocal relation within the semi-feudal political reality of Greece, "discipline-obedience to the state—respect-security from the state," as a pragmatic goal and at the same time as the only way of combating the void that has led to both the violence of December and the insecurity of the Economic Crisis. In other words, what the social-democratic governmental enclosure is doing, perhaps without realising it, is tempting the social imagination to conceive, rather than simply dream or fear, of a political and economic reality which works as an organic whole rather than as the sum of fragmented struggles of local and particular interests: the final arrival of modernity. It must thus be granted that the debt/guilt complex which forms the kernel of civil relations to the state during the present Economic Crisis is conditioned on a genuine if illusive promise for a new social contract, for a moment of salvation from the really existing anomic state of affairs in Greece and of delivery to a state of benevolent reciprocity; a kind of social utopia that will abolish the causes of the fundamental contradictions leading to civil strife and economic suffering in Greece in the last two centuries.

It is easy for the opposition, conservative or radical, to compete in condemning this promise as false, as a decoy or even as leading to a totalitarian nightmare. What is more difficult is to provide a meaningful and workable model as an alternative. Entrenched in its Welfare State protectionist nostalgia, the Left has proved incapable of providing just that. Stunned by the international woes of neoliberalism, the conservatives are splitting in ever more obscure parcels of populist obscurantism. And blinded by the rituals of invoking the return of the event-God by means of ever more grotesque and acts of wanton violence, the anarchists and other assorted radicals are equally impotent to face any real social, political, or economic challenge, let alone to attempt responding to it. Perhaps then this is the real end of the *metapolitefsi*: a time when the discourse of the state appears for the first time as the only thinkable and intelligible solution, as the only word whose effect has any pragmatic resonance and practical scope.

Christos Lynteris, May 2010

14

AN ECONOMY THAT EXCLUDES THE MANY AND AN "ACCIDENTAL" REVOLT

Yiannis Kaplanis

INTRODUCTION

Greece at the crossroads. Geographically an outer border of the European Union, economically the worst student of the monetary union experiment, historically living through the transformation from an outdated rigid public-sector-dominated capitalist economy to a modern flexible capitalist haven.

Greece at the crossroads between two events: the revolt following the killing of a 15-year-old schoolboy and the country's entrance into the era of the IMF/EU/ECB memorandum. Two periods intermingling with each other, not due to an organic link between the two events and not just due to pure chronological sequence. More than anything, these two events illuminate important ruptures in contemporary Greek history that simply cannot be ignored.

When the Greek youth demonstrated en masse in the streets for weeks in December 2008, commentators, journalists, analysts, academics, and politicians were unable to come up with answers and explanations for the revolt. Some of them talked about the rising tension between police and youth, others about the problems faced by the Greek education system, or the crisis of the political establishment, while some talked about the political culture of the Left and the antiauthoritarian movement in Greece that goes back to the 1970s and the uprising of the students against the Greek junta.[1, 2] Finally, economic interpretations were also discussed, for those who are keen on this kind of analysis. However, when the December revolt was sparked in 2008, the Greek economy was generally perceived as performing well, with rates of growth above the EU average and declining rates of unemployment. The international financial crisis had not yet hit hard in Greece and its only apparent weakness had to do with its banking sector, which the Greek government generously supported with a €28 billion gift package. But it is not necessarily the growing pie that matters, but also the slices of the cake. And the slice of the cake for the €700 generation was shrinking, as was the slice of the cake that goes to labour in comparison to capital.

It was only a year later, in December 2009, that the Greek economy entered an unprecedented crisis, with its credit reliability deteriorating into junk and the Greek government having to borrow at ridiculously high prices in order to refinance its debt.

All attempts by the government to boost its credibility, control the growing budget deficit, and meet its debt repayments by borrowing in the open market failed miserably. It was then in May 2010 that the Greek government signed the so-called "Memorandum of Cooperation" with the IMF the ECB and the EU (the so-called "troika"). As the memorandum laid out, Greece would borrow €110 billion from IMF and EU countries at a high rate of 5%, which was below the market rate but still quite high. At the same time the Greek government committed itself to imposing new economic austerity measures that would enable it to drastically reduce its budget deficit and restructure its economy along the lines of its lenders. General strikes and mass protests, called by the unions, the left, and the anti-authoritarian movements, brought thousands to the streets to oppose the memorandum and cancel its ratification by the Greek parliament. 5 May 2010 saw the peak of the protests and many felt it could be the start of a new uprising as the memory of the December riots was coming to haunt the present. Was the new "labour December" that did not take place when the crisis first started to evolve in late 2009 and the first austerity packages evolved in the early months of 2010 about to start?

The death of three bank employees that day by the irresponsible (if not criminal) acts of a nihilist group meant a freeze of the momentum that protesters had gathered that evening. Hundreds of thousands of them had surrounded the Greek parliament and only just fell short of storming inside.[3] This was one of the largest demonstrations in the *metapolitefsi* (post-dictatorial) era not only in terms of the numbers, the rage, and the variety of backgrounds of those who participated, but also in terms of the stakes on offer. After the tragic events of the day, the Greek government was given a great opportunity to extricate itself, and police embarked on a full-scale attack on radical political groups and social centres while the demonstrators retreated from the parliament after the confirmation of the sad death of the three bank workers. How things might have evolved if these events had not happened is difficult for anyone to estimate. It is also hard to understand when, how, and why revolts take place—they definitely do not take place by default, upon the deterioration of economic conditions (as the post-script of this book discusses). But does the economy matter, and to what extent?

A deterministic approach would expect social unrest, protest, and rise of class struggle in periods of austerity, deterioration of economic conditions, and suppression of workers achievements.[4] Judging from the period since the ratification of the memorandum in May 2010, this has not been the case, at least not to the extent that the worst retaliation on labour in the post-war era would lead somebody to expect. We had the killing of a 15-year-old boy and the "accidental" revolt of thousands of people with no apparent economic reasons driving them out to the streets. And now there is a full scale assault by the Government on wages, pensions, and whatever is left of the welfare benefits with relatively little reaction—at least when these lines were written in autumn of 2010...

But let's take things one at a time. In the next section, I give a brief overview of the Greek economy in the last decade and argue that things were not at all rosy even before the recent debt crisis. Then I try to see how, if at all, economic conditions might have fuelled the December revolt. Coming to the more recent situation, I briefly examine the economic transformation that the Greek state undertakes at the moment and discuss its importance for the antagonist movement.

GROWTH, BUT FOR WHOM?

The general perception as promoted by the official reports is that since the mid-1990s and until hit by the crisis, the Greek economy experienced a sustained path of growth and exhibited great economic successes. First, it grew with an average annual rate of 4.2% in the period 1998–2007, which was well above most European economies' growth rates and only second to Ireland's. Furthermore it managed to reduce unemployment from around 12% to 8% over the same period. In 2001, Greece satisfied most of the criteria of entry (except that of the public debt) and entered the European Monetary Union (EMU), something that was welcomed across nearly all the political parties. Entering a rich man's club like the EMU made the economic and political elite of Greece celebrate, and while the majority of the population initially seemed to share the general euphoria, it was quite soon that they would realise they were once again the ones to lose out. The adaptation of the Euro meant a gradual equalisation of the prices in the Eurozone area and as we can see throughout the last decade, inflation rates in the peripheral countries like Greece, Spain, and Portugal were higher than the average. And although it might be true that average real wages for these countries rose in the same period, large segments of the public ended up being worse off in the end. Average real wages do not take into account the wage distribution and the large inequalities prevalent there, as well as that inflation is not the same for all economic groups. When adjusting for these factors the gains of the workers are mediocre at best (see the INE Report 2010 for a relevant discussion), and it is not a surprise that a common slogan that people used is "we are becoming European in terms of the cost of living but not of the wages." Furthermore, it is very remarkable that the fall of the share of income that goes to labour has been declining steadily since the early 1980s (roughly by 10% in the period 1983–2008; INE 2010). This share takes into account the ratio of real remuneration per worker over real productivity, and although real remuneration increased over that period, the workers' productivity rose even further and thus they now gain less overall.

Focusing on the last decade, workers lost income shares with respect to capital for almost all countries of the Eurozone (with the exception of Ireland) and this can be attributed largely to the labour market policies that were pushed forward and the wage setting bargaining processes (RMF, 2010a). Germany experienced the largest decline in the share of income that goes to labour and this comes at no surprise since there was an important wave of labour market reforms implemented by chancellor Schröder in 2003 (Agenda 2010) that also gained the consensus of mainstream unions for minimal wage demands. This point is particularly relevant today when, under the guidance of the *troika*, the Greek government implements wage reductions in order for the economy to gain competitiveness compared to its economic partners and therefore follows Germany in a race to the bottom.

The best single measure to compare competitiveness in the Eurozone is the nominal unit labour cost. The trend for Germany is noteworthy, as it has remained almost flat throughout the period since the mid-1990s. However, nominal unit costs for peripheral countries (the so-called PIIGS: Portugal, Italy, Ireland, Greece, and Spain) have been rising steadily for the same period.[5] Then it might come as no surprise that Germany became an export champion and started to run high current account surpluses after the introduction of the Euro, while the current account deficits of the peripheral countries significantly deteriorated during the same period (RMF 2010a). This can also be seen when examining the bilateral trade balances of Germany with each of the periphery countries, which always show gains for Germany in the last decade (Dadush and Eidelman 2010).

There are other important elements of the Greek economy that contribute to the view that things had not been all that rosy during its years of growth. First of all, although in those years the unemployment declined (from 12% in 1999 to 8% in 2008), this general statistic might disguise other important processes that have been taking place in the labour market. It does not take into account the quality of the new jobs that have been created, regarding both the terms of the employment and also their remuneration. There has been a lot of commentary in Greece that the decline in unemployment was inflated by promoting training courses and internships for the youth (the so-called "stagiaires") and a general rise in precarious forms of employment (temping, part-time, undocumented employment, low-pay). There has been a systematic policy by successive governments to cover organic positions in the public sector and local government by hiring youth under traineeship programmes, often funded by the European Union, without insurance and with wages as low as €500–600. The stagiaires were employed in short-term fixed term contracts, but a significant proportion continued in successive stage programmes and ended up working more than two years as trainees. Since first initiated under the PASOK administration of Kostas Simitis (1996–2004), stage programmes offered an ideal solution for all governments of the period to cover their needs at the lowest possible cost as well as reduce unemployment. It was never clear how many people were employed in such programmes at the public sector, but estimates vary from 30,000 to 80,000.[6] It has also been common practice for the governments to use such programmes in order to satisfy clientilist relations with their electorate; the Conservative "New Democracy" recruited as many as 7,000 new stagiaires in the weeks just before the last general election of 2009.[7]

Besides the stagiaires, there are also around 35,000 workers employed by employment agencies to work for other companies (usually with terms and conditions inferior than if they had been hired directly by that company) and 80,000 employees who work under subcontracting arrangements, where a company has outsourced business functions to another company in order to reduce costs (Kouzis 2009). Sub-contracting has been quite prevalent in low-paid service work such as cleaning. Large public companies, like the Athens Piraeus Electric Railways (ISAP, the Greek overground), Hellenic Organization of Tele-communications (OTE, the Greek telecom giant), or even the universi-ties and ministries manage to minimise their administrative costs by outsourcing cleaning to specialised companies which then hire workers at low-wages and poor working conditions (hourly paid schemes with no benefits/leave, unpaid overtime, no unionisation, etc.).[8] But even jobs that we would not associate with precarity might fall under this category since there are many workers who are officially considered to be self-employed but are essentially employees who have to pay their own insurance and work with flexible arrangement conditions (e.g. this is the case for many engineers and architects).

Flexible forms of employment have been prevalent during the 2000s in Greece: by 2009, the proportion of temporary employment had exceeded 12.1% (Eurostat). Looking at different demographic groups, it is found that women and young people disproportionately work as temps, with percentages 14% and 27% respectively and rising trends in the last decade (Kaplanis 2010). A striking figure regarding job creation is that 70% of all new jobs in 2006 were part-time (Mo-nastiriotis 2009). A trend for rising employment polarisation might not be a Greek specificity, as it has also been documented at the European level as well as in the US (Goos et al. 2009; Autor et al. 2006; Kaplanis 2007). Recent research has shown that besides growing numbers of professionals and technicians in Greece, the next fast growing occupa-tion category is that of low-pay service jobs (Kaplanis 2010). Of course, these statistics do not take into account the informal economy that is suggested to form up to 30% of the GDP and constitutes an important element of the low-pay sector overall.

Temping, part-timing, and sub-contracting constitute flex-ible forms of employment that have been promoted systematically by the European Union and the Greek government in order to mi-nimise costs, combat unemployment, and stir an otherwise stagnating economy. Besides flexibility in the employment conditions, employers in Greece have relied for a substantial period on low wages in order to increase their profitability. Even before the most recent wave of crisis, Greece had the second lowest average wages in the EU15 (only second to Portugal) with wages at 82% of the European average (at current prices). And while the average wages had been rising over the last 15 years and converging slowly with the European average, these figures still hide what had been happening at the lower tail of the wage distribution. Specifically, almost a quarter of full-time workers earned less than €1,000 a month, and thus are officially classified as low-paid (i.e. earning less than 2/3 of the median wage; INE 2010). And although the General Confederation of Workers of Greece (GSEE) claimed to have managed to increase the minimum wage in real terms, this figure takes into account neither the higher inflation lower income groups face nor the rise in inequality. The minimum wage rose substantially less than the average wage, which is driven up by the high flying salaries of the high-earners, and thus their ratio deteriorated from 54% to 45% over the period 1990–2006 (INE 2010).

Indeed when looking at the income inequality (as the ratio of the richest 20% to the poorest 20%), Greece comes fourth after Latvia, Portugal, and Lithuania out of the EU25 (INE 2008). There is also 21% of the Greek population that lives below the poverty line,[9] while the respective figure for the EU25 is 16% and only Latvia performs worse than Greece. When examining the working poor, the proportion out of all workers is 14%, which is double the EU15 figure and places Greece at the worst position in the EU25 league. It should be noted that these official European figures (EU-SILC 2006) refer to the year 2006 alone, well before the world financial crisis and the Greek sovereign debt crisis. Overall, during this period of sustained growth for the Greek economy the poor remained poor (with stable poverty rates over 1995–2006), and the well-promoted case for prioritising the enlargement of the pie, with the expectation that the increased income will "trickle down" to the lower income classes never seemed to take place.

The high-growth years of the Greek economy were not based on great advancements in technology and infrastructure and well-planned developmental policies. Rather, they have been commonly suggested to come from credit expansion, the construction of public works and the boom of real estate. Generous funding under the European Community Support Frameworks along with rising public investment to serve the 2004 Olympic Games sustained high growth rates for the period starting in the mid-1990s and lasting until the recent economic crisis. Furthermore, the large influx of migrant workers from the Balkans and Eastern Europe in the 1990s enabled Greece to keep its wages low, increase its effective labour supply, strengthen the consumer demand and boost the economy. Many of these migrant workers worked without any insurance, with low wages, and under poor working conditions in agriculture, construction or services. Employment under the "galley" conditions in the Olympic sites was particularly notorious, with

154 reported work accidents and eleven dead workers in a period of just three years (2001–2003)—five of them were migrants (Georgakis 2003). "Legalisation" of earlier waves of migrants who have worked in Greece for some years gave them the opportunity to gain access to insurance and pension systems, improve their working conditions and to not live in fear of deportation at any moment. However, any attempts to integrate into Greek society have been very slow, with pronounced discrimination in the labour market and their daily transactions with the state alike.[10]

This brief overview of the economic situation up to 2008 presents a different image than the rosy one that was carefully portrayed by the officials and the media during the same period. According to official discourse there are a number of accomplishments that all Greek citizens should feel proud. Besides economic successes like the high growth rates, the entry in the Euro zone and the expansion of Greek businesses in the Balkans, we are supposed to believe that pride should also derive from the successful organisation of the 2004 Olympic Games. The Athens 2004 Olympics added a high economic burden to the public purse, since a small country managed to host the most expensive games ever, costing at least nine billion euros. This figure was later revised to 11 billion euros (around 6% of the GDP) by the crediting agency Standard & Poor's. If we were to include the extra cost coming from the intensification of the works to meet the deadline for the opening day of the games, the figure would be substantially higher. The estimated figure for the cost of the security of the games stands at one billion euros, for purchasing high-tech equipment and the deployment of thousands of policemen and agents in the city. The notorious scandal of the security CCTV system C4I that cost €255 million but never operated is a characteristic example; and questions are raised not only for the usefulness of such systems but also for the contracts and commissions to obtain them. Although C4I never worked, the thousands of police stayed in the streets[11] as well as the CCTV cameras so as to justify the money spent for them. And both were of great use to the authorities during the December 2008 revolt. But let's go now back to the future—to the revolt!

THE "ACCIDENTAL" REVOLT

The events of December 2008 [Dekemvriana] surprised many with their massive participation, intensity, and length, and with the sense of collective belonging that was shared amongst the people in the streets, and ingenious tactics of the movements participating. A further surprise was that the "accidental" killing of a 15-year-old school boy could spark the largest civil unrest in Greece since the years of the dictatorship, which was not directly rooted in a political, economic, or labour struggle. The picture was also blurred by the fact that the events of December did not put forward any specific demands nor was there any central committee, political party, or radical group to act as a main driving force. An extensive debate has evolved amongst commentators, analysts, journalists, academics, and politicians about the essence of December and its underlying causes.[12] Was it a riot, civil unrest, a revolt, a social movement? What caused that explosion of people to take to the streets, and especially the youth, after the killing of the 15-year-old Alexis Grigoropoulos on 6 December 2010 in Exarcheia?

The massive participation, its scale, and particularly its length suggest that the events of December were more than an explosion, a riot, or civil unrest. If that were the case, they would have calmed after the first two or three days. However the protests, occupations, general meetings lasted for over a month, while the massive violent confrontations on the streets with the police lasted for about two weeks and sporadically continued over the rest of the period. Furthermore, the Dekemvriana could not probably be characterised as a social movement, although they had a remarkable self-organisation of the struggle and initiatives like occupations of universities, of town halls, of the offices of GSEE, direct actions on the streets, markets, theatres, and media stations that constitute forms of organised struggles that we could associate with social movements. What probably distinguishes them is the spontaneity and intensity of the struggle at the same time that there was no single demand, group, collective, party, or force behind that drove it forward. The events surpassed the people who participated in them and belonged to organised radical political groups or collectives from the anti-authoritarian scene and the far left as well as the political parties (smaller or bigger). In that respect, the question of what was December had been answered in the streets by the same people who participated in it—*December was a "revolt."*

Looking for the causes that would enable us to understand better this "accidental" revolt, various hypotheses have been suggested. Namely, the crisis of the political establishment, the spectre of unemployment and the emergence of the €700 generation, the shortcomings of the educational system, the increased brutality of the police forces, and the rising tension with the youth or the political culture of the *metapolitefsi* era. There is no simple way to examine which of the above factors might have contributed to fuel the revolt and how. And although somebody might be persuaded from the earlier review that the economic conditions have been deteriorating over that time period, there is still not a straightforward way to suggest that they caused or fuelled the revolt.

One important point is given by the many accounts offered by participants that talk about the sharing of a common identity and belonging that was prevalent in the streets and that cut across employment and educational backgrounds. Students, stagiaires, unemployed, precarious workers, and young people, both natives and migrants, united in the streets of December crossing boundaries and backgrounds. As Sotiris (2010) argues despite the different social backgrounds, the youth in Greece share a common present and future—the deterioration of their employment prospects; and this unifying element was reflected vividly in December. Indeed, it is not only the high youth unemployment rate in Greece—which stood at 22.9% in 2007 and was the highest in the EU25 group of countries (Eurostat 2010). It is also the case that unemployment does not fall with educational qualifications, as it is the norm in most countries, but for those aged 20–29 the higher qualified ones face higher unemployment rates (Karamesini 2008; Sotiris 2010).[13]

The youth, the unemployed, the working poor, and the migrants were the ones who had nothing to lose and were giving the protests their particular character. The emergence of a new "precariat" at the dawn of the 21st Century might well be the outcome of the recent transformative processes of capitalism that advance deregulation, flexibility, and precarity. How the workers organise under such conditions is still to be answered. However, already from the mid-2000s, grassroots syndicalist unions emerged, especially in service sectors with poor working conditions and pay. Two notable examples are the Base Union of Workers Motor-Drivers that was created in 2006 and the Union of Waiters, Chefs, and Catering Workers that was created in 2007 and individuals from them were also active in the occupation of the GSEE offices during December 2008. There are also older unions with important syndicalist activism like the Union of Bookshop and Paper Workers (1992) as well as the Pan-attic Union of Cleaners & Domestic Staff (1999), whose general secretary, migrant worker Konstantina Kouneva, got attacked with sulphuric acid by employer-hired mafia in retaliation for standing up for cleaners' rights. That attack took place during December 2008 and was crucial in enriching December's discourse with the recent developments in the de-/un-regulated labour markets and the latest path of capitalist advancement.

Furthermore, another point worth considering is that it was the first time we saw a new emerging "*underclass*" participating in acts of civil unrest in Greece. This is not characteristic of the revolt overall, as it was mainly prevalent for one day, but still powerful and visible: Monday 8 December, day three of the revolt, was the day with the most massive participation in the protests and the most violent actions against the police forces, banks, and shops in Athens. By the night, the riots had escalated covering a very large part of central Athens, and there was large destruction of property and looting. The police were clearly unable to control the situation and the government held an urgent meeting to discuss its response and the possibility of calling a state of emergency. On that day, the poor sub-proletariat was actively involved and became visible for the first time in the recent political history of Greece. While expropriation of property might have been ideologically promoted by some radical groups, and while consumerist tendencies might have inflated the incidents, nobody can deny that poor fellow citizens that day had the opportunity to help themselves to a nice meal and some good quality clothes. There are many personal reports about elderly men and women who took food from smashed supermarkets or poor migrants who got meat from butcher shops.[14]

AFTER THE REVOLT...THE CRISIS! AND NOW?

If deteriorating economic conditions might have fuelled the revolt, why then do we not see a similar revolt or civil unrest nowadays that the sovereign debt crisis has unfolded fully and the effects of the harsh austerity measures have squeezed large segments of the population even further? Put simply, because history is not deterministic and the economic conditions do not spark revolts by default. It is the responsibility of the political subjects and movements to move things forward. Following the discussion so far, I can only hypothesise that due to the nature of employment of precarious workers (high turnover, short-period of employment, not fixed workplace, etc.) as well as the fact that only a tiny proportion of them are active in a union, it might be harder for them to mobilise and engage in organised labour struggles that would attract larger numbers of people. On the other hand, the fractions of workers that are hit the most so far from the government's measures like the public sector workers have probably lost most contact with radical mobilisations over the years of being under the auspices of state; while it would be naïve to expect the pensioners to lead the mobilisations. Taking into account the role of the media and the main trade unions

225

(GSEE-ADEDY) into building the necessary consensus desired by the government, it should be less surprising to see the relative social calm amidst Greece's financial storm. In this perspective, 5 May 2010 might have been a missed opportunity. Will there by any more opportunities? Only the future can tell.

In the meantime the third revised version of the memorandum is being prepared, where collective wage agreements and workers rights are thrown, almost without a blink of an eye, into the dustbin of history. The 2011 budget proposes further reductions to spending on education and health (in addition to the 2010 cuts) and an increase in heating oil tax rate, while there is a reduction of the tax rate for corporate profits from 24% to 20%. At the same time, the deregulation of the labour market would also now affect wages in the private sector, with expected cuts between 10–40% (depending on the different sectoral pay agreements that are being now subordinated to firm agreements). The latest figures show temporary work to have risen from 11 to 12.5% in the years between 2007–09 (Eurostat 2010) while the total unemployment mounts to 12.2% for August 2010 and is expected to reach 15% or so in year 2011. The revised estimates for the budget deficit provided by the Eurostat place it at 9.4% (higher than the target of 8.1%), while the public debt has soared to 144% for 2010. Such high debt is not sustainable, as the government would have to pay around 7.5% of its GDP each year just for interest on its debt. There are two ways the government follows in order to consolidate its debt and avoid default. The first is selling public assets and the second is a restructuring of its debt. The former means an unprecedented scale of privatisations and large sell-out of public property under the banner of "utilisation of the public land". Regarding the latter, since restructuring most likely would happen under the terms of the lenders,[15] a deep and prolonged recession period for the Greek economy has just started, under the "economic dictatorship" of the government, the IMF, and the EU. The economic crisis creates a permanent condition of emergency, and the opportunity for the government to pass unpopular structural reforms and austerity measures that it could not have done otherwise. In that respect, if the crisis did not exist, it would be in the interests of the establishment to create it. The Greek Prime Minister said it very succinctly on 3 May 2010, one day after the signing of the memorandum with the *troika*, the "crisis is an opportunity." It is not only an opportunity for curbing corruption and tax evasion (as they claim to be doing), but also an opportunity to deregulate the labour markets, cut labour costs, restructure the pension system, reduce the provision of welfare, and expand the private market to sectors such as energy, transport, health, and education. It is a class-based restructuring that serves the interests of the "big capital," both the local and its international partners. How the people and the movements will react and mobilise is an open question...

Yiannis Kaplanis, November 2010

NOTES

1 The peak of the resistance to the military dictatorship in Greece (1967–1974) was the uprising of the Athens Polytechnic in November 1973, which was crashed by the army on the early hours of 17th November.

2 For a more detailed discussion on various standpoints to the December events, see Kouki, this volume.

3 For a more detailed analysis of the impact of the events of May 5th, see Boukalas, this volume.

4 Though the political direction of the unrest might not necessarily be progressive; the rise of fascist regimes in the bankrupted Europe of the 1930s can show that all too loudly and dramatically.

5 As noted earlier, this does not mean that the workers in these countries faired better in terms of living conditions, since the nominal unit labour cost does not take into account inflation and distributional aspects.

6 Georgakis I. "Public Ending for the Stage: The Government Prepares Relevant Programme Exclusively for the Private Sector" Ta Nea, 20 October 2009 [in Greek].

7 Christou, M "Clarifying the Issue of Stage," Eleftherotypia, 20 October 2009 [in Greek] http://www.enet.gr/?i=news.el.article&id=93902.

8 As this book was about to go to print at the end of 2010, we heard the story of Emad Aziz, a 44-year-old Egyptian worker, who died while cleaning the windows of the Ministry of Labour in Athens. He was working there uninsured and unregistered on a Sunday, under a sub-contracting scheme, with poor safety conditions.

9 According to the official definition for 2006 that estimates the "risk of being poor," the threshold was annual income of less than €5,910 for an individual or less than €12,411 for a four-member household (of two adults and two children).

10 Furthermore, since the crisis started affecting the real economy in Greece, migrant workers have found increasingly difficult to secure work in order to renew their resident permit and not become "illegal" again. And of course, the more recent waves of migrants that came in the last five years to Greece were not covered by the last "legalisation" legislation of the government and thus have to work as undocumented workers in the informal economy.

11 It is not clear how large the police force is in Greece, but a low estimate would be 55,000, i.e. one police officer for every 200 residents.

12 At the same time, the participants of December who were supposed to give the answers to such questions were meeting elsewhere, at the occupied universities, town halls, schools, at the town's squares, neighbourhood gatherings, at the self-organised spaces, parks, and squats. They were discussing how to move the movement forward, how to deepen it, how to involve more people, more neighbourhoods, more groups, how to self-organise, how to communicate with each other, how to express themselves. For them, "December was a question…" and one still to be answered.

13 Karamesini, M. (2009) "Difficulties of Youth Employment in Greece," *Epochí* 18 January [in Greek] http://www.epohi.gr/portal/?option=com_content&task=view&id=2043.

14 For example see *VIMAgazino*, "Days of rage—December 2008—Athens," 21 December 2008 [in Greek].

15 Whose main concern is to protect the money of the German and French banks that was lent to the Greek state; thus the necessary writing off of the debt (aka "haircut") would be minimal and restructuring would mainly take the form of extension of its debt repayments.

15

THE GREEK DEBT CRISIS IN ALMOST UNIMAGINABLY LONG-TERM HISTORICAL PERSPECTIVE

David Graeber

In the corporate media, the Greek crisis is usually represented almost as a revolt of spoiled children: a population living beyond its means, rising up in a tantrum when forced to face the fiscal discipline it has for so long, and so unrealistically, resisted. This seems rather an extraordinary condemnation for a nation with one of the least developed welfare states in Europe, but it is the only narrative the corporate media really has to tell. After all, is not debt simply the rational measure of fiscal morality? And in geopolitical terms, is there any other morality that really matters? A nation in debt must have done something wrong, just as a nation with surpluses must be doing something right (no one seems to notice that you cannot have one without the other, so that for a German, for instance, to chide a Greek for his country's supposed fiscal irresponsibility is the equivalent of a heroin dealer chiding his client for having become addicted in the first place).

Curiously absent from these discussions is the one area where the Greek government, so penurious with its health and pension policies, seems remarkably open-handed: that is, in matters of military spending, or anything, for that matter, connected to what we like to call the "security services." Greece has the largest number of military personnel per capita of any NATO country (at 119 per 10,000, more than twice that of Bulgaria, the second runner-up), and the second highest ratio of police (33 per 10,000, or 1 cop per every 303 people).[1] Such a high level of securitisation is extremely expensive: of all NATO countries, Greece also spends the highest proportion of its budget (5.5%) on the military, a remarkable 3.1% of GDP. And this is almost certainly a low estimate. Real military spending numbers are just about everywhere shrouded in mystery, since governments tend to go to great lengths to obfuscate the real numbers, and as a result we have no idea if the case of Greece runs parallel, for instance, to that of the USA, where the size of the total military budget corresponds almost exactly with that of the federal deficit. However the role of the Greek government's interest in expensive German and French military equipment (jets, submarines), and its financing through money borrowed from German and French banks, has been well-documented.

Most commentators explain Greek military spending as the result of ongoing tensions with fellow-NATO member Turkey, as if the continued existence of these tensions is itself in no need of explanation. This is superficial. Sabre-rattling, as we all know, is a traditional technique for defusing social tensions at home; and if the Greek government does an unusual amount of it, it's because there are such an unusual lot of tensions to defuse. It's the same reason that the Greek police force is so large—the second largest in Europe—despite the fact that the crime rate is so low. Rates of most forms of violent crime (rape, murder, that sort of thing) are among the lowest in Europe, but the rate of political crimes (burning or looting banks, attacks on corporate or government offices) is veritably off the charts.[2] Clashes between police and leftists of one sort or another are an almost daily occurrence. In a very real sense, the Greek civil war, usually said to have lasted from 1946 to 1949, never ended. And while only a minority actively support the now largely anarchist-inspired resistance, the existence situation could never continue unless significant portions of the population at the very least passively acquiesce, seeing teenage squatters and even Molotov-throwing insurrectionists as at least as legitimate a political force as the police—who are, in fact, widely viewed as indistinguishable from the followers of the old fascist colonels. In many urban neighborhoods, police continue to be seen as occupying forces, and they often act as such, trashing social centres and cafes in leftist neighborhoods in the same way as gangs of right-wing thugs, who also exist, and with whom they actively collaborate. What has bankrupted the Greek government, in other words, is the cost of popular rejection of its basic institutions of rule; it has been forced to pour borrowed money into maintaining an endlessly expanding apparatus of coercion for the very reason that many of its citizens refuse to accept that apparatus as inherently legitimate.

The Greek situation is of course unique but I think it raises some very interesting questions about the connection between debt, organised violence, rebellion, and the state, because this connection has been a perennial feature of human history for at least five thousand years. To keep the focus on Greece—and this is by no means meant to imply any direct historical continuity, just as a particularly telling and well-documented example—in the late sixth century BC, at exactly the moment ancient city-states began to be incorporated into a larger commercial world, the immediate effect was a series of debt crises. The one in Athens, in which, according to Aristotle, "the poor became enslaved to the rich"—and many defaulters came to be literally sold abroad as slaves—led to the famous Solonian reforms, and set off a chain of social struggle that culminated first in the populist "tyranny" of Peisistratus, and ultimately in the establishment of Athens's democratic constitution. But similar things were happening everywhere: the new military classes, *hoplites*, sailors, whatever they might have been, were not willing to put up with debt peonage imposed by the former aristocrats and either supported populist coups (as for instance in Corinth), or made debt relief the principle focus of radical agitation, as in Megara, where the demos passed the famous *palintokia*, a law which not only banned all loans at interest, but did so retroactively, demanding all interest extracted over the principle on existing loans be immediately returned to the debtor. These debt crises appear to have been the main impulse beyond constitutional reform.

Neither—and this is an area where earlier scholars appear to have been largely mistaken—did they vanish during the rest of Greek history. In Athens, while the most abusive practices were banned, most citizens remained in debt, and the democratic state's solution was essentially military: to use the Athenian navy to establish an empire, and its economic power to acquire slaves overseas—most famously, the thousands set to work in the Laurium silver mines—and to simply distribute the spoils liberally enough (for instance, in public works projects, and fees for attending meetings at the *agora*). This was typical. While ancient Middle Eastern kingdoms had long been in the habit of pronouncing universal debt cancellations—starting with the Sumerian "freedom" proclamations of King Enmetena of Lagash in 2400 BC, where new monarchs would tend, on coming to the throne, to cancel existing consumer debts and allow debt peons to return home, and continuing through institutions like the Biblical jubilee—Greek city states almost never engaged in outright cancellations. Instead, they threw money at the problem.

This is important when one looks at the history of coinage, which, in the ancient world, was invented not for commercial purposes but largely for the payment of soldiers (probably, in the very earliest times, mercenaries) and secondarily, for taxes, fees, civic payments, and so on. Rather than being the cause of the early debt crises—which began before coins were widely in use—coins were really part of the solution, a way of detaching ordinary people from their traditional attachments to aristocratic patrons, who had converted their old allegiance into "debts," and instead linking them directly to the public institutions of the state.

As a result, most political crises in ancient Greek cities really turned on this sort of distribution of spoils. Here is one incident recorded in Aristotle (cited in Keyt 1997: 103 [1304b27–31]), who provides a (typically) conservative take on the origins of a coup in the city of Rhodes around 391 BC: The demagogues [i.e. leaders of the democracy] needed money to pay the people for attending the assembly and serving on juries; for if the people did not attend, the demagogues would lose their influence. They raised at least some of the money they needed by preventing the disbursement of the money due the trireme commanders under their contracts with the city to build and fit triremes for the Rhodian navy. Since the commanders were not paid, they were unable in turn to pay their suppliers and workers, who sued the commanders. To escape these lawsuits the trireme commanders banded together and overthrew the democracy.

Rome, significantly, was to pursue almost identical policies: after experiencing a series of bitter conflicts over debt in the early Republic, which periodically brought things very close to a mass defection of the plebs, and constitutional reforms. Yet debts were never quite cancelled, or the principle of debt was never challenged. Instead, Rome's rulers relied on a policy of the redistribution of spoils to keep the plebs from falling off the edge—which worked well enough in the late Republic and early Empire, though it began to fall apart again in the later Empire when citizenship became universal.

As a result, as the great Classicist Moses Finley (1960: 63) pointed out, in the ancient world, there was basically one single revolutionary program, voiced whenever the rural poor rose up: "cancel the debts and redistribute the land."[3]

Neither was this program limited to the ancient Mediterranean. Mesopotamian and Hebrew debt cancellations were clearly based on the fear of mass defection—"exodus," in the original sense of the term—where indebted farmers and labourers would flee to the desert fringes, away from the cities in the river valleys, joining pastoral nomads who threatened to eventually overwhelm the cities themselves. From the earliest times for which we have records, through the Middle Ages, and throughout the age of European colonial empires, whenever one finds people rising in rebellion one finds questions of debt first among the first of the grievances. This seems to be true everywhere—or everywhere where interest-bearing debt had not already been made illegal as a result of pressure from below. It is as true of peasant revolts in Japan as of colonial rebellions in India or Mexico. The burning of ledger books and legal records is usually the very first act in a successful uprising (with the storming of castles, mansions, and destruction of property cadastres or tax records only afterwards.) Certainly, far more rebellions have begun over debt than over slavery, caste systems, or the depredations of landlords, plantation foremen, or factory owners.

One might well ask why. What is it about debt, in particular, that sparks such endless indignation, and resistance? One could, perhaps, answer the question on a philosophical level. Caste, slavery, feudalism—all these are based on a presumption of inequality. Debt, alone, is not. A debt is a contract, an agreement, between two parties who stand—when they originate it—in a relation of legal equality. True, the terms of the contract are that one (the debtor) is in a position of subordination until the loan is repaid; but still, the entire point of the contract is that a debt should be repaid, and therefore, that the two parties ought to be restored to their original position of equality. If they are not, it's because the debtor is, in a certain sense, at fault. This is why words for "debt" and "sin" are, in so many languages—from Sanskrit to German to Aramaic to Quechua—originally the same word. Religious concepts of sin actually seem to derive from debt rather than the other way around (in fact, many of the key concepts in what are now considered sacred texts, from the Vedic notion of life as a debt to the Gods to the Biblical notion of redemption, were clearly framed in reference to arguments about debt and debt forgiveness that were at the very centre of political debate at the time). This then is the reason debt is so infuriating. It is one thing to tell a man or woman they are simply inferior. It is another to tell them they ought to be equals, but they have failed. On the one hand, it seems like an obvious way to tell those one has subordinated—usually through violence—that their troubles are their own fault. This is why conquerors and Mafiosi almost invariably tell their victims they owe them money—if only in the sense that they owe them their lives for not having simply murdered them. But these assertions almost invariably rebound if only because they do, ultimately, imply

233

a certain potential for equality. It's inevitable, once things are framed that way, that the victims will begin asking "But who really owes what to whom?"

This is, as I say, the philosophical explanation. There is also another one, which highlights the structural link between war, state power, and monetary policies that lead to mass indebtedness.

To understand this, however, I must pull back slightly and provide a few words about the history of money—the reality of which bears little relation to its representation in economic textbooks. We're all used to hearing the standard line: first there was barter, then came coinage, eventually, this led to the creation of elaborate credit systems of the sort which play havoc with economies like Greece today. In fact this history is precisely backwards. Credit, and even debt crises, came first.

I. AGE OF THE FIRST AGRARIAN EMPIRES (3500–800 BCE)

DOMINANT MONEY FORM: VIRTUAL CREDIT MONEY

Our best information on the origins of money goes back to ancient Mesopotamia, but there seems no particular reason to believe matters were radically different in Pharaonic Egypt, Bronze Age China, or the Indus Valley. The Mesopotamian economy was dominated by large public institutions (Temples and Places) whose bureaucratic administrators effectively created money by establishing a fixed equivalent between silver and the staple crop, barley; debts were calculated in silver, but silver was rarely used in transactions: payments were made in barley or in anything else that happened to be handy and acceptable. Major debts were recorded on cuneiform tablets kept as sureties by both parties to the transaction.

Markets, certainly, did exist, but most actual acts of everyday buying and selling, particularly those that were not carried out between absolute strangers, appear to have been made on credit. The habit of money at interest also originates in Sumer (it remained unknown, for example, in Egypt), and it led to continual crises, as in bad years farmers would grow hopelessly indebted to the rich and would begin having to surrender their farms and ultimately, family members, in debt bondage, forcing governments to announce general amnesties. (It is significant that the first word for "freedom" known from any human language, the Sumerian *amargi*, literally means "return to mother," since such declarations of debt freedom would also mean that debt peons would also be allowed to return home.) Such policies appear to have been commonplace:

from the Biblical Jubilee, whereby all debts were cancelled after seven years, to Chinese traditions indicating that coinage themselves were invented as part of government efforts to redeem debt pawns.

II AXIAL AGE (800 BCE–600 CE)

DOMINANT MONEY FORM: COINAGE AND METAL BULLION

From the Warring States period in China, fragmentation in India, to the carnage and mass enslavement that accompanied the expansion (and later the dissolution) of the Roman Empire, it was a period in most of the world of spectacular creativity, but of almost equally spectacular violence: of large, aggressive empires which combined the maintenance of standing armies and the mass use of war captives as slave labour, and an abandonment of old protections for debtors.

Remarkably, it also saw the simultaneous invention of coinage in China, India, and the Eastern Mediterranean—in each case independently, but in each case also, in almost exactly the same times and places that also saw the rise of the major world religions. This could hardly have been a coincidence. Coins, which allowed the actual use of gold, silver, and copper as media of exchange, even in ordinary day-to-day transactions, also made possible the creation of markets in the now more familiar, impersonal sense of the term. These appear to have arisen largely as a side effect of military operations, and coins were first used mainly to pay soldiers. It certainly was not invented to facilitate trade—the Phoenicians, consummate traders of the ancient world, were among the last to adopt it; the very first coins, issued by rulers of Lydia, were probably issued mainly to pay their Greek mercenaries. The result was what might be called—following sociologist Geoffrey Ingham—a "military-coinage-slavery complex," since the diffusion of new military technologies (Greek hoplites, Roman legions) was always closely tied to the capture and marketing of slaves, and the other major source of slaves was debt: now that states no longer periodically wiped the slates clean, those not lucky enough to be citizens of the major military city-states—who were usually protected from the clutches of lenders by the distribution of spoils—were fair game. The credit systems of the Near East did not crumble under commercial competition; they were destroyed by Alexander's armies—armies that required half a ton of silver bullion per day in wages. The mines where the bullion was produced were generally worked by slaves, captured in war. Imperial tax systems were consciously designed to force their subjects to create markets, largely to provision soldiers.

235

III. THE MIDDLE AGES (600 CE–1500 CE)[4]

RETURN OF VIRTUAL CREDIT-MONEY

If the Axial Age saw the emergence of complementary ideals of commodity markets and universal world religions, the Middle Ages was the period in which the new religions, mostly born as peace movements—forms of popular opposition to Axial Age militarism—effectively took over regulation of the market systems, with the result that coinage was largely abandoned, and the world moved back to virtual credit money (from tally sticks in Western Europe, to checking accounts in the Middle East, to the invention of paper money in China). It also saw, almost everywhere, the dissolution of the great empires with their standing armies,[5] the abolition or at very least extreme attenuation of chattel slavery, and the creation of some kind of overarching protections against the depredations of debt. Islam and Christendom of course banned lending money at interest entirely, along with debt peonage and related abuses; in China, this was the heyday of Buddhism, and Buddhist temples popularised pawnshops as a way of offering farmers an alternative to the local usurer (even as Confucian administrators enforced periodic debt relief). To get some sense of the degree to which things had changed, the Greek principle of *palintokia*, of the restitution to the debtor of all money extracted that exceeded the original principle—considered the utmost in extremist demagoguery by all existing Greek sources—was official Catholic doctrine by the 12th century; anyone identified as a usurer who did not make such restitution was to be excommunicated, could not receive communion, and could not be buried on sacred ground.

All this is not to say that this period did not see its share of carnage and plunder (particularly during the great nomadic invasions), but money, for the most part, was delinked from coercive institutions. Money-changers, one might say, were invited back into the temples, where they could be monitored; the result was a flowering of institutions premised on a much higher degree of social trust.

IV. AGE OF CAPITALIST EMPIRES (1500–1971)

RETURN OF PRECIOUS METALS

With the advent of the great European empires—Iberian, then North Atlantic—the world saw both a reversion to mass enslavement, plunder, and wars of destruction, and the consequent rapid return of gold and silver bullion as the main form of currency. The delinking of money from religious institutions, and its relinking with coercive ones (especially the state), was here accompanied by an ideological reversion to "Metallism." Internationally, the British Empire was steadfast in maintaining the gold standard through the 19th and early 20th centuries, and great political battles were fought in the United States over whether the gold or silver standard should prevail. All this is in dramatic contrast with the Middle Ages, where it was mostly simply assumed that money was a social convention that could be created or transformed more or less at will. This was all the more important since, in fact, the new capitalist hegemons (starting with Venice and Genoa, then the Dutch Republic, and finally the British and US empires) were driven at least in part by credit systems based on negotiable paper, and eventually, paper money. This paper money was a very peculiar form of credit money, consisting almost exclusively of government war debt, that is, wealth borrowed by governments to purchase the means for organised violence; a capacity for violence that was then used, in a kind of magnificent circularity, to enforce the claims of central bankers that that money those states now owed it could be lent out again, and used as legal tender in all commercial transactions.

V. CURRENT ERA (1971 ONWARDS)

RETURN, AGAIN, OF VIRTUAL CREDIT MONEY; OTHERWISE, UNKNOWN

The current age of virtual money—which might be said to have officially begun on August 15, 1971, when US President Richard Nixon suspended the convertibility of the dollar into gold—is thus nothing dramatically new. The financialisation of capital, the efflorescence of consumer debt, global debt crises, and of course the great meltdown of 2008, all appear in this long-term perspective as the likely birth-pangs of a new age whose form we could not possibly predict.

Still, some historical trends are obvious enough. Historically, as we have seen, ages of virtual, credit money have also involved creating some sort of overarching institutions—Mesopotamian sacred kingship, Mosaic jubilees, Sharia or Canon Law—that place some sort of controls on the potentially catastrophic social consequences of debt. So far, the movement this time has been the other way around: starting with the 1980s we have begun to see the creation of the first effective planetary administrative system, operating through the IMF, World Bank, corporations, and other financial institutions, largely in order to protect the interests of creditors. However, this apparatus was very quickly thrown into crisis, first by the very rapid development of global social movements, which effectively destroyed the moral authority of institutions like the IMF, and left many of them very close to bankruptcy, then by the current banking crisis and global economic collapse. The shape of what eventually emerges—and presumably, some new overarching system or systems will emerge—depends largely on the effectiveness of social movements. Those that arose at the end of the Axial Age largely managed to eliminate slavery across the Eurasian continent. Will it be possible to do the same with wage slavery? What sort of institutions will arise within the new virtual credit systems to prevent creditors from running completely amok?

What about the role of war and militarism in all of this? Well, for the moment, the world economy is still operating under the aegis of the US empire, whose financial system is organised in much the same way as earlier capitalist hegemons. Just as the Bank of England, for instance, was an ostensibly private institution given permission by the Crown to lend money that the King owed it in the form of paper money, so is the US system organised around the Federal Reserve— actually a consortium of private banks—which has the unique right to monetize the US debt. This is again, a war debt (as mentioned earlier, size of the US deficit corresponds almost exactly to the size of its military spending), the price of its coercive power, which is global in scope—there is no place on earth where the US military is not able to strike with relative impunity—just as there is no place on earth where the US dollar, which is essentially a promise for repayment by the US government for the means to maintain that military system, does not serve as the basic reserve currency.

The US empire does have one historically unique feature: it is the first empire to hold the official position that it is not an empire at all. This introduces a few peculiar kinks. Historically, aside from the Federal Reserve, the major purchaser of US Treasury bonds (financers of the US deficit) are foreign institutional lenders, which over the last forty years, have been US military client states: Germany (originally West Germany), Japan, South Korea, Taiwan, Saudi Arabia, Kuwait, and so forth. All are either covered with US bases, or directly under the US military umbrella in one form or another; all are in the habit of purchasing US bonds that never, in fact, mature, but are endlessly rolled over, creating a kind of indirect tribute system dressed up as US international debt (Hudson 2003). (Matters have become slightly murkier now that China has got into the game, since China is obviously by no means a US military client state, but if one examines Chinese policies in deep historical perspective, too, one finds that have long been used to playing this sort of game: Chinese imperial tribute systems always worked in reverse, showering wealth on foreign dependents (in fact, many of the same ones now maintained by the US—Japan, Korea, Taiwan—in exchange for political loyalty; which implies the long-term aim is reduce the US itself to a military client state of China; a military enforcer for East Asian capital. It's in no way clear if this will actually work.)

The result of this peculiar approach to empire is that debt ends up meaning different things to different people. US "debt" need never be repaid, in fact, in a certain sense, it cannot be repaid, since if the US did not maintain deficits, the international monetary system would cease to exist in exactly the same way that the British monetary system would no longer exist if the Queen actually paid back the original loan to the Bank of England. The debts of weaker nations, in contrast, are treated as absolute moral imperatives, tantamount to religious obligations, with the IMF in particular enforced to maintain the principle that no creditor, no matter how bizarre or foolhardy their original loan, should ever be forced to write down a single dollar. The recent bailout of the US financial system, even after they were caught engaging in transparent fraud, has revealed how this is now true on every level: banks, and any other corporations with a financial division, are allowed to basically make up money out of thin air through the manipulation of debt; ordinary citizens, who are obliged to backstop these efforts with their tax money whenever the bubble bursts, are under no conditions allowed to do the same: their debts are sacred obligations, matters of elementary morality, and should never be allowed the privilege of rescue or default.

The utter moral bankruptcy of such a system (to employ a metaphor that's almost not even a metaphor in this case) has now been revealed to all. The result? So far, it has been surprisingly weak: a kind of startled cynicism, or rage without direction, directionless above all because most people can no longer imagine what an economic system that wasn't morally bankrupt would even be like. The most common reaction perhaps is to simply reject the notion that morality exists on any level: as in the increasingly common habit, in the US, of homeowners simply walking away from "underwater" mortgages even if they do technically have the means to continue paying them. This does seem a logical reaction to the death-pangs of neoliberalism: "If we are all supposed to think of ourselves as tiny corporations, now, why can't we all be financial corporations? *They* can just make up money and, if they get in trouble, welsh on their debts. Well so will we." But it's hard to see how it could have much traction as a form of resistance to capitalism.

From the longer-term perspective I've been developing here, however, we can see that what we are witnessing is also a crisis in the redistributive function of the old capitalist empires—empires which are now, most likely, coming to the end of their 500-year historical run. Like the ruling classes of the Axial Age empires before them (e.g. Athens and Rome), the rulers of these more recent empires resisted earlier policies that challenged the very nature of debt. Such states, built above all on vast standing armies and navies, do not tend to indulge in jubilees, debt moratoria, or prohibitions against usury. Instead, they tend to insist on the sacred nature of debt, but at the same time, cushion certain privileged sections of the popular classes—above all, those that provide them with their soldiers and able-bodied seamen—by setting up systems to distribute the spoils of empire, directly or indirectly. Greek or Rhodian jury fees, Roman grain distributions (the "bread" part of the famous "bread and circuses"), and their innumerable Indian or Chinese equivalents, were designed above all to keep the military classes out of the clutches of the loan sharks. It's easy to see how North Atlantic social welfare policies of the post-War period operated in much the same way. They continued to operate with money that was, effectively, simply government debt, or debt created by private banks, and continued to insist that ordinary mortals treat the stuff as if it were some sacred moral trust, but then, at the same time, pursued redistributive policies that ensured that most citizens managed to keep themselves more or less above water. The new age of virtual money, starting in the 1970s, involved both stripping away those social protections, eliminating any remaining vestige of usury laws, and allowing the old North Atlantic working classes to essentially borrow their way into something like their old levels of prosperity (if not security). The solution was, clearly, a stop-gap—not really a solution at all. Empires simply cannot be maintained by destroying their core citizenry, and the crisis in Greece—with its tin-plated militarism, its perpetual posturing against Turkey, a kind of miniature comic-opera version of the grand US-EU imperial "war of civilisations" against Islam (whose militants, of course, reject the principle of interest-bearing debt entirely),[6] its dilapidated and inadequate welfare state run by a hostile and reluctant bureaucracy—all serve as a dress rehearsal for the likely fate of the global imperial system when it finally reaches its limits and the era comes definitively tumbling to a close.

And what shall follow? In a way, that's rather up to us. This is not the place to offer prescriptions. But it might help to suggest a few words of warning. Henry Ford—who as we all know was a fascist warmonger of the worst sort—once remarked that if ordinary people figured out how the banking system really worked, there would be a revolution overnight. He was referring, no doubt, to the fact that banks—and not only central banks—have been granted the right to, effectively, create money by lending it into existence. Perhaps so: but the objection is founded in a kind of false materialism that is itself a large part of the problem. Materialist ages, when it is assumed that gold and silver simply are money, and that money itself can be seen as a scarce commodity, are always scandalised by the fact that credit systems do not really operate this way, and never have. Consider for instance the words of Plutarch, on the depredations of usurers in Athens in the second century AD:

> And as King Darius sent to the city of Athens his lieutenants with chains and cords, to bind the prisoners they should take; so these usurers, bringing into Greece boxes full of schedules, bills, and obligatory contracts, as so many irons and fetters for the shackling of poor criminals …
> At the very delivery of their money, they immediately ask it back, taking it up at the same moment they lay it down; and they let out that again at interest the money they have charged in interest for what they have already lent.
> So that they laugh at those natural philosophers who hold that nothing can be made of nothing and of that which has no existence; but with them usury is made and engendered of that which neither is nor ever was.

> —Plutarch, *Moralia* 828f-831a

Compare that to this quote—almost certainly apocryphal, but extremely popular on the internet—attributed to Lord Josiah Charles Stamp, sometime director of the Bank of England, from a talk said to have been delivered in 1923:

> The modern banking system manufactures money out of nothing. The process is perhaps the most astounding piece of sleight of hand that was ever invented. Banking was conceived in iniquity and born in sin. Bankers own the earth; take it away from them, but leave them with the power to create credit, and with the stroke of a pen they will create enough money to buy it back again…. If you wish to remain slaves of Bankers, and pay the cost of your own slavery, let them continue to create deposits.[7]

The very fact that money is a social convention—a fact that was, as I've noted, simply taken for granted in the more enlightened Middle Ages—is now seen as itself intrinsically scandalous; and not, for instance, the fact that only some people are given the power to create and destroy money by mutual agreement, and other people are not. Not to mention that this power is ultimately rooted in privileged access to the instruments of violence. In a world that was not so organised around violence, such powers of creation would have to take a radically different form. Would we even be able to talk about money, debt, or credit in such a world? If nothing else, the meaning of all such words would change dramatically. In the final analysis, after all, a debt is nothing but a promise; and a promise, a form of social creativity, is a way of bringing something into being by agreeing it is there.

At the moment, we live amidst the rubble of a thousand broken promises: the promise of capitalism, the promise of technological progress, the promise of nationalism, the promise of the state. But if revealing the arbitrary nature of the power to create money out of nothing can lead to anything of ultimate worth, it should reveal the arbitrary nature of all these imaginary debts that our rulers claimed to owe us, and then, whenever it suited them, abruptly yanked away. Then we could begin to ask what kind of promises would genuinely free men and women make to one another, in a society where those structures of violence are finally yanked away. It is at moments of historical juncture like this one that we have the greatest chance of finding out. And the stubborn refusal of so many Greeks to accept the logic of *any* of these existing promises suggests that Greece is exactly the sort of place most likely to begin suggesting answers.

NOTES

1 Italy is number one. Encyclopedia "Where We Stand" data for 1997. The 2006 population was 10,688,000, of whom roughly a third were males between 14 and 65. This means one of every 50 adult males are actively serving in the security forces; if one counts army reserves, the numbers jump to one in twenty.

2 Statistics for specifically politically motivated crime are unfortunately unavailable, but consider the following, from the US government's "Greece 2010: Crime and Safety Report": "Statistics suggest that violent crime in Greece is considerably less prevalent than in other European countries. Athens is safer in terms of violent crime than comparably sized metropolitan cities. However, there has been a dramatic and steady increase in security related incidents involving improvised explosive and incendiary device attacks, as well as small arms, grenades, and other infantry style weapons. A majority of the increased attacks are politically motivated incidents that usually have a specific target of interest" (https://www.osac.gov/Reports/report.cfm?contentID=114049).

3 Mose Finley work was the earliest I managed to track down, but there are many. What he says for Greece and Rome would appear to be equally true of Japan, India, or China.

4 I am here relegating most what is generally referred to as the "Dark Ages" in Europe into the earlier period, characterised by predatory militarism and the consequent importance of bullion: the Viking raids, and the famous extraction of *danegeld* from England, in the 800s, might be seen as one of the last manifestations of an age where predatory militarism went hand and hand with hoards of gold and silver bullion.

5 It is a peculiarity of the age that, apart from China, which dissolved and was reconstituted several times, the only great empires of the period were created by nomads: from the Caliphate, to the Mongols, to the Tatars and Turks.

6 A word of clarification, lest the reader fall into the mistake of assuming that I believe the term "the West" in its conventionally accepted sense is in any way a meaningful concept. Some would challenge the idea the rivalry between Greece and Turkey is reflective of an "East/West" divide by arguing that both are, in effect, Oriental societies. My own preference is to go the other way. If "the West" means anything, over the last two centuries, it refers to that intellectual tradition that has tries to square Abrahamic revealed religion with the conceptual apparatus of Classical philosophy. But this means that Christianity, Judaism, and Islam were all equally Western, and that their current secularly-oriented epigones (such as for instance, Turkey) are equally so. The Greece-Turkey quarrel is very much a division within the West, and always has been.

7 Said to have been given at a talk at the University of Texas in 1927, but in fact, while the passage is endlessly cited in recent books and especially on the internet, it cannot be attested before roughly 1975. The first two lines appear to actually derive from a British investment advisor named L.L.B. Angas: "The modern Banking system manufactures money out of nothing. The process is perhaps the most astounding piece of sleight of hand that was ever invented. Banks can in fact inflate, mint and unmint the modern ledger-entry currency" (Angas 1937). The other parts of the quote are probably later inventions—anyway Lord Stamp never suggested anything like this in his published writings. A similar line "the bank hath benefit of all interest which it creates out of nothing" attributed to William Patterson, the first director of the Bank of England, and is likewise first attested only in the 1930s, and is also almost certainly apocryphal.

16

BURDENED WITH DEBT:
"DEBT CRISIS" AND CLASS STRUGGLES IN GREECE

TPTG

The only part of the so-called national wealth that actually enters into the collective possession of a modern nation is the national debt.

—Karl Marx, *Capital* vol. 1

Have these genealogists of morality up to now allowed themselves to dream, even remotely, that, for instance, that major moral principle 'guilt' [Schuld] derived its origin from the very materialistic idea 'debt' [Schulden]?... Where did this primitive, deeply rooted, and perhaps by now ineradicable idea derive its power, the idea of an equivalence between punishment and pain? I have already given away the answer: in the contractual relationship between creditor and debtor, which is, in general, as ancient as the idea of 'legal subject' and which, for its part, refers back to the basic forms of buying, selling, bartering, trading, and exchanging goods.... In order to inspire trust in his promise to pay back, in order to give his promise a guarantee of its seriousness and sanctity, in order to impress on his own conscience the idea of paying back as a duty, an obligation, the debtor, by virtue of a contract, pledges to the creditor, in the event that he does not pay, something else that he still 'owns,' something else over which he still exercises power, for example, his body... or his freedom or even his life....

—Friedrich Nietzsche, *On the Genealogy of Morals*

Through the constant terrorism of the media for almost a year now concerning "our" debt, the modern moralists, the preachers of the word of capital and money are trying violently to convince us, the "debtors," that in order to pay back "our" debt to "our" creditors we are obliged to take up our cross of torture and sacrifices, to place our faith in the orthodoxy of the Memorandum of Economic and Financial Policies and the Stability Pact, and are filled with awe to anticipate, in the fullness of time, the post-deficit life.

For months now, fiscal terrorism attempts to become more effective at targeting, through the collective responsibility of the debts, our own subjectivity. The storm of the imminent threats against "our" national economy aims at the internalisation of the crisis as fear and guilt: "our" debts [Schulden] should become our collective guilt [Schuld]. Thus, the original sin recurs even more violently to make us, paraphrasing Nietzsche, pledge our already low wages, our already labour-intensified life, our very expectations for a world where capitalist domination will be history. They want us to pledge our own claims for a life liberated of debts and guilt now and in the future; to become indebted with the burden of a depressingly insecure present so that we eliminate even from our imagination any possibility of abolishing this old, burdened with guilt and debt, world.

The terror of deficits now aims at creating an emergency in Greece, transforming it into a laboratory of a new shock-policy implementation. Certainly, this does not only reflect the aggravation of the global crisis and the particularity of its manifestation in Greece (as we will see below). It also reflects the catalytic effect of the December 2008 rebellion, which made the crisis even more acute, causing the delegitimisation of the previous government and the subsequent delay in taking the necessary pro-capital measures. In this sense, fiscal terrorism, along with police repression, could be considered to be a part of the ongoing counter-insurgency campaign that takes up—even in a preventive way—global dimensions.

Of late, Greece has been located at the heart of the continuing global capitalist crisis. The outbreak of the "debt crisis" and the implementation of a "shock-therapy" by the PASOK government in cooperation with the European Union and the International Monetary Fund have drawn internationally the attention of both capitalists and proletarians, since many people believe that the outcome of class struggles in Greece will greatly influence the outcome of the crisis on a global level. From this perspective, we believe that it is necessary to put the developments in Greece into a broader framework of analysis of the capitalist crisis; moreover, we should draw conclusions from the experience of the ongoing class struggles against the austerity measures in Greece since it has now become clear that similar "adjustment" programmes have already begun to be implemented in other European countries as well.

＊

The global economic recession of the previous years is nothing but the most recent manifestation of the permanent crisis of reproduction of class relations which started in the 1970s, a crisis that was never truly resolved.

The strategy followed by the "Capitalist International" since the mid-1970s was aimed at addressing the original cause of the reproduction crisis in the developed countries, i.e. the indiscipline and insubordination of the proletariat which in the late 1960s and early 1970s was extended to all spheres of everyday life, as the class struggles in the workplaces "came together" with the emergence of a multitude of new proletarian struggles (by women, minorities, the unemployed, etc.) in the sphere of distribution leading both to an exploitability crisis of labour power and to a legitimacy crisis of the capitalist state and its institutions. This strategy has assumed many different forms in the course of the years. A variety of different methods to restore profitability have been employed leading to recoveries which were proven to be only temporary:

＊ The real direct wages have been reduced in order to increase the rate of exploitation, and social expenditures have been restructured in order to discipline the workers through the imposition of workfare and the promotion of separations and atomisation. However, statistics show that even if the real direct wages have been reduced in the developed countries, this is not the case for the real compensation per worker which includes health care benefits and employers' shares of social security contributions.[1] At the same time, the labour productivity growth rates have decreased over the past four decades even if they have been higher than the growth rates of real compensation per worker.[2]

＊ In the capital-intensive sector of the economy, apart from the relative deindustrialisation that took place in the West and the relocation of a part of the production to developing countries, labour-saving technological innovations have been introduced aiming at the breaking up of the historical centres of working-class power and the disorganisation and control of the insurgent proletarians. As a consequence, these tactics faced the

247

necessity of economising on the employment of constant capital so that the organic composition of this part of capital would not be increased. But this process depends on many interrelated factors of the global accumulation circuit which have constituted a whole range of different terrains of struggle. These factors include the intensity of the labour process, the productivity of labour employed in the production of means of production, the concentration of the means of production, the length of the working day, the growth of employment, the education, skills, and discipline of the workers, the efficiency of organisation of the production process, the combination of "industrial labour" with "creative labour" in the services, the reduction of wastes, the prices of raw materials, etc. For example, educational struggles that have broken out in a number of different countries have undermined the reproduction of skilled labour power and the discipline of the collective worker; environmental struggles and peasant struggles against the expropriation of lands rich in raw materials in the so-called Third World have weighed down on the cost of raw materials and means of production; the relatively low identification of temporary workers with their job has had adverse effects on the intensity of the labour process as well as on productivity growth. *Therefore the increase of the rate of exploitation in relation to the increase of the cost of the constant capital employed has been, in total, rather mediocre.*

✳ After the mid-70s, the surplus capital that could no longer find a profitable outlet in production was transformed into money capital that was directed to the financial sector leading to its gigantic expansion and to the liberalisation of capital flows on a global level, playing also the role of the "watchman" of the global capitalist profitability, directing the flows of capital into locations of profitable investment. A significant part of this capital was employed in speculative investments betting on the future extraction of surplus value. At the same time, the removal of restrictions on the international flows of capital has become a basic instrument of the neoliberal strategy, accelerating processes of classic primitive accumulation in the periphery that have taken the form of the enclosures of communal land and of the violent proletarianisation of millions of people in South-East Asia, Latin America, and Africa.[3]

✻ A key driver of the above-mentioned process has been the "sovereign debt" as noted by Marx already since the 19th century.[4] However, the politics of the expansion of "sovereign debt" was not limited to the periphery. According to statistical data provided by OECD, since the end of the 1970s, the "sovereign debt" doubled or even tripled in all the developed countries in the West[5] for two reasons: one reason has been the successive reductions in the taxation of capital to prop up its burdened profitability; the other reason has been the inability to restrain government expenditures despite the restructuring which aimed at directing expenditures towards productive investments through the privatisation and monetisation of a significant part of the forms of reproduction of labour power.

✻ The welfare state has been partially transformed from an institution for the extended reproduction of labour power into an institution for the control of the marginalised proletarians and the imposition of low wages and poverty. The reforms of the welfare state have been also directed against the weakest parts of the working class—young workers, women, ethnic minorities, etc.—reinforcing the separations within the proletariat. However, this transformation has proven expensive and difficult to implement because of the high administrative and policing costs related to the control of the surplus population and due to the cost of the unemployment benefits which fluctuate according to the rate of unemployment. Despite the subordination of the state to the rule of money and the growth of relative surplus population, the national state still has to stabilize and secure the expanded reproduction of domestic capital and its integration into the accumulation of capital on a world scale. At the same time, the state has to guarantee the physical and social reproduction of the working class and the maintenance of social coherence and control. The rise of surplus population in a period of crisis does not exclude a rise in the absolute number of labour power which is valorised. So, the state still increases its social expenditures, but at a slower rate and in a more selective way.

✳ In parallel, the central banks' policies of low interest-rates and easy credit after the mid-1980s led to the expansion of every form of private debt—consumer, business and mortgage loans. As a result, some commentators started to talk about the appearance of "privatised Keynesianism" aiming at the promotion of effective demand on the level of society. The ephemeral boom of the mid-1980s was based on the decomposition of the working class and on the explosion of credit. Both the debt expansion and the restructuring of public expenditures have been used in order to promote the decomposition and disorganisation of the working class. The "socialisation" of the debt has integrated the better educated/specialised/productive part of the working class through a credit-sustained boom. The mirror image of credit-driven prosperity has been the exclusion of the weakest parts of the working class from consumer credit leading to their impoverishment and marginalisation. This had another effect as well: those proletarians managing to "participate" in this "prosperity" are disciplined by the fear of exclusion. However, the disciplining/divisive role of the debt expansion was seriously undermined in the years before the 2007 subprime mortgage crisis when the autonomisation of speculative investments in the derivative markets connected with consumer and mortgage debt led to a total relaxation of the rules and criteria for providing credit: in Greece even precarious workers could acquire cars with no advance payments, not to mention what happened in the United States with the housing loans, where even unemployed black families were able to get mortgage loans.[6]

The combination of an insufficient increase of the rate of exploitation with the failure to effectively economize on the employment of constant capital has led to a protracted crisis of overaccumulation. Despite temporary recoveries, the rate of profit has never returned to its "golden age" levels. Moreover, in the West, the liberal-democratic character of the integration of the proletariat into the capitalist state after the WWII has prevented the only definitive way out of the crisis: a wide devaluation or even physical destruction of unproductive capital through a generalised war for a fresh start of the capitalist machine of accumulation. All the more so, because in the beginning of the 1970s, when the crisis had first broken out, the capitalist state and its institutions faced a deep legitimisation crisis which made such an option totally unthinkable. Despite the promotion of separations within the proletariat in the decades that followed, the legitimisation crisis has not been weathered and this model of the integration of the working class into the capitalist state has not been abandoned. As we showed before, the decomposition of social relations and the deepening of separations within the proletariat, promoted by the debt expansion and the partial transformation of the welfare state into a penal state, have not proven adequate for the reconstitution of the circuit of social capital. This reconstitution entails the transformation of money into productive capital which presupposes the subordination of labour to an expanded extraction of surplus value: *the exploitation of labour must deliver rates of profit high enough to redeem debt and allow for an expanded and accelerated capitalist accumulation.* The fact that this has not been possible shows that the strength of the proletariat even at the moment of retreat has to be considered.

However, since debt and speculation cannot be used ad infinitum to boost capitalist development faster than it is warranted by the underlying flow of new value generated in production, the bubbles created by the excessive run-up of debt burst one after the other resulting in recurrent crises. In the beginning of the previous decade, the bubble of the so-called "new economy" burst in the United States. The resulting recession was dealt with on the one hand through the creation of a new bubble in the market of mortgage housing loans[7] and on the other hand through the burgeoning of the speculative investments in the markets of derivative financial products such as the Collateral Debt Obligations and the Credit Default Swaps (CDS), whose original function was the reduction of individual investment risk through its spreading within the market.[8] Ironically, the spreading of risk throughout the whole economy had disastrous consequences for financial capital. The bursting of these new bubbles in the beginning of 2008 brought the global banking system to the verge of total collapse and the global economy into deep recession. It seems that the financial sector played with money which didn't command labour, money which has lost its grip on labour. Credit represents abstract labour in the form of a claim on future exploitation, of surplus value that has not been produced yet. This fictitious surplus value appears to be a gamble. It is uncertain if it is produced.

All the governments of the developed capitalist states chose to deal with this situation through the even greater burgeoning of the "sovereign debt" with the provision of astronomical sums of money to bail out banks and boost capitalist growth. Naturally, this choice led to the transformation of the crisis into fiscal crises in a number of different countries: the first stop was Dubai with Greece following next and the rest of the PIIGS (Portugal, Italy, Ireland, Greece, Spain) waiting in the line. It seems that since the end of the 1970s, the monetarist dialectics of credit/debt sustained accumulation remains the principal way through which capital tries to maintain its domination.

The political choice to deepen the "sovereign debt crisis" exhibits great advantages for capital: the bogeyman of bankruptcy becomes a useful tool for a new cycle of violent primitive accumulation, in a similar fashion to what had happened in the countries of the periphery in previous decades. In the periphery the process of primitive accumulation takes the form of open looting, of enclosures of communal land and water resources, of the plundering of raw materials and resources resulting in the separation of millions of people from their means of production and subsistence, creating new, cheaper, and available for exploitation proletarian populations. On the other hand, in the West it takes the form of an attempt at the complete integration of the relatively decommoditised forms of social reproduction into capitalist valorisation as well as the form of labour power devaluation and disciplining: wage and pension cuts, reduction of the expenditures of public services and utilities, increase of the taxation of the working class, privatisations, reforms of social security, deepening of the separations between young and old workers, between permanent and temporary workers, between "idlers" and "industrious" workers. There is also crude violence and media propaganda against strikes and protests.

> [C]rises of capitalist accumulation find a temporary resolution in the imposition of conditions of primitive accumulation upon new populations, including the creation of new markets, discovery of new raw materials, and new and cheaper proletarians. Dispossession and expropriation are means of overcoming crises of capitalist reproduction. The werewolf hunger of capital for surplus labour, appropriating social labour time without an equivalent, develops through the expanded reproduction of dispossessed labour.[9]

> Primitive accumulation is a constantly reproduced accumulation, be it in terms of the renewed separation of new populations from the means of production and subsistence, or in terms of the reproduction of the wage relation in the "established" relations of capital. The former seeks to bring new workers under the command of capital and the latter to contain them as an exploitable human resource—the so-called human factor of production.[10]

At the same time, the privatisation of public services and utilities (public health, social housing, public transport, telecommunications, energy, water, etc.) leads to the release of a set of resources and assets at a very low cost, providing outlets to the surplus capital for capital-saving profitable investments. Finally, private investment in state bonds ensures profits which are extracted from the direct and indirect taxation of the workers aiming towards interest repayments.

Therefore, the "debt crisis" intends to become a productive crisis: a driver of primitive accumulation, dispossession and proletarianisation, a linchpin for the terrorising, the disciplining and the more effective exploitation of the proletariat through the curbing of class conflicts, proletarian desires and expectations.

Without a doubt, the selection of Greece as a laboratory for the implementation of a "shock-therapy" policy is related to the big problems which the imposition of neoliberal restructuring faced throughout the last 25 years due to the persistent eruptions of class struggles; in Greece the crisis of exploitability and disciplining of the proletariat is more intense than in any other country in Europe. This was explosively demonstrated by the rebellion of December 2008 which broke out simultaneously with the unfolding of the global economic recession. Even if only a proletarian minority participated in the rebellion, it however brought about a complete delegitimisation of the previous government and, as we mentioned before, a delay in taking the necessary restructuring measures for capital.

Apart from the consequences of the reduction of global economic activity during 2008 to the exports of Greek capital, especially in the shipping and the tourist sectors, the profitability of capital in Greece has been continuously slowing down in the last years because of the slow growth of productivity in relation to wages.[11] It is surely a fact that Greek capital and its state have made continuous attempts during the last twenty years to deal with the crisis of exploitability through repeated reforms of the welfare state; through the flexibilisation of labour relations of young workers; through continuous legal interventions for the imposition of discipline among immigrant workers and for the control of the flows of migration; through the cuts of allowances, wages, and social benefits in combination with the expansion of consumer credit.[12] In spite of the significant successes achieved by Greek capital in the period between 1996 and 2004 when the rate of exploitation and profitability rose, the crisis was not definitely resolved in favour of capital. As indicated by statistics, the rate of increase of productivity of labour has been continuously slowing down since 2004 to reach a negative growth figure of -0.5% in 2009, while real wages have been going up since 2007.[13] Productivity has risen in the period between 1995 and 2008 because of the public investments related to the Olympic Games, the influx of EU structural funds leading to the increase of constant capital investments and imports of capital goods, as well as the proliferation of a specialised work force through the rapid increase of workers with a university education. However, according to the report prepared by the Bank of Greece, the boost provided by these factors is exhausted. This is attributed by the capitalist think tanks to the relatively big size of the agriculture, trade, construction, and public administration sectors. The first three sectors are characterised by low capital/technological intensity, while the third one is attributed with a chronically low productivity performance. Also, they refer to the relatively small size of Greek enterprises, the limited connection of wages to productivity in individual workplaces as well as the "failures" of the education system. Furthermore, they do not hesitate to openly assert that the profitability slowdown is caused by our "maladjusted attitude" towards the aims of "national development," in other words by our indiscipline, by the "exalted" wages in the public sector and by the "excessive" raises agreed to by the Greek General Confederation of Labour (GSEE) and the Hellenic Federation of Enterprises (SEV) in 2008. The same reports also add that the privatisations of public utility companies, and deregulation, in general, have not proceeded as they should have, as well as that the labour market remains "rigid," aggravating the economic situation, and what's more, in a more permanent way. On the other hand, public expenditures related to wages in the public sector, health care, and so-called social protection (that is money for benefits and pensions) are continuously increasing in the last decade.

As a result, profitability started to fall from 2006 onwards, until it collapsed in the first half of 2009 by 51.5% in relation to the same period of 2008, because of the global recession. The fall of the turnover and of the profitability of private enterprises led in turn to a significant reduction of investments because of the increasing inability of private enterprises to get credit from the banks. Moreover, banks were directly affected since their profits dramatically declined because of the

254

significant increase of losses stemming from the overdue loans or even from the non-repayment of loans, having, in addition, a more general liquidity problem because of the global financial crisis.

Naturally, the state did not stay idle. It hurried to confront the problems that emerged because of the outbreak of the crisis by increasing its expenditures by 10.9% in 2009 in order to support capitalist accumulation, thus contributing to the GDP by 1.7%. At the same time, the state provided banks with funds of €28 billion, which is an amount that corresponds to 11.5% of the GDP of 2008, in order to save their profitability. This policy was continued by the government of PASOK which provided recently an additional amount of €40 billion. Besides, public expenditures were increased for other reasons as well, such as, for example, the payments of unemployment benefits since the number of unemployed workers has increased, while revenues from taxes and contributions decreased because of the recession, i.e. the decline of GDP (and what's more because of the consecutive decreases of the rate of taxation of profits in the last twenty years). Unsurprisingly, the result was that both public deficit and debt rose steeply to reach 15.4% and 126.8% respectively as a proportion of the GDP, according to the latest figures from EUROSTAT.[14]

However, the "debt" noir literature is an old affair in Greece, even if the hack writers of the ruling class try to present the "necessary sacrifices" for its reduction as something new. In fact, debt skyrocketed during the '80s. Until the end of the '70s, the government had managed to limit public expenditures related to wages and pensions. This tendency would be completely reversed in the beginning of the '80s, since the "socialist" government of PASOK was forced to increase both the direct and the indirect wages of the workers under the pressure of class struggles of the previous decade. Bound to balance between two basic, but contradictory state functions, the reproduction of capitalist accumulation and the legitimisation of exploitative social relations, the governments of that period agreed to "generous" wage increases in the public sector that also swept along the wages of the private sector. At the same time, they made investments in social welfare without securing new revenue through increased taxation of private capital or trying to reduce the shadow economy and tax evasion. Thus, the income policy and the creation of a rudimentary "welfare state," contributed to the expansion of public debt from 22.9% of the GDP in 1980 to 57.8% in 1985 and to 79.6% of the GDP in 1990.

Despite the increase of public expenses and debt, one cannot argue that the formation of social capital was carried out in the same way as in the developed capitalist countries. It seems that the aim of the welfare state during the 1980s was not so much the guarantee of the social conditions for the expansion of capitalist accumulation, but the management of the "social costs" of the reproduction crisis of the capitalist relation caused by the reduction of external revenue, the increase of social demands and class struggles and advancing deindustrialisation.[15] The low increase of productivity in relation to wages during the 1980s forced the PASOK government to change direction initiating an austerity programme in 1985 that was combined, on the ideological level, with a frontal attack against the "excessive demands" of wage workers, denouncing the workers of public utility companies as a "labour aristocracy," and trying to impose separations by blaming the workers of the public sector for enjoying "fat salaries" at the expense of the low paid workers of the private sector.

Initially, this policy led to a wage reduction of 12.5% and to a profit increase of 150% in the period between 1985 and 1987. Nevertheless, this policy was confronted by intense struggles of the supposedly privileged parts of the working class (teachers' strikes, strikes at public utility companies, bank employees' strikes, etc.) that continued to have offensive demands pushing the whole class upwards. These struggles forced PASOK to take back the austerity programme, leading, thus, to a reduction of the wage cuts by a half of their initial size. Although the "national unity" government in 1990 and the subsequent neoliberal governments took on the responsibility of the capitalist counter-attack, the "debt dynamic" was not checked, leading thus, to further debt increases. By the mid-1990s, debt had climbed to a figure of 97% of the GDP and was stabilised until the end of the decade around 95–100% of the GDP. In 2000 debt climbed to 103.4% of the GDP and in the following years it fluctuated around 100% of the GDP. It doesn't require much effort to recognize the common motto that politicians and journalists have repeated during the last twenty years every time they ask us to work more for less in order to "save the country from bankruptcy."

But let us return to the present developments. Since 2008, world financial institutions have decided to invest mainly in government bonds, which almost everywhere have multiplied because of the global state policies of bailing out banks. After the sovereign debt crisis of Dubai in October 2009 and the failure of the credit rating agencies in forecasting it, these agencies frantically downgraded Greek government bonds. This led in its turn to the rise of the CDS prices and spreads. The fact that the European Central Bank initially planned to raise the minimum credit rating for the eligibility of government bonds as collateral in liquidity provision from the start of 2011 encouraged the financial institutions holding Greek government bonds to dump them, precipitating the "debt crisis" and raising the interest, which in its turn raised the cost of debt refinancing.[16] Thus, public expenditures related to the payment of interest as well as forecasts for the increase of public deficit and debt have risen. The so-called "financial stabilisation mechanism" created by the EU and the IMF to "support" Greece through the provision of loans with a lower interest rate than the one that is determined in the market in "exchange" for the imposition of a strict structural adjustment programme should be seen in this context.[17]

It must be noted that the proportion of wage labour in Greece hardly reaches 65% of the economically active population, with self-employed people reaching a proportion of 22%,[18] while more than 90% of businesses employ less than ten workers. Therefore, the fact that 19,000 small businesses closed down in 2009, with a forecast that 45,000 small businesses will close down in 2010 and 60,000 in 2011, shows that the so-called "fiscal consolidation" assumes in Greece characteristics of a typical process of primitive accumulation with the proletarianisation of tens of thousands of self-employed people and professionals as well as small business proprietors.

In conditions of economic recession, businesses which are not adequately profitable and productive are forced to close down; the inefficient part of capital is destroyed so that a rising capitalist accumulation may start again. Of course, it is questionable whether this destruction of capital is adequate when the state provides astronomical sums to bail-out banks, which are "too big to fail." But, here we can also detect capital's tendency to concentrate: bank, transport and hospital merging negotiations are up and running.

An overview of the measures that the greek government tries to impose through the stability programme is sufficient to reveal the extent of the attack against us:

Repeal of 13th and 14th salary in the public sector. They are replaced by a €1,000 benefit but only for workers with gross salaries less than €3,000 per month. 7% pay cuts on the regular wages in the public sector. Pay freeze for three years for all public and private sector workers. 20% total cut down on the benefits in the public sector.

Repeal of 13th and 14th pension in the public and private sector. They are replaced by a €800 benefit. Pension freeze for three years in the public and private sector. 3% to 10% cut down on pensions of over €1,400 net.

Cut down on layoff compensation and increase of the number of workers that can be laid-off every month per workplace (especially in big companies).

Reduction in overtime costs.

VAT increase at all levels with the maximum reaching 23%. VAT base broadening. Increase of indirect taxes by 10% (fuel, alcohol, and cigarettes).

"Liberalisation" of closed-shop professions.

"Liberalisation"/privatisation of public transportation (buses, trains, etc.) and energy.

Pension system reform

Since the early 1990s the Greek government has made successive reforms of the pension system. One of the main aims of these reforms was the splitting up of workers in various categories with different ages of retirement, different minimum contribution periods for retirement, and so on. This has been further intensified by this reform.

Thus, despite the fact that from 2015 the age for retirement will be increased to the age of 65 and the minimum contribution period to 40 years for all the workers (equality between women and men), on the other hand there is a designation of a series of subcategories of workers with different requirements in order to get and determine their pension. Of course, the retirement age for these subcategories is also increased gradually to the age of 65 which will be applied for everybody from 2015. Apart from the workers officially hired before 1983 who are not affected by the new law, workers who have been officially hired up to 1993 are gradually assimilated to the new status from 2011 with an annual increase of the relevant requirements, while the workers that have been officially hired after 1993 are immediately subjected to the new pension limits.

Regarding the determination of the pension, there are also several new categories: for workers officially hired from 1983 to 2011, the pension amount will be calculated for the years of work until 2010 with the old law and for the years of work after 2010 with the new law. Here we must note that, according to the new reform, there is a significant reduction of the replacement rate for every category. Finally, the workers that will be officially hired from 2011 onwards will be subjected only to the new law. This situation leads inevitably to an individual determination of pension with obvious consequences on the potential collective workers' struggles in the field of social security.

From 2011, the amount of pension will be determined based on the wages throughout the work life and not on the best five years of the last decade before retirement, as it was until today.

Within the next two years, there will be a reduction of the supplementary pensions according to the economic status of each auxiliary fund.

A further reduction of pensions of 7% on average is planned, both in the public and the private sector.

Significant reduction of the professions that are ranked as heavy and health-hazardous occupations.

Revision of the framework for awarding disability pensions aiming at their reduction.

From 2020, there will be automatic adjustment of retirement age to life expectancy.

Suspension of all recruitments in public sector in 2010 and from 2011 implementation of the rule: one recruitment for every five retirements.

Establishment of lower wages than the minimum wage for entrants and the long-term unemployed.

Legislative regulations for the promotion of temporary and part-time contracts.

Legal predominance of labour contracts at enterprise level over contracts at sectoral level.

Cut down on public investments by €2 billion during the next two years.

Creation of a Financial Stability Fund with state financing (€10 billion) for the stability of the Greek banking system.

Reform of the "anti-terrorist" legislation. While in the previous "anti-terrorist" law there were some clauses whereby certain offences were not considered to be "terrorist acts" if they were done for the "protection of the democratic regime" and as an "exercise of fundamental individual, political and labour rights," in the new reformed law they have been repealed. Such offences (like "disturbance of the safety of transportation") are obviously related to an attempted stronger repression of class struggles and proletarian or political violence.

Restructuring of Higher Education. On top of the previous reforms (2006–2007), which proved unsuccessful to a certain extent because of the student movement, a series of new restructuring measures have been announced:

Reduction of expenditures through mergers, closures of institutions in the periphery and layoffs which will lead to a reduction of the number of students.

"Financial self-sufficiency": funding will be provided by the state on the basis of specific contracts with terms related to assessment of quantifiable targets such as research performance and the absorption of graduates in the labour market. In this manner, universities are being pushed to introduce student fees and to reduce their workforce.

Reform of the administrative structure of the universities: the participation of students' and professors' representatives in the administration will be abolished in effect through the establishment of a "Board of Trustees" organ which will be appointed by the government and will consist of CEOs and other representatives of the private capital in order to promote further entrepreneurialisation and commodification of studies. In parallel, it is obvious that this will lead in effect to the abolition of the academic sanctuary.

> Further intensification of student labour through the imposition of examinations acting as "filters" in the first year of the studies, as well as intensification of employee and teacher labour through the introduction of further assessment procedures and external evaluators.
>
> Individualisation and fragmentation of the academic diplomas through the division of studies into units in order to measure the academic performance of students and to align studies with business needs in a more effective way.
>
> *We must note that these measures are not taken once and for all but will be expanded (e.g. further VAT base broadening, further increase of indirect taxes, further reduction of recruitments in public sector etc.) during the next years as the Greek state continues the implementation of the "stability programme" and gets the scheduled payments of the instalment loan from IMF and ECB.*

✳

What follows below is an outline of the response of the working class since the beginning of the "debt crisis" which reached its climax in the strike demonstration of 5 May in Athens but has remained inadequate to the size of the attack that we are facing and the ferocity of the measures. (Indicative of the retreat of the response was the very small participation of 10,000 people in the general strike demonstration on the 8 July, which was the day that the pension reform act was passed in the parliament affecting almost all workers).[19]

Given the range of the attempted restructuring under the general name of the "austerity measures," apart from several "general strikes," a series of 24-hour, 48-hour strikes or work-stoppages have taken place in different key sectors (electricity, public transport, shipping sector, etc.) almost each month since February, as separate and sectional mobilisations, though, without any kind of coordination and communication among them.

The first general strike was called on the 24th of February 2010 with a participation ranging between 70–100% in the private sector and between 20–50% in the public sector. Two were the main features of the demonstration in Athens on that day: first, the noticeable participation of many immigrants not only "under the command" of left-wing organisations but also diffused in the body of the demonstration (the immigrants' presence was related to the new law for "the citizenship of immigrants," which creates divisions among them by categorising them into those few eligible for citizenship and those thousands condemned into the no-man's land of illegality). The second feature was the street fighting that took place between riot police and protesters who did not necessarily come from the anti-authoritarian/anarchist milieu as well as violent attacks against capitalist institutions like banks and stores and some looting. Although such incidents were not generalised, they certainly gave a quite different tone to what one might expect from the usual GSEE-ADEDY strike demos and showed the great impact of December 2008 revolt on the way of protesting. Despite the left-wing calls for "peaceful protest," there was certainly a general feeling of joy in releasing indignation against the cops and thus expressing the anger against the recent onslaught, so in this sense the strike and the demonstration functioned as a powerful antidepressant, although with a temporary effect.

On the 5 March, two days after the socialist government had announced the first new measures for the "salvation of the country," ADEDY (the umbrella organisation of the public sector unions) and GSEE (the corresponding organisation of the private sector unions) called for a three hour work stoppage, while other unions (both primary and secondary teachers' unions, public transport unions) called a day strike. Anti-authoritarians and younger people had a more visible presence that time and the atmosphere was tense from the beginning at Syntagma Square near the parliament where the Socialist Party was going to vote for the new measures. When the head of GSEE, Panagopoulos, made the mistake of trying to speak, he was attacked by the crowd (where certainly anti-authoritarians and leftists were in the majority), chased and beaten all the way to the entrance of the parliament where he took refuge among the riot police. Soon an angry crowd gathered just below the building and some fighting started between the enraged people and the riot squads which was generalised. About three hundred or more people were throwing stones at them (mostly anti-authoritarians but not only) and the rest remained there shouting and cursing for some time until the riot police made a heavy attack trying to disperse the crowd. The demonstration then started marching towards the Ministry of Labour (a clear effort on the part of the unionists to release the tension near the parliament) and although police presence became heavier, there were some incidents of smashing.

On the 11 March GSEE and ADEDY called for another 24-hour strike, in response to the climate of a general yet passive discontent with the announced austerity measures, attempting to retain a grain of legitimacy. The participation in the strike was higher than the previous one and the number of demonstrators was almost double than the demonstration on the 24 February. The composition of the crowd was also slightly different since there were more university students, a few high school students and more young workers while immigrants were absent this time. Moreover, a large number of demonstrators coming from almost the entirety of the anti-authoritarian milieu participated, too, dispersed into the whole body of the demonstration. That time both the police and the leadership of the union confederations were far more prepared: the riot squads tried to prevent an escalation of proletarian violence by closely following the demonstration from both sides using a more offensive tactics and the confederations unionists not only cooperated openly with the police but they actually gave specific commands to the riot squads to stop the demonstrators from the start in order to take the lead of the demonstration and avoid possible conflicts with the rank and file and a repetition of the events of the last demonstration. Thus, despite several confrontations with the police at various points, relatively fewer people not coming from the anarchist-antiauthoritarian milieu supported the street-fighting or actively participated in clashes with the police, something that may also be related to the more extended (and thus more conservative) composition of the demonstrators.

Until the 5 May the composition of the demos was different from the December 2008 demos. High school students did not show up at all, at least in recognizable blocks, except for a few ones on the 11 March demonstration, but university students began to participate as more and more general assemblies were called. In general, apart from the students, the precarious, "lumpen," marginal segments of the class which was the dominant subject of the riots was not present yet.

However, this changed on the 5 May demonstration. Although fiscal terrorism was escalating day after day with constant threats of an imminent state bankruptcy and cries for "sacrifices to be made," the proletariat's response on the eve of the voting of the new austerity measures in the Greek parliament was impressive. It was probably the biggest workers' demonstration since the fall of the dictatorship, even bigger than the 2001 demonstration which had led to the withdrawal of a planned pension reform, with strikes in almost all sectors of the (re)production process. But what was even more impressive was the fact that a proletarian crowd similar to the one which had taken to the streets in December 2008 (also called derogatorily "hooded youth" by mainstream media propaganda) was also there. Although there were instances when hooded rioters were booed when they attempted or actually made violent attacks on buildings, in general they fit well within this motley, colourful, angry river of demonstrators. The slogans ranged from those that rejected the political system as a whole, like "Let's burn the parliament brothel" to patriotic ones, like "IMF go away," and to populist ones like "Thieves!" and "People demand crooks to be sent to prison." As the demonstration was approaching the parliament, crowds of workers (electricians, postal workers, municipal workers, etc.) tried to invade the building from any access available but there was none as hundreds of riot cops were strung out all along the forecourt and the entrances. Despite the fact that the riot police made a massive counter-attack with tear gas and stun grenades and managed to disperse the crowd, there were constantly new blocks of demonstrators arriving in front of the parliament while the first blocks which had been pushed back were reorganising themselves. There was extensive destruction of property in the nearby streets and constant attacks against the cops. The fights lasted for almost three hours but soon the terrible news came about three or four people dead in a burnt-down bank! Although the accurate facts concerning this tragic incident are still relatively unknown, what seems to be closer to the truth is that at this particular bank, right in the heart of Athens on a general strike day, about twenty bank clerks were made to work by their boss, got locked inside "for their protection" and finally three of them died of suffocation. Initially, a Molotov cocktail was thrown through a hole made on the window panes into the ground floor and after some time the building got ablaze. The reversal was successful. Soon a huge operation by the riot police followed: the crowds were dispersed and chased away, the whole centre was cordoned until late in night and the prime minister would announce the news in the parliament condemning the "political irresponsibility" of those who resist the measures taken and "lead people to death" while the government's "salvation measures" on the contrary "promote life."

The consequences were visible the very next day: the media vultures capitalised on the tragic death representing it as a "personal tragedy" dissociated from its general context (mere human bodies cut off from their social relations) and some went so far as to criminalize resistance and protest. The government gained some time changing the subject of discussion and conflict and the unions felt released from any obligation to call for a strike the very day when the new measures were passed: just a few thousands gathered outside the parliament at an evening rally called by the unions and left organisations.

The sickening game of turning the dominant fear/guilt for the debt into a fear/guilt for a (violent) resistance against the terrorism of

263

debt had already started. In the case of the 5 May demonstration, a tragic event and the state propaganda that escorted it made this reversal possible: a huge and spontaneous violent crowd, ready to escalate the struggle, was pushed back and sent home, since spontaneity is extremely dependent on the feeling of the moment. Ever since there has been no massive response and on the contrary the trend of isolated strikes got stabilised without any indication that the thrust of the initial counter-attack could be revived.

In June, a three-day strike took place in the Athens metro against layoffs, but it stopped after some vague promises given by the Minister of Transport to the metro union, which is controlled by PA-SOK, that the workers would be rehired in other public organisations. Other strikes also took place in the transport sector. The employees of the OSE, the state-owned railway company, declared a 24-hour strike on 10 June against the wage cuts imposed by the government and the planned privatisation of the company as part of the broader attempts at cuts in the public sector. As a first step, the government decided to cut down on the operating costs of the company by abolishing railway routes that were not profitable. A 48-hour strike was decided by the employees of the suburban railway, a subsidiary company of OSE, on 22–23 of June. The employees of ETHEL, the state-owned bus company in the city of Athens, declared a 24-hour strike on 3 June and a 5-hour work-stoppage on 17 June against wage cuts and the government's plan to reduce the state subsidy to the company. Another 24-hour strike was declared on 1 July when the company failed to pay the salaries and the holiday pay to its employees on time.

The secondary school teachers who were going to mark the students' exams for the admission to the Universities decided to abstain from work, protesting against the decision of the Ministry of Education to cut down on their compensation for correcting the candidates' tests. In the end, OLME, the teachers' union, decided to show a "sense of responsibility" and put an end to this mobilisation. Since entrance to the university still has a major importance in the Greek society, OLME justified their decision by claiming that they did not want to "punish" the students.

In July, hospital doctors went on a five-day strike against the new reform of public health which aims at cutting down on public hospitals' expenditures, promoting the privatisation of some health services and adjusting the work conditions of doctors (especially the entrants) to a more flexible and precarious status. The strike was called by the Federation of Unions of Physicians (OENGE).

Bank employees went on a 24-hour strike against the oncoming takeover of the Agricultural Bank of Greece, which was the only Greek bank that failed the European "stress test."

The mobilisation of lorry-owners was the longest one and it also had a great impact on transports. In the end of July, the owners of public transport lorries announced a strike against the imminent law for the "liberalisation" of public transport. The main consequences of that law are (a) the devaluation of their licenses, which could be sold at a very high price until now and (b) the setting up of companies and the minimisation of self-employment. Some professions, such as lorry owners, pharmacists, lawyers, architects, and others are "closed shop" ones. For example, only a pharmacist can obtain a license to open a pharmacy and not an entrepreneur or a company without a pharmacist's specialty. Of course, in some "closed shop" professions, like lorry-owners, lawyers, or architects, companies already exist. But, at the present moment, capital is less concentrated in "closed shop" professions. Lorry owners' profession is the first one to be "liberalised" and the others will soon follow. In this sense, we can say that this "liberalisation" constitutes a crash test for the government's ability to implement such a measure. The insistence of the IMF, the European Central Bank, the European Commission and the Greek government on abolishing the "closed shop" status particularly of the Greek transportation shows the importance they lay on the concentration of capital in this particular sector increasing thus its profitability. We could say that the essence of the "liberalisation process" is the destruction/devaluation of small-scale capital, self-employment, and petit-bourgeois private property. Nothing is being "liberalised." On the contrary, capital is "tightening" itself in order to expand even further.

The road transport strike caused big problems for the distribution of commodities, especially fuel, and since it was called in the holiday peak, the government managed to isolate the lorry owners condemning them as "enemies of the public interest." On the fourth day of the strike the government made use of the "civil conscription" method on vehicles and drivers. Lorry owners defied the order and continued their strike and road blockades. The state decided to mobilize army vehicles and naval vessels to ensure the supply of fuel in "critical sectors" and break the strike. Private companies' fuel lorries were used in the same way, too. It is interesting to mention that most of the lorry owners' union representatives own transport companies although the vast majority of lorry drivers are self-employed. After nine days of strike, their leaders announced that they were going to cancel the strike, negotiate

265

with the government for side issues of their profession (insurance and taxation policy) and consider further action in September, when the law was going to be voted in the parliament. It is also important to mention that except for the combative attitude of this sector (clashes with riot police outside the Ministry of Transport in Athens, outside an oil refinery in Thessaloniki, road blockades, and scab beating), the social content of their struggle was totally sectional and not without nationalist features (Greek national flags and famous ancient Greek battle cries were used by the strikers!).

In the end of September the law was voted, while the "civil conscription" was still active. Lorry-owners were on an eighteen-day strike at that time and they continued even after the law was enacted. The state's response was the mobilisation of a scab-mechanism: the police escorted convoys of lorries, some drivers were arrested and the riot police cleared the road and port blockades. An aggressive propaganda against the strikers had been systematically used by the media. On top of that, the lack of any concrete social alliance led the strikers to become isolated and demoralised. Eventually, they were divided between a majority who went back to work defeated and a small minority of angry and desperate strikers who were labelled "extremists." Their actions (slashing the tyres of scab lorries and in some cases even shooting against them or burning them) and the formation of a strike committee were undermined and condemned by their own representatives. Finally, the strike was over.

In the public sector, many civil servants were on a kind of slowdown strike, delaying the function of their services. Especially those who work in ministries and civil services slowed down their work pace, creating problems and delays in the function of the state. An example of such a reaction was the air traffic controllers' mobilisation who initially announced a strike on 24 July which was ruled illegal (as it was in the peak of the tourist period in Greece). They chose to go on a work-to-rule strike using the strict international regulations for air traffic in order to block or delay airplane departures. Another example was the primary and secondary teachers' local unions' decision to reject the self-assessment process imposed by the Ministry of Education as the first step of the attempted disciplining assessment of both teachers and school units. Despite that, we could say that the overall response of the civil servants, who are excessively affected by the government's policy, has been rather lukewarm.

266   The mobilisation of temp workers in ERT (the national radio-television company) against the non-renewal of their contracts met with

the complete indifference of their permanent co-workers. The occupation of the ERT headquarters ended ingloriously after a negotiation between the PASOK-controlled temp workers' union and the management, without blocking the function of the TV stations and without exploiting the opportunity to take over the control and broadcast their demands all around Greece.

On 24 September, 2,000 temp workers from all over the public sector demonstrated outside of the Hellenic Supreme Court of Civil and Penal Law premises in order to press the court to issue a favourable judgement on the conversion of fixed term contracts of two cleaners working in a public company (OPAP, the official organisation of betting) into permanent ones since this judgement would be a res judicata for all similar future disputes. The recommendation of the rapporteur was negative for the workers but after a request by the union representatives the court decided to postpone the judgement until 20 January 2011 in an attempt to let off steam since the attitude of the demonstrators was rather combative. Afterwards, the demonstrators marched towards the parliament. When the demonstration passed outside of the Ministry of Interior, some eggs were thrown and some minutes later a bunch of temp fire fighters tried to invade the building after the main part of the demonstration had already reached Syntagma square. Their action was unsuccessful since only a hundred of them were there but it gave the opportunity to their union representatives to enter the building and deliver a resolution. At the same time, in Syntagma square, some right-wing unionists in a spectacular move got to the front and urged the demonstrators to chant the national anthem. Much to our dismay, many demonstrators joined in the chanting.

During September, the workers of OSE (the Hellenic Railways Organisation) went on a series of strikes and work-stoppages against the oncoming restructuring. The rationalisation process of OSE is a key matter for the restructuring and privatisation policy of the public transport sector in general. Using as an excuse the large deficit of OSE (about €11 billion), a deficit which was created by the previous state policies, the government is trying (a) to reduce labour and functional costs (cutting down on wages, overtimes and benefits, minimising the number of workers, closing down unprofitable lines), (b) to maximize OSE revenues by selling or using assets of the organisation (infrastructure) which remained idle until now and by increasing ticket prices, and (c) to create the conditions for the privatisation of parts of the organisation's services and functions. All these are accompanied with a new internal regulation and reorganisation of OSE's work relations and conditions. We should mention that the leadership of the union of OSE is controlled by PASOK and until now we have not seen any rank and file initiatives to create links with the "users" of the railway, i.e. other proletarians. The law for the restructuring of the national railways was voted in principle in the parliament in October.

✳

Although these struggles have created significant problems for Greek capital and its state in the course of the last eight months, they never-theless seem to have followed a general pattern: so far all the responses against the new measures have remained fragmented, unconnected, defensive, and totally controlled or sabotaged by unions. A typical ex-ample of how unions undermine the strikes is what happened during the general strike of 8 July when the union of the Metro employees, controlled by PASOK, contrary to what had happened during previ-ous strikes, decided on a complete blocking of the metro, preventing thus many strikers from demonstrating because they couldn't access the centre of the city.

The paralyzing and mediating role of the union apparatuses is best seen in the activities of the union confederations which are totally controlled by the socialist government and do their best to avoid any real resistance against the recent offensive.

The fact that GSEE has called six 24-hour strikes in the previ-ous eight months, while ADEDY has called, in the same period, eight 24-hour strikes and a few stoppages. A few stoppages should not be interpreted as a real effort on their part to promote struggles nor as an indication of a mighty working-class response. It must be noted that the declaration of these strikes was not accompanied by an effective union or other mobilisation in the workplaces. Without any preparation for the strikes, the percentages of the strikers gradually diminished after May and the demos degenerated, exhausting people, mainly function-ing in most cases as a "steam releaser." Thus, at the moment, it seems rather improbable that the crisis and the pressure exerted to those di-nosauric bodies by the rank and file will lead to major changes in their structure and function, if we consider the almost lethargic behaviour of the low in hierarchy union cadres of the socialist party who still win most of the votes in most workplaces. Although the "debt crisis" increasingly undermines their already weak function to guarantee the improvement of the conditions of the reproduction of the proletariat as labour power, still the power of the unions resides in the sectional and even individualistic use the proletarians make of them: the particular history of political clientelism in Greece is also evident within the unions, especially in the public sector, as voting for the socialist or right-wing unionists usually meant either climbing up the social ladder or at least some kind of legal advice. Thus, even if such material gains are limited now, they are not drastically cut yet; union cadres can still rely on social inertia and political clientelism that creates a relatively loose hierarchy and discipline in the public sector so as not to feel threatened and attempt major reforms in the union apparatuses.

As for the small, rank and file unions that have multiplied in the last years, whether leftist or anarchist, they are too impotent to mobilise workers in general apart from their politically affiliated members. Their militant practices (blockades of firms, taking part in demos) rely mostly on the active participation of anti-authoritarians who do not in fact belong to them.

As far as PAME's activities (the "labour front" created by the CP) are concerned, they probably seem impressive, taking into account the fact that in many cases PAME was the first one to call mobilisations, obliging GSEE and ADEDY to follow. It is possible that a plan for splitting GSEE and ADEDY and creating a third "independent" union confederation lies underneath this strategy. PAME has organised a number of spectacular moves, such as occupations of ministries, TV stations, the stock market, blockades of the port of Piraeus, etc.—in one case, PAME's members had blockaded the port in order to defend a strike of the shipworkers that was ruled illegal by the courts. However, these mobilisations were under the complete control of the party without a grain of initiative from the rank and file and it is certain that if the struggles escalate, the CP will again assume the role of the police repressing any radical initiative or action, as it has done many times in the past. Besides, this is clearly shown by its permanent tactics to prevent any contact and communication of its members with other strikers, organising separate and, above all, peaceful demonstrations. The present conjuncture constitutes an ideal terrain for the activities of the CP since the propaganda of the government itself and of the mass media about the alleged imposition of the tough measures by EU, international markets and speculators seems to confirm its rhetoric about "exiting from EU" and "resisting to monopolies and the big capital," which keeps repeating with religious devotion since the '80s. As one of the main political representatives of the working class (as a class of the capitalist mode of production and communication) inside the Greek state and its institutions, the CP proclaims the establishment of a nationalist "popular" economy where the working class will enjoy the merits of a social-

269

democratic capitalism with a flavour of Stalinism. As a matter of fact, the actions of the CP ensure the entrapment of struggles into the limits of capitalist institutions, and what is more, into the most fetishised of them, elections and the parliament since for the CP, voting for the party and getting organised in it constitutes the culmination of class struggle.

But, apart from the role of all kinds of unionist policing mediation, there is an almost total lack of autonomous proletarian action and of openly expressed radical contents of struggle going beyond the union/sectional demands. It is maybe frustrating, but the truth is that those strikes and demos that have attracted worldwide attention have been called and organised from above, be it the union confederations or federations that determined their time and content. The response of the greater part of the working class has remained to a considerable extent passive. It is true that the class combativeness of many strikers in the streets, against the cops and the trade union leadership, their joy in mixing with strikers of other sectors and in occupying the centre of the city (in the case of the first demos in February and March and on 5th May) reveal a deeper rebellious content which is however latent and has not been expressed in an autonomous and co-ordinated organisation of the struggle within the workplaces or in the neighbourhoods.

*

Partly, an explanation for the inadequate response of the proletariat to the attack called "debt crisis" can be traced back in the state's effective propaganda to legitimize it. In order to work more for less money we have to accept that we face a "problem" that is beyond our reach and control, something that needs our sacrifices. Thus, the cause of the crisis is attributed to an almost metaphysical but inescapable world of markets, statistics, rating agencies, speculators, and so on. This mystification veil is used in order to conceal the real cause of the crisis: the convulsive but persistent refusal of the global proletariat to become totally subordinated to capital and the circulation of its struggles, however limited it is.

Thus, in a period of acute crisis, capital's obsession with regaining control over the proletariat—especially when the command of capital and its state was recently questioned and delegitimised in a violent way—is transmuted into the invisible dark omnipotence of "economy" and the "markets" working above us, causing a generalised feeling of weakness and impotence. The hard austerity measures, this clear declaration of class war, has to become "naturalised": crisis has assumed the character of a natural catastrophe that cannot be reversed until it will come full circle after some years, as the economists-weathermen keep telling us in their forecasts.

The Greek state, under the PASOK administration, together with its European partners and the media scum, intensified the ideological terrorisation by also using a traditional but all-weather powerful "weapon": *national unity*. During crises, the partners turn into commanders and rivals; the unified European village whose inhabitants live harmoniously and co-decide democratically falls apart while a matter of utmost importance, the defence of the nation—this perennial deception—comes to the fore. In a few words, they try to persuade us that we will not work for our bosses but for the country's good.

The "debt crisis" offers the capitalist state a unique opportunity to re-impose the unification of the proletariat around the nation-state form and through that its disciplining, in the hope of an increasing productivity and higher profits. In the words of the Greek prime minister "…it is clear that the way in which we dealt with our finance affairs led us to lose a part of our national sovereignty. We have to take that part back by means of our credibility, our political programme and everyone's self-sacrifice." His "sacrifice" to "give away a part of the country's sovereignty" entails "our self-sacrifice" in order to "take it back." But we have to pay for this "part" with more work, less money, deeper divisions, and competition among us in the face of the increasing numbers of the reserve army of unemployed.

National unity is reinforced as a surrogate "collective" identity when, at the moment of economic and social disintegration, individualist roles within the reified social relations are shattered. In the last two decades, trade unionism and politics, which are both typically characterised by the use of collective means for individualist ends, tended to be less attractive and effective compared to the use of individual or household loans. The "sovereign debt crisis" and the imminent bankruptcy could entail a disaster on an individual and family level that most proletarians are not prepared to reverse in a class autonomous way. Passivity then under the flag of "national unity" can serve as a refuge and a rationalisation for those who, not willing to protest against their devaluation now, put their hopes for a future increase of the value of their *own* labour power in the increase of the competitiveness of the Greek economy. The non-strikers might even make verbal attacks against their fellow workers whose strikes would destroy this endeavour.

Since crisis is experienced as a multitude of personal failures bound together ("living beyond our means" summarizes the individual 271 "excesses" and "malfunctions" that led to a "national failure"), self-blame and guilt can take such epidemic dimensions, that certain defence-mechanisms are needed. Those defence-mechanisms are activated through the projection of the feeling of guilt onto the witch-hunted "extravagant" civil servants, tax evaders or even selected scapegoated "corrupt" politicians who "failed" to perform their high functions. The state ideologues, on their part, who know that in periods of crises capital and its state are no longer trustworthy since the "rewards promised" never came, they are all too willing to channel anger and fear to a path safer for the system.[20]

Nationalism and populism, however, can also emerge through another route as well: through the struggles themselves mainly because of the influence of the dominant left and leftist discourse and activity on them. Nationalisation of banks, self-management of key sectors of the national economy, different suggestions for the renegotiation of the debt by (this or another) government, emphasis on the "corruption" issue, ideas for a "productive" reorganisation of Greece are the most popular slogans of the left in these days—in sum, a capitalism confined within the borders against the three foreign evils (IMF, ECB and EC) and the "Quisling" Greek government.

Finally, to the "irresponsible" strikers who betray the "national cause" through struggle, the prime minister was clear when he declared: "Sacrifices are needed; we cannot afford blockades and strikes." It is obvious that the government and the capitalists are afraid of a social unrest which can burst out if all mediations and mechanisms prove ineffective. The ideologues of the system try to eliminate even the memory of the December 2008 rebellion as a nightmare that should not be repeated. When they demand social peace they know that they are walking on thin ice: their arsenal—be it union apparatuses and functions, individualism or doses of fear and guilt—may be exhausted. That's why while the government puts on its humanist-antiracist mask and speaks the language of the "common good," it holds the cop's bludgeon at the same time. Social consent must prevail by any means. No wonder the streets are full of cops that try to control every space that could become a field of struggle and clash. To return to Nietzsche: "this world deep down has never again been completely free of a certain smell of blood and torture"—something that the Minister of Labour reminded us when, some months ago, during the announcement of the new "hard but necessary measures" he declared: "there will be blood." Maybe, he unconsciously presaged the storm which is coming. A storm which may bring the recomposition of the struggles and will send the "public deficit" to the dustbin of history, together with the "life deficit," the only real one.

TPTG, August-October 2010

NOTES

1 See OECD Employment Outlook 1998, OECD Employment Outlook 2007 and America's Dynamic Workforce 2007 report by the U.S. Department of Labour.

2 L. Skoczylas and B. Tissot, *Revisiting recent productivity developments across OECD countries*, Bank for International Settlements Working Papers No. 182, October 2005, OECD Employment Outlook 1998 and OECD Employment Outlook 2007. One of the main reasons for the productivity slow-down has been the relative expansion of temporary and unskilled labour through the implementation of casualisation and flexibilisation policies mainly for the entrants in the labour market.

3 For example, primitive accumulation in China has provided a cheaper labour power than in the "West," which resulted in cheaper commodities for private consumption and also in cheaper means of production. Since the beginning of the '80s, the model of capitalist development in China has been based precisely on the gradual dissolution of the Maoist welfare state and on the permanent devaluation of labour power. China's economy has been completely dependent on extensive foreign investments of (cheap) labour-seeking and export-oriented global capital and, consequently, not on the expansion of domestic consumption. Rapid export growth led to ballooning foreign reserves which boosted debt-financed overinvestment in export-oriented sectors of the economy, whose maintenance hangs on the even greater export expansion. Thus, idle capacity has been soaring ever since the mid-1990s and it is estimated that 75% of China's industries are plagued by overcapacity. In parallel, over the past decade there has been a shift from exports of labour-intensive consumer goods to capital-intensive capital goods, parts, and components. Such a shift has made China's economy far more dependent on foreign demand as well as on the real effective exchange rate, which depends on the relation of wages to productivity. A drastic fall of foreign demand stemming from an economic recession due to the overaccumulation crisis in the West may have catastrophic results leading to an intense outbreak of enterprise bankruptcy and a destabilisation of the banking sector, which in its turn would hugely aggravate the global crisis of overaccumulation by directly influencing the credit stability of the United States. On the other hand, wage increases gained through class struggles or through "income redistribution programmes," labour legislation and a relative strengthening of the Chinese welfare state would prop up domestic consumption and would reduce both the dependence of China on foreign demand and the danger of a total collapse. Also, wage increases would provide a vast market for foreign capital, especially from the United States, supporting growth and employment overseas. Nevertheless, if such an option is not accompanied by a faster rise in productivity through higher worker retention rates, increased efficiency and higher skills—which is totally unsure given the spreading of industrial unrest throughout China's factories in the previous years— it would also lead to a reduction of exports as well as to an increase of the cost of

constant capital in the global economy, worsening the overaccumulation problem from a different route. If this situation seems like a dead end—which is reflected in articles and studies by organisations such as the "Financial Times" (e.g. *Tables turn on Chinese employers*, FT 4 June 2010)—it, however, originates from the character of the neoliberal project which is based on "spatial-temporal" fixes to global overaccumulation which do nothing more than switch the crisis from one territory of the planet to another territory of the planet—turning the recipients of surplus capital (in this case China) to exporters of surplus capital—or from one point of time to another point of time—through the reallocation of capital into financial and real-estate investments that delay the moment of profit realisation. In other words, neoliberal politics have not been able to constitute a new regime of accumulation, all the more so that this would require an extended devaluation and destruction of the non-productive capital. See Ho-fung Hung, *Rise of China and the Global Overaccumulation Crisis*, Review of International Political Economy, vol. 15, no. 2, 2008; Li Cui, *China's Growing External Dependence*, Finance & Development—A Quarterly Magazine of the IMF, vol. 44, no. 3, 2007 and David Harvey, *The Limits to Capital*, Oxford: Blackwell, 1982. (By the way, in the latter title as well as in a recent book by the same author, *A Companion to Marx's Capital*, some terms and themes of the present text are discussed more fully and thus they may be very useful to those who are not versed in Marxist lingo).

4 "The public debt becomes one of the most powerful levers of primitive accumulation. As with the stroke of an enchanter's wand, it endows barren money with the power of breeding and thus turns it into capital, without the necessity of its exposing itself to the troubles and risks inseparable from its employment in industry or even in usury. The state creditors actually give nothing away, for the sum lent is transformed into public bonds, easily negotiable, which go on functioning in their hands just as so much hard cash would." K. Marx, *Capital* vol. 1, chapter 31.

5 *OECD Economic Outlook*, No. 59, 1996; No. 71, 2002.

6 That was the case with the notorious Ninja loans (no income, no job, no assets) whereby the banks tempted the low income households. These Ninja loans offered the possibility of completely deferring the payment of principal during the first five years. In addition a "teaser rate" which was often below the market rate was agreed initially. However, it was replaced by an adjustable rate after some years.

7 Household debt in the United States has increased from around 68% in 1997 to around 98% of the GDP in 2007. It must be noted that non-mortgage loans as a share of disposable income remained relatively constant at 31–35% between 1998 and 2007 whereas mortgage loans as a share of disposable income ballooned in the same period from around 60% to 104%. In total, household liabilities rose from around 92% in 1997 to 135% in 2007 as a share of the disposable income. Moreover, the share of income devoted to servicing mortgage debt payments rose in the same period from 8.3% to 11.25%. If we look at the distribution of the household debt by income quintile in USA, the lowest fifth of households doubled their borrowing from 2000 through 2007 and the total value of their outstanding debt rose from 198 to 376 billion dollars. However, in absolute terms, the total borrowing by low-income households is relatively small, since the lowest first quintile accounted for just 4% of the total growth in all household debt, the second quintile for 5%, the third quintile for 14%, the fourth quintile for 28% and the fifth top income quintile for 49%, near half the growth in all household debt during this period. Furthermore, if we look at the percentage of families holding home

secured debt by income quintile in the period between 1998 and 2007, the proportion of families in the first quintile rose from 11.2% to 14.9%, in the second quintile from 23.9% to 29.5%, in the third quintile from 63.5% to 69.7%, in the fourth from 73.6% to 80.8%, and in the fifth top quintile from 73.0% to 76.4%. Last but not least, the average debt to income ratio is much higher in the lowest income quintile (around 260% in 2007) than in the other quintiles, which means that the poorest households have a far more difficult time in servicing debt payments. To a lesser extent the second, the third, and the fourth quintiles as well as the 9th decile face also difficulties in servicing their debt payments since the respective ratios are quite high around 150 to 180%, with the only exception of the top decile with a corresponding ratio of around 87%. Surely, these figures show why household debt has become unsustainable, putting the banking system of USA in jeopardy. The data were drawn from the following sources: Federal Reserve Survey of Consumer Finances 2007; OECD Economic Surveys 2010 United States; M. Baily, S. Lund and C. Atkins, "Will US Consumer Debt Reduction Cripple the Recovery?," *McKinsey Global Institute Report*, March 2009; G. Horn, K. Droege, S. Sturn, T. van Treek, R. Zwiener, "From the Financial Crisis to the World Economic Crisis. The Role of Inequality," *Macroeconomic Policy Brief*, October 2009.

8 Apart from the reduction of the individual investment risk, the derivatives market was supposed to have another prominent function: the universal supervision of the extraction of surplus value and the "disciplining" of individual capitals. Derivative financial products provide a measure of the efficiency of individual capitals through the calculation of the "discount" of surplus value corresponding to the individual capital stocks and securities. Therefore, in addition to contributing to the near collapse of the banking system, the burgeoning of speculative investments and the autonomisation of derivative markets also undermined this supervising and rationalising function.

9 W. Bonefeld, *Primitive Accumulation and Capitalist Accumulation: Economic Categories and Social Constitution*, draft working paper, CSE TransPennine Working Group.

10 W. Bonefeld, *The Permanence of Primitive Accumulation: Notes on Social Constitution*, Commoner, no. 2, 2001. Besides, Marx as well noted the incessant character of primitive accumulation: "The capitalist system presupposes the complete separation of the labourers from all property in the means by which they can realize their labour. As soon as capitalist production is once on its own legs, it not only maintains this separation, but reproduces it on a continually extending scale." (Karl Marx, ibid.)

11 According to the *European Economic Forecast—Spring 2010* official publication of the European Commission, "Widening competitiveness losses over the recent years [in Greece] are also reflected in the sizeable appreciation of the real effective exchange rate (REER) based on unit labour costs. The rapid rise of wage costs and mark-ups in excess of productivity growth, as well as the persistence of the inflation differential with the Eeuro area, has contributed to a wage-price spiral and resulted in high real-wage growth, well above productivity growth. The disconnection between wages and labour-market and productivity developments, including the still weak response of wages growth to the downturn, are set to come to an end in the short term, with positive impact on country's competitive position. Appropriate wage developments, in line with the moderation of public wages, would help to regain part of the lost competitiveness"

12 According to the Economic Bulletin of the Bank of Greece of May 2009, household

credit has increased in the period between 2002 and 2007 by a rather high annual rate of 28% because of the relaxation of the liquidity constraints of Greek banks due to the entrance of Greece in the European Monetary Union. Despite the fact that the rate of increase has slowed down since 2005, the total household debt (including both consumer and mortgage loans) has risen from 34.7% in the end of 2005 to 47.5% in the end of 2008 as a proportion of the GDP. It must be noted though that this figure is still lower than the average in the Eurozone, which amounted to 59.5% in 2008, as well as the average in OECD, which amounted to almost 80% in 2005. Nevertheless, according to Eurostat, the highest shares of the population living in households that had been in arrears with mortgage are found in Greece. According to another research conducted by the Bank of Greece in 2007, 6 out of 10 Greek households had been in arrears with mortgage, 7 out of 10 had been in arrears with consumer loans, 1 out of 2 had been in arrears with credit cards. The number of households on credit exceeded 51% in 2007 and that means 2.15 million are on some kind of credit. If the average household debt relative to disposable income per income quintile is considered, it can be seen that the poorest households have a much harder time in paying the installments of their loans. In the first quintile (the lowest one) the rate of debt relative to income is around 150%, in the second quintile almost 100%, in the third quintile about 80%, in the fourth quintile about 70%, and in the fifth quintile about 50%.

13 The average real gross wages have risen by 1.8% in 2008 and by 3.8% in 2009. This increase is mainly due to the rises in the public sector and the public utilities. Even if the annual average increase of the nominal regular wages was only 2.8% in the period between 2007 and 2009 for workers in the public sector, there have been special wage regulations (benefits, back pays, etc.) for juridical employees, military personnel and cops, doctors, nurses and teachers that have led to an annual average increase of the nominal gross wages by 5.9%. Furthermore, the workers in the public utilities managed to get annual raises of their average nominal regular wages in the same period of 6.2%. In the private banking sector the average nominal gross wages have stagnated in 2008 whereas in 2009 they have been increased by 6.8%. On the contrary, even if in the non-banking private sector the collective contract of 2008–2009 provided for annual raises of the average nominal regular wages by 5.8%, in 2009 the nominal wages paid fell below 2% because of the recession that led both to the reduction of overtime and of the average labour time (with a corresponding reduction in the wages) and in some companies to an outright reduction of regular wages. Nevertheless, this does not constitute an argument for the propagandists of separation, since the capitalist institutions themselves admit that in the period between 2001 and 2009 the increases of wages in the public sector and utilities swept along the wages in the private sector (see *Bank of Greece, Monetary Policy—Annual Report*, 2009–2010).

14 Relative figures for 2009 in other European countries for deficit and debt are respectively the following: UK 13% and 68.6%; Spain 11.25% and 54.3%; Ireland 10.75% and 65.8%; Italy 5.3% and 114.6%; and Germany 3.5% and 73.1%. The average figures of deficit and debt in Eurozone were in 2009 6.5% and 78.2% respectively with a tendency of increase.

15 With a paucity of public services for very small children, the lack of financial support for families—in Greece the family benefits are very low and the maternity benefits are the lowest of all EU countries—and the limited amount of provisions for "reconciling" family and employment, it is plausible to argue that to a large extent the Greek family substitutes for the welfare state in Greece. A situation which is unlikely to change as,

according to data, there has even been a strong increase in living with parents until about the age of 35 (in 1986 52% of men and 29% of women in the 25–29 age group were still living with their parents while in 1996 the proportion for the same age group were 65% for men and 44% for women) and it is certainly going to be stronger after the onset of the debt-crisis.

16 It is interesting to examine the distribution of the Greek sovereign debt among debt holders. According to the official data of the Greek government, 29% of the Greek sovereign debt is held by Greek investors, around the half of which is held by Greek banks. The rest 71% is held by foreign investors: to be more specific 60% of the Greek sovereign debt is held by EU financial institutions (23% UK/Ireland, 11% France, 9% Germany/Austria/Switzerland, 5% Netherlands, etc.). In this case as well, almost half of this part of the debt is held by EU banks. However, this estimation is provisory since these data refer to the moment of bond issuance and cannot grasp the current situation since bonds are exchanged in the financial markets. In any case, these data show that the nationalist propaganda spread by the Greek media about the role of the greedy foreign speculators is totally unfounded and fabricated since Greek banks and other Greek capitalists hold a significant part of the debt and, therefore, the imposed measures are also defending the interests of local capitalists. Recent developments reveal the mechanism that is employed by the EU and the European Central Bank to protect the stability of the European banking system (including Greek banks) and to avoid a possible contagion to other highly indebted European countries. During the last months the ECB has bought around €40 billion of Greek government bonds by French and German banks and in addition it has accepted as collateral €40 billion of bonds held by Greek banks to provide them with liquidity reaching about €90 billion. Furthermore, it is expected that the ECB will buy more Greek government bonds from other financial institutions dumping them and, therefore, it is estimated that soon it will hold around 35% of the Greek sovereign debt. In other words, the ECB has undertaken the risk reducing the exposure of the European banking system to the Greek sovereign debt. This is completely reasonable since the ECB can manage the risk in a much more efficient way than the isolated capitalist institutions, principally through its role in the imposition of the structural adjustment programme.

17 An overview of the measures is presented in the table that follows.

18 In some cases, in Greece, "self-employment" is the disguise of proper wage labour; it's a labour relation where, except for the direct wage, the cost of the reproduction of labour power has been shifted from the capitalists onto the "self-employed" workers.

19 For a more detailed analysis of strikes and demos since the beginning of the "debt crisis," one can have a look at our texts "There's only one thing left to settle: our accounts with capital and its state" and "In critical and suffocating times." Both can be found on our site http://www.tapaidiatisgalarias.org/?page_id=105

20 Another aspect of the general feeling of "weakness" in the face of the enforcement of the austerity measures and the "alien forces of economy" that control our lives can be traced in the rise in the number of people who ask for help from psychiatrists and psychiatric institutions. According to some specialists, specific mental disorders like depression, panic crisis, or anxiety disorder are explicitly connected with the rise of unemployment, individual indebtedness and the general feeling of uncertainty. Reports from two of the major Mental Hygiene Centres in Athens show a significant

increase of the number of people who asked for help in 2009 compared with 2008 and an additional rise in the first three months of 2010. Unfortunately, there are no overall data or public researches for the general mental health in Greece. But this rising tendency is also confirmed by the increase in the sales of psychiatric medication, especially antidepressants, anxiolytics and hypnotic pills since January of 2010. We should also add a slight but not insignificant rise in the number of suicides, during the last ten months, often because of an inability to repay debts.

17

NO ONE IS REVOLUTIONARY UNTIL THE REVOLUTION!

A LONG, HARD REFLECTION ON ATHENIAN ANARCHY THROUGH THE PRISM OF A BURNING BANK[1]

Christos Boukalas

The first word of the face is the "Thou shalt not kill." It is an order. There is a commandment in the appearance of the face, as if a master spoke to me. However, at the same time, the face of the Other is destitute; it is the poor for whom I can do all and to whom I owe all.

—Levinas 1985: 89[2]

ANARCHY, A KILLER?

Supposing for a moment that the indispensible condition for society is that, upon the meeting of two faces, a simple communication is mutually understood: *do not kill me!* Until recently, Greek Anarchy has been respecting this primordial convention. It is well known: (neo)liberals kill the poor and the idle; fascists kill the foreigner, the mad, and the perverted; large sections of the left kill the delinquent, the lumpen, the heretic; conservatives kill assortments of all previous categories—and so on. While the existential core of every political force involves both symbolic and actual killing, the exclusion/extermination of some otherness, Anarchy is bereft of such bloodlust. Thus, in the 35 years that Greek Anarchy has been the political force that persistently and systematically includes among its practices low intensity violence, confrontation with the police, and property destruction, its actions never resulted in loss of life or in the symbolic death of a social category.

It is no surprise that political forces that perpetually evangelise social peace are ceaselessly producing hecatombs of victims—given that their "peace" is an order that depends on the death of those who do not fit in. Similarly, there is no paradox when a political force that promotes the escalation of social antagonism—Anarchy—proves to be innocent of homicide or genocide: its order knows no misfits. So, when Greek Anarchy does finally kill, and kills the people it was always expected to fight with and for, the resulting aporia is devastating, the questions raised rip at the core of Anarchy's existence.

Explaining, at this point, what I am talking about is likely to benefit the reader—especially as the incident may not be widely known outside Greece, and some historical distance is bound to set in between the time this is being written (September 2010) and the time of it being read. In mid-April 2010, due to an allegedly unsustainable public debt, the IMF and the EU took over Greek economic policy in exchange for making future lending available to the Greek state at reasonable rates. True to Freedmanite form, the IMF takeover launched a massive attack on the material conditions of the population: drastic reduction of public expenditure, expansion of working life, shrinking of the public sector, reduction of wages and pensions by over 20%, privatisations, and rapid increases of indirect taxation combined with lowering the taxes for big (international) capital. Practically every government since 1990 has tried to introduce elements of this neoliberal agenda, and they have invariably been met with resistance by affected sectors of the population. Now, in a typical "shock doctrine" move,[3] the full treatment is introduced all at once, in the wake of months of market-orchestrated, media-amplified panic. Still, the paralysis and disorientation anticipated after generous "shock" inductions did not materialise: within a fortnight, the scattered gestures of resistance were already combining into a massive force, culminating with the general strike and the Athens demonstration of 5 May. The demonstration was attended by 200,000 people, and its defining feature was the rage displayed by those attending: despite extremely heavy treatment by the riot police, the march spent most of its course "out of control," putting the parliament building and those inside it under immediate threat, and injuring a large number of police personnel, clearly suggesting to everyone (participants, cops, Greek and European politicians, technocrats, *and peoples*) that an insurgency was forthcoming. Anarchy participated in the march with several blocks, congregating a few thousand people. A few splinter groups were moving alongside the march, damaging banks' and shops' facades. They attempted to burn down a bookstore and a super-market that where doing business during the strike, but were physically prevented by other anarchists, worried about the fate of the people inside. One of the splinter groups managed to approach a Marfin Bank branch, which was also open. They attacked it with Molotov cocktails, indifferent to the presence of people within. The building caught fire and three workers died. It was later established that the building had neither a fire-extinguishing system nor an emergency exit and that the workers were forced to work on the day of strike under threat of immediate dismissal.

Still in order to know what we are discussing, I must explain what I mean by "Anarchy." To provide a faithful and concise description of it would be next to impossible. Its configuration is such, that anarchist/anti-authoritarian people, organisation, and activity are referred to neither as a "movement" nor a "scene," but a "space" [χώρος]. It can indeed be seen as a space of flows, (inter)action, and belonging, defined and reproduced by, and containing, a multitude of individuals, organised into looser or tighter groupings, formed on the basis of a combination of personal bonds, locality, and confluence of theory and/or action, that are in turn linked together selectively, in a looser or tighter fashion. While this sounds more or less like the condition of Anarchy everywhere, perhaps it should be noted that in the Athenian case the theoretical framework that shapes its analyses and informs its practices, has never been purely anarchist. From its onset in the late '70s, the "space" was theoretically forged not only by anarchist thought (from Bakunin, say, to Bookchin) but also by select radical-revolutionary Marxist thought. The Situationists have been a permanent and hugely influential fixture in the theoretical landscape, and so has Autonomy, in different configurations among its three main strands: the French (esp. Castoriadis), the Italian (e.g. Negri) and the German. So, the designation "Anarchy" is from my part a somewhat artificial and arbitrary construct that puts in the same bag a multitude of groupings ranging from anarcho-communists to anti-authoritarians, to autonomous.

It must also be added that, due to its inclusive character, Anarchy has been the political force in which people (especially youth) of what the sociologists would call "delinquent" or "anomic" behaviour (i.e. those who their inadequate fit into the social order is reflected in their daily behaviour) could participate and/or organise in a political framework—provided they wanted to do so. Over the years, Anarchy consolidated almost like a natural hub for this section of society. As a result, low-impact delinquency was typically present in Anarchy—it was in fact one of the features that co-defined it. Anarchy was never all smooth sailing: since there is no hierarchy, no legislators, and no police to impose order, the latter was always determined through the interaction among people prescribing to some general principle and delimited by the order of a broader society which they do not accept. Every political organisation is a socialisation platform, and same goes for Anarchy. Except that here "socialisation" acquires an unusually strong sense: in the absence of cathexis, the very society in question is created by its participants. In reference to the perpetrators of the 5 May incident, there is no question of this function being discontinued or registering a "failure." This would imply that an amount of people, proclaiming themselves as anarchists, have managed over a period of time to co-exist in the same places with thousands of anarchists from all kinds of tendencies, and never talked to or collaborated with any of them. The socialising function of Anarchy continues as well or as badly as always; the question is what does this socialisation consist of or, in other words, what are the dominant meanings and tendencies in Anarchy today, into which newcomers become socialised.

Finally, it should be noted that there are important reasons for consideration with Greek Anarchy in the current conjuncture. Not only does it constitute one of the most populous forces anywhere in Europe and North America, and one with great impact on overall society; but it is also *the first radical force to experience the ravaging of society by a full-blown capitalist attack*, and mobilise against it. In this sense, Greek Anarchy is the first to confront issues that will become the immediate concern of all comrades throughout the "western" world in the immediate *present*.

WITH SO MANY REVOLUTIONARIES...WHO NEEDS A REVOLUTION?

The killing on 5 May, a specific action of a tiny (sub-)grouping at the fringes of a large, varied political "space," is neither accidental nor isolated, but refers to long-developing, deeply rooted, dominant tendencies in large parts of Anarchy. It is symptomatic of the present condition of Athenian Anarchy, and it therefore involves it in its entirety. Not a folly by some crazed youth, but the high (or low) point in a trajectory. Some of its main trends (e.g. hatred towards the middle class; a "serves you right" attitude towards dispossessed groups; the "critique" of "democracy") have appeared at different moments in the last two decades and, since the December 2008 uprising, they have combined and crystallised in form. By now, they effectively describe what Greek Anarchy is about: *a fetishisation of the "revolutionary" identity*, precisely at the moment when Anarchy *ceases to be a revolutionary force*.

282

Something unique happened during December 2008: Anarchy *de facto* found itself at the leadership of an ample and hugely varied sector of society, set to create situations that often challenged the social institution. While most of the practices employed by the uprising[4]—its organisational forms[5], its demands[6], its discourse, etc.—have all been practiced by Anarchy for decades, they suddenly become the property of wide parts of the population and viewed with aspiration, awe, and/ or empathy even by people not involved in the uprising. A marginalised, persecuted, and defamed political force triggered the release of forces beyond its wildest dreams (and, it is now clear, beyond its comprehension), and became their point of reference and aspiration. It thus gained an historical opportunity to open up to society: to explain, propose, mobilise, organise, discuss, understand, convince, change, and be changed, thus helping to widen and deepen the fronts of resistance, and prepare the real (i.e. the social) conditions for a revolutionary counterattack. Presented with this unique opportunity to make a deep, lasting, and game-changing impression on society, Anarchy reacted by rapidly severing all, actual and tentative, ties with it.

The accounts of the uprising by almost all anarchist publications, including the most advanced,[6] were dominated by a radical division of the participants between "insurgents" and "non-insurgents," where the latter category included leftists, democrats, slackers, unionists, etc.—i.e. everyone who was not anarchist. To be sure, in many instances where the course of action had to be determined, these differences were both pronounced and important. Yet, in most instances these differences were a prefabricated pattern for self-indulgence and ego-tripping. But what matters here is that, (a) these differences were elevated to the status of ontological categories, where the positions of the subjects are fixed, there is no possibility for criss-crossing and/or overlapping, no room for reversals; (b) the power to make this categorisation is exclusively reserved for the "insurgents," and with it the capacity to call into being subjectivities and attribute (fixed) qualities to them, regardless of their self-perception or potentiality; and (c) the employment of "revolutionary violence" became, with time and grace, the sole criterion informing this categorisation. At the crucial moment when an historical opening was within grasp, Anarchy closed itself down to fortify its purity.

A possible explanation for this is Anarchy's reluctance to engage in "hegemonic" politics.[8] Understood (mistakenly) as a mode of domination based on a blend of force and subterfuge, Anarchy would, of course, steer clear from it. Yet, the (healthy) aversion towards this (distorted) notion of hegemony may have had the side effect of hollowing out the social address of Anarchy altogether. Thus, when a chance to genuine (counter-)hegemony is thrown to it by society, the chance to establish (variations of) its practices, objectives, and meanings at the heart of the agenda of broad social forces, Anarchy is not only reluctant, but plainly incapable of responding. A different explanation is that, as the anarchist/insurgent/revolutionary becomes an existential identity certified through "confrontational practices," when ample parts of society employ such practices, then, in order to save his/her identity the revolutionary can only escalate the degree of confrontation.[9] These two explanations converge on the crucial point of Anarchy becoming an ontological category and an existential identity *differentiated from* the rest of society; they essentially point to a relation of *alienation* between society and the anarchist/Anarchy.

From thereon, we have experienced a robust fetishisation of the "insurgent" (i.e. ourselves) and an automatic, self-evident, justification of whatever we may come up with: from a rich and varied fauna of behaviours showing open disregard towards residents at the "free-zone" of Exarcheia; to armed robberies that—when involving grenades— may cause indiscriminate injury; to bombings not always planned in a manner that makes injury to others impossible. It seems that our self-categorisation as "revolutionaries" not only constitutes us as "different" and "special" vis-a-vis the rest of society; it also ascribes us to a different, more lenient and permissive, moral code—it situates us not only apart, but also above society. It also seems that, in practice, the category is premised on the capacity to use "revolutionary violence." And, as "more violent" equals "more revolutionary," the fetishisation of our political identity reaches paroxysm when it comes to armed guerrillas. This is hardly surprising since the hard coin for the distinction between "revolutionary" and "reformist" is the employment of "confrontational" practices, rendering an observable and tangible character to the distinction. Observable and tangible also mean measurable: the "more" confrontational the practices, the "more" revolutionary the subject that adopts them. There is thus an implicit hierarchy of status within the people and entities that comprise the "revolutionary" camp. In this context, Anarchy not only expressed full and unconditional solidarity to comrades effectuating "armed struggle," but also, in its desire to approach the hefty heights of *revolutionarity* scaled by the armed comrades, it expressed this solidarity in historically novel forms. In all previous cases of comrades accused of "armed violence," Anarchy responded that those comrades were targeted because of their prolific activity in social struggles, and that they were being morally/ideologically defamed and physically exterminated on the pretext of accusations that were *false*, because the comrades were *innocent*. This time (April 2010), solidarity was expressed on the basis that the comrades are *guilty* of armed struggle, they are indeed "terrorists," and *so are all of us*. Given that Anarchy has been meticulously vague about its stance in relation to armed guerrilla struggle for over 30 years, mounting expressions of solidarity in terms of affirmation of it tends to conclude an issue that has not been discussed.[10] It is, of course, understandable that a political force that has faced the most brutal repression from left, right, and centre and which has only the bonds of solidarity to count upon would be reluctant to leave anyone from its ranks on their own. And it is categorical that Anarchy never abandons the practice of solidarity: solidarity, as both an ontological and normative condition of social relations, is Anarchy's very essence. Yet, certain characteristics of specific gestures of resistance should be considered. Indeed, what occurs here is a reflex-solidarity that endorses a practice post-festum and only on the grounds that some comrades undertook it. In this manner, Anarchy comes to endorse armed guerrilla struggle, even when the vast majority of comrades would never contemplate such means and/or reject the practice. The dangers generated by such a haphazard stance should be obvious: from infiltration by agents-provocateurs, to signalling encouragement for younger comrades to undertake a "heroic" practice that no one cared about to begin with, to a critical mutation of the values and purposes of Anarchy, to—lo and behold!—Wednesday, 5 May 2010.

While the solidarious comrade accumulates revolutionary capital along these lines, the rest of society becomes simply indifferent. Anarchy's reply to the existential agony of the middle class under the ongoing, intensifying capitalist attack has been "*it serves you right*." From posters ("Maybe You Went Bankrupt During the Nineties?") blaming the middle class's contemporary hardships on the greediness they displayed two decades earlier; to slogans like "butchers of peoples/petit bourgeois/you look a treat/drowning in debt" shouted by the anarchist blocs throughout the December marches; to the endless—and so ironically dated!—association of the petite bourgeoisie with the "neo-rich" in most analyses, the hostility to the middle class is both pronounced and self-flattering. The origin of this trend can be traced to Autonomy (especially with the rise of the German influence in its Greek circles in the mid-1990s), as part of an analysis to which it remains consistent to date. This is somewhat ironic: the analysis whose (mis)appropriation by Anarchy provided a platform for the building of a certain mentality that contributed to loss of life, was provided by a force (Autonomy) that, for many years now, is in fierce disagreement with the rest of Anarchy precisely regarding street violence. But, of course, direct lines of causality/intentionality in social dynamics are rather rare; and, in any case, this piece *does not attempt an evaluation of theoretical analysis, but an identification of how certain appropriations thereof have contributed towards a given outcome.* Put extremely schematically, the "German" Autonomy analysis is based on locating the relevant position of each class in the framework of the contemporary configuration of capitalist relations of production. On this basis, it identifies a revolutionary subject—an actual or potential subjectivity whose existence constitutes the negation of the social framework. All other social classes and forces are considered integral to the system. In this context, the crucial task is to safeguard the autonomy of the revolutionary subject—of its material conditions, its logic and ideology, its forms of organisation and practice—so that it remains uncorrupted and un-co-opted by capitalism, and therefore retains and advances its revolutionary potential. The indispensable contribution of this analysis is that, through its grounding in the social relations of production, it can overcome the fragmentation, isolation, self-referentiality, mutual incompatibility, and utter integration-ability that "post-structuralism" attributes to instances of "resistance"; it can unify them and give them a truly transcendental dimension. Furthermore, it can help evaluate our and others' struggles, estimate their potentiality, and, on this basis, map out a field of interventions and coalitions. Finally, it provides an important emphasis on the need for constant critical assessment of our relations and actions at the "micro-social" level. It is nonetheless immensely problematic inasmuch its subjectivities are determined by and "locked" on the structure of the relations of production: it ignores the inner contradictions, dynamics, and clashes resulting to/from the placing of each subjectivity in the capitalist structure; it ignores internal differentiation and struggle within each subjectivity (are teachers and policemen the same—middle class—thing?); it ignores the difference between class-origin and class-relevance (how come so many anarchist/autonomous comrades are of middle-class origin?); and it does not permit any room for meaningful intervention, not even by revolutionary elements, not even in the context of socially explosive conjunctures (leaving Anarchy open-mouthed to the reality of shop-owners and taxi drivers smashing banks alongside the December marches). In this manner, the thrust of the analysis can lead to terrifying misunderstandings. First, the antisocial one: discounting people due to the structural position of their class, starting with the petit-bourgeois, continuing to workers' aristocracy, small farmers, qualified workers, and so on, until it is determined that over 95% of the population are reactionary scum. And, second, the trap of narcissism, given that our main duty is to safeguard the purity of mind and the uncompromised character of the action of the revolutionary subject.[11]

What seems to underlie this double antisocial/narcissist move is what some comrades very aptly call "an incomplete understanding of the mechanisms of the molecularisation of power."[12] In this sense, the petit-bourgeois is not the—always contingent and traversed with contradictions—outcome of the complex reproduction of relations of power and resistance at a social and personal level, but merely a local micro-despot. Similarly, the revolutionary is not the contingent outcome of dynamic social relations, but the Avenger from the Fifth Dimension. Precisely on the interface between narcissism and the antisocial mindset, the posters issued by different collectivities to honour an armed comrade murdered by the police, show Anarchy declaring in all tones the supremacy of the "revolutionary," culminating in the conviction that everyone else "might as well have not existed." There is, then, no cause for wonder when the "revolutionaries" engage in reckless acts, form search-and-destroy splinter groups, or, eventually, kill a few forced-labourers inside their gulag. These people might as well have not existed.

So far so good—if you are a "revolutionary." The trouble is that the thinly veiled animosity and the proudly paraded contempt for society cause some unexpected problems regarding the "revolutionary" identity. Namely, if "revolutionaries" face the rest of the population with indifference, scorn, and hostility, then with whom do they hope to make the revolution? For whom do they hope to make the revolution? And, what kind of revolution will that be, with the entire society excluded and marginalised from the get go? We are not dealing with an attempt-to-"vanguard" here: society is not seen as masses to be led by the enlightened; we are dealing with an identity whose main aspiration is to entrench and fortify itself in order to adore it. We are dealing with socio-political self-indulgence.

Furthermore, Anarchy has abandoned "democracy" not only as an objective, but also as a form of social and internal organisation. This process is about ten years old. It is difficult to trace it back to theory given that no known theorist of anarchism, anarcho-communism, or autonomy has taken a similar stance. Their analyses typically uphold

287

democracy both as a desired point of arrival (whether as "direct-" or "inclusive-" democracy, and/or as "council communism" or "communisation"), and as a platform for launching an attack against capitalist "democracy" as a mockery of the real thing. In short, the standard positioning of antiauthoritarians in relation to democracy is a rejection of capitalist (pseudo-)democracy as a politico-ideological mechanism of incorporation, combined with an urgent, constitutive aspiration for genuine democracy. That was very much the case in Greece too, until the early '00s when the first "against democracy" posters and brochures equalised democracy with the capitalist-democratic regime, permitting no other meaning to the notion.[13] Since then, variations of this approach have taken root in most tendencies of Anarchy, to the extent that in their assessments of December 2008 just a handful of collectivities[14] would mention the direct-democratic aspects of the uprising as something positive.[15]

While the sanity of leaving the concept of "democracy" to the exclusive use of the bourgeoisie without contestation is certainly questionable, what happened post-December was the abandonment of direct democracy as an organisational form. During the uprising, the "insurgents" lost a couple of assemblies, given that their open character allowed all sorts of riffraff from society to come in and have a say. In these "contaminated" assemblies, the identity of the "insurgent/revolutionary" was forged in opposition to that of the "democrat." Rather than reflecting on their (occasional) failure to convince under extremely favourable conditions, large segments of Anarchy chose to ditch democratic procedures altogether in favour of "initiative" action, decided in the context of closed "affinity" molecules. Leaving aside the high originality of the concept of the anarchist as anti-democrat, created for the first time in Athens 2009, this new-found dichotomy causes another round of problems for the "revolutionary" identity. Namely, by dropping democracy, Anarchy has no organisational model to propose to society—before, during, or after the revolution. The idea that any social process can continue for any length of time organised solely on conspiratorial principles and do-as-you-please initiative is laughable—but it is the only model Anarchy has got left. So, the "revolutionaries" have no answer regarding not only the "by whom" and "for whom" of the revolution, but also regarding the "what" and "how" of it.

In short, by constructing a "revolutionary" socio-political identity as separate and above society, Athenian Anarchy has effectively excluded itself from any kind of revolutionary process, thus voiding the very identity it had so lovingly constructed.

Finally, a note regarding tactical acumen. We know that they knew that the 5 May march would be a "difficult" one; we know that they know that banks are a prime target for demonstrators; then, right in the path of a huge, wild march, we see a bank belonging to the upcoming champion of Greek (i.e. international) capital, open for business. How on earth is it possible that we swallowed this bait? How could we fail to immediately consider the implications of an attack for the broader course of social antagonism? Indeed, at the time when capital imposes a savage and deep restructuring of society through a process that will evolve over a length of time, are we certain that "instant insurrection" can be an effective counterstrategy—even if we could force/ will society into an insurrection? This is not a cynical assessment of tactics and strategy on the backs of three dead people. It points to the same violent disjunction between identity and practice, between social reference and lack thereof. The virtual disappearance of Anarchy from the frontline of social antagonism since 5 May clearly shows that there is a stock of social conscience—and shame—among the bulk of our comrades. But it also points out the utter bankruptcy of the "revolutionary" identity and its assorted "militant" tactics. The end result is that, precisely at the moment that society needs its Anarchy the most, the latter has no choice but to recede and engage in a long, bruising, and uncertain struggle against itself in order to redefine it.

ANARCHY ~~REFLECTS~~ CONCLUDES

The events of 5 May have sent ripples through Anarchy. A host of collectivities publicised their reaction to, and reflections on, them. A small number of texts focuses exclusively on the magnitude and fierceness of the march, and merely mention the lethal arson as an accidental event that mobilised the state-capital-media complex to a massive crackdown and an orgy of propaganda.[16] Of course, the vast majority of the texts do discuss the arson to some considerable extent. These can, very schematically, be divided into two broad categories: those who seek to separate the position of the collectivity from the practices and/or attitudes seen as provoking the incident; and those that see it as the contingent outcome of a trajectory involving—to varying extent— Anarchy as a whole.

The texts that seek to differentiate their authors from the dynamics leading to the incident can again be divided in two sub-categories. The first consists of a tiny number of texts that devalue Anarchy in its entirety. These originate from some "post-" tendencies, and blame anarchists as ideologically fixated into a grand-narrative, which constitutes them as an authoritarian, (crypto-)fascist vanguard claiming exclusive possession of an absolute truth.[17] On this basis, they set to associate the anarchists with a strange assemblage of events, ranging from past assassinations of comrades by the Greek police, to the Soviet invasions in Hungary and Prague. These accusations hold testimony to the seriousness of the analysis informing them: they are symptomatic of a mechanistic application of a dogma into a lived reality they seem to know nothing about—and to which they hardly refer to. Indeed, the analysis contains nothing else than a resounding affirmation of the authors' dogma, and moralistic indignation expressed in dramatic over-tones. As contributions to a meaningful dialogue, these texts are absolutely inconsequential.

On the contrary, the second sub-category includes texts by some of the largest, most active, and most influential collectivities in Greek Anarchy—the anarchist "mainstream." These texts portray the perpetrators and their informing mentalities as in collision with Anarchy itself.[18] The groupings responsible for the incident are seen as sliding into a separation of violence from its political rationale and objectives, constituting it thus as a fetish, and introducing it firmly in the universe of the spectacle. De-politicised and self-referential, this violence is inherently nihilistic and anti-social. It becomes a dynastic force, the diametrical opposite of Anarchy (and its counter-violence) that constitutes the par excellence liberating force in/of society. The groupings responsible for the arson act in the name of Anarchy, but never discuss or inform others about their tactics and intentions. They are therefore acting parasitically, exploiting Anarchy while distorting its worldviews and practices into their complete opposite. Most of these collectivities acknowledge some responsibility for the 5 of May. It consists in admitting to having tolerated the hatching of such mentalities in their proximity over the years; and in rooting them out from now on. Essentially, these texts try to draw a bold separation of Anarchy into unconnected, uneven, and hostile camps, with real and proper anarchy on one side, and pseudo-anarchist, nihilist thuggery on the other. In a typical "bad apple" move, the responsibility they pretend to acknowledge is firmly fixed on the other side. Reflection on whether problematic practices and attitudes have—occasionally or systematically—crept into the repertoire of the groups now throwing anathemas is ruled out, and self-reflecting is eclipsed by self-congratulating. Here, Anarchy proceeds to a rare and significant move: it identifies and ostracises its own heretics and misfits. This symbolic extermination of someone within one's own ranks was pertinent to leftists, liberals, conservatives, etc.—the forces identified early in this piece as having a clear, specifying difference with Anarchy, precisely on this regard.

By contrast, there is a multitude of texts that consider the incident an outcome of deeper, persistent trends within Anarchy, implicating it therefore in its entirety. Yet, while making this acknowledgment, and stressing the imperative of a searching self-critique, most texts do not specify said responsibilities or suggest a direction for self-reflection.[19] The texts that attempt to do so tend to identify the same ills that the "bad apple" approach does, with the crucial difference that they do not attribute them to imposters, but acknowledge their bearers as genuine and bona fide comrades. Hinging on the use of political (counter-)violence, the criticism is addressed to its fetishisation/spectacularisation, that inserts techniques of popular (counter)violence to the bourgeois value framework. This trend is attributed either to a disregard for democratic processes and political communication, which has taken root in ample parts of anarchy in the course of years; or to Anarchy's failure to instil its values in the sudden, mass influx of people during and after the 2008 uprising.[20]

Starting from the later point, one of the most impactful texts on the events[21] retorts that the failure to introduce the youth to an anarchist value framework lies neither with the youths themselves, nor with the comrades that approach and help them organise. It lies squarely with the anarchist leaders ("anarcho-fathers") that monopolise the time in assemblies, inhibiting and discouraging newcomers to have a say. In an astonishing reversal, the entire list of accusations mainstream Anarchy fired against its misfits is now squarely laid on its doorstep. The anti-political character of many youths' groupings is a direct result of their exclusion by Anarchy, its reluctance to permit them the capacity to co-determine its shape and character through dialogue. Furthermore, the presence of "wild youth" in Anarchy is not a sudden apparition, but a constitutive element of the latter for thirty odd years. And, it is not these elements that exploit Anarchy, but vice versa: Anarchy has historically been content to approach the "wild youth," use them as muscle power and watchdogs, and introduce them under the "anarcho-fathers" command into the constellation of feuds that map out its territory. Finally, the responsibility that weighs upon Anarchy is not its tolerance towards the mindless violence of the wild youth or the "warlords" that organise them, but its protracted tolerance of its commanding "fathers."

While the above text unleashes an attack to the anarchist mainstream and seeks to defend the groupings directly responsible for the arson without defending their strategies, tactics, or worldview, a couple of other texts attempt exactly this. Here, an "individualist-nihilist" current tries to establish itself as a legitimate tendency within Anarchy.[22] Their operative word is "war." Social struggle is conceptualised exclusively as open war—a condition that is both omnipresent and should be brought about by the revolutionary forces. The enemy is not just the abstract entities of state and capital, but is located in society, especially in the "neo-rich" middle classes (in a similar vein, the dead workers of Marfin bank are post-mortem baptised "bank executives"). Given the revolutionary duty to bring about social warfare, the necessary tactic for Anarchy is to agitate mass events, pushing them to the direction of uprising and violent upheaval. Indeed, anarchist action is understood in very tight association to armed guerrilla struggle. Furthermore, the actuality of warfare renders democratic procedures "unproductive." Instead, the objective is the organisation of a "revolutionary militarism," on the basis of groupings intervening confrontationally in social life. My argument in the previous section anticipates many of these declarations, so there is no use repeating it here—except to add three quick points. First, my dialectic capacity is not developed enough to conceptualise a condition (open social war) as both impending and actual. I still see it as an either/or situation, in which case a good part of the justifying basis of the comrades collapses. If open warfare is an actuality, then what is the purpose of all these tactics for bringing it about? If it is a potentiality, then how are we so certain that everyone is an enemy, and that we are in such an emergency as to cancel democratic procedures and organisation? Second, the logic for cancelling or "limiting" democracy because of its restricted "efficiency" is stereotypical of dictatorial and liberal regimes. Seeing it invoked by anarchists is a very unpleasant surprise—and possibly symptomatic of an ascription to a bourgeois value-framework. Furthermore, the designation of the murdered clerks as "executives" provides a glimpse into the seriousness of the process of enemy-designation. Interestingly, it also parrots neoliberal discourse (where every Starbucks waiter is termed as a "manager" of some description) and is equally convincing with it. Finally, since even the vast majority of the ruled and the exploited are enemies, who is there to be awakened by confrontational interventions and dynamic escalations? Or does this not matter, the latter practices being necessary in/for themselves?

All in all, it seems that the 5 May incident has forced Anarchy to confront all kinds of issues that have, for many years, been hastily hidden under the carpet. Its organising structures, its relations to democratic decision making and/or initiative-based action, its attitudes and practices towards the broader society, its designation of enemies, the means of its struggle and their appropriate employment, the legitimacy of de facto hierarchies, the accommodation and socialisation of newcomers, its socio-political objectives, the strategies and orientations of its struggle—a swarm of crucial issues that were left to take their course, are now, under the double pressure of a critical event within a critical conjuncture, demanding urgent resolution. This can be seen as a hopeful sign, an indication of a healthy political force that, even in the last minute, dares to engage in painful self-reflection. Yet, these same texts show that what passes as "self-critique" or "reflection" is in most cases an entrenchment of each collectivity in their own worldview, coupled with attempts to deny the legitimacy of opposing understandings of anarchy. It is like the 5 May never happened: each collectivity—even those whose tactics directly caused the incident—proceeds to a robust confirmation of their principles and action (with all cringes and contradictions ironed out), and engages in "public dialogue" only to eulogise itself and castigate others. On this basis, and given the absence of democratic forums and culture, civil war looks more likely than dialogue, and this is as depressing as the event itself. It shows Anarchy incapable of comprehending the importance of 5 May for it, as an event that threatens to dramatically decimate its ranks and cut it off from any goodwill from the broader society; and its own importance for society in the current conjuncture. While Anarchy is the only force that can convincingly suggest meaningful alternatives to/for society; and while most groupings seem to realise that the current struggle will be long-term, and hence uprising tactics should play second fiddle to a widening and deepening of ties with social forces and their struggles; it is more than likely that, due to 5 May, said social forces will avoid Anarchy like the plague. Perhaps this realisation has dawned upon the collectivities whose texts do not attempt to salvage or confirm a "party line." The numbness of their reaction—their vague calls for self-critique, their pleas against certain mentalities—seems to indicate such realisation, but also an impotence to act on it. The short- to mid-term future of Greek Anarchy seems bleak. Yet, if there is to be a future at all, this will lie with precisely these presently depressed comrades that seem to take their responsibility for 5 May to heart, as part of their responsibility towards society. Similarly, if Anarchy's ranks are decimated over the next months, this will result in a diaspora of comrades in other spheres of social activity: workplace, neighbourhoods, shop-floor unions, etc. It wouldn't be surprising if in the long run they came to constitute the critical mass for radical organisation and struggle, "away from the flag." In any case, this is a crossroads. It seems to me that the first decision that every individual and collectivity must make is whether anarchy exists primarily in, by, and for society; or for its own integrity, reason, and purpose. Whether it is an integral part of social dynamics (implying that its direction and meanings may shift in conjuncture thereof, even in ways we cannot fully determine), or a platform for our personal gratification and self-fulfilment. Crucially, whether our gratification and self-fulfilment can be achieved regardless of their relation to, and their impact on, social dynamics. I think that agreement on this decision—and the commitments that follow it—will largely determine whether Anarchy will manage to re-establish itself as a social and political force, or be castigated to a marginal existence as an ever-shrinking, universally detested, and socially irrelevant niche.

NOTES

1 Not yet published, and this piece has attracted intense (but friendly) criticism. It has been accused of over-generalising, and of lacking sensitivity towards its subject. Both criticisms are, in a sense, correct. The text is (over?) generalising. This is because its purpose is not to "accurately" attribute "responsibility," or to establish a grade-system that will show the extent to which each group partakes in mentalities and practices I consider problematic. Its purpose is to expose the *general line of force* that the multitude of ideas, attitudes, and actions were combining into on the eve of 5 May. Each group or comrade can—however partly—recognise themselves in some of the tendencies I describe, and either agree or disagree on whether they are problematic. Possibly, Greek comrades may use this piece as a platform for self-reflection, while comrades in other countries as a call for caution.

The piece also lacks sensitivity. It nowhere acknowledges the tremendous importance of keeping a genuinely different vision and practice of society visible in the Greek political agenda—or the heavy personal cost that each comrade has to pay daily for doing so. Yet, it is my conviction that, in the present conjuncture, the only anarchist sensitivity that matters is that of the *anarchist towards the broader society*; anarchist-to-anarchist sensitivity at a time when Anarchy displays palpable symptoms of arrogance is a dangerous self-indulgence—to which I decline to contribute.

On this note, I hope that Telemachos Antonopoulos, Stefi Christidou, and Chris Witter (who have offered the above criticisms and much more help) will forgive me for thanking them for their contribution: it not only enabled the production of this piece, but also made writing it worthwhile.

2 Emmanuel Levinas "*Ethics and Infinity*," p.89; Duquesne University Press, 1985.

3 For a description of the capitalist strategy in question see: Naomi Klein *The Shock Doctrine*, Allen Lane 2007.

4 From "free public transport" to occupations of buildings, from savage clashes with the cops to high-voltage "happenings."

5 General assemblies in neighbourhoods and occupied buildings.

6 No demands—meaning, among others, no negotiation.

7 E.g. TPTG-*Ta Paidia tis Galarias* [Τα Παιδιά της Γαλαρίας],vol.14, October 2009; Blaumachen vol.3, July 2009. In fact, the only exceptions to this trend seem to be Babylonia [Βαβυλονία] issue 51, January 2009; and Eutopia [Ευτοπία], vol.17, June 2009.

8 For an interesting discussion see: Richard Day "*Gramsci is Dead*," Pluto Press 2005.

9 Fabrica Yfanet Occupation "*Social Revolution or Barbarity?*" [Κατάληψη Φαμπρικα Υφανέτ "*Κοινωνική Επανάσταση ή Βαρβαρότητα;*"], 24 May 2010. Autonomy had given timely warning about such a post-December escalation of violence (Serajevo, vol.25, January 2009).

10 To my knowledge, the autonomous are the only groupings that have taken a clear, consistent, public—and negative—position in relation to armed struggle.

11 Characteristically, the autonomous (Serajevo, vol.41) dismiss the 5 May demonstration as a "regime"-march, and the demonstrators as nostalgists of the "prosperous past"(?). Compare with Katsiaficas, whose analysis not only designates 1/3 of the population as outside the capitalist relations of production, permitting it thus some revolutionary potential; but it is also permeated by a deep need for dialogue and synthesis: political, theoretical, philosophical. (George Katsiaficas "The Subversion of Politics," Humanities Press 1997).

12 Fabrica Yfanet, ibid (note 9). The text (possibly the best analysis of the 5 May event) applies this explanation regarding only the "antisocial" tendency. I am responsible for its extrapolation to the "narcissist" one.

13 Characteristic of this consistent equation of democracy to capitalist rule: in the 1,700 words under the title "*Democracy: There Is No Escape*" ["*Δημοκρατία: Καμία Διέξοδος*"] (Blaumachen, vol.4, July 2010) the word "democracy" does not appear once. The word "capital" and its derivatives appear 23 times.

14 *Collectivity* possibly sounds somewhat strange in English. While *collective* is used to refer to a particularly structured association, and therefore designates a defined entity, *collectivity* can refer even to very loose, temporary, and fluid associations. I prefer it, therefore, as a common denominator, when referring to anarchist groupings. (The distinction is clear in Greek: "*συλλογικότητα*" and "*κολεκτίβα*").

15 E.g. *Babylonia* and *Eutopia* (see note 6).

16 E.g. Skaramanga Occupation "The Assassins 'Mourn' their Victims" [Κατάληψη Σκαραμαγκά "*Οι Δολοφόνοι 'Θρηνούν' τα Θύματά τους*"], 5 May 2010; Elea Occupation "Text about 5/5" [Κατάληψη Ελαία "*Κείμενο για τις 5/5*"], 11 May 2010; Naxos's Autonomous Initiative "Bulletin on Crisis and 5 May" [Αυτόνομη Πρωτοβουλία Νάξου "*Προκήρυξη για Κρίση και 5η Μάη*"], 15 May 2010; Serres "Serres's Anarchists' Announcement on the 5 May Events" [Σέρρες "*Ανακοίνωση Αναρχικών Σερρών*

για τα Γεγονότα της 5ης Μάη"], 11 May 2010; Baruti-Veroia "Plain Announcement Regarding the Incidents of 5/5" [Baruti-Βέροια "Λιτή Ανακοίνωση για τα Περιστατικά της 5/5"] , May 2010; Kouvelou Mansion Occupation "Wednesday 5 May" Κατάληψη Έπαυλη Κουβέλου "Τετάρτη 5 Μαΐου"], unknown date.

17 See: Autonomy or Barbarity "About the Dead in Marfin" [Αυτονομία ή Βαρβαρότητα "Για τους Νεκρούς της Marfin"], 7 May 2010; Flesh Machine "The Sickening Explosion of Ideology" [Flesh Machine "Η Νοσηρή Έκρηξη της Ιδεολογίας"], 10 May 2010.

18 E.g.Syspeirosi "No Haven and No Tolerance to the 5 May Assassins, their Logics and Practices!" [Συσπείρωση "Καμία Υπόθαλψη και Ανοχή στους Δολοφόνους της 5ης Μαΐου, στις Λογικές και στις Πρακτικές τους!"], 11 May 2010; AK/Athens "Antiauthoritarian Motion's Announcement on the Events of the 5 May March" [AK Αθήνας "Ανακοίνωση της Αντιεξουσιαστικής Κίνησης για τα Γεγονότα της Πορείας της 5ης Μαΐου"], 6 May 2010; AK/Thessaloniki "Announcement of Thessaloniki's AK about Marfin," [AK Θεσσαλονίκης "Ανακοίνωση της AK Θεσσαλονίκης για τη Marfin"] 11 May 2010; Thersitis, Resalto, Anarchists from the Western Quarters of Athens and Piraeus, Assembly of Insurects from Perama, Keratsini, Nikaia, Korydallos, Piraeus, Anarchists from Piraeus, Egaleo Anarchists' Initiative "On the Events of 5 May and the Tragic Death of Three People" [Θερσίτης, Ρεσάλτο, Δυτικά, Συνέλευση Εξεγερμένων από Πέραμα, Κερατσίνι, Νίκαια, Κορυδαλλό, Πειραιά, Αναρχικές/οι από Πειραιά, Πρωτοβουλία Αναρχικών Αιγάλεω "Για τα Γεγονότα της 5ης Μάη και τον Τραγικό Θάνατο Τριών Ανθρώπων"], 12 May 2010; Patrai "With or Without Salary, Some are Working for the State" [Πάτρα "Με ή Χωρίς Μισθό, Κάποιοι Δουλεύουν για το Κράτος"], 15 May 2010; Black Flag "Anarchy is Struggle for Life, Freedom, and Dignity" [Μαύρη Σημαία "Η Αναρχία είναι Αγώνας για τη Ζωή, την Ελευθερία, και την Αξιοπρέπεια"], 11 May 2010; Occupation Rosa Nera "The 5 May March and the Three Dead" [Κατάληψη Rosa Nera "Η διαδήλωση της 5ης Μαΐου και οι Τρεις Νεκροί"] unknown date; Herakleio "On the Events of 5 May" [Ηράκλειο "Για τα Γεγονότα της 5ης Μάη"], 12 May 2010; Common Solidarity Action "About the Strike's Demonstration and the Events of 5/5" [Κοινή Δράση Αλληλεγγύης "Για την Απεργιακή Πορεία και τα Γεγονότα της 5/5"] , 7 May 2010; Vogliamo Tutto "Social Counterviolence or Countersocial Violence?" ["Κοινωνική Αντιβία ή Αντικοινωνική Βία;"], 24 May 2010; Cybrigade "The 'work accident' in the 'revolutionary' factory" ["Το Εργατικό Ατύχημα στο Επαναστατικό Εργοστάσιο"], 11 May 2010; Self-administered Place at the Old Chemistry Faculty "About 5 May 2010," 13 May 2010; Steki Antipnoia "Moronic Murderers, the State Would Have Paid You For This Work!"

19 Autonomo Steki "We'd Better Not Remain Silent!" [Αυτόνομο Στέκι "Καλύτερα να μη Σωπάσουμε!"], unknown date; Editions/Journals: Panopticon, Xenon, Stasei Ekpiptontes, Exarxeia, Mauro Piperi tou Euboikou, Nyxtegersia "Anarchy is Struggle for Life, Not Death" [Περιοδικά/Εκδόσεις: Πανοπτικόν, Εκδώσεις των Ξένων, Στάσει Εκπίπτοντες, Το Μαύρο Πιπέρι του Ευβοικού, Νυχτεγερσία "Η Αναρχία είναι Αγώνας για τη Ζωή, όχι το Θάνατο"], unknown date; Saltodoroi-Chania "On the Political Strike of 5 May, the Three Dead, and the Struggle" [Σαλταδόροι-Χανιά "Για την Πολιτική Απεργία της 5ης Μάη, τους Τρείς Νεκρούς, και τον Αγώνα"], 19 May 2010; Occupied London "Really, What do we have to Say about Wednesday's Event?" ["Αλήθεια, Εμείς τί έχουμε να πούμε για το Γεγονός της Τετάρτης;"]unknown date.

20 Libertarian Place Pikrodafni "Announcement" [Ελευθεριακό Στέκι Πικροδάφνης "Ανακοίνωση"], 16 May 2010; Anarchists for Social Liberation "Announcement by the

Collectivity for the Events of 5 May" [Αναρχικοί για την Κοινωνική Απελευθέρωση *"Ανακοίνωση της Συλλογικότητας για τα Γεγονότα της 5ης Μαΐου"*]; Rioter "On the March of 5/5 and the Three Dead Bank Clerks" [*"Για τα Γεγονότα της 5/5 και τους Τρείς Νεκρούς Τραπεζοϋπαλλήλους"*], 13 May 2010; Fabrica Yfanet Occupation, ibid (notes 8, 11); Terra Incognita Occupation "About the Events of 5 May" [Κατάληψη Terra Incognita *"Για τα Γεγονότα της 5ης Μάη"*], 12 May 2010; Apatris Street Newspaper "Opportunism is Oil in the Grind of Power—About the Three Dead in Marfin" [Εφημερίδα δρόμου Απάτρις *"Ο Τυχοδιωκτισμός είναι Λάδι στα Γρανάζια της Εξουσίας—Για τους Τρείς Νεκρούς στη Marfin"*], 12 May; Counter-information Team Kaka Mantata "We Do Not Stop Here…We Have the Entire World to Gain!" [Ομάδα αντιπληροφόρησης Κακά Μαντάτα *"Δεν Σταματάμε Εδώ… Έχουμε Ολόκληρο τον Κόσμο να Κερδίσουμε!"*] 19 May 2010.

21 Some Anarchists from Thessaloniki *"Fables and Nightmares"* [Κάποιοι Αναρχικοί από τη Θεσσαλονίκη *"Παραμύθια και Εφιάλτες"*], 17 May 2010.

22 A Group of Comrades that Contributed to the Destructive Activity in the Centre of Athens During the 5 May March "On the 5 May Events, and the Stance of a Part of the Anarchist Space" [Μια Ομάδα Συντρόφων που Συνέβαλε στην Καταστροφική Δραστηριότητα στο Κέντρο της Αθήνας κατά τη Διάρκεια της Πορείας της 5ης Μάη *"Σχετικά με τα Γεγονότα της 5ης Μάη και τη Στάση ενός Κομματιού του Αναρχικού Χώρου"*], 14 May 2010; Conspiracy of Cells of Fire "Announcement Regarding the Recent Events of 5/5" [Συνομωσία Πυρήνων της Φωτιάς *"Ανακοίνωση Σχετικά με τα Πρόσφατα Γεγονότα της 5/5"*], 19 May 2010.

18

FOR THE INSURRECTION TO SUCCEED, WE MUST FIRST DESTROY OURSELVES

Alex Trocchi

Sky News ran into difficulty about five minutes ago when they attempted to go live to one of their reporters on the ground. She appeared to lose her temper as students standing around her began to pitch in with comments like "Ladies and gentlemen, the insurrection has started."

—Paul Lewis, *Guardian* coverage of London protests against austerity measures, 10 November 2010.

We are surrounded by the picturesque ruins of all explicitly *political* ideas: schools at which no one learns, families bereft of love, banks whose coffers are empty, armies that only lose wars and laws that are merely expressions of "anti-terrorist" paranoia. What does this mean for any kind of *new* politics—if "politics" is even a suitable word? This question must be answered because strangely enough, insurrection against the entire social order is increasingly the only option left on the table. After all, everyone knows *nothing works*. To be realistic, a system in the midst of both global resource depletion and a global fall in the rate of profit could not possibly concede any sort of demand even if it was in its best interest to do so. In election after sorry election, people are throwing out their so-called representatives—*¡Que se vayan todos!*— yet they are not really voting *for* anyone, but they vote *against* politics itself using the only feeble expression of politics remaining to them, the ballot. The youth know better, as the absenteeism that increases in every election shows. Even though the vast spectacular machine of the empire will never admit its own litany of failure— a failure self-evident since the financial crisis of 2008 – for the first time in generations, from Greece to France to even Britain, the kids of the planetary bourgeoisie are getting hip to this truth.

The entire imperial apparatus is no longer held together on a mass scale by objective evidence or even faith in "progress," but only by a certain mixture of depression and repression. The bitter fruit of the end of history is the lack of any horizon even in the face of the collapse of our present. So what occult forces maintain this world? In an inversion of Hobbes's classic argument, only fear can maintain the present order, and there is no fear more terrifying than the fear of an untimely death. The murder of Alexis Grigoropoulos was precisely the kind of untimely death necessary to prop up a failed state, a human sacrifice intended by the police to restore a respect for their elders in the increasingly restless youth. The Greek police did not invent this recipe: the formula of state-sanctioned murder of those who refuse to assimilate has been repeated with miraculous results in other more "civilised" states. When an African-American youth is murdered by the police in the United States of America, the murder is not even mentioned in the back pages of newspapers unless somehow the act itself has been caught on film and released on the Internet, as befitting the most spectacular society on the planet. It should be no surprise that eventually police murder as an act of social control would come to Greece, and it is not even surprising that riots would follow, as very intense rioting also happened after the death of Michalis Kaltezas there in 1985. What was new about the murder of Alexis Grigoropoulos was that what began as a riot soon was on the road to becoming an insurrection against the totality of capitalist life that generalised throughout high-school students to immigrants in Greece. Just in time for Christmas, the spectre of insurrection haunted Europe yet again. Putting a few people in prison in France, murdering a youth in Greece, declaring all anarchists to be "terrorists"—all of these acts by the state are unable to restrain the rising tide of insurrection. Even if the most pacified of countries like Britain and the United States, buildings are occupied, demonstrations run riot, and tears are wept by politicians over broken windows. And they all know, a broken window is just a *sign* of disorder—and soon the *real* disorder may arrive.

Around the world, anarchists of the previous generation are puzzled. Why, after such a long absence, are *the People*—who we were never sure we even believed in—back? Even more puzzling, two years later in Greece, in the very the country that seemed closest to the brink of collapse after the financial crisis, the anarchists have (at least temporarily) foiled their own insurrection after the accidental killing of three people in the burning of the Marfin bank. While it is true that such an accident could have easily occurred in earlier protests, the timing of this event was almost tragic on a world-historical scale (and all too convenient for the Greek state), for it happened just at the very moment that the insurrectionary process was generalising even to Greek workers. In the months after this event, it was as if the momentum has been knocked out of the coming Greek insurrection.

Perhaps what is missing in these times is no longer action, but a certain collective intelligence that can both surpass the previous height of insurrection in 2008 and push through its nadir mid-2010. So in addition to the practice of Molotovs and barricades, a collective revolutionary theory that can account for both the current concepts and actions in terms of an insurrectionary process is necessary for any insurrection to avoid simply fizzling and dying. What we mean by this strange term "theory" is a certain strategic debate amongst those on the front lines of the global social war, the war in which the death of Alexis was merely one attack by the state and the insurrection of December but a single social response.

A THEORY OF SOCIAL WAR

Hitherto the murders and seditions had been internal and fragmentary. Afterward the chiefs of factions assailed each other with great armies, according to the usage of war, and their country lay as a prize between them... the Senate, fearing lest they should be surrounded by war, and unable to protect themselves, garrisoned the sea-coast from Cumae to the city with freedmen, who were then for the first time enrolled in the army on account of the scarcity of soldiers. The Senate also voted that those Italians who had adhered to their alliance should be admitted to citizenship, which was the one thing they all desired most.

—Appian, *The Civil Wars*

In an era when the global economy is so intertwined that the primary conflict between nation-states involves demolishing their borders for "free trade," a military war on the scale of the Second World War is simply a financial impossibility. Increasingly, such traditional military war is reduced to the periphery of empire, while a *different* kind of war is waged inside the centre of empire. What is this new kind of war, and is it actually just the return of a forgotten form of warfare? What is the geneaology warfare? Historically, the Greeks recognize two different kinds of war, the civil war [*emfylios*] and the social war [*koinonikos polemos*]. 301

The civil war, *emfylios*, is the primordial taking of positions that binds together opposing collectivities. From the perspective of the state, civil war can be a war interior to itself, such as the English Civil War or the French Revolution of 1789, but it can also be a war before and beyond the existence of the state, ranging from the various religious wars that came before the formation of the modern nation state to the Commune of Paris in 1871 or the revolt in Oaxaca in 2006. It is this last kind of civil war that gains increasing importance as the form of the nation-state mixes with the universalised state of empire. Inside empire, civil war polarizes an otherwise uniform citizenry, forcing them to take either the side of the partisans or the side of the empire itself.

Let us remember that a civil war is between any collectivities that may be latent within a state, and these collectivities may very well be counter-revolutionary, as the phenomenon of political Islam in the Middle East shows all too well. Even in Greece, as the possibility of the actual dissolution of the Greek state became increasingly possible, counter-revolutionary fascist collectivities like the Golden Dawn arose, who are trying to create an ethnically clean stronghold in Ayios Panteleimonas,[1] not too far from Exarcheia. Luckily, the first civil war in Europe since the financial crisis of 2008 was not between a quasi-fascist nationalism and a neo-liberal state (a very real possibility glimpsed in the revolt of 2008 in Bulgaria), but between anarchist-inspired revolution and the state in Greece. As no individual nation-state stands as an island due to their interlocking into the global state of empire, so the insurrection in Greece also naturally raises the possibility of global civil war against empire. The true nightmare of empire is revealed: The seeming historic abnormality of civil war is *always* present even within the so-called "peace" of capitalist representative democracy, and global civil war will return to the stage of history as that very image of "peace" rapidly unravels in the wake of the financial crisis.

While in the era of the formation of modern capitalist nation-states—ranging across the American Civil War to the emergence of the Greek state in the 1940s—civil war is primarily military, in the era of empire civil war takes a more subtle form. The insurrection of December in Greece is a perfect example of such a post-militaristic civil war, in which previously isolated collectivities such as students took a position with anarchists and immigrants to form a new kind of partisan war machine. This new kind of form is revealed even in how civil wars are brought to their end by the state. While earlier civil wars such as the Paris Commune were destroyed through military massacre, something changed after World War II. Remember that DeGaulle defeated the civil war of May 1968 in France by ordering the police to not fire a shot, and then ordering an election instead. The same sequence emerges in Greece: the brutal military repression of the original Polytechnic revolt reduced the popular tolerance of the military junta, which was one of the factors that eventually led to its collapse in 1974—a fact not lost upon Karamanlis. So in the footsteps of DeGaulle, Karamanlis did not order traditional military (or even police) repression against the insurrection of December. How is it that civil war can now be averted without military repression, by only deploying generalised "counter-terrorist" arrests and elections? The answer may yet be another kind of warfare.

In Greek, *koinonikos polemos* means the *social* war. *Koinonikos polemos* is separate from civil war, although in other languages there is only a single word for both kinds of war, like *Burgerskrieg* in German. Although the term "social war" is often thrown around in a sloppy and confused manner in anarchist propaganda, yet the history of this term reveals that a certain powerful concept is being deployed, a concept that can help us understand a distinct transformation in the form of warfare since the Second World War. The concept of "social war" should directly address the repressive side of the transition from the localised nation-state to the global state of empire—as the function of counter-insurrection is too often ignored by certain ivory-tower theorists, but of immense and immediate concern to practising revolutionaries.

In contrast to civil war, which signifies the breakdown of the apparatus of the state, social war is the low-intensity war by the state against the social relationships of its own population in order to maintain its continued existence. The social war then encompasses the totality of everyday life: To be alive today is to be at war, to never sleep properly, to awaken at odd hours to work, to be constantly surrounded by surveillance and police. A further recital of the various symptoms is unnecessary. Unlike in military war, demands of any kind are futile: demands would only make sense as long as the social war was limited in time and space, yet the capitalist form of life today encompasses the entire globe and imagines its reproduction extending into the infinite future. Another response is to pretend the social war doesn't exist—perhaps the most popular option. More so than in any other moment in history, the temporary relief that bread and circuses provide a population from the social war has been transformed into an entire global industry. One does not win a war by pretending it does not exist. One does not even survive a war in that manner. One wins a war by understanding the terrain and acting accordingly. So a theory of social war will be our weapon against the social war itself, allowing us to recognize our common terrain and devise a strategy to end this state of affairs.

Historically, social war emerged during the same time as the concept of empire itself. The first mention of "social war"—the war between allies (*socii* in Latin, also denoting companionship and hence related to *social* in English)—occurred when Athens failed to transform its confederacy of allies into an empire. So let us not forget that Athens, the long-reputed originator of democracy in the West, nonetheless was also the first aborted empire of Europe. When Athens created a confederacy of city-states in its war against Persia, it was the first among equals, the proto-imperial capital of the Delian League. The true intent of Athens became crystal clear to the other city-states after the Athenians massacred the islanders of Milos, who had in "good faith" believed that they could preserve their independence from the Athenian Confederacy. Increasingly threatened by Athenian domination, the former allies of Athens revolted to preserve their equal standing in the confederacy, and so shattered the prospects for a unified Athenian empire. However, the fall of Athens destroyed only a possible materialisation of empire, not the concept of empire itself. A generation later, the same ambitions re-emerged with Alexander the Great's failed universal empire. What Alexander realised too late was that military war is not enough to establish an empire: Empire can only be created by universalising a form of life, which Alexander took too literally by having his Greek soldiers marry Persians. Again, Greek attempts to become empire-builders were foiled by their adherence to the concept of citizenship as a blood-right, rather than understanding citizenship as a form of life involving language and customs regardless of ancestry.

The first true social war occurred at the birth of the first actual empire in the West: the Roman Empire. Before becoming an empire, Rome was an unimpressive little city-state built upon seven hills, far from the glories of Athens or Babylon. After nearly losing their independence to the Etruscans, the Romans discovered that the best defence was a good offence, and thus began the long and bloody transformation of the Roman Republic into the Roman Empire. The Romans gathered a league of Italian allies around them in return for a share of the bounty of their wars. Yet secretly the Romans also determined that Rome would be the first amongst equals, and kept the wealth and land accumulated from their conquests to themselves, slowly building massive slave plantations instead of parcelling out the spoils amongst Italian freemen from other cities. The former allies of Rome demanded to be treated as equals and declared themselves a new republic—known as

"Italia"—with its capital at Abruzzo. Let it not be said that history lacks a sense of irony; at the G8 in 2009, the new Roman empire of late capitalism had its most imperial of meetings on the earthquake-devastated rubble of Abruzzo.

After decades of bloodshed between the former allies, Rome emerged triumphant and granted all of those that did not revolt the right to become Roman citizens. By this act, the Roman empire expanded Roman citizenship outside of Rome, a process that soon spread across all of the Mediterranean world. Even those who had revolted could become Roman citizens if they submitted themselves at the feet of a Roman praetor! Why was this forgotten war between Rome and the other city-states a *social* war, rather than a *military* war? Unlike a military war where the vanquished are either enslaved or slaughtered, the Romans created a new kind of asymmetric war in which the war was won by transforming the vanquished into citizens.

What does it mean to think through the social war not as a historical event, but as a strategic concept? Which is worse: to die in a military war or to become a citizen in a social war? At least a slave can dream of insurrection against his master: the insurrection of Spartacus against the Romans followed shortly after the social war. Part of the strategy of social war is to avoid the inevitable slave revolt of those excluded from citizenship with its concomitant framework of rights. Yet to be a citizen is to adopt a whole new form of life, a form of life taken from the outside either willingly or through the threat of force: *Death or citizenship!* In contrast to the Greek concept of citizenship that ensured the barbarians would always be excluded, the Romans re-conceived the notion of the citizen to be based on shared customs, shared language, and being bound to a single legal-juridical framework—transforming the ethnic nation-state into an expansive empire capable of expanding across the entire world, at least in theory.

Advocates of empire would have us believe there are two phases to its expansion, which always occur in succession: the first phase of conquest and bloodshed and the second one of peacefully assimilating the conquered into empire as citizens. This is a lie—the social war shows that the assimilation of citizens into empire is just a different kind of war, one that takes place simultaneously via outward military forms of colonisation and via a more inward war on social relationships that begins before and continues long after any military operations have ended.

The social war is a war between forms of life in which the victorious form of life subsumes the conquered one. A form of life evades definition; it exists as the totality of lived material conditions, whose very basis is the social relationships that compose a world. We find ourselves always expressed by and taking part in such forms of life. They are more real than the very concept of the individual, for they are something that simultaneously conjoins and forms the foundation for objective conditions and subjectivity.

Subsumption is the primary tactic of social war, as via subsumption a form of life can be replaced with another form of life. A form of life acts as a configuration of habits and a sort of certain order of life; subsumption reconfigures these habits and re-orders these differences. Social war does not result in destruction for the vanquished: the subsumed do not disappear into ashes like the victims of Hiroshima, but instead the losers of the social war are remade in the interest of the dominating form of life, be it Rome or late capitalism. Subsumption was originally theorised by Kant in terms of the application of abstract concepts to the particulars of the vast manifold; some concepts allow us to register "red apples" despite the fact that each apple is on some metaphysical level indescribably different in tone and hue. Something in Kant still rings true, for the violence of subsumption destroys the concrete particular, reshaping reality into the image of a concrete universal.

In a social war, the concrete universal takes the form of the citizen, the *being without social relationships*. The only relationship allowed to the citizen is that of being dominated by the state, which today has expanded its power via domination by commodities. The particular is all forms of life that resist incorporation into the state apparatus. To ward off civil war, citizenship must expand to subsume all other forms of life, which is only possible by having a new kind of war that destroys the possibilities for social relationships. Under late capitalism, this is accomplished by constantly consuming citizens with work or by isolating people via artificially instilled fear of each other (as done via primitive scaremongering around race or religion). The citizen is not just stripped of social relationships by the social war, but also re-composed in terms of language, habits, and inclinations. Witness the mania for learning English in Greece—the surest sign of the spread of empire is a universalising language! The Roman form of life spread in lock-step with the Latin language, much as English is spreading over the entire world as the new lingua franca of global capital. The social war even expands into the very geography of a town (as Baron Haussmann realised all too well); where once each city had its own building style, the skyscraper is the monstrous form of life of capitalism made real, an inhuman abode fit only for capital. It is not by accident that every metropolis appears eerily similar and that everywhere the same miserable citizens rush to and fro, driven mad by work. Even in Greece, one can see in Ermou Street the eternal return of shopping in the form of anorexic girls and strangely "American"-looking men wandering amid the sterile display of commodities, with Athens being no different than any other metropolis. The victory of the social war is complete only when the citizen feels deep metaphysical anguish at witnessing the destruction of commodities and other violations of "private" property and fails to wince at the death of living beings.

A form of life can be destroyed by attacking and dissolving the social relationships that compose its autonomous world one by one, replacing them with relationships to images and dependence on the state and capital. In order to transform indigenous populations to citizens, the state must also strategically destroy their relationships to each other (families, tribes, friends) and their connections to the natural world, substituting a wholly imaginary relationship to the idea of the nation and absolute dependence on wage labor for these primordial relationships. In this way, the social war of the present empire is far more advanced than the social war of the Roman era, since today the military war is always limited to living bodies while the social war has the unlimited scope of social relationships. As the primary goal of social war is the elimination of any social relationships outside domination, social war is inherently *anti-social.*

It is true that the Greeks invented tragedy, and so perhaps more than superficial Americans they take the death of one of their own with a proper measure of seriousness. Yet their insurrection reflects also that many Greeks intuitively understand the horizon of what lies ahead for the future of this world far better than the most well-read of activists. It is no surprise that Alexis was murdered by the police—it was the most predictable response of the empire of capital when faced with a renegade youth who refused to become a citizen, instead inclined to loiter in Exarcheia amongst the excluded. The empire needs such examples, just as Rome needed to hang the bodies of rebellious slaves on the highways. Far from an accident, police killings of those who refuse the assimilation of the social war will doubtless become increasingly common as the social war intensifies. Again, what was surprising was that the consequent December insurrection generalised to attack the totality of the symbolic order of capitalism itself, reaching its height in the torching of Europe's largest Christmas tree. It was not in terms of violence that the events of December stepped outside the normality of Greek anarchist demonstrations, as Molotov cocktails are often to be seen in Greece at large demonstrations. What was abnormal even to

Greece was that those outside the anarchist milieu *also* simultaneously aimed for the transformation of everyday life while assaulting capital in acts of pure negation. In this way, the insurrection is a rupture with the previous forms of protest that emerged over the last ten years even in Greece: the first battle of a new sequence in the global civil war.

THE LIMITS OF THE ANARCHIST IDENTITY

From 1969 on, the spectacle, in order to still be believed, had to attribute to its enemies incredible actions, and in order to still be accepted, it had to credit proletarians with unacceptable actions, and thereby ensure sufficient publicity so that people who allow themselves to become frightened always choose "the lesser evil," namely the present state of affairs.

—Gianfranco Sanguinetti, *On Terrorism and the State*

One hypothesis that has been put forward for the power of the insurrection of December was the incredible strength of the anarchist movement. Credit must be given to the Greek anarchists, as it was their quick response that sparked the events on the evening of Alexis's death. Furthermore, the tactical forms of the anarchist movement did diffuse throughout other sectors of the population like students and immigrants. Yet in retrospect, the insurrection of December was both the apogee and the limit of the insurrectionary anarchist movement in Greece. For what the hypothesis of giving all credit to the "incredible Greek anarchists" does not account for is their subsequent paralysis. On the anniversary of December in 2009, as students took the streets again in Athens, many of the anarchists remained surrounded by police and isolated in their squats—the most visible example being the raid of the anarchist space Resalto in Keratsini, Piraeus.

In the midst of a general strike in May 2010 that nearly led to the storming of government buildings, a handful of anarchists burned down a bank, accidentally killing the three bank employees inside. This event was ready ammunition for the state and media, and used to full effect to nearly abort what appeared to be an even more wide-scale insurrection against the austerity measures being imposed on Greece by the IMF and EU. Although it is true that many people—far more than three—are likely to die in any insurrection, and that it was almost sheerly a matter of luck almost that such events did not occur earlier, the deaths in May 2010 led to massive demoralisation and infighting, including the departure of many of the voices of intelligence like those from the journal *Flesh Machine*.[2]

While revolutionaries must never in bad faith attack other revolutionaries that in good courage put themselves on the front line, nothing should be above analysis and critique from comrades who are involved in the same struggle. To avoid analysis and critique would lead anarchists to the same sort of ideological blindness that stopped many communists from critiquing Stalin (which shockingly many authoritarian communists in Greece somehow *still* refuse to do). Analysis is a sign of fidelity to insurrection and critique is honesty to our sisters and brothers in insurrection. We do not want to assign blame, like collaborators with the state. It is obvious that the deaths were caused by both a lack of care on the part of insurrectionaries and the twisted logic of capital that caused the boss to demand them to be at work on the day of a general strike. Instead, we want to understand why the aftermath of such an event could so easily thwart a growing popular insurrection.

One possibility is that it was the resurgence of a kind of anarchist identity in Greece after December that led to a careless cult of militaristic attack by anarchists, which in turn let the state and media isolate anarchists from the general population. Our counter-hypothesis is that the anarchist identity—as developed in Western Europe and North America since the 1980s and taking hold increasingly in Greece—is structurally counter-revolutionary. If this is true, while the first step of insurrection may be started by insurrectionists, for it to be complete the insurrectionists themselves must destroy their identity as "insurrectionists" so that the insurrection can generalise.

Following Badiou, the modern European sequence of insurrections starts with the Paris Commune, which expressed in a few days the ability of people to self-organise their lives without the accumulation of capital or domination of the state.[3] However, the Paris Commune was short-lived, as it was unable to defend itself from the inevitable military war that massacred it. The result of this failure of form was thirty years of successful counter-insurrection until revolutionaries adopted the form of the Leninist party, which adopted the Fordist factory-form—a strict discipline and hierarchy—to the revolution in order to create a revolutionary army that could withstand the capitalist counter-offensive (and did, after the insurrection in Russia). While the form of the Leninist party could defend an insurrection, such a centralised form failed to abolish relationships of domination, leading to the worst of all worlds: the professional revolutionary activists used "communism" as an attempt to intensify capitalism in pre-industrial societies.

After decades of further counter-insurrection, May 1968 identified the crux of the problem that Lenin failed to understand —that capitalism was based on social relationships rather than merely military domination. Yet the abortive insurrection of May 1968 failed to find a new form outside of the Leninist party, and so was incapable of generalising into a global insurrectionary process. Focusing on social relationships but unable to comprehend the new historical positioning of capital and the state, the movements of May '68 could only articulate the necessity for a revolution in social relationships in terms of recognition of the differences in domination, rather than their commonality. This led these movements to fall into an increasingly schizophrenic identity politics that was ultimately only compatible with further subsumption, via the creation of new markets around identity. However, the memory that it *could* have been otherwise still haunts the state. It is not by accident that Sarkozy stated in response to the December insurrection in Greece that "We don't want a European May '68 in the middle of Christmas."[4] In the last round of struggle, the anti-globalisation movement finally developed an alternative to the Leninist party through the network form of organisation, but was unable to develop any further revolutionary content, instead becoming trapped in the identity politics of 1968.

In contrast to the revolutionary anarchist tradition of those like Bakunin, anarchism as a specific "countercultural identity" is a relatively new phenomenon that developed after 1968, although traces of it can be found in historical movements such as the nihilists of pre-revolutionary Russia and the moralism of the Spanish revolution. In its current form, the anarchist identity as the "hooded one in black" descends—in dress, at least—from the German Autonomen. The Autonomen first appeared in Germany at the tail end of the seventies; their open street-fighting was a self-conscious rejection of the tactical stance of armed guerrilla groups like the Red Army Faction. This new generation (who were called the "Black Bloc" first by the media, and then by themselves) are best understood as revolutionaries whose discontent came not in particular from the exploitation of their labor at their jobs (contra traditional Marxism), but from the capitalist subsumption of their own daily life. This accounts for the fact that this generation's most elementary form of resistance was cultural: the "barbaric" inversion of bourgeoisie morality known as punk. The tradition of wearing black occurred as if by accident, although the tactical advantages of remaining anonymous were soon obvious to all and repeated with success.

This subcultural anarchist identity was globalised with the rise of summit-hopping at the turn of the millennium. Yet while this anarchist identity must be given due credit for helping reinvigorate an explicitly anti-capitalist trajectory in street protests, the anarchist identity never fully disassociated from the more confused reformists of the anti-globalisation movement, as exemplified by the explicitly social democratic pretensions of Naomi Klein and Ya Basta! This is likely due to the dissolution of the proletarian insurrectionary anarchist movement in Europe and the United States after the crushing defeats like those of the Industrial Workers of the World and the Spanish Civil War, which led to a veritable erasure of the revolutionary anarchist tradition. So the new anarchists of the 1990s made an almost infantile return to a sort of radical democracy and Proudhon-inspired federalism, despite the fact that such ideologies were anathema to revolutionary anarchists generations before, who learned all too well the theoretical and practical failures of these dead-ends. While there is no doubt that the anti-globalisation movement led to the valuable development of techniques and a renewed internationalism, the anti-globalisation movement was more a global petite bourgeois movement for the reform of empire into a global democracy than an explicitly insurrectionary movement. Anarchists were either side-lined as a sort of "out of control" element or fell into a sort of confused radical democratic posturing, as witnessed by the fetish of many anarchists for formal consensus even when such consensus exiled the Black Bloc to the fringe of the movement.

Let us give an honest funeral oration for the anarchist identity and the anti-globalisation movement from which it emerged. In precious few years, the form of networks pioneered by the anti-globalisation movement was able to produce a new kind of decentralised organisation that took the power of capital and the state off guard, an answer to a Leninist party for the 21st century. It was as if a new Internationale had materialised out of thin air. However, are networks revolutionary merely by virtue of their form? If somehow networks are indeed always structurally revolutionary, what a curious agreement between Silicon Valley marketing firms and autonomist theory! Our second hypothesis is that this absurdity results from a fundamental confusion between content and form, one that must be solved for the insurrection to proceed. The anti-globalisation movement pioneered a new form, but failed to provide it with revolutionary content.

From the standpoint of those enslaved to the centralised Fordist factory-form, the anarchic network-form seemed inherently revolutionary, perhaps even anti-capitalist. What is obvious in retrospective is that the network form has been given the content of capital. Soon after the anti-globalisation movement had taken centre stage, other groups with less-than-revolutionary content also began forming networks. Police were creating affinity groups and corporations like Google organised themselves in a decentralised fashion. When the reactionary elements of political Islam also adopted the network form, within a day the shockwaves set off by the events of 11 September 2001 destroyed the momentum of the anti-globalisation movement. At the present moment, the situation has become even more deranged. Invented by Indymedia, digital user-generated content is the heart of capitalist production. More and more youth belong to digital social networks like Facebook that serve as unimaginable treasure troves for police and surveillance. Given that Israeli military strategists read Deleuze,[5] one cannot help but agree with Fredric Jameson that there is something about Deleuze that strangely resonates with contemporary capitalism.[6]

Forms like networks (or hierarchies) are methods of organisation, but their content is the intentions that fill the form. While there can be no content without form and no form without content, the two do not necessarily march together hand in hand, but can even become dislocated temporally. Each historical epoch has its own limits, and so the determination of revolutionary content requires historical analysis. What was revolutionary in St. Petersburg in 1909 or Seattle in 1999 may not be revolutionary in Greece in 2009. If capitalism can be thought of as a particular form of life, any content is revolutionary insofar as it seeks to completely abolish this form of life and replace it with a new form of life without monetary exchange or domination. An insurrection in turn is a concrete event that, to a greater or lesser degree, expresses the emergence of this new form of life and negates the power of capital and the state.

Identity as such forms when the image of a form of life the possible social relationships, and therefore the proliferation of identity-based politics and subculture is merely another form of spectacular society. So it should be of no surprise that even as faith in neo-liberal capitalism collapses, a politics based on identity remains as strong as ever, as even self-professed revolutionaries are trapped within a politics based on images. Why is it so hard to overthrow the yoke of image-based politics? Could it be because the social relationships of the citizen under capital are almost gone, and so the citizen needs to have the image of social relationships—an "identity"—to avoid complete breakdown? Citizens express themselves only as a certain shifting pastiche of identities: the nationalist, the feminist, the punk, the hippie, the homosexual, the exercise-nut, the sci-fi fan, the person rediscovering their "ethnic" roots. Since subsumption has nearly stripped each person of any ability to hold onto her own presence, identities come and go, no more afflicting than a passing crush or the value of stock. These identities at their core are then just new brands of citizenship in the social war, the most advanced techniques thus far of subsumption. One can be a citizen while maintaining one's individuality and "unique" style.

While the anti-globalisation movement created new forms of organisation, its content was still held hostage by identity politics. When the anarchist re-emerged in the anti-globalisation movement, its insurrectionary content was also neutered by an inability to supersede the image of being an anarchist. Instead of focusing on actually creating social relationships without domination or exchange and strategising how these relationships could be cultivated into an insurrectionary process capable of bringing about revolution, anarchists became identified with a particular kind of image as given by dress and music, as well as pre-defined taboos on eating and consumption. For example, in Berlin one can go from one anarchist bar to another every night for months— living and eating only with other black-clad vegans—and never leave this bubble.

One of the most refreshing aspects of Greece until recently was the relative lack of anarchist identity. One could not easily identify "an anarchist" sipping a frappé coffee on the streets of Athens. Although sometimes vaguely counter-cultural, anarchists in Greece were not easily identifiable by dress or mannerisms, unlike areas like the United States or Germany where a veritable anarchist uniform developed. Isolated linguistically and geographically from mainland Europe, anarchists in Greece also remained isolated from identity politics that became integrated within anarchism elsewhere, and Greek anarchists kept loyal to a concept of revolution that still meant the overthrow of the state. There are many diverse factors responsible for this divergence from mainstream anarchist identity politics, ranging from the unique geography of the Balkans to the still-living memory of junta in the older generations in Greece. While some Greek anarchists did travel and take action in the major summit protests that rocked Europe, they participated in these summits by arriving and acting as they did in Greece, Molotov cocktails included where possible. Despite the rather maddening paranoia of the Negriists that the Black Bloc in Genoa was composed entirely of cops and fascists, the carefully planned script of Ya Basta! was at least partly interrupted by Greek anarchists who just didn't care about such absurd-scripted battles with the police. While there was some traffic between the various insurrectionary anarchist milieus, the Greek anarchists' attempts to invite the dying anti-globalisation movement to the protests against the EU Summit in Salonika in

2003 only brought out a few internationals.[7] Further attempts to gain international contacts, such as the European Social Forum in 2006, led only to further splits (with no less than four separate anarchist counter-forums organised). To a reader of the book *We Are Everywhere*,[8] the anti-globalisation movement would seem to be everywhere but Greece, despite Greece having the largest anarchist movement in Europe.

Attracted by the images of policemen on fire and destroyed streets, anarchists from across the globe showed up in droves to Greece after December 2008. While this solidarity is part of a long and honourable tradition exemplified also by the International Brigades in the Spanish Civil War, anarchists from outside Greece also brought with them an increased emphasis on the anarchist identity. When the insurrection failed to generalise into a full-scale revolution after December, instead of strategically analysing what tactics could sustain the insurrection, factions of the anarchist tendency in Greece retreated into an anti-social politics based around identity, perhaps unconsciously blaming the wider population for not having the courage to rise up. Some anarchists also decided that the decreasing quantity of attacks could somehow be compensated by their increased intensity, and so there was a distinctly anarchist revival of the long tradition of the armed guerrilla in Greece.[9] This led to increased activity after December by older socially-oriented anarchist armed groups like Revolutionary Struggle and the formation of new anarchist armed guerrilla groups like the "Conspiracy of the Cells of Fire" around a more anti-social and individualist ethos. So while the anarchist identity re-emerged specifically in Germany as a rejection of the form of the armed guerrilla, in Greece the content of the anarchist identity and the form of the armed guerrilla were more compatible. While there are clear historical reasons for the difference between the Greek and German experience of the guerrilla cell, there are also metaphysical reasons that connect nihilism with the armed struggle.

Perhaps the anarchist identity of the free individual—despite a superficial rejection of capitalism—is at the same time the most refined moment of bourgeois metaphysics. The "anarchist" is free only insofar as he rejects any force that may interfere with his desires. Expressed positively, this concept of the individual led to the Enlightenment project of human rights, democracy, and freedom. The individual was promised the satisfaction of her ever-expanding desires by capitalism, which in turn are defined by and define the absolute freedom of the individual. When this fairy tale comes up against the harsh reality of the decline of capitalism and the consequent inability of this world to satisfy their desires, a certain nihilist individualism is produced. As history proved that the Enlightenment project resulted solely in nightmares and so, the only remaining option for genuinely "free" individuals is to exercise their freedom to destroy the totality of the world, despite the fact that their own categories of thinking are subsumed by capital. The entirety of a social and collective revolutionary force is displaced onto the individual, who not surprisingly, then shows the inevitable signs of stress and burn-out as she cannot individually defeat the systematic social domination of capital. In honest desperation, the sign of true devotion to the cause becomes the intensity of the attack, nothing more. "Insurrection" is reduced to a series of actions, applying the same quantitative logic of commodity consumption to the number and ferocity of their individual attacks. To negate capitalism through acts of destruction is the first step, but to go beyond capitalism requires new metaphysical foundations for social relationships outside that of the individual and their desires.

This anti-social nihilism has unfortunately become an ever-increasing component of the anarchist identity in Greece. Forgetting its origins as a tool of empire, the social war is deployed by the anarchist themselves against anyone who does not share their identity. The anarchists can then in good conscience declare war against anyone involved in capitalism, mirroring the indeterminacy of the attack of police. While there is a truth that all citizens are complicit within global capital, so are the anarchists themselves, who exist both within and against capitalism. It is not just that the anarchists are fighting the social war *badly*, but that they engage in the social war with the goal of transforming others into anarchists *like themselves*. Taken to an absurd extreme, are people to be killed if they don't dress in black, eat the wrong kinds of food, aren't friends with the "right" people? More realistically, the taking up of indiscriminate social war by anarchists lets them conceive of themselves a permanent minority always in a losing war with wider society, never capable of actually achieving wide-scale revolution.

So when the events of May 2010 confirmed Victor Serge's maxim that "carelessness on the part of revolutionaries has always been the best aid the police have," the police had the perfect excuse to isolate and eliminate the anarchists in Greece.[10] The combination of anarchist armed struggle groups and a certain careless anti-social nihilism allowed for them to be painted by the state and media as some spectacular monsters, whose incredible actions might even target the average man-on-the-street. This contradicts the efficacy of the "hit and run" street actions that for many years did not go wrong and the very

315

real targets (banks, politicians, police) that armed struggle groups actually aimed for. However, it was difficult for many citizens to distinguish between reality and the spectacle, and the anti-social tendencies of anarchists prevented the truth of the insurrection—which will include a certain responsibility for carelessness and the taking of whatever measures are appropriate to prevent it in the future, from being communicated to former allies at the critical juncture in May. This led to the isolation of the anarchists and the halt of the insurrection, despite the fact that even some fellow employees understood it was the threat of being fired that kept the employees at the bank during the strike and so the bank was responsible at least in part for the deaths.[11] The social war by the state upon the general population is the self-evident current state of affairs, but the declaration of social war by anarchists against the general population is suicidal.

The crux of the problem is identity itself, not anarchism. Instead of creating an actual collective force based on shared experience, identity politics creates imaginary collectivities that are easily manipulated by capitalism as a way to divide and conquer potential revolutionaries. From the standpoint of the state and capital, identity is to be encouraged insofar as to label one as "different" and so capable of being discovered and isolated by the state's social war. As long as any group—the blacks, the anarchists, the Muslims, the Jews, the armed guerrilla—can be isolated in terms of identity, they can be destroyed. The anarchist actions after the death of Alexis exploded precisely because many youth in Greek high schools could identify with Alexis and many immigrants could identify with the hatred of capital and the police displayed by the youth. Had the anarchists been a completely isolated element in the population, then the murder of Alexis would not have been noticed by those outside their circles. It was precisely the lack of a separatist anarchist identity in Greece that led the events of December to be a success, as diverse and formerly divided sectors of the population did come together. At the limit of any insurrection, the identity of the insurrectionaries must be destroyed or become an obstacle to insurrection itself. Far better that the insurrectionaries destroy their identity than be physically imprisoned or killed by the state apparatus.

THE LAST CHANCE TO SAVE THE INSURRECTION IN GREECE

> Fire is physical time, absolute unrest, absolute disintegration of existence, the passing away of the "other," but also of itself; and hence we can understand how Heraclitus, proceeding from his fundamental determination, could quite logically call fire the notion of the process. He further made this fire to be a

real process; because its reality is for itself the whole process, the moments have become concretely determined. Fire, as the metamorphosis of bodily things, is the transformation and exhalation of the determinate; for this process Heraclitus used a particular word—evaporation (anaqumiasis)—but it is rather transition.

—G.W.F. Hegel, *Lectures on the History of Philosophy*

The lesson of May 2010 should be clear: Greece cannot repeat the 1970s in Italy. To repeat history due to a certain lack of creativity would betray the true potentiality of the events of December. In contrast to what we hope is the beginning of a new cycle of struggle in Greece, Italy was the last dying upsurge of 1968, an explosion particularly strong due to a certain failure of subsumption in the very peculiar industrial development of that country. Towards its decline in the late 1970s, the Italian movement also joined armed guerrilla groups and adopted a certain workerist ideology that was already historically out-dated. Perhaps it should be even less surprising that some of its theorists, like Negri, later found themselves as the leading voices of the anti-globalisation movement, since this movement was itself the activists 1968. We must go beyond 1968 and beyond Seattle 1999, and the events of December in Greece give us a path towards a new authentically insurrectionary content capable of giving such momentum to the forms pioneered in the last decade by the "anti-globalisation" movement. It is easy to be "revolutionary" with an almost religious zeal in eras when the counter-revolutionary tide seems to make questions of strategy and tactics impossible—so why not simply get yet another coffee and read another book about bygone revolutions? In revolutionary times, to be a revolutionary requires one to confront truly difficult questions of strategy and tactics with courage and intelligence.

If the very act of identification is counter-revolutionary, the first act of insurrectional content should be the desertion of the subcultural anarchist identity and the ideology of the "insurrectionary" as separate from the general population. The insurrectionary question should transform from "How to increase the intensity of the attack?" to "How can the number of people involved in the attack increase?" As the primary maneuver of the social war is to isolate pro-revolutionary individuals in order to prevent them from forming networks that could spread insurrectionary practices to the general population, insurrectionists should seek to *multiply* their social relationships. Since the image of "being an anarchist" constrains the kinds and types of relationships that one can have, insurrectionists should seek to have relationships that criss-cross the terrain of a society ghettoised into identities. To fight back in the social war, the insurrection must create and increase the *social relationships* it is founded upon.

The insurrection may have more friends than we suspect. It is through the politics of identity that capitalism staves off its true nightmare: that the majority of the population wishes to destroy the capitalism itself. To be revolutionary is to believe that the idea of insurrection can be majoritarian. Being revolutionary is the concrete destruction of the domination of the state and capital in everyday life of the population—not just inside a few anarchist enclaves. The maxim of Bakunin holds as true today as when it was first uttered, "The freedom of all is essential to my individual freedom."[12] The truly important thing about the December insurrection was this majoritarian aspect—that a large part of the Greek population was in open sympathy, and that groups that had previously been outside the anarchist identity, like students and immigrants, took to the streets to attack the police and occupy spaces. Only then was the previously invincible police and machinery of the state revealed to be as flammable as a paper tiger.

After December, the question of insurrection in Greece became not how to "start" the insurrection—where, when, and how to attack— but how to sustain it. This involves far more than spectacular terrorism or printing even more posters; answering the question of insurrection affirmatively requires seriously proving to the population that this condition can sustain life better than capitalism. Technical and practical questions come to the forefront: how to self-organise sustenance and the necessary production, how to raise children, how to build defences, how to care for the wounded and elderly. In other words, not just how to open the space for a new form of life, but how to create the space so that a form of life outside capitalism can *reproduce*. When the insurrection dissolves, it is can be because even after generalising outside of a set of given identities devised by capital (anarchists, students, immigrants), the insurrection failed to answer the question of how to sustain itself.

Luckily, it will not be too difficult for the insurrection to sustain the world better than capitalism. From the perspective of future generations, it will be evident that this is the best of times for insurrection, as the reproduction of the capitalist form of life is in crisis. Greece is likely only the beginning; the crisis of 2008 and the subsequent jobless recovery points to the possibility that capitalism is itself in an ongoing a crisis due to the over-accumulation of capital. To simplify dramatically, the innovative technologies behind the factories that produce commodities have accumulated to such an extent across all industries that profit is decreasing and the further production of real commodities requires little in the way of "new jobs," leading to a paradoxical situation of an over-abundance of commodities and a scarcity of jobs, as has been more elegantly said by others.[13] The only way to increase profit is to move investment further into speculative sectors in the form of financialisation as done from the 1970s onwards, but these kinds of speculative commodities are increasingly impossible to assign a value to, leading to financial crisis. Capital is by virtue of its own internal dynamics at a period of crisis, both the moment of its highest development and its immanent end.

Despite the mule-like insistence of politicians that there must be jobs—there are no jobs either now or in the future. The increased over-accumulation of capital makes even industrial jobs less necessary, even the workers find themselves soon-to-be-unemployed. The bet of the social war waged against this ever-increasing mass of unemployed is that they can be subsumed as citizens. Still, there is a point of contradiction, for under capitalism citizenship is equated also with being a worker. Yet as there are no more jobs, the social war of the state can no longer offer citizenship and global capital's financial markets have no other option than to desiccate the state through austerity measures in order to maintain profit. As the future of ever-increasing unemployment is nowhere clearer than in Greece, it is not surprising that the sector of the population most vulnerable to unemployment, the youth, are the first to join in an insurrection. It is precisely at school where the relations of production (the assignment to jobs) are reproduced, but in Greece even a newly minted doctorate speaking half-a-dozen languages is lucky to find a job as a waiter. The second to revolt will naturally be the immigrants, who are sensitive to the disappearance of even the most precarious jobs in the underworld of the economy. The last to revolt will always be the workers, whose identity and life is most strongly invested in the reproduction of capitalism, and who have benefited the most over the last years. The workers, the last of revolutionaries, are now joining the insurrection in Greece, as shown by their behaviour in May 2010, despite the Communist Party of Greece desperately trying to police them.

What is the spring from which the insurrectionary process in Greece swells, despite the social war of the state? The answer is obvious to anyone who has been to the country: the source of the insurrection in Greece comes from multitudinous social relationships of the people there. Walk in the streets of Exarcheia or even a small Greek village and what is striking in comparison with the desolate city streets of Northern Europe or North America is that there are simply people everywhere, chatting, sipping frappés, laying about—not *working* at all. In Greece, almost unique in modern Europe, life is still intertwined with innumerable rich social relationships, letting the streets of Athens essentially remain a social space. What is self-evident is that the source of their insurrectionary strength comes from the historical fact that Greece never went through industrial capitalism and the attendant process of subsumption: the bulk of the population went straight from an agrarian world to that of post-modern late capitalism. So social relationships are still mostly intact; one still sees extended families living together, people returning to one's family village and the islands for the summer, gangs of friends growing up together in a single neighbourhood, the Orthodox church engaging in strange rituals of fire—and warning against multinational corporations that "have no face." The general populace does not trust the state, and rightfully views it at best as something to be robbed or destroyed, and capitalism as a practice best left to the family or individual. Not so much a metropolis in the sense of Paris or London; Athens can be considered a mega-village in process of transformation to a proper capitalist metropolis, a hopeless amalgam of social relations based on friendship, gossip, and family (and thus often repressive in a regressive manner). Contra Negri, Greece was not transformed into a "social" factory (much less the use of Facebook!) leaving the subjectivity of Greeks as a bulwark of resistance to capital. What the murder of Alexis of December did was to provoke and mobilise this pre-capitalist subjectivity—which like any pre-capitalist subjectivity, has a notion of blood-debt that is foreign to the careless murder part and parcel of capitalism.

This pre-capitalist subjectivity serves as a possible hidden social reservoir of resistance to capitalist subsumption, but is it unique to Greece? Of course not—if anything these pre-capitalist subjectivities are the submerged around the globe. Due to the generalised betrayal and destruction of any sort of "progressive" anti-capitalist politics at the hands of Stalinism and the inability of the renewed anarchist movement of the last two decades to escape its own minoritarian identity politics, in times of crisis the general population falls back increasingly on to pre-capitalist subjectivities. Some of these are classical nationalist or ethnic "right-wing" movements, although many of them are at least superficially for the reduction of the state (such as the Tea Party in the US) or religious international forces (political Islam). Further subjectivities like these can be compatible with capital and so are simultaneously recuperated as its very vanguard. This is to be expected, as the false dichotomy between objectivity and subjectivity is itself a product of capital, and many of these "pre-capitalist" subjectivities are at least in part creations of spectacular capitalism itself.

The situation of Greek subjectivity serving as the basis for the insurrection shows that even these pre-capitalist subjectivities can express a truth that is antagonistic to capital, a truth that can burst forth as an insurrection. In this historical period, a homogeneous internationalism cannot be majoritarian. The only abstract truth reflected by "identity politics" is that the mass of subjectivities have at their heart particular truths of domination. However, must the insurrection rely on pre-capitalist subjectivities? By this logic, there is no hope for insurrection among the more fully subsumed forms of life in places like the United States, the United Kingdom and Germany—except possibly from those non-integrated immigrants and permanent underclasses (African Americans, Celtic minorities, Turkish groups). Worse, the insurrectional process could be combined with a sort of half-baked nationalism—"of course they are having an insurrection, that's just what they do in Greece." This concoction fails to take into account the most elementary of truths: Empire is the truly universal condition of catastrophe created by capital.

This common condition of catastrophe, brought about by the subsumption of all forms of life to capital, is the real abstraction that provides grounds for unity across all differences and so can provide real content to a new Internationale. To the extent that this lived experience of domination and destruction is common, it reduces all differences to contingencies, although of course the insurrectional process must take these regional variations in subjectivity into account. As capital is a historical rather than transcendental force, it is not surprising that the level of subsumption varies from region to region. Yet insurrectionists should neither wait till the forces of subsumption equalise (which while theoretically possible, is unlikely due to both regressive forces and the crisis) nor depend on an imported identity. Instead, insurrectionists must first explore the common conditions of their home in order to discover how each pre-capitalist subjectivity expresses a particular resistance to the universal truth of capitalist subsumption. This requires revolutionaries to both affirm the differences in their life-worlds on the level of tactics and unite globally on the level of strategy. In Greece, the insurrectionists must be carefully attuned to the themes of civil war and total freedom that resonate throughout a society that lived for centuries under foreign rule, while in Great Britain, insurrectionists should attune

321

themselves to the violent expropriation of the land from the peasantry (and thus the love of the land and animals deeply imprinted on British subjectivity) and historic defeat of the worker's world by Thatcher. The history of every pre-capitalist subjectivity should be understood in order to make the concept of insurrection resonate in the widest possible circles and instead of looking to the past, the insurrection needs to create a new kind of subjectivity whose horizon is a living anarchy yet to come.

Insurrection can—and must—be re-thought in a majoritarian manner. While it may be impossible to destroy identity entirely, insurrectionists can abolish their identity "as insurrectionaries" by acting in such a way that tends to dissolve the boundaries inherent in a social terrain divided up into identities, rather than just falling back into the even more isolated subjectivity of "the anarchist who has a critique of identity." The kinds of acts that dissolve any separatist identity are those—from propaganda to direct action to daily life— that show there exists some new collective force against the social war, an "open conspiracy" where anyone can participate in and form new social relationships in some meaningful way. The insurrectionary process is not the social war of a few lonely anarchists condemned to being a permanent minority; it is the renewal of humanity's social relationships that ends the social war, revealing all relationships as immediately social by abolishing the mediation of the commodity. As the insurrection spreads, the sign of its success will be that revolutionaries will become indiscernible from the wider population, the concrete realisation of what even Marx glimpsed in his theory of the self-abolition of the proletariat.

Revolution is the horizon that insurrection aims towards, otherwise all acts become mere resistance to a supposed permanent state of capitalism. Instead of wholesale abandoning the collective knowledge of the anti-globalisation movement, the insurrectionary process can breathe new revolutionary content into form of the network by opening this knowledge to everyone—but from the perspective of insurrection. The first step is to open the storehouse of technical knowledge to the general population, rather than sharing these techniques only with those who "fit" some absurd identity. The act of creating a Molotov cocktail should not be the secret technique of "summit-hopping" anarchists, but a technique that is known by every schoolchild. The ability to grow food and build houses should not be confined to bourgeois hobbyists, but part of the common heritage that every parent should teach their young. The courage to speak in an assembly should not be the province of a few "professional" anarchist men (who tend to always say the same thing) but an ability shared by even the most self-effacing of men and women. There are some that believe that somehow the anarchist identity as ideology is necessary to spread the opposition of authority to the general population. What is necessary to spread opposition to authority is not yet another identity or book about why authority is "bad." Opposition to authority—a genuine lived anarchy—can spread through the real collective social relationships involved in learning how to get organised, so the population has the material base to resist authority. Otherwise anarchist ideology remains pure idealism, with no means to prevent authoritarian power dynamics.

Open assemblies are the primary form that allows insurrectionary content to resonate with anyone interested enough to attend, and so spread networks with revolutionary content. It is almost sad that the focus on the fire and flames of Greece led many outside observers to miss the open assemblies in the occupied Universities that spread throughout even union-halls and small villages. Assemblies and occupations of buildings provide a space where new kinds of social relationships could form and multiply, so that people previously isolated and atomised from each other could form a collective force. Of course, in Argentina such assemblies were eventually co-opted by authoritarians and leftists. To prevent this, insurrectionary assemblies should differ in quality from any so-called "constituent" assembly that creates another state in embryo, and the more self-conscious insurrectionary elements should force out any signs of state collaboration or professional activism, although care should be taken to not impose a singular viewpoint—or worse, identity—on the assembly. The form of these assemblies will differ from activist consensus meetings. For most things, consensus matters little (although of course, it may be used as necessary); what matters is the development of a common feeling and space to debate tactics and strategy.

These insurrectionary assemblies should ask new kinds of questions that go beyond street protests. In an era where all political ideas are dead, it is in these assemblies that the post-political material questions about how to seize control of life from capital can be asked: How to raise children and nurse the wounded, how to never work at a job again yet provide bread and wine at the table, how to both destroy an economy and survive without one? Any particular open assembly will not have all the answers; often the requisite technical knowledge may simply be elsewhere, so the insurrection must grow and encompass more and more people. The assembly may need to go to the despairing workers of factories, to the elderly farmers of the fields, the isolated technicians of computers, to the outcast immigrants who still preserve their form of life, and it must gather their complicity by asking them directly and honestly: How can we create a new form of life without capitalism? Given the asylum of the University occupations in Greece, hosting an open assembly on insurrection is considerably easier there than in many other countries, but in any country such assemblies can form. After the excitement of the riot ends, the open and insurrectionary assembly is of utmost importance to *continue.*

The relationship of action to the growth of the insurrection is complex. The level of technique ideally spreads in step with the generalised level of civil war, as not to prematurely isolate the insurrection. Of course there is a tendency to go clandestine as soon as repression attacks public forms of insurrection like demonstrations or assemblies. However, more important than the amount of damage inflicted is the growth of public support for insurrection. One tactic is to focus on actions that can be easily replicated, as this undermines the spectacular relationship of passive citizens to professional "insurrectionaries." We know that in Greece even some schoolchildren can make barricades and fight cops in the streets. Dangerously, the power of the spectacle can even spread the insurrection, as the burning Christmas tree spelled for all of Greece that the capitalist symbolic order was dissolving and something new was happening. The important aspect then is not the attack by itself, but whether or not the attack spreads the insurrection in combination with other activities —which is precisely what an attack on the Christmas tree did in connection with thousands of posters calling to gather in the Polytechnic or elsewhere to discuss what to do next and thousands of other attacks. Direct actions are the spread and self-defence of a new kind of form of life, and so can even create new and more intense social relationships amongst all who are complicit, whatever the level of involvement.

With every new form of life, there is also a new metaphysics. This new way of being comes only with a little shift, but one that makes all the difference. This new kind of metaphysics is not mere idealism, but a new material manner of being in the world. For example, let us consider an assembly in a public space to plan a demonstration. To be in a meeting in the light of a capitalist metaphysics of isolated individuals, an individual who advocates an action may appear to be very brave, while another individual who expresses some fear that the plan will go wrong could be thought to be a coward. By being in an assembly through the lens of a new metaphysics that takes social relationships as the foundation of reality, one person may be expressing a sort of bravery that resonates with everyone, but the other is expressing equally validly the concerns and fear that everyone in the assembly feels but has been too cowardly themselves too articulate. These fluxes of fear and courage roll over the assembly like waves, until eventually it either dissipates into mere individuals or there is a phase transition into a new kind of collectivity, leading to the articulation of a plan by the assembly as a single body. The action itself becomes an articulation of a collective intelligence.

If Italy in the 1970s was the last gasp of the abortive revolution of May 1968, the insurrection of 2008 in Greece was something new: the first strike in a new round of global civil war after the financial crisis of 2008. The terrain of battle has inevitably changed. The social war cannot be fought against by the militaristic means of a vanguard party, even if that vanguard party has the content of anarchist activism or nihilism rather than the content of Leninism. Instead, the social war can only be fought by multiplying new forms of social relationships, and this can be done by taking the friendships that emerge temporarily in a riot or an occupation and determining what material organisation is necessary to sustain them to the point where they can reproduce of their own accord. The social war can only attack us when we are alone, but in open assemblies or in our most private of bedrooms, one by one, the lonely citizens can help form the collective intelligence necessary to defend and spread the insurrection. Anarchists no longer have to be content to be the perpetual losers of a social war, but can escape their identity to become only the first of those touched by the spreading common feeling for insurrection, and thus must bear the responsibility to bring its material organisation into being by re-appropriating the dead forms of activism and giving them life with insurrectionary content.

The events of December in 2008 were the first moment in a global insurrectionary process, a process that may (or may not) take years to develop in other countries to the same level as in Greece. Unfortunately it was to be expected that the Greek insurrection would not to spread outside the country except amongst a few isolated anarchists. Worse, after the events of May 2010 the fire that seemed to spark in Greece appeared to have evaporated. Yet what appears to be the evaporation of the insurrection may only be the dislocation in time of the Greek insurrection from the other moments of global insurrection. Further intensification of the pacifying operations of the social war has already led to its backfiring, as people globally become unemployed and so find it increasingly difficult to avoid the profound existential crisis of capitalist labour, and may thus be forced by the material breakdown of capital to take sides. The long-term case for global insurrection is compelling given the decline of capital's global rate of profit and possible limits to growth. In the short-term, insurrections may also break out overnight, and each insurrectionary moment will take on its own character. In France in 2010, the student and the youth from the banlieus, whose revolts were formerly entirely separated by their identities in 2005 and 2006, merged forces in common cause against capital with striking workers, and without a strong anarchist movement providing exemplary actions. Even after May 2010, all signs point to the fact that the people of Greece will be unable to tolerate further austerity cuts, so that the Greek insurrection could return with renewed ferocity at any moment. The insurrectionary process should not become trapped as merely a series of concrete insurrections, evaporating after each of these moments ends, but link each concrete visible moment into a global one.

It can be the task of our generation to fulfil the potential of all failed insurrections. This means that the future insurrection in Greece must go beyond the limits of 2008: rather than merely the destruction of shopfronts in some sort of fiery apocalypse, insurrection signals the difficult transition to a new form of life beyond capitalism and the state. This new form of life must come with a new kind of metaphysics no longer based on individual identity, and it is this new collective metaphysics that we glimpse when we lose ourselves in a rave, fall in love, join in a riot—which is precisely why we return to such events again and again. On a more subterranean level it is even possible such a feeling is spreading throughout the everyday life of the citizens of empire. This is revealed best by this real story that could also be apocryphal:

> As the financial crisis continued to take its toll on Greece, a British magazine did an expose revealing that Greeks were—against all tenets of being good citizens!— spending money on parties and absurdly expensive gifts. When the BBC reporter asked one of the Greeks why he was enjoying himself in the midst of a crisis, a party-goer said that 'everyone deserves a beautiful life'.

Other ways of having a beautiful life are possible; one sees such beautiful smiles on the faces of those who remember the insurrection of December. Just as the metaphysics of Western civilisation was born in Athens, so it must die there. May something more beautiful emerge in its wake.

NOTES

1 Also see Dalakoglou and Vradis, this volume.

2 For the dissolution text of the Flesh Machine project, see http://www.occupiedlondon. org/blog/2010/05/11/289-the-morbid-explosion-of-ideology/.

3 Badiou, A. "The Communist Hypothesis" *New Left Review* 49, Winter 2008.

4 As quoted in Campbell, M. "Sarkozy drops reforms amid fears of riots" *The Sunday Times*, 21 December 2008.

5 See Weizman, Eyal "The Art of War" http://www.frieze.com/issue/article/the_art_ of_war/.

6 See Frederic Jameson's quote on G. Deleuze and F. Guattari, *A Thousand Plateaus* (Minneapolis: University of Minnesota Press, 1987).

7 In fact, the EU Summit protest made a much longer-lasting impression in Greece due to its causing a split between the insurrectionary anarchist movement and the more leftist and populist anti-authoritarian movement.

8 See *We Are Everywhere, The Irresistible Rise of Global Anticapitalism*, http://www. weareeverywhere.org/.

9 In Greece the tradition of the guerrilla cell led back generations to their war against the Nazis and junta rather than the spectacular failure of the Red Army Faction.

10 Serge, V. *What Everyone Should Know About Repression*, (1926). http://www. marxists.org/archive/serge/1926/repression/index.htm.

11 See http://www.occupiedlondon.org/blog/2010/05/05/an-employee-of-marfin-bank-speaks-on-tonights-tragic-deaths-in-athens/.

12 Bakunin, M. *Man, Society, and Freedom* (1871).

13 See in particular *Endnotes* and Benanav, A. "Misery and the Value Form" *Endnotes* (2), 2010. http://endnotes.org.uk/articles/1.

19

CAPITALISM BY DEFAULT

Occupied London Collective

default, de · fault, / dïfôlt/
1. Act of failing to meet a financial obligation.
2. Nonpayment: loss resulting from failure of a debt to be paid.
3. Loss due to not showing up; "he lost the game by default."
4. Default option: an option that is selected automatically unless an alternative is specified.

"*At the time when these lines were written*": a disclaimer running through many contributions in this book, an acknowledgment that these are fluid times in which we find ourselves, an understanding that things might be—that they probably *will* be—completely different by the time writers have completed their articles, by the time the book goes to print, by the time readers get to hold it in their hands.

At the time when these lines were written, then, the Greek state was "about to" throw itself into the turmoil of emergency elections and by the looks of it—to default. This long "about to" moment has conveniently thrown much of the likely resistance in limbo; it is not easy, after all, to resist something supposedly not happening yet... *Not yet?* Wild, almost unimaginable changes have been sweeping the country since the revolt of 2008. In these two, long years we saw the end of post-dictatorial social consensus—the end of whatever welfare state that had ever existed around here, the end of workplace relations as we knew them (hell, for so many—the end of workplaces altogether), the end of public and free education. We saw a frantic increase in policing, and an end to whatever tiny crumbs of tolerance to migration that ever existed. So many "ends," all pointing at the end of capitalist order as-we-knew-it; the shattering of all those tiny bits that held together the mosaic of normality.

In a sense the future is already here. The welfare state, mild capitalism, post-WWII consensus, the American dream and all its regional variations are well and truly gone. Yet the past still haunts us. The state of emergency as a mode of rule; that old things-are-bad-ask-no-questions trick hasn't come out of the rulers hat for the first time. The state of emergency is pumped out to an extreme—brute force is more brute and longer-lasting than ever, and as wall poster in Athens reads: "As carrots run out sticks become plenty."

What times! The certainties of capitalist rule crumble and fall, one after the other. Why won't the rulers even bother to prevent the unveiling of the humanist façade of their rule—is this some obnoxious-ness on their part? Hardly so. A systemic crisis is, after all, exactly that: *systemic*. It would take more than a few obnoxious leaders (or clumsy, inexperienced, totalitarian, or simply too "progressive" and "lenient" ones for that matter) to destabilise the existing system of order. Change simply runs much deeper than any single one of them. Why is capitalist rule nakedly exposing its ruthlessness then—could it be out of fear? After all, the wounded animal will sometimes grind its teeth; a show of force can be a sign of desperation.

The 2008 uprising in Greece, the troubled fall of 2010 in France, the string of revolutions in Tunisia, Algeria, Libya, and Egypt in the same year show that there is good reason for fear to nest in the minds of the rulers, fear that people might, and in fact can rise up. In 2008 Greece, in Exarcheia, a cop's bullet and a dead boy was the spark that caused the boiling rage of many to spill out onto the streets. In 2010 France the rage was against the nude new capitalist realm as a whole. A single pretext was no longer necessary. Have we reached that point, that moment in time when sparks are not even needed, when people will rise up against order, period?

How easy and convenient it would be to think so. But the Greek experience in the time of the IMF so far has taught us a few bitter lessons.

Lesson number one—a revolt does not happen by default. Just because "things are too difficult," people won't automatically become active. And if they do, it might be for the wrong reasons altogether.

Lesson number two—when a revolt does happen, as in 2008, its legacy is precious. It gets inscribed in our spaces of the everyday, it livens up our practice and inspires us as a possible direction into which change may head.

Lesson number three—the legacy of an unfinished revolt can also be a burden. It remains as a painful memory of change that came to a halt; of the counter-insurgency launched by authority, of the limit inherent in some of our own practices even, which can become a counter-insurgency force in itself—as the deaths of 5 May in Athens were sure to show.

We take these lessons into the time of post-revolt and we move on. Every part of this book reads what happened in December as a mostly unwritten, unfinished chapter—as the first instant of a long, long moment of transition in which we stand.

Here we stand, staring at the frantic collapse of reality as we knew it, just as frantic as mass euphoria had been only a few years ago in this part of the world, when the local variation of capitalist rule seemed to be taking after its elder western siblings.

Here we stand, in our collective not-yet-awake moment, just when the dream turns into a nightmare, when the past defaults and crumbles but doesn't quite fall. For now, and now only, it remains by default.

Here we stand, between a present yet to pass and a future still to come.

Occupied London Collective, Spring 2011

A BRIEF TIMELINE OF MAJOR PROTESTS AND REVOLTS IN ATHENS BETWEEN NOVEMBER 1973 AND DECEMBER 2010

17 NOVEMBER 1973. After several days of anti-junta protests situated mainly in downtown Athens and particularly around the universities, tanks, police, and soldiers storm the Athens Polytechnic. Clashes follow and more than forty protesters are killed. To this day, this date is a point of reference for the antagonistic movement in the country.

1979–1980. The first post-junta mass student movement. Universities and schools are occupied by students against the so-called educational reform. The Prime Minister, Konstantinos Karamanlis (Senior), is forced to withdraw the education act.

17 NOVEMBER 1980. During the march commemorating the 1973 revolt, barricades are erected and clashes with the police take place around the House of Parliament. On that night the worker Stamatina Kanelopoulou and the student Iakovos Koumis are murdered by the police. No police officer has ever been held responsible for the two deaths.

DECEMBER 1984. Hotel Caravel in Athens is attacked by thousands of anarchists and far-leftists, causing the cancellation of an extreme-right conference where Jean-Marie Le Pen of the French National Front had been invited to give a speech.

17 NOVEMBER 1985. During the annual march commemorating the 1973 revolt, fresh clashes erupt between youth and the police. In these street fights, 15-year-old Michalis Kaltezas is shot in the back of the head by MAT officer Athanasios Melistas. Major clashes follow in Athens. The Chemical School and the Polytechnic are occupied on the same night. On the next day, police are given permission by the university authorities to storm the building and make arrests in what was the first withdrawal of the "constitutionally secured" academic asylum. Melistas is sentenced to a suspended two-and-a-half-year sentence. In 1990, the sentence was overturned at the court of appeal, a decision which led to fresh clashes with the police in the major cities of Greece.

1990–1991. A new student movement that would resist and eventually prevent another governmental attempt to "reform education"—namely to limit the provision of free public education—emerges. More than 1,500 high schools and most universities were fully occupied for several weeks after the respective decisions of their assemblies. Demonstrations of several thousand people flooded the streets of every Greek city and town and severe clashes with the police and attacks on governmental buildings took place on a weekly basis while the occupied schools became cells of political activity, discussion, and popular resistance to the government. Eventually, joint operations by police and members of the governing party (ND) attacked schools and tried to remove the protesting students and teachers. Nikos Temponeras, a mathematics teacher, was murdered by right-wing thugs while defending his school. His assassin was Kalampokas, a distinguished member of ND's local branch in the city of Patras. Temponeras's death was followed by two days of major protests and clashes in Patras, Athens, Thessaloniki, and other cities.

17 NOVEMBER 1995. During the events commemorating the 1973 anti-junta revolt, anarchists occupy the Athens Polytechnic. The occupation was in solidarity with the prisoners of Greece's largest prison of Korydallos, who were in revolt those days, as well as with the imprisoned anarchist hunger strikers Christophoros Marinos and Kostas Kalaremas. The assembly in the occupied Polytechnic numbered more than a thousand participants, while clashes with riot police were taking place all night long in the streets around the Polytechnic. Once again, the PASOK government would revoke academic asylum, and riot police would storm the institution, arresting more than 500 occupiers the next morning.

1996–1997. Teachers' unions all around the country go on strike for several weeks, halting most schools' operation in order to resist the reform of their working conditions. Marches, road blockades, and clashes with the police take place almost every week across the country.

17 NOVEMBER 1998. During the commemoration events for the 1973 revolt, 153 anarchists are arrested outside the gates of the Athens Polytechnic during a joint operation by riot police (MAT) and the Communist Party's Youth (KNE), which in the previous few years had emerged as the self-appointed steward of the commemorative demonstration. This event signified the long distance that KNE had travelled towards conservative practices and Stalinist authoritarianism, a process that was inaugurated by the KNE condemnation of the 17 November 1973 uprising.

1998–1999. Fresh attempts to vote in an education reform bill give birth to a new high school student movement that storms the country: high schools and universities are occupied while tens of thousands of students march in Athens. An attempt by the Communist Party to hijack the movement fails as autonomous students take political control of most schools.

SEPTEMBER 2000. Activists from Greece quickly join forces with the movement against the globalisation of sovereignty. Soon after the battle of Seattle, many hundreds of Greek far-leftists and anarchists travel to Prague to protest against the IMF/WB summit in the city.

JULY 2001. Several thousand anarchists and far-leftists from Greece travel to Italy to take part in the Genoa anti-G8 mobilisations.

DECEMBER 2001. Hundreds of Greek activists travel to Brussels to participate in the pan-European trade unions' demonstration, during and against that year's EU summit. EU leaders were discussing the European constitution and common policies on privatisation, asylum, unemployment, security, surveillance, and "terrorism."

JUNE 2003. Greece hosts the EU leaders' summit in the northern city of Thessaloniki. During the protests, a more than 4,000-strong black bloc marches through the city while several thousands from the left participate in the demonstration.

2004. The year of the Athens Olympic Games. During the previous three years, several constitutional rights were withdrawn, special anti-terrorist laws came into force, and armed police presence had increased dramatically in public spaces. One year before the Games, Athens resembled a city occupied by police brigades, while more than 1,000 police-operated CCTV had appeared. Still, the introduction of CCTV was resisted en masse by anarchists who organised several actions sabotaging the majority of these cameras. In the name of a "successful" Olympiad, public money was wasted on useless infrastructure, most of which has remained unused ever since. Major construction contractors monopolised the building of expensive infrastructure such as stadiums, highways, and airports. This allocation of enormous amounts of public money to private businesses paved the way for the crisis that would follow a few years later.

MAY 2005. The closing demonstration of Athens Social Forum gathers the unexpected number of circa 70,000 participants. Making visible a growing part of the population which identifies with left and anti-authoritarian ideas but does not have any explicit political group or party affiliation.

2006–2007. Yet another attempt by a Greek government to reform higher education, this time following the guides set by the neoliberal EU Bologna agreement for higher education. The attempted reform triggers a student movement that spreads across the country. General assemblies of students decide university occupations and protest against the plan to limit the free public education. During one of these demonstrations, a policeman guarding a ministry in Athens shoots into the air trying to intimidate the protesters. Parliament eventually voted the law in during major clashes outside the building.

AUGUST 2007. Vast forest fires destroy some of the most beautiful parts of the country. It is clear to most people that the economic interests of developers played a major role in the fires. The underfunding of the fire service leaves neither enough firefighters nor enough firefighting equipment available. The Prime Minister, Costas Karamanlis, claims that "Greece was under attack." Other governmental sources spread information that either anarchists or the political opposition have set the fires. A rally several thousand strong takes place in front of the House of Parliament protesting against big developers and the government.

FEBRUARY 2008. A few dozen neo-Nazis attempt to march in central Athens and several hundred anti-fascists organise a counter-march, with clashes erupting all around, in what was one of the largest and most intense anti-fascist street fights in recent years.

NOVEMBER 2008. Approximately 8,000 prison inmates revolt and participate in a mass hunger strike, demanding more humane jail conditions. A strong prisoner solidarity movement is formed only weeks before the December revolt.

6 DECEMBER 2008. Alexis Grigoropoulos, a 15-year-old high-school student, is shot in the chest by police officer Epameinontas Korkoneas. The murder triggers a profound revolt across and beyond the country's borders.

17 NOVEMBER 2009. Almost 100 people, mostly teenagers, are detained in Athens during and following the events commemorating the 1973 anti-junta revolt. The police talk of "pre-emptive detentions," admitting these people had not committed any illegal acts.

6 DECEMBER 2009. Several thousand people march in the major cities of Greece to commemorate the revolt of December 2008. Almost 1,000 people are detained or arrested before and during the marches.

5 MAY 2010. The Greek parliament votes to receive a €110 billion loan from the IMF/ EU/ECB, effectively making Greece the first euro zone country to ever agree to an IMF loan. During the vote, hundreds of thousands demonstrate outside the House of Parliament. Protesters attempt to storm parliament and clashes erupt for hours all over Athens. A bank branch on Stadiou Street is set on fire and three bank clerks die from the fumes.

6 DECEMBER 2010. For a second consecutive year, several thousand demonstrators gather to commemorate the revolt of December 2008 in Athens and most Greek cities.

15 DECEMBER 2010. General strike against the austerity measures imposed by the government and the IMF/EU/ECB, the seventh in that year alone.

GLOSSARY

17 NOVEMBER: Originally refers to 17 November 1973. On that date, tanks, the army and police attacked students and other protesters who had occupied the Athens Polytechnic protesting against the dictatorship. Since then, a commemorative march has taken every year in Athens, from the Polytechnic to the US Embassy.

ACADEMIC ASYLUM: A constitutional provision for safeguarding academic freedom, under which the police and armed forces have no right to enter university grounds without prior permission of the university's asylum committee.

ANTAGONIST MOVEMENT: Deriving from the 1970s tradition of the autonomia in Italy, this is an all-encompassing term used to describe the far-left, anti-authoritarian, and anarchist movement.

ANTARTIS[ML]; ANTARTISA[FML]: A guerrilla. The term was used to describe those who joined the Resistance against the Axis occupation of Greece in WWII (1940–1944), especially those who went to the mountains. The same term was used for those who joined the communist forces during the civil war (1946–1949).

ANTIPAROCHI: A system for building apartment blocks, applied en masse for several decades in Greece following WWII. Antiparochi brings together in a single joint venture operation a landowner and a (small) building contractor, who jointly divide the built property produced by the latter on the owner's parcel. Antiparochi received tax privileges and profited from the general increase in construction coefficients in 1968, becoming the sole system for condominium building until the late 1970s (Maloutas & Karadimitriou 2001).

BASE UNIONS: First degree workers unions developed mostly in precarious workplaces during recent years, partially in an attempt to overcome the reformism and bureaucratic structures of already existing unions.

DEKEMVRIANA (LIT. "[EVENTS]OF DECEMBER"): At the end of 1944 the command of British troops stationed in Athens ordered the complete disarming of all Resistance organisations within ten days. In response, EAM (National Liberation Front, which initiated the largest and most active Resistance group during the occupation) called for a demonstration in central Athens. On the day, more than 200,000 marched through the city. The police, along with British Forces and former Nazi collaborators of the X group, who had been re-employed by the new regime, opened fire on the demonstrators, killing twenty-eight of them. This attack led to thirty-seven days of clashes between EAM and British troops, who fought on the side of smaller Greek armed units faithful to the enforced government. The Dekemvriana ended officially with the peace treaty of Varkiza. The term Dekemvriana has also been used in reference to the December 2008 revolt.

EMFYLIOS (CIVIL WAR): The war between the Greek Governmental Army and the Democratic Army of Greece (DSE) between 1946 and 1949. This is considered to be the first major conflict of the Cold War, because the UK and USA supported the governmental army while the socialist regimes of the Balkans supported DSE. DSE was fundamentally controlled by KKE and was formed mostly of former guerrillas who had fought for years against the Axis occupation of the country. The governmental army faced severe losses and failures until 1948, yet increased foreign aid combined with DSE's decreasing international aid resources and numerical strength ultimately led to DSE's defeat.

POLYTECHNIC GENERATION (GENIA TOU POLYTECHNEIOU): Those involved as young students or workers in the anti-junta struggle and particularly in the November 1973 Polytechnic uprising. The term often has negative connotations when referring to politicians, journalists, or other figures of power who will mention their Polytechnic credentials in order to justify their subsequent reactionary practices or discourses.

GOLDEN DAWN: A neo-Nazi group founded in the early 1990s. The leader of the group won a seat on the city council of Athens in the 2010 municipal elections, the first time Golden Dawn had been elected to political representation.

JUNTA: The seven-year-long colonels' dictatorship (1967–1974) that started on 21 April 1967 when a group of colonels under Georgios Papadopoulos staged a coup supported by the US government. It ended with a transition of power to civilian politicians in 1974 and elections in November 1974. Whether the post-dictatorial state inherited several of the dictatorship's legacies remains a contested issue, especially in terms of its oppressive state apparatus.

KOUKOLOFOROI (LIT. HOOD-WEARERS): Somebody who wears a hood or a balaclava during demonstrations. The corporate media use the term pejoratively and often almost as a synonym for "anarchist."

338   KOUKOLONOMOS (LIT. THE HOODS' LAW): A law introduced in the summer of 2009 which dictated that all petty crimes committed by protesters in hoods or balaclavas

would receive an enhanced sentence. The introduction of the law has been directly linked to the aftermaths of December's revolt.

METAPOLITEFSI (LIT. POLITICAL TRANSITION): The term used to describe the historical period of modern Greek history that follows the end of the colonels' dictatorship (1974). Many believe the revolt of December 2008 to signify the end of *Metapolitefsi*.

POLYKATOIKIA (LIT. MANY RESIDENCIES): The most common type of housing building in Athens. These are multi-storey buildings made mainly out of concrete. Their mass construction started after WWII and boomed during the 1960s and 1970s. They were promoted by the authorities through antiparochi (see above). With the vertical segregation of its residents (higher classes living in upper floors) and their mixed use (commercial and housing), the polykatoikia played a key role in shaping the character of contemporary Greek cities.

POLYTECHNIC UPRISING: The anti-junta protest of university students that started on 14 November 1973 and which escalated into a popular uprising and an occupation of the Athens Polytechnic by students and other protesters, lasting for three days. Thousands joined the protests, but in the early morning of 17 November 1973 an army tank crashed the front gate of the Polytechnic, followed by a full-scale attack by police and the army resulting in the deaths of at least forty protesters.

REVOLTED (EKSEGERMENOI [PL]): The term has been used widely within the antagonist social movement in Greece to describe participants in the 2008 revolt. The use of the term—otherwise uncommon in English—has been deemed necessary in order to describe the composition of the revolt's participants: neither exactly insurgents (which would imply more war-like characteristics) nor simply protesters.

STEKI [SNGLR], STEKIA [PLRL] (LIT. "HANGOUT," WHERE PEOPLE HANG AROUND OFTEN): In the Greek social antagonist movement, the term steki has been used to describe spaces—rented or occupied, in universities or other urban areas—used by a single group or by groups in close affinity with each other. While most stekia are open to the public, they are distinctively different to social centres in that they are most often associated with a much tighter group or politics.

SYNASPISMOS: The Coalition of the Left of Movements and Ecology, a parliamentary party which originates from KKE (int) [see acronyms]. In late 1980s was an electoral coalition of both KKE and KKE (int), but soon became a new party mostly identified with KKE (int.) agenda. Today is the largest party of SYRIZA [see acronyms].

KEY PLACES AND PEOPLE

ALEXANDROS (ALEXIS) GRIGOROPOULOS: the 15-year-old student murdered by the police officer Epameinondas Korkoneas on 6 December 2008 in Exarcheia.

ANDREAS PAPANDREOU: Prime Minister of Greece 1981–1989 and 1993–1996 (Social Democrat).

ASOEE: The campus of the Athens University of Economics and Business, located on Patision Avenue a few blocks north of Polytechneio [See Acronyms].

ATHENS POLYTECHNIC (POLYTECHNEIO): The historical building of the National Technological University of Athens, located in Patision Avenue. It was the epicentre of the 17 November 1973 anti-junta uprising. Much anarchist and other radical activity has been centred there since then.

CHEMISTRY SCHOOL (CHIMEIO): The old building of the Chemistry School of the University of Athens, located on Solonos Street.

COSTAS SIMITIS: Prime Minister of Greece 1996–2004 (Social Democrat).

EXARCHEIA: The central Athens neighbourhood where radical, anarchist, and far-left spaces and political activity are concentrated. Alexandros Grigoropoulos was murdered there on 6 December 2008.

GEORGE PAPANDREOU: Prime Minister of Greece since 2009 (Social Democrat).

GEORGIOS PAPANDREOU (SENIOR): Prime Minister of Greece, 1944–1945, 1963, and 1964–1965.

IAKOVOS KOUMIS: A university student murdered by police on 17 November 1980 during clashes between demonstrators and the police in front of the House of Parliament in Athens.

KOLONAKI: The most bourgeois district of central Athens, with the highest property values and expensive boutique shops, high-class bars and cafés. It is adjacent to the House of Parliament but also to Exarcheia.

KONSTANTINOS KARAMANLIS (SENIOR): Prime Minister of Greece 1955–1963 and the first post-dictatorial PM (1974–1980).

KOSTAS KARAMANLIS: Prime Minister of Greece 2004–2009 (Conservative).

LELAS KARAGIANNI: One of the oldest anarchist squats in Athens, located on Lelas Karagianni St.

MESOLOGEIOU: One of the most vibrant street in Exarcheia, also the site of assassination of Alexandros Grigoropoulos.

MICHALIS KALTEZAS: The 15 year-old student killed by a police officer of the riot police unit (MAT) on 17 November 1985, during clashes in Exarcheia.

NAVARINOU PARK: A self-organised open-air space in Exarcheia, located next to the site where Alexandros Grigoropoulos was assassinated.

NIKOS TEMPONERAS: A high-school mathematics teacher assassinated in the city of Patras by a right-wing thug of the then governing ND party in 1991.

NOMIKI: The Law School of the University of Athens. Located on Akadimias Street, it is one of the central Athens university campuses.

OMONOIA SQUARE: The most central square of Athens.

PANEPISTIMIOU AVENUE: The avenue passing in front of the neoclassical refectory of the University of Athens, the National Library and the Academy of Athens. It connects Athens's two most central squares of Athens, Syntagma and Omonoia.

PANTEION UNIVERSITY: The primary social and political sciences university of Athens. Located on the edge of the city centre, in the district of Kalithea.

PATISION AVENUE: The avenue connecting the centre of Athens with the northern district of Patisia. It runs in front of the Athens Polytechnic and on several occasions in the past forty years has been the battlefield between protesters and police.

PROPYLEA: The square at the front of the University of Athens refectory, located on Panepistimiou Avenue. It is one of the most central university facilities in Athens and is protected under the academic asylum legislation. It is one of the most common sites for rallies take place and marches to start.

STAMATINA KANELOPOULOU: A worker killed by police on 17 November 1980 during clashes between demonstrators and the police in front of the House of Parliament in Athens.

SYNTAGMA SQUARE: The square in front of the House of Parliament in Athens.

TROIKA: Common name for the three organisations (IMF, EU, ECB) which gave a loan to the Greek government on May 5, 2010.

VILLA AMALIAS: The second-oldest anarchist squat in Athens, located in Aharnon Street.

BIBLIOGRAPHY

Agamben, G. (1995) "We Refugees," *Symposium* 49 (2) pp. 114–119

— (2005) *State of Exception*, Chicago: Chicago University Press

— (2007) *The Coming Community*, Minneapolis: Minnesota University Press

Amin, A. (2003) "Unruly Strangers? The 2001 Urban Riots in Britain," IJURR 27 (2)

Angas, L. L. B. (1937) *Slump Ahead in Bonds*, New York: Somerset Pub. Co

Arendt, H. (1986) *The Human Condition*, Chicago: Chicago University Press

— (2006) *Between Past and Future*, London: Penguin

Austin, J. L. (1975) *How to Do Things With Words*, Oxford: Clarendon Press

Autor, D. H., Katz, L. F. and Kearney, M. S. (2006) "The Polarisation of the US Labour Market," *American Economic Review Papers and Proceedings* 96 (2), pp.189–194

Badiou, A. (2005a) *Being and Event*, London: Continuum

— (2005b) *Metapolitics*, London: Verso

— (2007) [1988] *Being and Event*, New York: Continuum

Bagguley, P. and Hussain, Y. (2008) *Riotous Citizens: Ethnic Conflict in Multicultural Britain*, London: Ashgate

Baldassare, M. (1994) *The Los Angeles Riots: Lessons for the Urban Future*, San Francisco: Westview Press

Bank of Greece (2009) *Monetary Policy 2009–2010*, Athens: Bank of Greece [in Greek]

Bauman, Z. (1994) *Alone Again: Ethics after Certainty*, London: Demos

— (2006) *Liquid Fear*, Oxford: Polity

— (2007) *Liquid Time*, Oxford: Polity

Benjamin, W. (2003a) "Berlin Childhood Around 1900," in Benjamin, W., Bullock M. P., and Jennings M. W. (eds) *Walter Benjamin: Selected Writings Volume 3 1935–1938*, Boston: Harvard University Press

— (2003b) *Paris, Capital of the 19th Century*, Hotel des étrangers (Thessaloniki), 4 [in Greek]

— (2004) "Critique of Violence," in Benjamin, W., Bullock, M. P. and Jennings, M. W. (eds) *Walter Benjamin: Selected Writings Volume 1 1913–1926*, Boston: Harvard University Press

— (2006) [1942] "On the Concept of History" in Benjamin, W., Bullock, M. P., and Jennings M. W. (eds) *Walter Benjamin: Selected Writings Volume 4 1938–1940*, Boston: Harvard University Press

Blaumachen (2009) *December 2008: An Attempt to Detect the Strengths and Limits of Our Struggle*, Thessaloniki: independent edition [in Greek]

Boltanski, L. and Chiapello, E. (2005) *The New Spirit of Capitalism*, London and New York: Verso

Bourdieu, P. (1990) *The Logic of Practice*, Oxford: Polity Press/ Blackwell

— (2000) *Pascalian Meditations*, Oxford: Polity Press/ Blackwell

c/krümel (2005) *Between a re-fractured arrow and a straight line*, Athens: Primitive [in Greek]

Castells, M. (1983) *The City and the Grassroots: A Cross-Cultural Theory of Urban Social Movements*, Berkeley: California University Press

Clastres, P. (1989) *Society Against the State: Essays in Political Anthropology*, New York: Zone Books

Dadush, U. and Eidelman, V. (2010) "Germany: Europe's Pride or Europe's Problem?," in Dadush, U. (Ed.) *Paradigm lost: the Euro in crisis*, Carnegie Endowment, Washington DC.

Day, R. (2005) *Gramsci is Dead*, London: Pluto Press

Deleuze, G. and Guattari, F. (1986) *Nomadology: the War Machine*, New York: Autonomedia

Dikeç, M. (2007) *Badlands of the Republic: Space, Politics and Urban Policy*, Oxford: Blackwell

Douzinas, C. (2008) "Polis, Kratos, Kosmopolis: on Space, Law and Democracy," unpublished paper presented at the International Conference A-ktiston: Space and Democracy, Athens, December 19–20th, 2008

Eurostat (2010) *Unemployment Rates, Temporary and Part-Time Employment*

Faraklas, Y. (1997) "The Revolution as Revenge," Athens: *O Politis* 43 [in Greek]

Foucault, M. (2003) *Society Must be Defended: Lectures at the Collège de France, 1975–76*, New York: Picador

— (2006) *Psychiatric Power: Lectures at the Collège de France, 1973–1974*, London: Pelgrave Macmillan

Gavriilides, A. (2010) "The Professors of Nothing: Counter-Insurgency as Political Science," *Theseis* 113 [in Greek]

Goos, M., Manning, A. and Salomons, A. (2009) "The Polarisation of the European Labour Market," *American Economic Review Papers and Proceedings* 99(2), pp.58–63

Gortsos, K., Markou, A., Camoutsis, P. (2008) "Trends in the Transformation of the Use of the Coastal Areas of Attica from Areas of Second and Resort Accommodation Into Main Accommodation the Social and Spatial Transformations in the 21st Century Athens," Athens: National Centre for Social Research [in Greek]

Graham, S. (2004) "Cities as Strategic Sites: Place, Annihilation and Urban Geopolitics," in Graham, S. (ed.) *Cities, War and Terrorism: Towards an Urban Geopolitics*, Oxford: Blackwell

Guha, R. (1983) "The Prose of Counter-Insurgency," in *Subaltern Studies* II, New Delhi: Oxford University Press India

Hardt, M. and Negri, T. (2000) *Empire*, Cambridge, MA and London: Harvard University Press

Harvey, D. (2008) "The Right to the City," *New Left Review* 53

Hoare, Q. and Nowell Smith, G. (1971) *Selections from the Prison Notebooks of Antonio Gramsci*, New York: International Publishers

Hobsbawm, E. (1965) *Primitive Rebels: Studies in Archaic Forms of Social Movement in the 19th and 20th Centuries*, New York: W.W. Norton

Hudson, M. (2003) *Super Imperialism: The Origins and Fundamentals of U.S. World Dominance*, London: Pluto Press

INE/GSEE-ADEDY (2008) *The Greek Economy and Employment*, Annual Report, Athens [in Greek]

— (2010) *The Greek Economy and Employment*, Annual Report, Athens [in Greek]

Internationale Situationniste (1979) *Land planning*, Athens: Akmon Publications [in Greek]

Jacobs, R. (2000) *Race, Media, and the Crisis of Civil Society: From Watts to Rodney King*, Cambridge: Cambridge University Press

Kaplanis, I. (2007) *The Geography of Employment Polarisation in Britain*, London: Institute for Public Policy Research (IPPR)

Kaplanis, I. (2010) "Greece: An Economy That Excludes the Many and the Rise of the New 'Precariat,'" Vienna, Austria: EURS Conference, 16-9-2010

Karamesini, M. (2008) *The Entry of University Degree Holders in the Labour Market*, Athens: Dionikos [in Greek]

Katsiaficas, G. (1997) *The Subversion of Politics* New York: Humanities Press

Keyt, D. (1997) *Aristotle: Politics Books VII and VIII*. Oxford: Clarendon Press

Klein ,N. (2007) *The Shock Doctrine*, London: Allen Lane

Kouki, H. (2009) "Where Do We Go From Here?" *Naked Punch* (12)

Kounalaki, X. (2009) "The Cities Lose Their Colour," *Kathimerini* 5/12/2009 [in Greek]

Kouzis, G. (2009) "The Panorama of Job Insecurity and Precarious Employment," mimeo, accessed at: http://evelixia-stop.blogspot.com/2009/12/blog-post_5773.html

Kuriyama S. (1999) *The Expressiveness of the Body and the Divergence of Greek and Chinese Medicine*, New York: Zone Books

Lapavitsas, C., Kaltenbrunner, A., Lindo, D., Michell, J., Painceira, J.P., Pires, E., Powell, J., Stenfors, A., Teles, E. (2010) *Eurozone Crisis: Beggar Thyself and Thy Neighbour, Research on Money and Finance Occasional Report*, accessed from http://www.researchonmoneyandfinance.org/media/reports/eurocrisis/fullreport.pdf

Lefebvre, H. (1996) *Writings on Cities*, Oxford: Blackwell

Levinas, E. (1985) *Ethics and Infinity*, Pittsburgh: Duquesne University Press

Löwy, M. (2005) *Fire Alarm: Reading Walter Benjamin's "On the Concept of History,"* London: Verso

Lukacs, G. (2000) *A Defence of History and Class Consciousness; Tailism and the Dialectic*, London: Verso

Massey, D. (2001) *Philosophy and Politics of Spatiality.* Athens: Papasotiriou [in Greek]

Michalis (2007) *Exarcheia Reloaded, Blackout in the Social Factory, No. 9* [in Greek] http://blackout.gr/keimena/95

Monastiriotis, V. (2009) *"Economy (Greece),"* in Central and South-Eastern Europe 2010, Europa Regional Surveys of the World Series, London: Routledge

Moore Jr., Barrington (1968) *Thoughts on Violence and Democracy*, Proceedings of the Academy of Political Science, 29 (1)

Moroni, P. (1999) *Self-Managed Social Centres, Nomadism, Rhizomes, and Desires at the Space and the Time of the Metropolis*, Athens: Agriogata [in Greek]

Mose, F. (1960) *Slavery in Classical Antiquity: Views and Controversies*, Cambridge: W. Heffer &

Nietzsche, F. (1989) *Genealogy of Morals*, New York: Vintage Books

Pallasmaa, J. (2005) *The Eyes of the Skin, Architecture and the Senses*, Oxford: Wiley-Blackwell

Purcell, M. (2002) "Excavating Lefebvre: The right to the city and its urban politics of the inhabitant," *Geojournal* 58

Rancière, J. (1991) *The Ignorant Schoolmaster: Five Lessons in Intellectual Emancipation*, Stanford: Stanford University Press

— (2003) *Short Voyage to the Land of the People*, Stanford: Stanford University Press

— (2004) "Introducing disagreement," *Angelaki* 9(3)

— (2004)"Who is the Subject of the Rights of Man?" *The South Atlantic Quarterly* 103(2/3)

Roth, P. (2004) *The Plot Against America*, London: Random House

Schmitt, C. (1985) *Political Theology: Four Chapters on the Concept of Sovereignty*, Cambridge, MA: MIT Press

— (1996) *The Concept of the Political*, Chicago: Chicago University Press

— (2007) *Theory of the Partisan: Intermediate Commentary on the Concept of the Political*, New York: Telos Press

Sennett, R. (1994) *Flesh and Stone: the Body and the City in Western Civilisation*, London: Faber and Faber

Sevastakis, N. (2004) *Banal Country: Perspectives of Public Space and Antinomies of Values in Contemporary Greece*, Athens: Savvalas [in Greek]

Sotiris, P. (2010) "Reading Revolt as Deviance: Greek Intellectuals and the December 2008 Revolt of the Greek Youth," Paper presented at the 38th Annual Conference of the European Group for the Study of Deviance and Social Control, Mytilene, Lesvos

Ssorin-Chaikov, N. (2003) *The Social Life of the State in Subarctic Siberia*, Stanford: Stanford University Press

Stafylakis, K. (2009) "Against the Event: the Role of Aesthetics in the events of December 2008," *Kaput Art Magazine* (05) [in Greek]

Thompson, E.P. (1971) "The Moral Economy of the English Crowd in the Eighteenth Century," *Past and Present* (50)

Vaiou, D. (2007) "The Map of Immigrant," Athens: Research Group for Urban and Regional Planning, NTUA [in Greek]

Wacquant, L. (2008) *Urban Outcasts: A comparative Sociology of Advanced Marginality*, Cambridge: Polity

Weizman, E. (2002) "Maps of Israeli Settlements," in *The Politics of Verticality*, available at http://www.opendemocracy.net/ecology-politicsverticality/article_631.jsp

Woditsch, R. (2009) *Plural Private and Public Spaces of the Polykatoikia in Athens*, Berlin, Technical University (Dissertation)

Zibechi, R. (2010) *Autonomies and emancipations, Latin America in the Move*, Athens: Alana [in Greek]

Žižek, S. (1999) *The Ticklish Subject*, London: Verso

— (2002) *Welcome to the Desert of the Real*, London: Verso

10 December 2008

People standing at one of the barricades of Patision Avenue in Athens on the third day of the revolt, during a brief respite from the street fighting, waiting.

ABOUT OCCUPIED LONDON

Occupied London is an anarchist collective writing on all things urban. Since 2007, the collective has worked together to publish an irregular journal, offering a platform for discussion within the global social antagonist movement, and featuring contributions by writers and collectives from around the globe, including Nasser Abourahme, Zygmunt Bauman, Franco Berardi, Klara Jaya Brekke, Manuel Castells, Mike Davis, Dimitris Dalakoglou, Christos Filippidis, David Graeber, Richard Pithouse, Marina Sitrin, Antonis Vradis, and many, many more. Since 2008, the collective has maintained a wildly popular blog, "From the Greek Streets," providing up-to-the-minute coverage of the urban revolt of December 2008 in Greece, and examining the impact and legacies of the revolt and the crisis that followed.

http://www.occupiedlondon.org | http://www.occupiedlondon.org/blog

ABOUT AK PRESS

AK Press is a worker-run, democratically-managed publisher of anarchist and radical literature. Founded in 1990, AK Press is a ten-person collective of committed anarchists, spread between Oakland, Baltimore, and Edinburgh, working hard to publish more than twenty new titles each year, and distributing thousands of other titles from like-minded publishers around the globe. No bosses. No bullshit. Great books.

http://www.akpress.org | http://revolutionbythebook.akpress.org

Consider signing up for the Friends of AK Press Program. $25 a month ($30 for non-US customers) gets you a copy of every book AK Press publishes during the course of your membership, including fantastic titles like this one. Your monthly contribution goes directly into our publishing account, and ensures that we'll be able to make even more books available in the coming years. Email friendsofak@akpress.org for more information or to join.